Financial Investments

Howard Griffiths PhD
Senior Lecturer in Finance
Polytechnic of the South Bank

McGRAW-HILL BOOK COMPANY

London · New York · St Louis · San Francisco · Auckland
Bogotá · Caracas · Hamburg · Lisbon · Madrid · Mexico
Milan · Montreal · New Delhi · Panama · Paris · San Juan
São Paulo · Singapore · Sydney · Tokyo · Toronto

Published by

McGRAW-HILL Book Company Europe

SHOPPENHANGERS ROAD, MAIDENHEAD, BERKSHIRE, ENGLAND SL6 2QL
TELEPHONE MAIDENHEAD (0628) 23432
FAX 0628 770224   TELEX 848484

British Library Cataloguing in Publication Data
Griffiths, Howard, 1951–
  Financial Investments.
  1. Financial markets
  I. Title
  332
  ISBN 0-07-707206-5

Library of Congress Cataloging-in-Publication Data
Griffiths, Howard, 1951–
  Financial Investments/Howard Griffiths.
     p.   cm.
  Includes bibliographical references.
  ISBN 0-07-707206-5
  1. Investments. 2. Portfolio management.   3. Capital market.
I. Title.
HG4521.G735   1990   89-13660
332.6–dc20   CIP

To
Anne, Huw and Rhys

2345 CL 9321

Typeset by Vision Typesetting, Manchester
and printed and bound in Great Britain by Clays Ltd, St Ives plc

Contents

Preface

This book has been written as a result of the courses I have presented both at the University of Witwatersrand and at the Polytechnic of the South Bank during the last ten years. It is designed for final year undergraduates, postgraduates and MBA students studying capital market theory and investment analysis. It will also be of value to those sitting professional examinations and to those just wishing to gain a deeper understanding of the operation of the markets. The amount of literature on financial theory and financial markets is prodigious and I cannot claim to have covered it all. However, I would like to thank all those whose work and research has formed the foundations of this book.

The text falls into three parts. Chapters 1 to 3 give the student an introduction to financial markets, the principal legislation, the statistical and economical tools of analysis necessary for the following chapters and the efficiency of the operation of the markets. Chapters 4 to 7 form the second section, which first develops modern portfolio theory and then presents a critique before showing how the theory has been used in practice. The final four chapters deal with the assets which can be purchased in financial markets, together with traded options, equities, debentures and futures. However, with these expositions are included two topics of great contemporary importance and interest—mergers and acquisitions and the crash of October 1987. Mergers and acquisitions are usually covered in corporate finance rather than investment analysis texts. However, given their influence on the stock market during the last few decades, it seems more than appropriate to include them in a text on financial markets.

I would like to thank my wife for her forbearance while this book was being written, my reviewer who supplied many valuable suggestions and my colleagues at the Polytechnic of the South Bank for their support and advice.

H. R. Griffiths
Department of Business and Finance
Polytechnic of the South Bank

1. An introduction to financial markets

Introduction

The term investment may be defined as the deployment of resources in order to make a financial gain. In general two types of investment may be distinguished. The first is physical investment whereby resources are converted into physical assets in order to produce commodities or services which may be sold to make a profit. The second is financial investment in which resources are converted into financial assets (certificates of ownership, rights to transact, and/or debts or credits) which involve the acceptance of risk in order to make a profit.

For the great majority of people in this country, or any western industrialized country for that matter, financial investment consists of the purchase of a house (although this is a physical investment which produces a service to the owner it also has a financial aspect as the great majority of house buyers expect to make a capital gain) and/or subscription to a contractual savings scheme. Despite recent attempts to foster an equity-owning democracy, most people will only have an indirect ownership of equities through their membership of a pension fund or the ownership of a life insurance policy. It might be true to say that more people understand and indulge in 'investments' on the turf than in company and government financial assets. London's financial markets remain the preserve of market professionals and those with the money, time and ability to make their own investments. Yet the financial markets are as important for the economic life of the nation as retail and wholesale markets, if not more so.

Most markets are obscured by custom and jargon and financial markets are no exception to this. Custom and tradition have left their mark on the methods and terms used in financial markets. The growth of specialized language and practices has distanced the financial markets from ordinary people. The proliferation of professionals, experts and analysts has produced a jargon exclusive to financial markets. Fowler[1] has described jargon as 'the sectional vocabulary of a science, art, class, sect, trade or profession, full of technical terms'. Fowler went on to observe that 'so copiously does jargon of this sort breed nowadays, especially in the newer sciences such as psychology and sociology, and so readily does it escape from its proper sphere to produce POPULARIZED TECHNICALITIES—words that cloud the minds alike of those who use them and those that read them.' London's financial markets have experienced this sort of development and it is no surprise that popular and even professional misconceptions and misunderstandings abound.

All financial markets in the UK and in other countries have one or more of the following characteristics:
1. the demand for, and supply of, financial assets and services;
2. the sale and transfer of risk;
3. the demand for, and the supply of, the prospect of future income streams;
4. the demand for, and the supply of, the prospect of speculative gain.

These characteristics imply that financial markets are primarily involved with the trade of non-physical or paper assets. However, within this loose classification we may include commodity markets whose primary activity concerns the transfer of risk and the creation of the prospect of speculative gains. In virtually all of the commodity markets the acceptance of the physical

1

commodity forms a very small part of the actual activity. Therefore the following types of markets may be included within the above classification:

1. Stock markets dealing in equities, government and corporate debt, and all the other varieties of corporate ownership and obligations. This includes both the primary market in which capital is raised for fresh ventures and secondary markets which are involved in transactions concerning second-hand financial assets.
2. Traded options and financial futures markets.
3. Long- and short-term insurance markets.
4. Commodity markets.

The term 'market' implies an activity rather than a place. It is the case that many of these activities take place within a specific place, however, it is also true that many of them do not. For example, the primary market for equities and gilts takes place in the London Stock Exchange (LSE). On the other hand, the market for long-term insurance is as physically dispersed as are the people who buy the products and services offered by the insurance industry.

Financial markets are primarily concerned with the transfer of capital and risk. They provide a means whereby large amounts of capital may be accumulated and transferred to those who want to use it. The other side of this particular coin is the provision of income-bearing assets to the owners of capital. However, any commercial undertaking involves risk and the other function of financial markets is the dissipation of this risk. This is achieved in two ways: first by spreading the ownership of an enterprise among a large number of people and second by the explicit sale of commercial risk to people other than the direct owners of the enterprise.

Origins of the stock market

Financial markets have grown in response to the demand for risk capital generated by the growth in trade. For example, the earliest modern marine insurance contracts came from Palermo and Genoa in the thirteenth century. In England the practice of modern marine insurance began rather later, in the first half of the sixteenth century as transatlantic trade started to grow. The long sea voyages required greater amounts of capital and entailed much greater degrees of physical and commercial risk than did the coastal and continental trades. Consequently, the required capital was raised from large numbers of subscribers and part of the risk of these enterprises was sold to the growing number of marine underwriters who were prepared to incur the risk of future catastrophy in return for a present payment.

England was not alone in developing capital markets at this time. Indeed it was not in the forefront of this movement. During the sixteenth and seventeenth centuries it was the Dutch who were the most advanced. The pre-eminence of the Dutch capital markets did not end until the extended occuption by the French during the Revolutionary and Napoleonic Wars. The capital market in Amsterdam raised loans for domestic and foreign governments and businessmen, capital for direct investment abroad, and became an active secondary market in foreign securities.

By the end of the seventeenth century the market in Amsterdam had developed most of the sophisticated services that are taken for granted today. For example, an investor in seventeenth-century Amsterdam could sell his shares short, buy and sell call and put options, and deal in commodity futures. In the 1630s the Dutch produced one of the first speculative manias; not in stocks and shares but in tulip bulbs. At the height of the bubble in 1637, the highest recorded price for a tulip bulb was 20,000 guilders.

The Bank of England

In England these activities grew and developed during the seventeenth century at a more sedate pace than in Holland as the country gradually became a major trading power with an increasing number of overseas colonies and chartered joint stock trading companies such as the East India Company. The major distinguishing feature of the capital markets of these years was the transferability of the ownership of financial investments without affecting the capitalization of the original venture. This enabled the creation of a secondary market which is so important in the pricing of financial assets.

The existence of a 'second-hand' market ensured that the original investors could sell their investments. It also created the second potential for gain or loss. The original investment, if held, offered the prospect of profit and the repayment of capital in the event of the venture being successful, or loss in the event of disaster. However, the secondary market offered the original investor the means of withdrawing or holding according to his expectations of the fortunes of the venture. It held out the opportunity for investors to capitalize on any price increase or to minimize any losses they might expect to bear. Hence, the transferability of ownership increased the marketability of investments and increased the attractiveness of the nascent market to potential investors and made it more efficient as a means of raising larger and larger sums of capital for commercial and government ventures.

Capital markets in England are not readily discernible before the 1680s. However, a spate of flotations during the 1680s and 1690s produced enough tradable stock for the growth of a recognizable market. By 1688 there were 15 joint stock companies and by 1695 this had risen to 140. Of these, the most important was the Bank of England, floated in 1694.

The accession of William III in 1688 ensured that Britain would be involved in every major European war during the following 130 years. The scope and cost of these wars very quickly meant that new forms of financing had to be found. Fortunately for the Crown, its demand for cash could be met by an increasingly affluent society which was proving itself very successful in trade and colonial exploitation. In 1694 William Patterson and his colleagues offered the Crown a perpetual loan of £1.2 million (equivalent to about 2 per cent of the annual national income of that year) in return for a Royal Charter incorporating the subscribers into a bank, and an annual interest charge of 8 per cent. There were some 1,300 subscribers to the issue and on average they each invested £900. Despite some opposition from the private bankers, the whole subscription was raised in 12 days.

The Act of Incorporation allowed the bank to issue notes, buy and sell bullion, deal in bills of exchange and make advances. Each time the charter was renewed the amount loaned to the Crown was increased. Furthermore, during the first 50 years of the bank's existence it repeatedly lowered the rate of interest on the national debt and consequently in the economy as a whole. For instance, in 1709 and 1742 the bank made interest-free loans to the Government of £0.4 million and £1.6 million respectively. These loans reduced the interest charge on the national debt to 3 per cent by 1742. Henceforth, the stock of the Bank of England became an indirect form of state debt as the dividend originated with the Government.

The South Sea Bubble

The market in the shares of joint stock companies had grown up in and around the London coffee houses. Even at this early stage of development there was growing separation of function between stock-jobbers and brokers. The former were regarded with suspicion and were the subject of many a pamphlet recommending their demise. This opprobrium continued for much of the eighteenth century. Dr Johnson's dictionary defined a stock-jobber as 'a low wretch who makes money by buying and selling shares in the funds'. On the other hand brokers, being licensed by the Lord Mayor of London, were more socially acceptable. Their broking activities were not confined to shares, but included commodities, shipping and insurance.

The London market, once established, produced its speculative booms just as the Amsterdam market did during the 1630s. One of the earliest and most infamous was the 'South Sea Bubble' of 1720 (this had almost an exact parallel in France during 1719–1720 in John Law's *Compagnie d'Occident*). The way in which the Bank of England had been incorporated in 1694 had set something of a precedent. The Government seemed to have found a very lucrative source of finance. Acts of Incorporation could be used to raid the capital of companies in return for trading monopolies. The incorporation of both the New and United East India Companies (1698 and 1702 respectively) involved the investors subscribing to new government loans. The most ambitious exercise of this type was the incorporation of the South Sea Company in 1711. In return for a monopoly of South American trade and an annual interest payment of £568,000, £9 million of unfunded government debt was converted into South Sea Company stock at par. Immediately, this produced an opportunity for speculative profit as government debt was selling in the market at a discount of some 40 per cent.

The opportunity for further speculation on a much larger scale occurred some eight years later when the war with Spain ended and the doors to the legendary South American market were opened. As the price of its stock began to rise the company proposed to take over $31 million of government debt at a reduced rate of interest. In April 1720 Parliament gave its assent to the scheme. Through a combination of market manipulation and public relations exercises the company was able to push up the price of its own stock. Thus it could redeem government debt with only a fraction of the authorized issue of stock, leaving the remainder to be sold for pure profit.

The price of South Sea stock peaked at £1,050 and £100 nominal. The success of the South Sea subscriptions during 1720 inspired a host of other companies, mostly proposing ventures in trade or insurance. Many of the promotions were impractical and fraudulent, and most of them were issued on a partly paid basis as was the stock of the South Sea Company itself.

Much of the demand for the shares was financed with credit (buying on margin or using 'leverage' or 'gearing'). The rationale for buying without the means to pay the total price of the share was to sell and reap a profit before the next cash call came from the issuing company. The practice of buying partly-paid shares on margin effectively meant that investors were using leverage twice. First, by making a down payment on a share for which they had no intention of paying the full price, and second, by making the down payment with borrowed funds. The part payment aspect enabled people to buy many more shares than if the full price were demanded and in addition it effectively lowered the entry price into the market so that many more people of limited means could gamble with their wealth. The use of credit enabled speculators to inflate the already enlarged demand for the partly paid shares. Buying on margin ensured that any price rise in the stock was converted almost completely into profit as all the excess of revenue over and above the purchase price accrued to the speculator.

The crash started as people began to try to take their profits. The principal culprits in this respect were some of the directors of the South Sea Company itself. Public confidence in the stock collapsed and the price started to fall precipitately as the leveraged positions began to unwind leaving people with debts backed by unsaleable and virtually worthless stock. This episode resulted in the 'Bubble' Act which prohibited the formation of joint stock enterprises without a Royal Charter or incorporation by Act of Parliament. From 1720 to the early years of the nineteenth century the stock market in London was largely confined to trading in government debt and the shares of those few joint stock companies which had survived the crash of 1720.

The development of the stock market

Between the start of the War of Jenkins's Ear in 1739, and 1816, the year after the Battle of Waterloo, the national debt increased from £44 million to £709 million. The events of the 'Bubble' had largely discredited the practice of 'ingrafting' government debt into corporate capital. As a consequence, the Government sold its debt direct to the public. Nominal interest was invariably fixed between 3 and 5 per cent, but considerable variation was achieved by selling most of the stock in conjunction with some form of lottery or life annuity. These devices were used because successive governments during the eighteenth century were opposed to selling national debt with high coupons or large discounts. As the number of the types of financial assets were limited the stock market's development during these years was rather sedate. Trading continued to take place in the coffee houses as it had done at the turn of the century. It was not until 1801–02 that the brokers and jobbers got together to organize the construction of a building for the conduct of their business.

It is quite apparent that the 'Bubble' Act of 1720 was no impediment to economic growth during the eighteenth century. All the large trading enterprises had already been incorporated by Act of Parliament or Royal Charter before 1720. The growth in manufacturing, mining and transport was mostly financed by individuals or partnerships. However, because of the development of more expensive technology and the growth of the size of individual enterprises the need for capital outstripped the ability of partnerships or individuals to supply it by the end of the eighteenth century.

During the first two decades of the nineteenth century the obstacles to joint stock incorporation were largely worn away. In 1811, in a case concerning a cooperative flour milling company, the courts ruled that the provisions of the 'Bubble' Act did not apply when it could be shown that the enterprise was in the interest of the public at large. In addition, the Act was circumvented by the use of trustees. If an unincorporated joint stock company appointed a board of trustees to act for the shareholders and to control the property of the company, the company did have a legal status and could therefore enforce contracts and collect monies due. The best example of this device was the Sun Insurance Office which remained unincorporated until 1891. Not only did company promoters try to circumvent the Act, they also resorted to far more questionable tactics. Each stock market boom in the first quarter of the new century produced a crop of flotations based on the proposition that petitions had been lodged with Parliament for bills to acquire incorporation. This led to fraudulent promotions and a backlog of bills which Parliament could hardly cope with. The consequence of this was that the 'Bubble' Act was finally repealed in 1825, although joint stock corporations were not to enjoy limited liability. This was only achieved in 1855.

Despite the legal difficulties of incorporation before 1825 the London stock market developed and matured as new types of company were promoted. Canals, docks and insurance companies were among the most common at this time. If insurance companies were by no means new to the stock market they suffered from a high rate of mortality and hence there was a perpetual stream of new companies coming to the market during the nineteenth century. A good example of a fashion in company promotions was the early railway boom. During the 1820s and 1830s railway promotions became increasingly common, until the railway 'mania' took place in the 1840s.

The market developed more or less like a layer cake. As each new manufacturing and commercial development and fashion occurred a spate of new companies would be introduced to the market. Even though many of the more injudicious schemes failed, a residue of commercially viable companies would be left. Invariably, this residue would be further reduced by amalgamation as the industry matured.

This type of development has most recently been observed in the Unlisted Securities Market (USM) between 1980 and 1985. Three distinct phases can be discerned to date; oil exploration and production, electronic and computer manufacturing, and leisure stocks. At the time of writing the electronics and computer stocks have already experienced a shake out while the oil shares are currently undergoing their second bear-market (a protracted fall in share prices) resulting from the oil price collapse during the first half of 1986.

The provincial exchanges

Although the main activity of the LSE during the eighteenth century was the trade in government securities this does not mean that industrial shares were not traded elsewhere. For example, canal shares were sporadically traded in the provinces during the 1790s. The fashion for canal building was inspired by the Duke of Bridgewater's Manchester to Worsley canal of 1761. This trend culminated in the canal 'mania' of 1791–94 when 81 Acts were passed by Parliament allowing the construction of canals. The important feature of these ventures is that they depended on local financial support. During the mania of the early 1790s most promotions were heavily oversubscribed by investors living along the routes of the proposed canals. After the turn of the century local businessmen turned their attention to public utility companies such as water works and gas companies (mainly street lighting). Other fashions in company promotion after the 1820s included banks, railways and insurance.

The two most important centres for company promotion outside London were Liverpool and Manchester. During the first 6 months of 1836 approximately one hundred companies were promoted in Liverpool involving a nominal capital of nearly £27 million. This promotional activity naturally led to the formation of a stock market by the local Liverpool brokers in April 1836. Only a month later the same speculative promotional boom persuaded the Manchester dealers to set up their own market.

The following boom in railway stocks during the years 1844–46 produced another crop of provincial exchanges. Most of these were based on some sort of precedent such as occasional auctions of stock and informal gatherings in local coffee shops and the like. Exchanges were established in the cities Sheffield, Leeds, York, Hull, Bradford, Huddersfield, Halifax, Leicester, Nottingham, Newcastle, Glasgow, Edinburgh, Aberdeen and Bristol. Some of these were short-lived and activity hardly outlasted the boom that inspired their creation.

In most of the smaller markets the principal activity was agency business. It was only in the larger markets like Liverpool and Manchester that there was any jobbing activity. In the larger markets there was a mix of single (jobbers or brokers but not both at the same time) and dual (both jobbing and broking) capacity firms. As the provincial markets established themselves there also developed a good deal of arbitrage in railway stocks. Speculators called 'shunters' would buy in one market to sell in another to make a profit. The shunters also indulged in selling short: i.e. selling the stock in one market before buying it in another to complete the deal. This practice became more common with the development of the telegraph in the 1870s. Shunters could get up-to-date prices from jobbers in the London market and use the information to their own advantage while they still had a monopoly on it.

As most of the provincial markets arose out of occasional share auctions it is not surprising that most of them continued to operate as auctions after the exchanges were formally organized. This type of system has become known as a call market. The basic method of operation is to fix the prices of each financial asset traded on the market twice a day. At the appointed time all the brokers and dealers with an interest in the particular share would gather and sit in a semicircle or circle around a chairman and, through bargaining, fix a price which would be the official market price. This market price would then act as a guide for all subsequent transactions until the next fixing.

During the 1960s the regional stock exchanges along with the LSE and the Irish Stock Exchange combined to form the Federation of Stock Exchanges in Great Britain. The principal objective was to standardize regulations and operations in order to raise standards and improve the public image of the provincial exchanges.

The modern stock markets in London

London's financial markets have developed and specialized according to the type of financial assets concerned. Thus the stock market is concerned with corporate and government financial assets, the USM is concerned with smaller companies which want a cheaper and easier method of raising equity capital and the Over-the-Counter (OTC) market is a collection of brokers and licensed dealers who specialize in trading the shares of small (often family) concerns, to the public.

Additional to the above 3 markets is the more specialized traded options market. Although physically part of the Stock Exchange it is solely concerned with the exchange of risk. Options on the right to buy or sell corporate equities and government stocks at some future date may be purchased in the market. Its primary function is to transfer risk from those who do not wish to bear it to those who do (see Chapter 6).

Until October 1986 the London stock market operated a dealing system which was unique in the world. This system, known as 'single capacity,' separated the functions of principal and agent between jobbers and brokers respectively. Under a system of single capacity, jobbers acted as principals and traded on their own account. They made their money on the spread between their buying and selling prices. On the other hand brokers were not permitted to act as principals with investors and consequently earned their income from the commissions generated by their agency services to the private investors. The brokers' function was to find the best possible price from the jobbers for any transaction being undertaken by the private investor.

The separation of function had occurred to some extent with the genesis of the London market in the last quarter of the seventeenth century. However, this seems to have been done by accident rather than by design and the practice was subsequently strengthened by custom and tradition. By the end of the eighteenth century the system was well entrenched in the sector of the market that dealt in government debt. As each new industrial sector was added to the market the practice was copied in a rough and ready way. Although separation of capacity did exist in the corporate sectors of the market, it was not as well defined as in the government debt sector.

In 1847 the Stock Exchange's rule book expressly forbade the adoption of dual capacity by any of the member firms. Single capacity worked well for those stocks and shares in which there was a large and frequent trade, but it appears not to have been so beneficial for the less active shares. Jobbers acting as principals were supposed to quote both buy and sell prices without knowing the direction of the possible transaction coming from the broker. In this way the interests of the private investor were supposed to be protected without recourse to any legal system of regulation. However, in the less traded shares not only did some jobbers refuse to quote a price without knowing the direction of the transaction, but very often did not make a market in the share at all. As a consequence the markets for the less popular shares operated almost on the principle of matched bargains (modern examples of this are the markets run by Granville and Co. in its sector of the OTC). Towards the end of the nineteenth century this situation was exacerbated by the dual capacity markets operated in US stocks and South African mining shares.

After several ineffectual attempts, this situation was clarified by the new rules of 1908. These held that members of the Stock Exchange should only deal with other members unless the brokers could find better terms for their clients elsewhere. Single capacity worked well in the LSE until the sixties and seventies. During these years considerable changes took place due to the different types of investor coming to the market.

A major cause of change in the LSE has been the growth of the investing institutions since the fifties. In 1963 the investing institutions held only 30 per cent of listed company shares and individuals held 54 per cent. By 1981 this had been reversed with individuals holding only 28 per cent while the institutions held 58 per cent, (see Table. 1.1).

The increase in the importance of the investing institutions reflected major changes in British

Table 1.1   The growth of institutional holdings

Holdings of the investing institutions (£million)

	UK equities				Foreign equities			
	Investment trusts	Unit trusts	Pension funds	Insurance companies	Investment trusts	Unit trusts	Pension funds	Insurance companies
1976	2711	1705	10068	8246	2459	463	1114	1062
1977	3729	2572	14791	12358	1891	411	1178	940
1978	3734	2732	17180	13122	2067	594	1674	1162
1979	4160	2758	19690	13820	2139	688	2026	1155
1980	4620	3357	26005	17978	3042	1081	4325	2059
1981	4673	3566	30129	20464	3514	1454	6321	3110
1982	4604	4457	39257	27127	4256	2229	9742	5051
1983	5306	5954	50990	35126	6570	4091	15566	7711
1984	6322	7925	66047	45134	7259	4943	17998	10130
1985	8069	11138	80580	55315	7820	6097	21862	12278
1986	8661	16423	100054		9549	11816	31078	
	UK gilts				*Land and property*			
1976	164	32	4285	4917	n/a	n/a	2826	5254
1977	321	32	6829	8834	n/a	n/a	4268	6637
1978	232	32	7945	9260	n/a	n/a	4927	9446
1979	320	52	9511	11340	n/a	n/a	6242	10330
1980	266	72	12011	14632	n/a	n/a	8305	12362
1981	183	175	13022	15429	n/a	n/a	9782	14490
1982	199	322	18984	22782	n/a	n/a	10654	15993
1983	310	415	22631	25794	n/a	n/a	11293	17169
1984	306	567	24505	27608	n/a	n/a	12359	18693
1985	464	522	27233	30456	n/a	n/a	12929	20162
1986	261	539	29224		n/a	n/a	13941	

Sources: Annual Abstract of Statistics 1988, Tables 17.16, 17.17, 17.18.

society. Rising prosperity and standards of living for the majority of the population have resulted in more consideration being given to contractual savings for retirement. Occupational pension schemes have been particularly important. The scale of this change is well demonstrated by the fact that the largest pension scheme at the end of 1984 was that of the National Coal Board with assets worth £5,750 million. This was equivalent to approximately two per cent of the total market value of equities quoted on the LSE at that time. The state pension was, and is, considered by most workers to be inadequate and consequently people have made an additional provision for their retirement. Furthermore, the favourable tax treatment of pension and life assurance contributions (until 1984) encouraged the use of the investing institutions. The institutions also provided people with an investment service which was especially important to those who had neither the ability, nor the time, nor the inclination to acquire the knowledge and skills to invest their savings on the LSE.

The insurance companies and pension funds have become large and risk-averse investors whose business has been eagerly sought by both jobbers and brokers. The increase in Stock Exchange turnover during the period 1965–87 is shown in Table 1.2. The size of the individual transactions have become very much larger and under the old system of single capacity and fixed minimum commissions brokers and jobbers experienced a period of great prosperity. However, for the jobbers at least, the increased size of the bargains brought a concomitant increase in risk.

The increased size of each transaction has meant that any mistake on the part of the jobber could more easily result in ruin. In addition, the institutions, all having access to the same information and analyses, have tended to make the same buy and sell decisions at the same time. The result of this is the creation of one-way markets in which the jobber is faced by orders of one kind only. The

Table 1.2   Stock Exchange turnover 1965–86

	£ billion Equities	£ billion Gilts
1965	3.48	16
1966	3.57	16.61
1967	5.8	27.97
1968	9.12	21.04
1969	8.71	19.46
1970	8.8	27.35
1971	13.38	47.4
1972	20.07	32.74
1973	17.08	35.41
1974	12.62	38.26
1975	17.55	67.24
1976	14.16	81.92
1977	20.17	135.76
1978	19.22	103.68
1979	24.11	128.95
1980	30.8	151.7
1981	32.39	146.06
1982	37.41	203.39
1983	56.13	210.76
1984	73.11	268.68
1985	105.55	261.53
1986	181.21	424.42

Source: *Stock Exchange Quarterly* and *Quality of Markets Report*, various issues.

main implication of one-way markets for jobbers is that they are forced to adopt very large long (buying more shares than they have sold) and short positions (selling more shares than they have bought). A long position requires a lot of capital which is then tied up in a financial asset, the price of which may fall before it can be sold. The short position involves the considerable risk of not being able to acquire the share at favourable prices for settlement purposes. Therefore, to absorb such business the jobbers have amalgamated to become larger and at the same time have resorted to wider spreads between their buying and selling prices.

The enlargement of the member firms (both brokers and jobbers) has been a gradual process. Some of the landmarks are worth noting. The first occurred in 1967 when the LSE permitted partnerships to exceed 20. More importantly, in 1969 the LSE allowed member firms to re-form themselves into limited companies and sell 10 per cent to outsiders. This move was not particularly successful due to the tax advantages of remaining as a partnership as opposed to a limited company. However, it marked the thin edge of the wedge by setting a precedent for further involvement of outsiders. In 1982 the LSE raised the limit of outside participation to 29.9 per cent. This limit avoided any difficulty with the regulations of the Panel for Takeovers and Mergers (see page 19). By the end of 1986 the limit on outsider participation in member firms was swept away with the 'Big Bang'. Many of the major broking and jobbing firms have been taken over by the commercial and merchant banks, both domestic and foreign. Table 1.3 shows the general reduction in the number of jobbing and broking firms over the period 1920–89.

The consumer power of the investing institutions has had several effects on trading practices in the LSE:

1. In response to pressure from the institutions the LSE has reduced the scales of its minimum commissions. The institutions had claimed that the agency work involved for the broker was

Table 1.3   Jobbing and broking firms

	Brokers Firms	*Members*	*Principals*	*Others**	*Jobbers* Firms	*Principals*	*Others**
1920	475	4 055	1 513		411	1 465	
1950	364	3 890	1 743		187	791	
1960	305	3 432	1 886	1 173	100	545	254
1965	270	3 413	1 893	1 358	60	417	333
1970	192	3 287	1 810	1 438	31	273	349
1975	284	4 117	2 129	1 849	21	231	438
1980	240	4 067	2 104	1 923	19	203	384
1985	199	4 495	2 144	2 148	17	209	382
1986	207	5 009	2 189	2 518	18	247	441

Member firms after deregulation

	Firms	Members
1987	357	5 433
1988	350	5 255
1989	389	5 114

* Associate Members and Authorized Clerks.

Source: *Quality of Markets Quarterly*, Appendix 3, various issues.

little different for a transaction for 100 shares than one for 10,000, yet the commission paid on the larger deal was far greater than on the smaller deal. The brokers argued that the minimum commission system paid for the analysis given to the institutions in every transaction. However, this carried little weight as the institutions themselves employed financial analysts to select their purchases and sales.

2. Further reductions in institutional dealing costs were effected by the brokers offering discounts on the scale of minimum commissions.

3. To further reduce the costs of institutional dealing the brokers in recent years have been operating 'put-through' deals. This involves the broker in matching buyers and sellers, and then getting the jobber to rubber stamp the transaction and absorb any excess stock due to slight mismatches for a reduced spread (reduced because the risk of the transaction has already been greatly lowered by the activity of the broker).

4. The reduction in the number of jobbing firms by amalgamation in order to secure a larger capital base has led to a situation where many of the less actively traded shares (the majority) are not easy to buy and sell as few, if any, brokers make markets in them. This also raises the possibility that lack of activity and difficulty of trading in these shares leads to incorrect pricing. The market value of any asset is correctly set when there are large numbers of buyers and sellers making a large number of transactions.

The second development which has had a major impact on the operation of the single capacity system at the LSE has been the complete removal of foreign exchange control in 1979. Since the collapse of the 'Bretton Woods' system of fixed exchange rates between international currencies in 1971 there has been a gradual but progressive liberalization of the world's financial markets. The removal of exchange controls has coincided with a substantial improvement in international communications. These two developments have combined to produce a global market for financial assets in which the national markets have become constituent parts, each competing for a bigger share of the available business. This has had the effect of increasing the level of competition in the market by exposing the domestic firms to foreign competition both in terms of foreign firms competing in the domestic market and in terms of the greater availability of foreign securities.

Not only have domestic and foreign merchant banks been making markets in foreign and domestic shares but they have also evolved a dealing system for British securities that bypasses the LSE completely. This is known as the ADR (American Depository Receipts) transaction and is primarily of benefit to US investors and financial intermediaries. British (and other) securities are deposited with an American bank and then the depository receipt issued by the bank (usually for 1,000 shares) is traded. This avoids any costs of listing on the American markets and also the payment of British stamp duty on each transaction.

The third major impetus for change was the referral of the whole of the LSE's rule book to the Restrictive Practices Court by the Government in 1976. This meant that the court would assume that every rule in the book was against the public interest unless proven otherwise. The LSE made a settlement with the Government in 1983. In return for dropping the referral to the Restrictive Practices Court, the LSE committed itself to abolishing the minimum commission system by the end of 1986. This has led to the adoption of dual capacity. However, the capacity in which any firm chooses to deal is discretionary and there is a mix of both dual and single capacity firms, although all the market-makers will have dual capacity.

The last major change in London's securities markets worth mentioning is the growth of the Eurobond market. This is a market without any central place of business. If a physical market can be said to exist it is a telephone and telecommunications network between the major merchant banks. This market is solely concerned with the issuance of national and corporate debt in any currency that the borrower wishes to denominate. Eurobonds have become popular with borrowers because of their flexibility and because the market is almost totally unregulated in a formal legal manner although there exists an informal self-regulation which, if ineffective, would be superseded by a statutory system. In addition, many Eurobond issues are in bearer form which can facilitate tax evasion by the lenders as there is no central register of ownership for authorities to go to for information. However, the extent of this rather apocryphal practice is uncertain. The size of the new issue market in Eurobonds is vast. In 1985 the LSE raised £4,800 million in new corporate equities. In the same year the Eurobond market raised £154,700 million in commercial and national capital. None of this passed through the LSE.

The 'Big Bang' 27 October 1986

The media paid a lot of attention to the proposed changes in LSE rules and practices between 1984 and 1986. These changes may be summarized as follows:
1. Dual capacity replaced the single capacity system and separate functions. Any member firm of the LSE can now set itself up as both agent and principal in the business of trading stocks and shares.
2. The prohibition on the membership of foreign firms was removed.
3. All restrictions on the ownership of member firms were removed.
4. Minimum brokerage commissions were scrapped.

The move to dual capacity brought with it the serious problem of conflict of interest. To guard against malpractice the LSE introduced some modifications to trading practices:
1. Business can only be done intrafirm if the in-house jobber offers a price at least as good as the best offered by the market.
2. In order to ensure the above is carried out, all transactions must be time stamped so that they can be checked with LSE records if necessary.
3. The LSE has explicitly banned the use of suspense accounts. These enabled multiple fund managers to make a purchase of stock without naming the purchaser until a later date in order to take advantage of a movement of the price after the purchase had been made.

The new dealing system has been called the 'competing marketmaker system'. It is flexible enough to allow any number of firms to make markets and places no restrictions on the numbers of shares in which the firm makes markets. The LSE only requires that marketmakers continuously quote two way prices in the shares to which they are committed. The whole system is underpinned by the new LSE computerized share price quotation system SEAQ (Stock Exchange automatic quotation system, see Fig. 1.1). This will allow transactions to take place instantaneously off the floor of the Stock Exchange and it will keep a record of the previous 3 years' worth of transactions, each of which may then be checked for malpractice if necessary.

The new dealing system is very similar to that operated under the old single capacity regime and hence will not cause too much upheaval in terms of jobbing practices. The biggest organizational change has been the installation of the SEAQ system in each of the member firms.

The amalgamation of the LSE and the Eurobond dealers association (AFBD) resulted in a

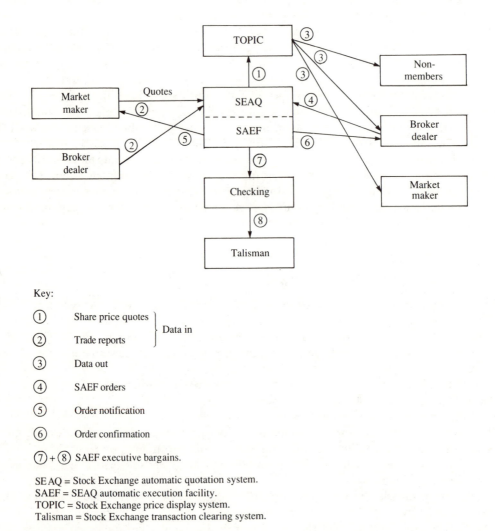

Key:

①   Share price quotes   ⎫
                               ⎬ Data in
②   Trade reports   ⎭

③   Data out

④   SAEF orders

⑤   Order notification

⑥   Order confirmation

⑦ + ⑧ SAEF executive bargains.

SEAQ = Stock Exchange automatic quotation system.
SAEF = SEAQ automatic execution facility.
TOPIC = Stock Exchange price display system.
Talisman = Stock Exchange transaction clearing system.

Figure 1.1   The International Stock Exchange information and dealing systems.

change of name for the LSE to the International Stock Exchange (ISO). The Stock Exchange has developed, and continues to develop, a set of information and bargain execution systems during the seventies and eighties. The system has been built up piece by piece in response to various needs. For example, in 1972 the merchant banks belonging to the Accepting Houses Committee set up a computer-based system of share trading called 'Ariel'. However, the Stock Exchange responded by reducing brokerage charges on the larger bargains and the system never attracted many customers and was soon discontinued.

TOPIC is a video system which displays share and stock data to over 8,000 subscribers. It draws from the ISO's main computer (EPIC) which has data on some 3,000 securities. TOPIC is also used to display information from the ISO's other computerized systems.

SEAQ, which became operational in 1986, is the ISO's means of allowing marketmakers to quote prices for the shares in which they are prepared to deal. SEAQ divides the shares into 3 types:
1. Alpha (102 equities in June 1987), these are the largest and most commonly traded companies. Marketmakers quotes are firm.
2. Beta, these shares are generally smaller and their markets are not as liquid as those of alpha stocks. The quotes for beta shares are also firm.
3. Gamma, these shares constitute the majority of the small companies listed on the exchange and as their markets are not very liquid the quotes made by marketmakers and shown on SEAQ may only be indicative.

In addition to quotes, the ISO requires both marketmakers and broker–dealers to report immediately to SEAQ all the details of the share transactions that they have made. SEAQ also displays fixed interest security prices and the prices of some 600 international stocks quoted by nearly 50 marketmakers.

SAEF is the SEAQ automatic execution facility which enables member firms to trade with each other over the computer links rather than by telephone. This has meant the SEAQ now receives order information from participating firms as well as data on deals and price quotes. Once an order is received by SEAQ, SAEF matches it against the best available quote and the bargain is automatically reported to the ISE central checking system which validates the transaction and then to 'Talisman' for settlement.

Talisman was installed in 1979 to automate the transfer and registration of ownership of securities. It replaced a system which had been in place for nearly 100 years but which had grown excessively clumsy and expensive, with the market employing over 5,000 people on settlement business. Total costs were in the region of £100 million per annum. In addition, this decentralized method required the employment of over 1,000 registrars maintaining share registers for some 9,000 securities.

Talisman is based on the operation of the Stock Exchange Nominee Company, SEPON, which holds shares when they have been sold on a temporary basis until a buyer is found. It also facilitates the trading of shares without certificates which eliminates the risk of losing the certificates and makes it easier for the company to stay in contact with its own shareholders. In addition, it helps the Inland Revenue and potential bidders by maintaining an up-to-date list of the company's owners.

Talisman is undergoing further change and adaption with the introduction of two new systems in 1989—TAURUS and INS. The first of these, TAURUS (transfer and automatic registration of uncertified stock), is a computerized share depository which will transfer stock by book entries and remove the need for much of the paper which travels back and forth across the City every day. This, it is hoped, will speed up and improve the accuracy of settlement and transfer, thus avoiding the creation of backlogs during periods of heavy trading as in the summer of 1987. The second development is INS (institutional net settlement) which will enable the institutions to trade with each other on a net basis without having to go through the Talisman–Taurus systems.

Market regulation and practice

The regulation of financial markets is of necessity an adaptive process. All markets change as they grow or decline. The natures of both the products and the participants change and as a consequence of this so do the rules which govern market operations. Although changes take place almost continuously in the market, the rules change only periodically when they can be seen to have long outlived their usefulness. Hence the law is always behind current practice and its changes are often large and sometimes disruptive.

Any legal framework must ensure that the investing public is protected, as far as is possible, from fraudulent practitioners. In addition, any legal framework should facilitate rather than hinder the operation of the market. These two functions are to some extent contradictory in that the scope necessary within the legal framework for the efficient operation of the market may also facilitate fraudulent practice. Whatever the details of the legal framework and the methods of practice the result must be a large measure of trust from the investing public and capital raising corporations in the 'fairness' of the market. This essential ingredient of trust may be created either by custom and tradition or by law or by a combination of both. Without this trust the market will not perform the necessary functions of raising capital and pricing financial assets.

London's financial markets have a unique system of regulation and supervision. This is based on a mixture of law, self-regulation and custom. The market enjoys an incomparable legacy of trust despite recent cases of fraud. However, the more infamous cases of financial failure and fraud of the early 1980s induced the Government to make a review of the legal framework for investor protection. The outcome of this exercise was the publication of the *Review of Investor Protection* by Professor L. C. B. Gower[2] in January 1984 and, after a period for consultation with the interested parties, the Financial Services Act (FSA) of 1986.

Professor Gower has described the system of investor protection as being dependent on disclosure of information. There has never been any rigorous system of supervision—statutory or otherwise; and the new FSA continues this tradition despite the plethora of self-regulatory organizations. However, Gower also shows that it is difficult for private investors to check the accuracy of the published information. Indeed, some of the most effective supervision comes from the press rather than from the Government and its agencies or from the self-regulating bodies of the financial markets.

Since the Prevention of Frauds Act 1939 most of the legislation affecting financial services has followed a similar pattern. Each Act defines the areas of business with which it is concerned (common to all legislation) and sets up the conditions for doing business. Thus, each piece of legislation sets up a system of licensing or a procedure for exemption from licensing. In each case the Act will nominate a designated agency to carry out the supervisory duties that it sets up. These agencies vary from the Bank of England to the Department of Trade and Industry (henceforth referred to as the DTI) to various bodies set up by the practitioners involved. The principal functions of the designated agencies are to operate the licensing/exemption system, to set up and enforce a code of conduct and to impose penalties on those practitioners who transgress the law or the code of conduct. Finally each Act has paid increasingly specific attention to the use of advertising material in the normal conduct of business. The remainder of this chapter will be confined to giving a brief description of those pieces of legislation which have a direct bearing on the operation of the stock market.

Outlines of the Acts

The Company Securities (Insider Dealing) Act 1985

The practice of insider dealing was broadly defined by a Government White Paper published in

1977 (Cmnd. 7037) as being the use of privileged information which had a significant bearing on the future value of the security in question. The Act of 1985 put this definition into practice by prohibiting any individual connected with a company in the preceding 6 months from dealing in the securities of that company on any recognized stock exchange if he or she was in possession of price sensitive information. The connection is specified as employee or officer but not director (see the Companies Act of 1985). This also applies to those consultants.

In addition, the Act makes it illegal for individuals to use price sensitive information which has been acquired on a second-hand basis. This is specifically extended to takeover situations. For example, a director planning takeover of a company may not buy the shares of the target company for his or her own account. The penalties for insider dealing are an unspecified fine and/or a maximum of 2 years' imprisonment.

Insider dealing is difficult to define and identify. It is virtually unique in that in almost every market the practice is condemned yet it is essentially a 'plaintiffless crime'. However, the existence or non-existence of a victim is irrelevant to the importance of the crime. The practice may, if unchecked, lead to a loss of confidence in the essential 'fairness' of the market and the resultant lack of trust will undoubtedly impair the market's ability to raise and price capital.

The Financial Services Act 1986

This Act accompanied the 'Big Bang' and replaced the Prevention of Fraud Act 1958. However, the philosophy is largely unchanged as investor protection is still based on self-regulation, maximum disclosure of information and *caveat emptor* enforced by fines and prison sentences. Even if the philosophy behind the Act hasn't changed, it does constitute a compilation of the best features of investor protection from recent legislation. The objectives of the new framework of investor protection are efficiency, competitiveness, confidence in the system and flexibility. It embodies the proposition that these objectives will be best achieved if market forces operate properly and tries to create a system of rules which are easily understood and are easily implemented.

The Secretary of State for Trade and Industry is empowered to delegate authority and responsibility for investor protection to a 'designated agency' which in this case is the Securities and Investment Board (SIB) which is a private limited company.

The Act defines 'investments' as follows:
1. shares, debentures (including certificates of deposit), all forms of government stocks, warrants and options, and futures contracts;
2. unit trusts;
3. participatory rights in real assets such as plantations and bloodstock.

The Act defines 'investment business' as follows:
1. transactions involving 'investments' either as agent or principal (except for personal portfolios);
2. managing 'investments' and unit trust schemes;
3. selling investment advice, and publishing promotional material about investments or issuing tip-sheets (except financial journalism).

The SIB (the 'designated agency') must establish a compensation scheme for those investors who suffer losses if an authorized firm becomes insolvent. At present, the Stock Exchange has a compensation scheme, and NASDIM and AFBD have made insurance arrangements to cover their investing clients. The scheme is to be funded by contributions from the investment businesses and will compensate investors up to 100 per cent of their total loss with a maximum limit of £30,000, and 90 per cent of the next £20,000. In addition, the SIB must set up a system for investigating complaints against authorized investment businesses and self-regulatory organizations (SROs). To meet this obligation, the SIB proposed the appointment of an ombudsman.

Investor protection will be implemented through a system of SROs authorized and supervised by the SIB. Each SRO will draw up a set of rules regulating the business of its members. Furthermore, the SROs are expected to discipline errant members and to facilitate this function they have been given legal immunity from prosecution by its members. However, the members have been given the right of appeal to the SIB. In May 1986 the SIB proposed to recognize the following SROs:

1. The Stock Exchange and the International Securities Regulatory Organization (ISRO); now combined to become the Securities Association.
2. The Association of Futures Brokers and Dealers (AFBD).
3. The Life Assurance and Unit Trust Regulatory Organization (LAUTRO).
4. The Financial Intermediaries Managers and Brokers Regulatory Association (FIMBRA).
5. The Investment Management Regulatory Organization (IMRO).

To simplify the administration of the regulatory framework, the SIB has insisted on one SRO being designated as being senior where there is an overlap of coverage.

In 1987 the Stock Exchange and ISRO (principally Eurobond dealers) had 208 and 193 member firms respectively. The AFBD has 142 member firms, mostly concerned with LIFFE, LME, and the London Commodity Exchange (LCE). LAUTRO has 200 member firms including insurance companies, friendly societies and unit trusts. IMRO has no member firms at the moment but has a potential membership of about 1,000 among the merchant banks, pension fund managers, unit trust managers and insurance companies. Lastly, FIMBRA has a membership of 1,180 firms. The membership of FIMBRA consists of the smaller securities dealers involved in the OTC market and the small independent brokers of life assurance and unit trusts. It is possible for an investment business to be a member of more than one SRO in the case where the operations of the firm extend beyond the coverage of one SRO. In the event of multiple membership the SIB requires that one SRO should be the leading regulator so that authority remains unambiguous. In addition, the SIB is empowered to recognize professional bodies and individuals for the purpose of carrying out investment business. There are about a dozen professional organizations including those of the accountants and solicitors which will apply or are in the process of applying to the SIB for recognition.

The SIB is empowered to recognize investment exchanges. The essential prerequisite for recognition as an exchange is the existence of adequate clearing arrangements and recording facilities for all transactions. The following have been recognized:

1. The Stock Exchange.
2. The UK Commodity, Financial Futures and Options Exchanges.
3. The Association of International Bond Dealers.
4. Certain other overseas exchanges such as the New York Stock Exchange (NYSE).

The principles which must underlie the rules of the SROs for the conduct of business may be summarized as follows:

1. All investment business must be based on a principle of fair dealing. There must be a 'best execution' rule and the complete subordination of interest by market intermediaries whether operating as agent or principal.
2. All investment business must include safeguards so that transactions are handled with due care, skill and attention.
3. Full disclosure of interest on the part of the investment business.
4. All investment business must be recorded.

The SIB has attempted to ensure that there is a common minimum standard for the rules of the various SROs and professional bodies by insisting on 'equivalence'. This means that the rules laid down must offer the investor an equal level of protection to that provided by the rules and regulations laid down by the SIB itself and as the SIB changes its own rules so must the SROs and professional bodies.

The rules and regulations of the SIB include the following:

1. *Independence*. All investment advisers must be independent of any influence that may prejudice their advice to their clients.
2. *Investment advertisements*. In addition to the obvious requirements of honesty and integrity, adverts will carry risk warnings about the volatility, liquidity and future liabilities of the advertised investment.
3. *Published recommendations*. Not only do tipsheets have to be adequately researched but their recommendations must be substantiated.
4. *The 'know your customer' rule*. This almost constitutes a *caveat vendor* rule as investment advisers must know the character and substance of their clients so that their advice is 'appropriate'.
5. *Off-exchange securities*. When a security is not traded on any recognized exchange the client must be informed of the fact and of any problems that the investor may experience when he or she sells the security. Furthermore, when a firm is the only institution to make a market in an off-exchange security it must inform the potential investor of the fact.
6. *Transactions*. All transactions must be time-stamped and all deals must be executed immediately.
7. *Fund management*. The SIB is attempting to prevent excessive trading ('churning') by discretionary fund managers. Churning is designed to increase the income of the manager rather than improve the performance of the fund. The SIB hopes to deter this practice, increasng surveillance on unusually actively managed funds.
8. *Cold-calling*. The practice of unsolicited calling on an individual is prohibited by the Act, but it does allow certain exceptions which the SIB has interpreted as follows:
   (a) calls on professional investors;
   (b) calls concerned with contracts that may be cancelled during the cooling-off period as specified by the Insurance Companies Act of 1982;
   (c) calls on individuals who have given their written consent.

The Companies Act 1985

The Companies Act regulates the formation and registration of both UK and foreign companies in every part of the United Kingdom and as such plays a very important part in protecting investors by regulating those who come to the capital markets in search of risk capital. It is concerned with the creation and management of capital, the publication of reports and accounts, the qualifications and duties of directors, the conduct of shareholders' meetings, and the liquidation and winding-up procedures for registered companies. Like the other legislation concerned directly or indirectly with the regulation of financial markets this Act relies on the disclosure of information to protect investors and prevent fraud.

All companies seeking capital through the medium of the stock market must make the following information available:

1. *The Articles of Association*. The articles of association will include provisions outlining the variation of shareholders' rights, alteration of capital, notice and procedure for general meetings, borrowing powers, the powers and duties of directors, the publication of accounts and the procedures to be followed in the event of winding-up the company.
2. *Prospectuses*. When a company offers securities (not required for rights issues or a placing) to

the public a prospectus must be issued in which the following information must be presented:
(a) the number of founders' shares and the nature and extent of their interest in the property and profits of the company;
(b) the names, descriptions and addresses of the directors and proposed directors of the company;
(c) the voting and dividend rights of each class of share, the minimum number of shares that may be subscribed for, the amount payable on application and the details of any options or warrants attached to the securities on offer;
(d) the financial history of the company. The prospectus must include up to 5 years' profit and loss accounts (this has been reduced to 3 years for those companies floated on the USM). In addition, it must display the last audited balance sheet of the company and give details of its interests in subsidiaries and other companies;
(e) the assets acquired or to be acquired with the funds raised in the issue (this does not apply to property or assets that are acquired in the course of the company's normal business);
(f) auditors. The prospectus must contain the name and address of the firm of auditors that has prepared the accounts.
3. *Alteration of capital.* If authorized by its Articles, a company may change its Memorandum in order to raise new share capital by creating and selling new shares. It may also attempt to improve the marketability of its shares by either consolidating existing shares or splitting the shares into smaller units. In addition, a company may reduce its authorized capital if permitted by the Articles of Association or the passing of a special resolution at the annual general meeting (AGM), and the confirmation of the resolution by the courts. This may be achieved in one of three ways:
(a) cancel or reduce the liability on partly paid share capital;
(b) cancel paid-up capital which is no longer represented by assets;
(c) redeem any paid-up capital which is in excess of the company's requirements.
Lastly, a company may purchase its own fully paid-up shares on a recognized stock exchange if authorized to do so by its Articles of Association or after an ordinary resolution has been passed at an AGM. However, off-market purchases can only be made if they are first sanctioned by a special resolution passed at an AGM.
4. *The major shareholders.* It is materially important to existing and potential investors in a company to know of any investor who has built up a substantial holding which may affect the control and value of the company. The Act requires an investor to inform the company when 5 (this figure may be reduced during the course of 1989 or 1990) per cent of the ordinary equity has been acquired. These disclosure provisions also apply to alliances of investors known as 'concert parties' which try to create controlling holdings in the company.
5. *Meetings.* There are two types of meeting, the AGM and the extraordinary general meeting (EGM). Every company must hold at least one AGM each year. In the event of no AGM being called any shareholder may request the DTI to hold an AGM. The AGM is used to declare a dividend, for the consideration of the accounts and the directors' and auditors' reports, and for the election and dismissal of directors.
6. *The directors.* A company is an abstract legal entity and requires human agents to act on its behalf—directors. The Act is concerned to define what qualities and behaviour are fit and proper for directors of public companies;
(a) it stipulates a compulsory retirement age of 70 for public companies;
(b) individuals may not be appointed as directors if they are undischarged bankrupts, or of unsound mind, or been convicted of fraud, or who have been a director of 2 companies which have gone into liquidation within the previous 5 years;
(c) the duty of the directors is to manage the company for the shareholders;

(d) company directors are not automatically entitled to remuneration for their services although shareholders may approve fees at AGMs.

The Act attempts to prevent directors from abusing their positions for personal gain:

(e) directors must declare their holdings of shares or debentures in the company;

(f) it makes it an offence for directors and their families to trade in options on the shares of the company;

(g) it makes property transactions between the company and the directors and their families illegal;

(h) it prohibits the directors and their families taking loans from the company outside its normal business.

The City Panel on Takeovers and Acquisitions

The Panel's Code sets out 14 general principles regarding the way in which takeovers and mergers should be conducted; these may be summarized as follows:

1. All shareholders of the target company must be treated equally in respect of the offer and the information supplied.
2. The shareholders of the target company of the takeover bid should be given sufficient information to judge the merits of the offer.
3. The directors of the target company are to act in the best interests of the shareholders and seek independent advice about the offer.
4. If the acquirer gets more than 50 per cent acceptances, the offer must be extended to all the undecided and dissentient shareholders.

The Code insists that all takeover advertising must be created with the same discretion as prospectuses. However, as a consequence of the extensive use of 'knocking copy' during the spate of takeovers during 1985–86 the Panel required firms to use more propriety in their advertising.

When a holding of 30 per cent has been created, the Panel requires the investor to make a general offer for the rest of the shares. After the announcement of the general offer, the investor is prevented from acquiring additional equity for 7 days unless the offer has been made unconditional or the investor has control of a majority of the voting rights.

Lastly, the Fair Trading Act 1973 (amended by the Competition Act of 1980) also tries to protect the consumer by preventing the creation of monopolies. An offer will be referred to the Monopolies Commission if the enlarged company controls 25 per cent or more of the supply of a particular commodity. In practice this has been avoided by the creation of a revised offer which involves the disposal of assets so as to prevent the creation of a monopoly position. For example, both Guinness and United Biscuits revised their bids for Distillers and the Imperial Group respectively, to avoid the delay of a reference to the Monopolies Commission.

The Panel has no statutory powers. Its authority stems from its acceptance by the financial community in London. Therefore, its principal sanction is public censure which may well have a detrimental effect on the reputation of the individuals and companies involved. In response to criticisms made about its lack of supervision of some of the larger acquisition battles in 1986 the panel published new guidelines in February 1987:

5. All shareholders with 1 per cent or more of a company's shares are required to make daily disclosures of the extent of their holdings during the course of a takeover bid.
6. For each trade in the shares of a company involved in a takeover bid which brings an investor's holding to over 1 per cent it will be necessary for the investor to declare his or her interest.

The intention of these new guidelines is to identify concert parties involved in share price support operations.

Notes

1. H. W. Fowler, *A Dictionary of Modern English Usage*, 2nd edn, Oxford University Press, 1968.
2. L. C. B. Gower, *The Principles of Modern Company Law*, Stevens, 1971.

Further reading

Clayton, G., *British Insurance*, Elek, 1971.
Cockerell, H. A. and E. Green, *The British Insurance Business, 1547–1970*, Heinemann, 1976.
Commission of the European Communities Report, 'Supervision of the securities markets in the member States of the European Community', Parts I and II, 1979/1981.
Gower, L. C. B., *The Principles of Modern Company Law*, Stevens, 1971.
Hamilton, A., *The Financial Revolution*, Penguin, 1986.
Kindleberger, C. P., *A Financial History of Western Europe*, Allen and Unwin, 1984.
Lipson, E., *The Economic History of England*, Vol III, The Age of Mercantilism, 6th edn, Adam and Charles Black, 1956.
London Stock Exchange Report, 'The choice of a new dealing system for equities', July 1984.
McRae, H. and F. Cairncross, *Capital City*, Methuen, 1985.
Morgan, E. V. and W. A. Thomas, *The Stock Exchange*, Elek, 1962.
The Building Societies Act 1986.
The Companies Act 1985.
The Company Securities (Insider Dealing) Act 1985.
The Financial Services Act 1987.
The Gower Report, 'Investor protection', Cmnd. 9125, 1984.
The Wilson Report and Evidence, 'The functioning of financial institutions', Cmnd. 7937, 1980.
Thomas, C. D., *Company Law for Accountants*, 2nd edn, Butterworths, 1988.
Thomas, W. A., *The Provincial Stock Exchange*, Frank Cass, 1973.

Questions

1. Discuss the point of view that any legal framework devised to regulate the stock market can only be as good as the efforts made to implement and enforce it.
2. To what extent can the new operational systems in the stock market claim to have been responsible for uncovering the Guinness Affair?
3. Describe and critically discuss the main factors that induced the London Stock Exchange to change from single to dual capacity in 1986.
4. Gower has argued that the protection of the investor under English law is effected by a combination of maximum disclosure and *caveat emptor*. Has this been changed by the Financial Services Act of 1987?
5. What is gearing or leverage and why was it so important in the affair of the South Sea Bubble of 1720?
6. Why was the Government so important in the creation of a stock market during the eighteenth century and why were the provincial exchanges so important in the nineteenth century?
7. Why might the investing institutions be described as the 'major engine of change' in the stock market over the last forty years?
8. Discuss the proposition that the increase of competition implied by the Big Bang has been incompatible with the concept of self-regulation in the stock market.
9. Big Bang was a highly dramatic episode in an evolutionary process; how and why has the market developed since 1986?
10. What are the advantages and disadvantages of a system of self-regulation and would there be any benefit to the market of changing to a statutory system of control?

2. Risks and returns

Introduction

Any investment, whether physical or financial, involves individuals in sacrificing current consumption of wealth in return for an increase in future wealth. To be more accurate the increase in future wealth is expected, it is never guaranteed. Every investment will involve a degree of risk. Hence, any investment can only be assessed for its expected returns and the risk of those returns.

Marketmakers on the London stock market, specialists on the New York Exchange and underwriters (both insurance and those who underwrite new issues) make their returns solely by taking risks. Their activities are not unlike those of the bookmaker who takes wagers on horse-races and other sporting contexts. All of these individuals accumulate a portfolio of risks, any one of which may materialize. The skill and expertise of these risk-takers is to set their premiums, spreads or odds to ensure that in the worst scenario there is a small excess of income over payouts. Therefore, the marketmaker and specialist must continually reset his or her bid and offer prices to reflect the changing balance of demand and supply for the securities in which they trade. One of the primary tasks is to ensure that the inventory carried at any one time is not so large that the trader's capital is eliminated by any change in price of any one of the securities in the inventory (the term inventory is used here as the securities are only held temporarily by market traders in order to sell them again as soon as possible and it would be inaccurate to call this holding a portfolio as it is held as a tradable asset rather than an investment).

Similarly, the underwriter can set insurance premiums to reflect the probability of an event so that income will invariably exceed payouts. This task is immeasurably easier in life assurance— due to the reliability and accuracy of actuaries' mortality tables—than it is for the insurance of objects. For example, the probability of a hurricane (albeit small by international standards) striking the south-eastern part of the UK is extremely small as the last known similar event took place in the eighteenth century. Yet this is exactly what happened in October 1987.

When insuring an object the underwriter must estimate the probability of having to pay out on a claim. For example, if it was established that on average there were 200 incidences of house fires in a population of 100,000 similar houses then by using the past as a proxy for the future the underwriter may calculate the probability of each event as:

$$(200/100,000)(100) = 0.02\%$$

If the average market price of this type of house was known to be £50,000, then the total amount insured would be:

$$(£50,000)(100,000) = £5,000 \text{ million}$$

and assuming on average a ratio of 60 per cent between the payout and the average value of the house, the total amount expected to be paid out would be:

$$(£50,000)(200)(0.6) = £6 \text{ million}$$

Therefore the financial risk may be expressed as the expected payout compared with the total value of property insured:

$$(£6 \text{ million}/£5,000 \text{ million})(100) = 0.12\%$$

The minimum rate the underwriter would expect to charge to cover expected payouts would be 12p for every £100 of property insured. Hence, the minimum charge for the average house would be:

$$(£50,000/100)(0.12) = £60$$

To this minimum charge would be added considerations for administrative and production costs as well as an element of profit. This process will work well for all but very exceptional cases such as the hurricane which hit the south-east of England in October 1987.

Under normal circumstances the underwriters' activities are very similar to those of the bookmaker as there will be very few 'winners' to pay. The bookmakers' task is to set the odds so that under any circumstances a small profit will be made. In the event that so much money is placed on one horse (the favourite) that the odds cannot be adjusted, these bets will be 'laid off' by the prudent bookmaker; i.e. a process of sub-underwriting or reinsurance. In the case of the 'Totalisator' (Table 2.1) a slightly different system operates in which the final payout odds are adjusted after the betting has finished in order to leave the Board with a small fixed (as a proportion to the total amount taken on the race) surplus revenue after every race.

Table 2.1   A simplified totalisator with no place payouts

Horse	Total bets	Odds	Winnings	% Payout
A	1 600	9 : 4	3 600	82.76
B	900	3 : 1	3 600	82.76
C	600	5 : 1	3 600	82.76
D	500	6 : 1	3 500	80.46
E	200	17 : 1	3 600	82.76
F	100	35 : 1	3 600	82.76
G	100	35 : 1	3 600	82.76
H	100	35 : 1	3 600	82.76
I	100	35 : 1	3 600	82.76
J	100	35 : 1	3 600	82.76
Total	4 300			

Note: Only in the case of horse D does the chosen payout result in unusual ex-post odds (31 : 5), an unfamiliar combination to most who wager on horses, so in this case the odds have been rounded to give 6 : 1 and a slightly reduced payout (i.e. the most favourable result for the Tote).

Financial probability

This chapter looks at the nature of expected returns on investments and the statistical methods necessary to make a rigorous analysis of risks and returns. The second part of the chapter goes on to examine the theoretical considerations that underlie the economic decisions to invest or not to invest. The remainder of the chapter examines the construction and usefulness of stock market indices such as the FT 30, the FTSE 100 and the FT Actuaries All Share Index.

Returns as random variables

The return on any financial investment may be defined as the change in the price of that asset (capital gain or loss) plus any dividend or interest payment:

$$r_{i,t} = (d_{i,t} + p_{i,t} - p_{i,t-1})/p_{i,t-1} \qquad (2.1)$$

where d=dividend per share (or interest payment per debenture in the case of debt)

p=price of the share or debenture

i=particular share under scrutiny

t=time period

In Eq. (2.1) both capital gain/loss and dividend are treated as known quantities; hence the rate of return on the left-hand side of the equation is also defined as a known quantity. We need to redefine this equation to allow for uncertainty:

$$r_{i,t}^* = (d_{i,t}^* + p_{i,t}^* - p_{i,t-1})/p_{i,t-1} \qquad (2.2)$$

In Eq. (2.2) the asterisk denotes a random variable and the expected operator E (used in Eq. (2.3) below) denotes the mean expected value which is calculated as follows:

$$E(r_i^*) = \Sigma\, r_{i,t} P(r) \qquad (2.3)$$

where $P(r)$ is the probability of occurrence of the return and Σ is the mathematical symbol indicating that all legitimate values of r should be summed. Although the mean expected value has an asterisk it is not strictly a random variable, being a unique number determined by the probability distribution of $r_{i,t}$.

For example, suppose an investor is considering buying the shares of Southbank plc which might be described as a general engineering firm with a steady, but uninspired, track record for profitability. Suppose also that the purchase price is 50p per share and the investor makes the assessments detailed in Table 2.2 about dividends and capital gains for the next 12 months.

Table 2.2 Expected mean and variance

Time	Expected return (p)	$(p_i - p_m)$	$(p_i - p_m)^2$
$t+1$	8	−0.5	0.25
$t+2$	7	−1.5	2.25
$t+3$	13	4.5	20.25
$t+4$	5	−3.5	12.25
$t+5$	11	2.5	6.25
$t+6$	5.5	−3.0	9.0
$t+7$	8	−0.5	0.25
$t+8$	7.5	−1.0	1.0
$t+9$	12	3.5	12.25
$t+10$	8	−0.5	0.25
Total	85		64.0

Then, from Table 2.2:

Expected mean return, $E(r^*) = 85/10 = 8.5$

Expected variance, $\sigma_{r^*}^2 = 64$

Expected standard deviation, $\sigma_{r^*} = \sqrt{64} = 8$

The expected mean return of 8.5p per share is equal to 17 per cent when the purchase price of 50p is taken into consideration.

The expected mean return is not guaranteed. It is a risky return and the investor should be aware of the extent of that risk. Using the same information used to calculate the $E(r_i^*)$ the investor may calculate the variance and standard deviation of the return (see Table 2.2).

The variance and standard deviation may be formally expressed as follows:

$$\sigma^2_{(r*)} = E[r* - E(r*)]^2 = [r - E(r*)]^2 P(r) \tag{2.4}$$

Hence, the variance of a random variable, $\sigma^2_{(r*)}$, in this case the return on an investment, is the sum of the squared differences from the expected mean, weighted by the probability distribution, $P(r)$. The standard deviation is merely the square root of the variance and may be defined as follows:

$$\sigma_{(r*)} = \sqrt{\sigma^2_{(r*)}} \tag{2.5}$$

Advantages of using the normal distribution

The assumption of a normal distribution for the expected returns on an investment confers certain advantages on any subsequent analysis (Fig. 2.1). The use of the normal distribution permits large quantities of information to be represented by just two parameters, the expected mean and standard deviation. In addition, these two parameters are relatively unaffected by the event of an exceptional observed or expected return which would destroy the usefulness of a parameter like the range of a distribution. The first major advantage over any other distribution is that the normal distribution is unimodal and hence considerably simplifies any subsequent calculations. For example it enables the easy calculation of the probability of any level or range of expected returns.

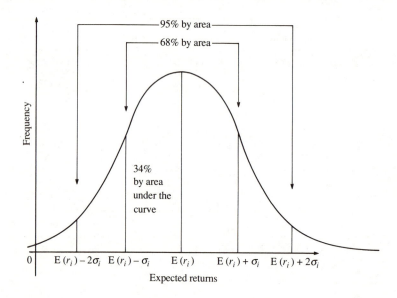

Figure 2.1 The normal distribution.

The standard deviation of any normal distribution represents a specific portion of the area under the curve. One standard deviation represents 0.3413 of the area under the curve. Using the previous example where the expected mean return was 8.5p and the standard deviation was 8p, the probability of the return falling between 8.5p and 16.5p is 0.3413. The probability of the return being within one standard deviation either side of the mean (between 0.5p and 16.5p) is $2(0.3413) = 0.6826$. The probability of the return falling within two standard deviations either side of the mean is 0.9550. The probabilities of any event in terms of standard deviations is known without reference to the actual values of the expected means and standard deviations of the returns of the investment under consideration.

Using this property of the normal distribution the probability of any specific level or range of returns may be calculated merely by expressing the return in terms of its own standard deviation (sometimes called 'z' scores):

$$z = [r_i^* - E(r_i^*)]/\sigma_{(r_i^*)} \qquad (2.6)$$

Suppose an investor is considering Southbank plc as an investment and has made a subjective assessment of the future returns (Table 2.2) and from these has calculated the expected mean and standard deviation. With this information the investor can calculate the probability of making a loss, i.e. a negative return.

$$z = \text{Abs}(0 - 8.5)/8 = 1.0625$$

A return of zero is 1.0625 standard deviations away from the mean (the sign is not important in this usage and so is ignored by taking the absolute value of the calculation). Using Table A1.1 (areas under the normal curve) in Appendix 1 this z score gives a coefficient value of 0.3554. The hatched area under the normal curve in Fig. 2.2 may be calculated as a residual as follows. The area to the right of the mean value is equal to 0.5 or 50 per cent of the area under the curve; the area between the mean and the hatched section has been shown to be equal to 0.3554 or 35.54 per cent of the total and hence the remainder is equal to:

$$1 - 0.5 - 0.3554 = 0.1546$$

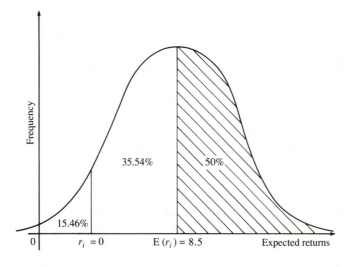

Figure 2.2   Using the normal distribution (I).

Therefore the estimated probability of incurring a loss is 15.46 per cent. If the investor then wishes to know the estimated probability of making a return of greater than 10 per cent a similar calculation is necessary (Fig. 2.3).

$$z = \text{Abs}(10 - 8.5)/8 = 0.1875$$

Ten per cent is 0.1875 standard deviation away from the mean and using Table A1.1 in Appendix 1 this z score gives a coefficient value of 0.0754 (the z score has been rounded to 2 decimal places).

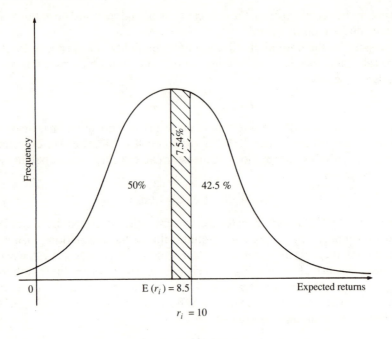

Figure 2.3 Using the normal distribution (II).

As in the previous example the probability of receiving more than 10 per cent may be estimated as a residual:

$$1 - 0.5 - 0.075 = 0.425$$

The estimated probability of receiving more than 10 per cent is 0.425.

This technique may also be used to estimate areas under the normal curve not in the tails of the distribution. Suppose the investor next asks for an estimate of the probability of receiving between 5 and 10 per cent (Fig. 2.4).

This calculation involves estimating and adding together the areas under the curve. The area under the right-hand tail has already been calculated in the previous example, so it remains to calculate the area under the left-hand tail

$$z = \text{Abs}(5 - 8.5)/8 = 0.4375$$

Using Table A1.1 this gives a coefficient of 0.1331. Hence the probability of receiving between 5 and 10 per cent is:

$$0.075 + 0.1331 = 0.208, \text{ or } 20.8 \text{ per cent}$$

The second major advantage of using the normal distribution is that the sum of two normally distributed variables is also normally distributed. In addition, the variance of the sum of two independent normally distributed variables is the sum of their variances. (The proof for this quality is in Appendix A at the end of this chapter.) This has been of considerable importance in the development of Markowitz's[1] theory of risk and return and the subsequent developments by Sharpe[2] and Lintner[3] (see Chapters 4 and 5).

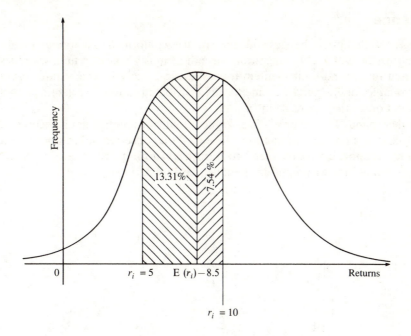

Figure 2.4   Using the normal distribution (III).

Using the normal distribution in practice

In practice, the population mean and standard deviation of a random variable such as the expected return on an investment are never known. Consequently, they have to be estimated from a sample. The sample data are drawn from past returns rather than from some subjective process of estimating the likelihood of the future returns (e.g. the process employed in the previous worked example).

Using sample data the mean is calculated as follows:

$$\bar{r}_i = \sum_{i=1}^{n} r_i / n \tag{2.7}$$

where r_i is the ith observation and n is the number of observations in the sample. It should be noted that in the calculation of the sample mean each observation is weighted equally as the sum is divided by n rather than $n-1$. However, the calculation of the sample variance is as follows:

$$s^2(_r) = \sum_{i=1}^{n} (r_i - \bar{r})^2 / (n-1) \tag{2.8}$$

Note: A small 's' is used here to distinguish the sample standard deviation and variance from the theoretical population parameters.

The sample standard deviation is merely the square root of the sample variance:

$$s_{(r*)} = \sqrt{s^2_{(r*)}} \tag{2.9}$$

It was stated above that the mean and standard deviation of expected returns is never known. In fact, it cannot be stated with certainty that the distribution of expected returns is normal. Consequently, it is very necessary to be able to test for normality in the sample data.

The evidence

The first suggestion that price changes and hence returns conformed to a normal distribution was made by Bachelier in 1901.[4] This suggestion was not seriously taken up until the fifties. In 1959 Osbourne[5] used the central-limit theorem from statistical analysis which states that there is a tendency for samples of independent, indentically distributed random variables to conform to a normal distribution as they increase in size.

On the other hand Mandelbrot[6] has argued that the central-limit theorem does not automatically lead to a normal distribution. He argued that observations in stock market returns and many other economic variables tend to form *leptokurtic* distributions in which there are concentrations around the mean and in the tails (see Fig. 2.5).

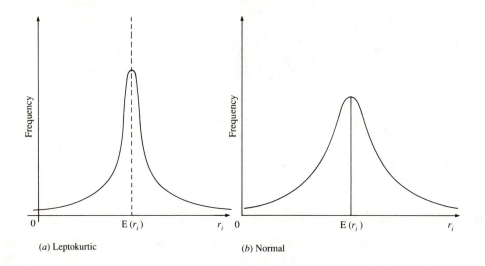

(a) Leptokurtic   (b) Normal

Figure 2.5   Normal and leptokurtic distributions.

Mandelbrot pointed out that many of the price changes observed in the stock market are not related to new information. What this amounts to is that a high percentage of the small price changes that are observed every day may not relate to new information, while a smaller, but still significant, number of the larger price changes which do relate to changes in information about corporate financial status will tend to form the tails of a leptokurtic distribution.

Mandelbrot's work inspired others to look at the distribution of price changes but the overwhelming simplicity of the normal distributions and its implications have not been abandoned. The reason for this is that the statistical tools available to analyse stable non-normal distributions are inferior, both in power and sophistication, to those available for the normal distribution.

Market indicators

Market indicators give an overall assessment of the movement that a market has made over any given period. The London International Stock Market is well supplied with such indicators— more commonly referred to as indices.

Indices measuring the progress (or lack thereof) conform to the following general formula:

$$I = \sum_{i=1}^{n} (p_i^1 w_i^1) \Big/ \sum_{i=1}^{n} (p_i^0 w_i^0)$$
(2.10)

where I is the index in question, p_i^1 is the price of security i in period 1 and w_i^1 is the weight allotted to security i in period 1. Thus I measures a weighted average divergence from the base value (period 0).

There are 3 principal indices used to measure the performance of the London International Stock Exchange. The Financial Times 30 (FT 30) was the first to be created for the British market, in 1935, with a base value of 100. It is not strictly an index, but is a geometric average of 30 major share prices whose weights ('w' in Eq. (2.10)) are all equal to 1. The FT 30 is a sample of the domestic securities quoted on the London International Stock Market. However, it is biased in that its constituents are the 'blue chips' (Table 2.3).

Table 2.3   Constituents of the FT 30 Index January 1986

Allied Lyons	BOC	Grand Met	P & O
ASDA-MFI	Boots	Hawker-Siddely	Plessey
BICC	Cadbury-Schweppes	ICI	Tate & Lyle
BT	Courtaulds	Imperial	Thorn EMI
BTR	Distillers	Hanson Trust	Trusthouse Forte
BP	GEC	Lucas	Vickers
Beecham	GKN	Marks & Spencer	
Blue Circle	Glaxo	NatWest Bank	

Since January 1986 the list has changed as ASDA-MFI has been split up by a management buy-out of the MFI section of the conglomerate, Distillers has been taken over by Guinness, and Imperial has been taken over by Hanson Trust. Not only are the smaller companies left out, but as the list shows, it is heavily biased towards industrial shares at the expense of financial, commercial and other types of company. Even so, the constituents of the FT 30 usually account for about a quarter of the total capitalization of domestic UK shares. In addition to being biased, the FT 30 is deficient in that the sample weightings are all equal to unity and therefore do not reflect the practical investment opportunities in the market being measured. The most common method of achieving this attribute is to assign weights that are equal to the ratio capitalization of the firm to capitalization of the sample as a whole.

The deficiencies of the FT 30 were long recognized (by statisticians at least), but a practical solution to these problems could not be attempted until the advent of computers. In 1962 the Financial Times–Actuaries All Share Index was created (Table 2.4). At present the 'All Share' Index has 710 constituent shares, which is a considerably larger sample of the market than the FT 30. Furthermore, this sample is drawn from every significant sector and sub-indices have been created for each. Hence, an investor wishing to monitor the market performance of shares in the electronics industry can keep track of the relevant sub-index which contains 31 shares. Not only is the sample very large, it is also representative of those shares with a listing on the London International Stock Exchange. Lastly, the All Share Index uses the firm's market capitalization as the weight in an arithmetic calculation.

As the sample is so large it still takes a considerable time for the index to be updated. At present the All Share Index is updated only once a day (although this may change if the computerization of

Table 2.4 The Financial Times—Actuaries All Share Indices

FT–ACTUARIES SHARE INDICES

These indices are the joint compilation of the Financial Times, the Institute of Actuaries and the Faculty of Actuaries

Friday July 22 1988

EQUITY GROUPS & SUB-SECTIONS

Figures in parentheses show number of stocks per section

Section	Index No.	Day's Change %	Est. Earnings Yield% (Max.)	Gross Div. Yield% (Act at 25%)	Est. P/E Ratio (Net)	xd adj. 1988 to date	Thu Jul 21 Index No.	Wed Jul 20 Index No.	Tue Jul 19 Index No.	Year ago (approx) Index No.	1988 High	1988 Low	Since Compilation High	Since Compilation Low
1 CAPITAL GOODS (209)	805.72	−0.9	9.93	3.93	12.46	14.06	812.80	813.17	802.75	998.02	813.17 20/7	706.80 8/2	1038.07 16/7/87	50.71 13/12/74
2 Building Materials (29)	1009.50	−0.8	11.15	4.19	11.02	18.65	1017.10	1020.74	1002.63	1293.27	1049.17 18/3	937.68 8/2	1381.08 16/7/87	44.27 11/12/74
3 Contracting, Construction (37)	1607.48	—	10.23	3.33	12.78	26.91	1606.97	1597.61	1558.81	1836.30	1623.61 22/3	1385.83 4/1	1951.50 16/7/87	71.48 2/12/74
4 Electricals (12)	2188.69	−1.5	8.62	4.56	14.34	48.13	2222.81	2200.90	2181.79	2667.80	2222.81 21/7	1946.87 6/4	2733.45 20/7/87	84.71 25/6/62
5 Electronics (31)	1770.13	−1.3	9.60	3.37	13.27	21.33	1792.57	1792.14	1769.75	2162.25	1792.57 21/7	1423.66 9/2	2234.70 17/7/87	1229.01 8/10/85
6 Mechanical Engineering (56)	421.87	−1.2	9.69	4.14	12.80	8.32	426.78	427.52	425.09	529.91	429.70 15/7	367.20 8/2	544.57 14/10/87	45.43 5/1/75
8 Metals and Metal Forming (7)	505.93	−0.6	9.19	3.70	13.42	7.95	509.08	507.67	503.42	572.66	509.92 14/7	424.40 19/2	596.47 9/10/87	49.65 6/1/75
9 Motors (14)	282.71	−1.1	11.58	4.54	10.00	5.22	285.81	287.19	284.06	389.12	295.13 10/3	259.79 5/4	411.42 13/10/87	19.91 6/1/75
10 Other Industrial Materials (23)	1316.80	−0.5	8.85	4.23	13.48	27.43	1323.85	1327.11	1313.52	1634.50	1350.28 6/7	1191.01 8/2	1736.80 22/9/87	277.55 15/1/81
21 CONSUMER GROUP (186)	1097.12	−0.5	8.97	3.59	14.09	17.13	1103.16	1105.25	1092.99	1357.62	1107.97 23/6	996.55 8/2	1406.32 16/7/87	61.41 13/12/74
22 Brewers and Distillers (21)	1116.57	—	10.63	3.65	11.86	17.67	1117.13	1112.26	1099.74	1241.28	1141.54 15/6	951.87 8/2	1269.35 16/7/87	69.47 13/12/74
25 Food Manufacturing (21)	1007.44	−0.6	8.58	3.62	14.92	17.45	1013.16	1014.88	999.30	1046.56	1014.88 20/7	803.48 6/4	1092.25 16/7/87	59.47 11/12/74
26 Food Retailing (16)	2000.25	−0.6	8.67	3.33	15.27	21.46	2012.29	2026.97	2002.49	2519.94	2179.42 10/3	1964.63 7/6	2649.96 16/7/87	54.25 11/12/74
27 Health and Household (12)	1836.01	−0.9	6.77	2.66	17.13	17.98	1853.45	1867.34	1856.71	2583.59	1927.94 10/3	1708.33 13/1	2699.85 16/7/87	175.38 28/5/80
29 Leisure (30)	1339.21	−0.5	8.62	3.73	14.85	24.56	1346.11	1343.27	1331.64	1427.37	1360.27 11/7	1142.19 4/1	1504.79 13/10/87	54.83 9/1/75
31 Packaging & Paper (17)	528.46	+0.1	9.32	3.81	13.77	9.15	528.09	528.98	526.07	716.79	537.00 8/7	473.11 6/4	739.46 16/7/87	43.46 6/7/75
32 Publishing & Printing (18)	3527.72	+0.1	8.08	4.33	15.59	72.37	3522.84	3542.33	3482.68	4468.81	3632.86 4/3	3625.99 25/4	5070.66 5/10/87	85.88 6/1/75
34 Stores (34)	814.29	−0.8	10.19	4.00	12.90	14.57	820.97	821.87	813.24	1129.63	859.85 28/1	789.39 10/2	1160.58 29/7/87	52.63 6/1/75
35 Textiles (17)	609.32	−1.0	11.33	4.46	10.36	12.51	615.44	611.32	599.39	828.90	620.72 27/4	546.27 19/2	914.52 2/10/87	62.46 11/12/74
40 OTHER GROUPS (93)	894.22	−1.1	10.94	4.37	11.21	17.30	904.60	905.40	899.82	1145.27	918.89 1/7	834.42 8/2	1192.48 16/7/87	58.63 6/1/75
41 Agencies (19)	1152.92	−1.1	7.57	2.57	16.68	15.71	1165.33	1171.98	1156.09	1739.58	1219.02 18/3	1016.74 18/3	1795.57 17/7/87	870.35 4/12/87
42 Chemicals (21)	1061.70	−1.2	11.38	4.63	10.74	24.96	1074.60	1081.25	1086.28	1423.51	1121.06 6/1	971.71 5/4	1545.46 5/10/87	71.20 1/12/74
43 Conglomerates (13)	1206.98	−1.0	10.39	4.43	11.09	20.98	1219.06	1222.64	1212.50	1465.25	1227.15 8/7	1095.37 4/1	1547.01 8/10/87	975.19 10/11/87
45 Shipping and Transport (12)	1903.38	−0.8	11.25	4.70	11.77	34.04	1918.32	1916.71	1896.23	2396.93	1992.59 23/3	1718.96 4/1	2497.85 16/7/87	98.80 29/6/82
47 Telephone Networks (2)	950.13	−1.8	11.72	4.68	11.07	20.38	967.96	967.90	960.02	1119.52	1011.82 1/7	880.24 12/1	1274.14 9/6/87	517.92 10/11/84

	Index No.	Day's Change %	Earn. Yield % (Max.)	Gross Div. Yield %	P/E Ratio (Net)	xd adj. to date	Jul 20	Jul 19	Jul 18	Year ago	High		Low		High		Low	
48 Miscellaneous (26)	1196.13	−0.4	11.34	4.31	10.07	20.93	1200.83	1192.23	1184.76	1638.67	1217.48	23/3	1096.28	19/5	1773.70	5/10/87	60.39	6/7/75
49 INDUSTRIAL GROUP (488)	978.22	−0.8	9.76	3.89	12.75	16.74	986.08	987.30	977.21	1221.98	990.94	11/7	887.00	8/2	1268.86	16/7/87	59.01	13/12/74
51 Oil & Gas (12)	1834.40	−1.3	10.89	5.80	11.80	39.80	1858.07	1863.23	1831.87	2316.76	1881.96	21/6	1699.17	13/1	2458.68	16/7/87	87.23	29/5/62
59 500 SHARE INDEX (500)	1050.78	−0.9	9.92	4.16	12.61	18.74	1059.94	1061.48	1049.65	1314.92	1064.20	11/7	958.79	5/2	1369.68	16/7/87	63.49	13/12/74
61 FINANCIAL GROUP (122)	708.08	−0.9	—	4.80	—	15.53	714.51	713.27	708.42	855.90	720.68	14/6	630.02	8/2	896.67	13/10/87	55.88	13/12/74
62 Banks (8)	688.92	−1.1	20.78	6.10	6.45	18.03	696.53	689.08	688.42	878.91	696.53	21/7	610.26	7/4	898.38	16/7/87	62.44	12/12/74
65 Insurance (Life) (8)	1049.56	−1.1	—	4.78	—	24.97	1061.03	1067.27	1049.28	1127.56	1076.52	8/7	938.43	9/2	1285.72	9/10/87	44.88	2/1/75
66 Insurance (Composite) (7)	549.04	−1.0	—	5.39	—	13.82	554.35	555.44	547.25	636.94	567.92	10/6	481.43	8/2	707.58	13/10/87	43.96	13/12/74
67 Insurance (Brokers) (7)	996.97	−1.2	9.66	6.39	13.38	31.54	1009.11	1009.09	1004.94	1353.72	1022.51	27/6	823.41	6/4	1399.56	17/7/87	65.86	16/12/74
68 Merchant Banks (11)	359.22	−0.1	—	4.02	—	7.03	359.58	357.71	357.32	495.54	378.23	9/6	334.73	5/4	547.59	12/10/87	31.21	7/1/75
69 Property (51)	1209.58	−0.8	5.05	2.66	25.43	13.66	1218.80	1222.48	1210.79	1296.99	1258.31	15/6	975.44	4/1	1374.86	16/7/87	56.01	20/4/65
70 Other Financial (30)	380.47	−0.5	10.30	4.96	12.17	9.27	382.47	382.69	385.00	590.81	401.37	22/3	370.51	8/2	603.48	16/7/87	33.29	17/11/74
71 Investment Trusts (78)	917.86	−0.6	—	2.97	—	12.04	922.95	927.77	924.30	1124.86	935.58	13/7	784.91	4/1	1207.90	5/10/87	71.12	13/12/74
81 Mining Finance (2)	538.16	+0.7	8.90	3.50	12.70	8.12	534.24	534.27	521.90	631.17	556.12	23/6	385.04	8/2	727.93	3/8/87	66.31	30/9/74
91 Overseas Traders (8)	1164.83	−0.8	9.89	4.50	11.88	29.22	1174.37	1178.18	1163.60	1147.71	1203.16	8/7	969.88	4/1	1364.12	13/10/87	97.37	6/1/75
99 ALLSHARE INDEX (710)	962.01	−0.8	—	4.22	—	17.60	970.11	971.14	961.03	1192.66	974.10	11/7	870.19	8/2	1238.57	16/7/87	61.92	13/12/74

	Index No.	Day's Change	Day's High	Day's Low	Jul 21	Jul 20	Jul 19	Jul 18	Jul 15	Year ago
FT 100 SHARE INDEX	1844.8	−19.6	1857.0	1844.8	1864.4	1867.2	1844.8	1849.3	1861.5	2346.9
	1879.3	22/6	1694.5	8/2	2443.4	16/7/87	986.9	23/7/84		

trading systems continues at the current pace). The need for a continuously updated index was met in 1985 by the creation of the Financial Times Stock Exchange 100 Index (FTSE 100, more commonly known as Footsie). This was given a base value of 1000 on 3 January 1984. It is made up of the 100 largest domestic shares by market capitalization and uses the same criterion for its system of weights in an arithmetic index. It has been intentionally biased towards the larger companies because its intended users were and are the institutional fund managers who tend to concentrate their investments in the larger companies. As such it represents an actual portfolio of domestic shares (unlike the FT 30) which can be continuously updated.

Despite the deficiencies of the FT 30 it is still widely used to monitor the movements of the market and as a yardstick for portfolio assessment. This is mainly for two reasons: many investors are unaware of its statistical deficiencies, and, due to its longevity, it gives a historical perspective to the current performance of the market.

The three types of index are compared in Fig. 2.6.

Table 2.5 illustrates how two types of index calculation lead to different views of the market progress. Five hypothetical shares are followed over a period of 10 weeks (the time period is irrelevant as the intervals could be in days or months etc.). The numbers of shares are given in each case so that the market capitalization can be calculated and used as the basis for a system of weights. The first index generated is a simple geometric average like the FT 30 and the second is a weighted index such as the FTSE 100.

The results of Table 2.5, if plotted on a graph (Fig. 2.7), clearly illustrate the differences between the FT 30 and the FTSE 100 as indicators of market progress. However, this sample is rather too small to show the second major difference which is that the FT 30 is less volatile than the FTSE 100.

Although this section has discussed only the indices measuring the progress of the international stock market in London, there are of course indices for almost every regularly active market. Hence, there is an index for the USM complied by Datastream, there are indices for the price

Figure 2.6(a)   The FT 30 Share Index 1982–88. Source: *Stock Exchange Quarterly*.

Figure 2.6(b)   Financial Times–Actuaries All Share Index 1982–88. Source: *Stock Exchange Quarterly*.

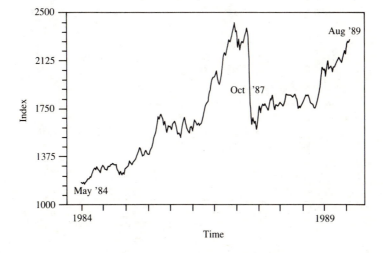

Figure 2.6(c)   FTSE 100 Share Index 1984–89.

Table 2.5 Simulated Stock Exchange indices

Share	No. of shares	Wk1	Wk2	Wk3	Wk4	Wk5	Wk6	Wk7	Wk8	Wk9	Wk10
						Prices in the period					
A	10m	200p	185p	180p	167p	178p	195p	210p	229p	241p	260p
Mkt Value £m		20.0	18.5	18.0	16.7	17.8	19.5	21.0	22.9	24.1	26.0
Weight		0.025	0.024	0.022	0.020	0.021	0.022	0.024	0.026	0.026	0.027
B	50m	61p	62p	60p	58p	57p	59p	62p	64p	60p	60p
Mkt Value £m		30.5	31.0	30.0	29.0	28.5	29.5	31.0	32.0	30.0	30.0
Weight		0.037	0.040	0.037	0.035	0.034	0.033	0.036	0.036	0.033	0.032
C	35m	140p	135p	133p	138p	147p	146p	145p	159p	169p	185p
Mkt Value £m		49.0	47.3	46.6	48.3	51.5	51.1	50.8	55.7	59.2	64.8
Weight		0.06	0.061	0.063	0.059	0.061	0.058	0.059	0.062	0.065	0.068
D	80m	70p	65p	63p	61p	60p	63p	61p	65p	60p	60p
Mkt Value £m		56.0	52.0	50.4	48.8	48.0	50.4	48.8	52.0	48.0	48.0
Weight		0.069	0.067	0.063	0.059	0.057	0.057	0.056	0.058	0.053	0.051
E	150m	440p	420p	439p	455p	465p	489p	476p	488p	500p	521p
Mkt Value £m		660	630	659	683	698	734	714	732	750	782
Weight		0.809	0.809	0.820	0.827	0.827	0.830	0.825	0.818	0.823	0.822
Total											
Capitalization £m		816	779	803	825	843	884	866	895	911	950
FT 30 Index		100	95.9	94.6	93.3	95.5	99.8	100.9	107.2	106.9	111.4
FTSE 100 Index		100	95.4	100.3	104.5	107.0	112.6	109.4	111.9	115.3	120.4

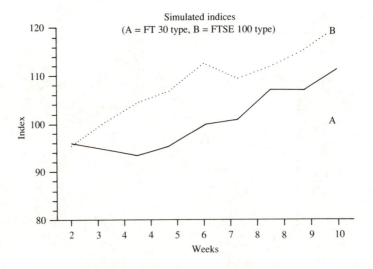

Figure 2.7 Simulated market indices.

movements of British Government Securities, there are indices compiled for every major world stock market—not only those calculated domestically but *The Financial Times* in conjunction with Goldman Sachs and Co., and Wood Mackenzie and Co. Ltd., also publishes indices for a wide spectrum of international markets and groups of markets by geographical area. The FT–Actuaries World Index is shown in Table 2.6.

Before moving on to consider the behaviour of investors a warning should be sounded. Although indices like the FT All Share Index are used as proxies for calculating the returns on market investments (see Chapters 4–6), no market index includes dividend payments and therefore cannot give a totally accurate picture of investment returns.

The behaviour of investors

Having taken a look at the concept of risks in investments, it is now time to consider the manner in which investors behave when confronted by these uncertainties. As all the 'players' in financial markets are economic agents it is to neo-classical microeconomics that we must look for an appropriate analysis for human behaviour. Neo-classical microeconomics is not a monolithic body of thought and analysis. There are competing strands and emphases. The subject, not being dead, undergoes a continual process of development. Very frequently, yesterday's revolutionary ideas have become today's orthodoxy and may be superseded by the current heresies.

The classical analysis of utility presented in the majority of university economics texts operates within an environment of certainty. In economics the satisfaction or happiness derived from the ownership or use of a good (whether it be a commodity or a service) is called utility. In general it is assumed that a good with a positive utility (as opposed to one whose utility is negative and causes dissatisfaction and/or unhappiness) will afford the owner or user greater amounts of satisfaction the more that he or she uses or owns. However, this is qualified by the observation and assumption that all goods have diminishing marginal utility: i.e. that each successive unit consumed or owned will yield the consumer or user successively smaller increments of satisfaction or utility during any specified period of time. This assumption is based on the observation that needs are finite over any specific period of time and therefore are capable of being satisfied. Thus the utility of a loaf of bread to a hungry man may be enormous yet it may not assuage his hunger completely. The second loaf of bread is still wanted but without the urgency of the first. Hence, it is inferred that the second loaf afforded less utility than the first to the hungry man. This line of reasoning is applied to all goods and services including money and income.

It should be noticed that the foregoing section discussed differences in utility in ordinal rather than cardinal terms. That is to say that no numerical values were assigned to the utilities of the first and second loaves of bread. This is a result of a second observation that satisfaction or utility cannot be objectively measured. As a consequence, the same ordinal comparison is used between products as between successive units of the same product. This, then, is the system of analysis of personal wants and desires known as ordinal utility which reached its apogee in Hicks' *Value and Capital*.[7]

Following the above, the total utility function for wealth should be a concave function, (Fig. 2.8). However, financial markets, indeed all markets, are subject to risk; the purchase of a commodity does not guarantee the satisfaction of a personal need. An investment in a financial asset certainly does not ensure an expected level of return or even a positive return at all. Hence, our analysis of utility so far is deficient in that it does not take into account risk. Although classical economists like Adam Smith[8] specifically included risk in their analyses of the net advantages of an occupation, the later neo-classicists such as Marshall[9] avoided analysing choices involving risk with ordinal utility

Table 2.6 FT–Actuaries World Indices

FT–ACTUARIES WORLD INDICES

Jointly compiled by the Financial Times, Goldman, Sachs & Co., and Wood Mackenzie & Co. Ltd, in conjunction with the Institute of Actuaries and the Faculty of Actuaries

NATIONAL AND REGIONAL MARKETS Figures in parentheses show number of stocks per grouping	FRIDAY JULY 1988					THURSDAY JULY 21 1988			DOLLAR INDEX		
	US Dollar Index	Day's Change %	Pound Sterling Index	Local Currency Index	Gross Div. Yield	US Dollar Index	Pound Sterling Index	Local Currency Index	1988 High	1988 Low	Year ago (approx)
Australia (89)	150.71	+0.5	128.38	123.34	3.61	149.92	128.74	122.80	150.71	91.16	149.30
Austria (16)	87.05	+0.8	74.15	82.64	2.51	86.39	74.19	82.48	98.18	83.72	98.60
Belgium (63)	115.99	+1.4	98.80	110.55	4.56	114.36	98.20	110.55	139.89	99.14	128.27
Canada (129)	125.91	−0.5	107.25	109.23	3.07	126.50	108.63	109.69	128.91	107.06	135.13
Denmark (39)	129.21	+0.0	110.06	122.13	2.38	129.20	110.95	122.88	132.72	111.42	113.58
Finland (26)	132.84	+0.2	113.16	121.06	1.42	132.62	113.89	121.60	139.53	106.78	
France (129)	93.35	+0.7	79.52	90.24	3.63	92.70	79.61	90.16	99.62	72.77	108.46
West Germany (100)	75.59	−1.1	64.39	71.80	2.58	76.42	65.63	72.99	80.79	67.78	98.06
Hong Kong (46)	108.20	−0.9	92.16	108.47	4.22	109.23	93.80	109.53	111.86	84.90	134.26
Ireland (18)	144.16	−0.1	122.80	138.33	3.43	144.25	123.87	139.02	144.25	104.60	138.65
Italy (102)	72.58	−0.2	61.82	73.23	2.75	72.73	62.46	73.93	81.74	62.99	95.07
Japan (456)	163.74	−0.2	139.47	135.22	0.53	163.99	140.82	137.04	177.27	133.61	135.91
Malaysia (36)	153.67	−0.5	130.90	155.21	2.37	154.42	132.61	155.97	154.42	107.83	182.09
Mexico (13)	163.10	+1.0	138.94	407.75	1.33	161.56	138.73	403.89	180.07	90.07	309.33
Netherland (38)	106.07	−0.3	90.36	99.78	4.63	106.38	91.35	100.67	110.66	95.23	126.58
New Zealand (21)	79.90	+2.6	68.06	63.50	5.90	77.90	66.90	62.14	84.05	64.42	109.92
Norway (25)	124.39	+0.1	105.96	112.27	2.69	124.31	106.75	113.01	132.23	98.55	152.36
Singapore (26)	131.76	−0.5	112.24	123.57	2.10	132.44	113.73	124.57	132.44	97.99	161.30
South Africa (60)	124.64	−1.3	106.17	94.77	4.54	126.33	108.46	95.22	139.07	118.10	179.03
Spain (43)	148.89	+0.6	126.82	136.65	3.25	148.04	127.12	136.60	164.47	130.73	129.52
Sweden (35)	119.24	+0.1	101.57	111.07	2.57	119.07	102.25	111.58	125.50	96.92	118.87
Switzerland (55)	80.04	−0.1	68.18	75.32	2.27	80.15	68.82	75.95	86.75	75.60	102.41
United Kingdom (325)	134.17	−0.1	114.29	114.29	4.38	134.30	115.33	115.33	141.18	123.09	153.96
USA (582)	107.54	−1.1	91.60	107.54	3.65	108.75	93.39	108.75	112.47	99.19	126.01

NATIONAL AND REGIONAL MARKETS

Figures in parentheses show number of stocks per grouping	FRIDAY JULY 1988					THURSDAY JULY 21 1988			DOLLAR INDEX		
	US Dollar Index	Day's Change %	Pound Sterling Index	Local Currency Index	Gross Div. Yield	US Dollar Index	Pound Sterling Index	Local Currency Index	1988 High	1988 Low	Year ago (approx)
Europe (1014)	106.68	−0.1	90.87	96.68	3.73	106.79	91.70	97.48	110.82	97.01	124.74
Pacific Basin (674)	161.02	−0.1	137.16	133.56	0.73	161.24	138.46	135.24	172.26	130.81	134.49
Euro-Pacific (1688)	139.30	−0.1	118.66	118.83	1.66	139.48	119.77	120.17	147.53	120.36	130.64
North America (711)	108.52	−1.1	92.44	107.66	3.61	109.70	94.20	108.83	113.29	99.78	126.50
Europe Ex. UK (689)	89.63	−0.1	76.35	85.72	3.17	89.72	77.04	86.36	92.99	80.27	106.60
Pacific Ex. Japan (218)	128.28	+0.1	109.27	112.84	3.80	128.12	110.02	112.79	128.28	87.51	141.51
World Ex. US (1890)	138.72	−0.1	118.16	118.40	1.73	138.92	119.30	119.70	146.49	120.26	131.43
World Ex. UK (2147)	125.93	−0.5	107.27	114.65	2.13	126.56	108.68	115.94	131.77	111.77	126.87
World Ex. So. Af. (2412)	126.66	−0.5	107.89	114.74	2.33	127.24	109.26	116.01	132.39	113.26	128.96
World Ex. Japan (2016)	108.87	−0.7	92.74	104.17	3.67	109.62	94.13	105.14	112.43	100.00	127.10
The World Index (2472)	126.65	−0.5	107.88	114.61	2.35	127.23	109.26	115.87	132.38	113.37	112.00

Base value: Dec. 31, 1986 = 100; Finland, Dec. 31, 1987 = 115.037 (US $ Index), 90.791 (Pound Sterling) and 94.94 (Local)
Copyright: The Financial Times, Goldman, Sachs & Co., Wood Mackenzie & Co. Ltd 1987
Belgian market closed July 21 and 22.

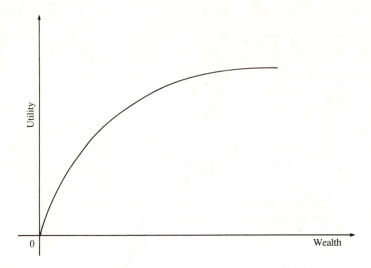

Figure 2.8   The total utility of wealth (I)—concave.

arguing that if the satisfaction gained from gambling is greater than the expected net return then the activity was 'impure' and beyond rational economic analysis.

The omission of risk from the neo-classical analysis of economic behaviour is rooted in the belief in the concept of diminishing marginal utility. When this concept is applied to wealth and its uses without modification, it leads to the conclusions:

1. A unit of wealth yields less utility to a rich person than to a poor person.
2. The indulgence in lotteries, football pools and the like by poor people is irrational and beyond the scope of economic analysis.

Yet the concept of insurance discussed earlier in this chapter and the wide scope of its use by individuals rich or poor suggests that people recognize risk and derive utility from paying out part of their wealth to escape from it. In terms of the utility analysis described above, the utility loss involved in the damage to the commodity or activity insured is far greater than the loss involved in the expenditure on the premium. However, most individuals who purchase insurance in one form or another to escape some risk actively seek risks when they gamble. Therefore, we have the contradictory situation in which a very large proportion of the population (of any country) pay premiums on the one hand to escape from risk and on the other to indulge in risk.

Choices between risky investments involve probability distributions of possible returns. Assume for the moment that a risky investment (X) offers a return of R_1 with a probability of p_1 where $0 < p_1 < 1$, and a return R_2 with a probability of $(1 - p_1)$ and assume that $R_2 > R_1$. Lastly, assume that there is a riskless alternative investment Y which yields a return of R_0. Therefore the expected utility from investment X will be

$$E(U(X)) = p_1 U(R_1) + (1 - p_1) U(R_2) \qquad (2.11)$$

Hence, investment X will be preferred if $E[U(X)] > U(Y)$. If $E[p_1 R_1 + (1 - p_2)R_2] = R_0$ the choice is described as being a 'fair game' and if the investor still opts for the risky alternative we may infer that $E[U(X)] > U(Y)$. On the other hand in this situation if the investor selects investment Y we may infer that he or she prefers certainty and is *risk averse*.

In order to illustrate the difference between insurance and gambling assume that R^* is a riskless income with the same utility as $E(R_x)$ (i.e. the 'certainty equivalent'). If $R^* > E(R_x)$ we may deduce that the investor has a preference for risk (and the opportunity of receiving an income of R_2); on the other hand if $R^* < E(R_x)$ we may conclude that the investor is risk averse. This is more easily demonstrated from Fig. 2.9. Each diagram depicts a total utility of income curve (ABC) for a risk-averse investor (a) and a risk-preferring investor (b). In diagram (a) the utility curve is concave to the horizontal axis and the slope of the curve reduces as the income increases suggesting a diminishing marginal utility of income. In diagram (b) the utility curve is convex to the horizontal axis giving a rising slope as income grows implying an increasing marginal utility of income. In each case the extreme points A and C represent R_1 and R_2 respectively. These two points are also joined by a straight line ADC. In each case point D divides the vertical distance between A and C indicating the probabilities of R_1 and R_2. Hence, the vertical distance between D and the horizontal axis is equal to the expected outcome $E(R_x)$. Therefore if the investor is risk averse and experiences diminishing marginal utility of wealth, $R^* < (ER_x)$, the investor is willing to forgo income up to the value of BD in order to escape from risk in his or her investments. In Fig. 2.9(b), the condition of increasing marginal utility of wealth produces the situation in which the investor is willing to forgo a certain income of BD for the pleasure of gambling on the outcome being R_2 rather than R_1.

Friedman and Savage[10] take this analysis a step further and suggest a shape to the utility curve

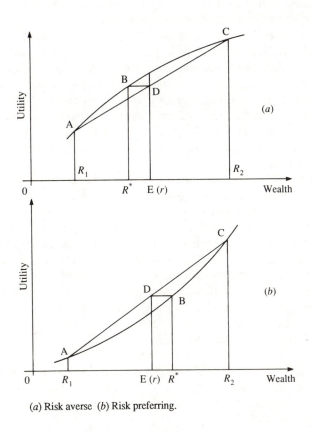

(a) Risk averse (b) Risk preferring.

Figure 2.9   The utility f alternative risky incomes. (a) Risk averse. (b) Risk preferring.

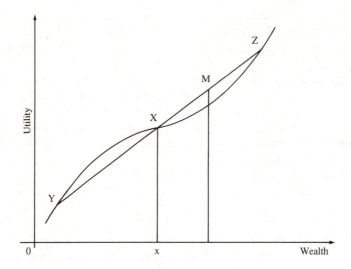

Figure 2.10   The Friedman–Savage total utility curve.

which will explain how individuals on low incomes can indulge in both insurance and gambling at the same time (Fig. 2.10).

If an individual is situated at point X he or she will be risk averse about losing wealth and/or income and so take out insurance to escape loss, but on the other hand will be willing to gamble in order to have a very small chance of obtaining an income of Z. However, this formulation is deficient as Markowitz has pointed out.[1] An individual at a higher income at M would take a fair bet to reach Z which is unlikely as the size of the loss is equal to the size of the win (i.e. the individual would be prepared to contemplate an income of X in order to have a chance of obtaining an income of Z). In addition an individual with an income only slightly inferior to Z would be unwilling to purchase insurance against loss. Markowitz suggested that utility is related to changes in income rather than absolute levels.

We are left with the following sustainable implications about investors' behaviour:
1. Utility functions are unique to both individuals and time.
2. Even in the condition of diminishing marginal utility of wealth and/or income investors will always prefer more wealth to less wealth at the end of the period under consideration.
3. Investors are risk averse implying that they will reject a fair gamble, and the opportunity to win or lose an equal amount with identical probabilities will be turned down. This implies that a condition of diminishing marginal utility applies and the utility function is going to be concave to the horizontal axis. However, this does not mean that there is a total absence of risk-neutral or risk-seeking investors who will be either indifferent to or will accept the fair gamble, merely that the investors' usual behaviour will be risk averse.
4. The above development of utility theory may be used to analyse the behaviour of investors confronted by risky and riskless rates of return.

Assume that two investors (A, B) are confronted by two investments. The first offers a riskless rate of return R^*, and the second offers a risky return $E(R_x)$ which is an expected mean of two possible outcomes R_1 and R_2:

$$E(R_x) = p_1 R_1 + (1 - p_1) R_2$$

It can be seen from Fig. 2.11 that the risk-free return R^* affords a greater level of utility to investor

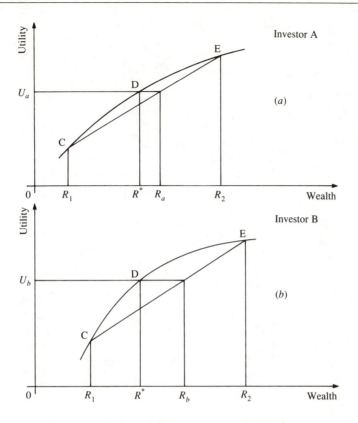

Figure 2.11 Degrees of risk aversion. (a) Risk preferring. (b) Risk averse.

B than to investor A. Using each investor's utility function (CDE) the risky return with the equivalent level of utility to the riskness return may be found by finding the point of intersection of the relevant level of utility with the diagonal CE. In the case of investor A the necessary level of expected return to make the individual indifferent to either the risky or riskless investments is R_a and in the case of investor B the relevant rate of return is R_b. Each investor is clearly risk averse but it can be seen that B is more averse to risk than A. The incremental rate of return needed to compensate B for forgoing the riskless rate of return is much larger than in the case of A.

The above has distinct implications for the shape and slope of the indifference curves (or isoquants) of each investor. If more investments are added to the diagrams additional risk return coordinates could be observed so that a family of indifference curves could be identified for each investor. From the observations and assumptions about investor behaviour and preferences that have already been made it clearly follows that any investor will obtain a greater level of utility under two circumstances:

1. where the investor can obtain a greater level of expected return for a given level of risk;
2. where the investor can obtain the same level of expected return for a reduced level of risk.

It follows then that in the risk–return space depicted in the diagrams of Fig. 2.12 utility increases as the locii of the indifference curves move toward the top left or north-west of each diagram. Before looking at the indifference curves of investors A and B we should consider the two extremes of investor behaviour and preferences—complete abhorrence of risk and complete indifference to risk. For the former, the only way in which utility may be increased is by a reduction in risk regardless of the opportunity cost in terms of the expected return, hence the indifference curves are

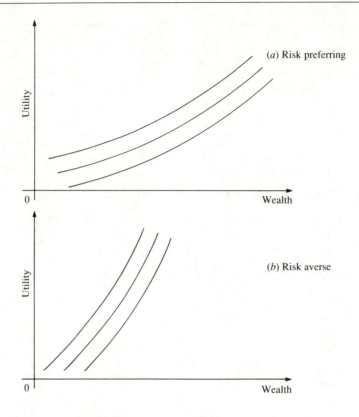

Figure 2.12   Investor indifference curves.

vertical. In the case of the latter, increases in utility are only gained from increases in the level of expected return, therefore the indifference curves are horizontal. Apart from these extremes, the bulk of investors are assumed to be ranged along a spectrum of greater or lesser risk aversion. Two such were depicted in Fig. 2.12. Those of (b) are much steeper than those of (a) indicating a higher degree of risk aversion.

Lastly, the shape of the indifference curves must be explained and justified. The two investors A and B that were used earlier were both risk averse and although the former might be described as aggressive and the latter as timid with regard to risk, both families of indifference curves were convex to the horizontal axis.

The slope of any investor's indifference curve is measured by the marginal rate of substitution (e) between the expected level of return and the level of risk. In the current analysis risk is measured by a proxy, the standard deviation of the expected returns:

$$\left(\frac{E(r_x)}{\sigma_x}\right) \times \left(\frac{\partial \sigma_x}{\partial E(r_x)}\right) \tag{2.12}$$

The positive slopes of the indifference curves shown in Fig. 2.12 indicate a positive value for e. This must be so for two reasons:

1. Risk yields a negative utility to all investors but inveterate gamblers.
2. Wealth is subject to the condition of diminishing marginal utility for all investors except inveterate gamblers once more.

This means that starting from a position of very little return and small risk, additional expected return has a high marginal utility and additional levels of risk have low levels of negative marginal utility. Hence, even the most timid of investors will be prepared to take on some extra risk in order to have a greater expected return. As a consequence, the lower section of each indifference curve will either be flat or have a very small slope. However, if this process of substitution is continued, taking on greater levels of risk for additional expected return, each additional increment to the expected return yields successively smaller increments to total utility and each increase in risk yields successively larger levels of negative utility. Therefore, each unit increase in risk must be compensated for by larger and larger increases in expected return and the slope of each indifference curve must get progressively steeper. The overall result is that each family of indifference curves must be convex to the horizontal axis for any risk-averse investor whether they be timid or aggressive.

Appendix A: The variance theorem

Assume there are two distributions which may be described as follows:

$$r_{(1)} = a_1, b_1, c_1, \ldots \text{ to } n_1 \text{ observations, mean } \bar{r}_{(1)}$$
$$r_{(2)} = a_2, b_2, c_2, \ldots \text{ to } n_2 \text{ observations, mean } \bar{r}_{(2)}$$

Let $R = r_{(1)} + r_{(2)}$,

$\therefore R = a_1 + a_2, a_1 + b_2, a_1 + c_2, \ldots + b_1 + a_2, b_1 + b_2, \ldots$, making $n_1 n_2$ observations. Summing over all the $n_1 n_2$ observations:

$$\Sigma R = n_2(a_1 + b_1 + c_1 + \ldots) + n_2(a_1 + b_1 + c_1 + \ldots),$$
$$\therefore \bar{R} = \Sigma R / n_1 n_2 = \Sigma r_1 / n_1 + \Sigma r_2 / n_2 = \bar{r}_1 + \bar{r}_2$$

The mean of any distribution can be made equal to zero if a constant equal to the mean is subtracted from each observation. This will not affect the distribution apart from shifting the mean; for example, the standard deviation will remain the same. As $\bar{R}$ was shown to be equal to $\bar{r}_{(1)} + \bar{r}_{(2)}$ it will also be equal to zero,

$$\therefore \sigma^2_{(1)} = \Sigma r_1^2 / n_1 \, ; \, \sigma^2_{(2)} = \Sigma r_2^2 / n_2 \, ; \, \sigma^2_{(R)} = \Sigma R^2 / n_1 n_2$$

However,

$$\Sigma R^2 = (a_1 + a_2)^2 + (a_1 + b_2)^2 + \ldots + (b_1 + a_2)^2 + (b_1 + b_2)^2 + \ldots$$
$$= n_2(a_1^2 + b_1^2 + c_1^2 + \ldots) + n_1(a_2^2 + b_2^2 + c_2^2 + \ldots)$$
$$+ 2(a_1 + b_1 + c_1 + \ldots)(a_2 + b_2 + c_2 + \ldots)$$
$$= n_2 \Sigma r_{(1)}^2 + n_1 \Sigma r_{(2)}^2 + 2\Sigma r_{(1)} r_{(2)}$$

The last term vanishes as r_1^1 and r_2^1 are equal to zero, therefore the last equation reduces to:

$$\Sigma R^2 / n_1 n_2 = \Sigma r_{(1)}^2 / n_1 + \Sigma r_{(2)}^2 / n_2$$

i.e.

$$\sigma^2_{(R)} = \sigma^2_{(r1)} + \sigma^2_{(r2)}$$

Appendix B: Indices

It is worth noting the essential difference between stock market indices and those used to calculate the rate of price inflation. There are two basic methods used to measure price inflation:

1. *The Laspeyre index.*   This measures the increase in the cost of buying base year quantities at current year prices, hence:

$$L = \sum_{i=1}^{n} p_i^1 x_i^0 \bigg/ \sum_{i=1}^{n} p_i^0 x_i^0$$

where x represents each type and quantity of good included in the basket of goods being measured, and p is the price of each unit of each type of good. The superscripts '0' and '1' indicate the time period.

2. *The Paasche index.*   This index uses the current year's basket of goods rather than that of the base year as the yardstick for comparison:

$$P = \sum_{i=1}^{n} p_i^1 x_i^1 \bigg/ \sum_{i=1}^{n} p_i^0 x_i^1$$

Consequently, the second index is similar in concept to those capitalization-weighted indices used in stock exchanges such as the FTSE 100. However, most retail price indices are of the Laspeyre type as they require less effort to calculate since the basket of goods is fixed for many years. This of course necessitates periodic changes of base year for the RPI and the creation of a new series.

Notes

1. H. Markowitz, 'The utility of wealth', *Journal of Political Economy*, Vol. 60, 1952.
2. W. F. Sharpe, 'A simplified model for portfolio analysis', *Management Science*, Vol. 9, 1963. W. F. Sharpe, 'Capital asset prices: a theory of market equilibrium under condition of risk', *Journal of Finance*, Vol. 19, September 1964.
3. J. Lintner, 'The valuation of risky assets and the selection of risky investments in stock and capital budgets', *Review of Economics and Statistics*, Vol. 47, 1965.
4. L. Bachelier, *La Théorie de la Spéculation*, Paris, 1901.
5. F. Osbourne, 'Periodic structure in the Brownian motion of stock prices', *Operations Research*, 1959.
6. B. Mandelbrot, 'The variation of certain speculative prices', *Journal of Business*, 1963.
7. J. R. Hicks, *Value and Capital*, Oxford University Press, 1939, pp. 1–30.
8. A. Smith, *The Wealth of Nations*, Pelican, 1970, pp. 202–222.
9. A. Marshall, *Principles of Economics*, 8th edn, Macmillan, 1920, p. 135.
10. M. Friedman and L. Savage, 'The utility analysis of choices involving risk', *Journal of Political Economy*, Vol. 54, 1948.

Further reading

Alchian, A., 'The meaning of utility measurements', *American Economic Review*, Vol. 43, 1953.

Questions

1. What are the advantages of being able to assume that the distribution of expected returns from a financial investment is normal?

2. Calculate the following probabilities when the expected average annual return on an investment is 12% and the standard deviation of that return is 10%:
   (a)   The probability of the return being above 15%;
   (b)   The probability of the return being below 5%;
   (c)   The probability of the return being between 5% and 15%;
   (d)   The probability of the return being above 15% or below 5%;
   (e)   The probability of the return being negative.
3. Critically discuss Mandelbrot's critique of the assumption of the normal distribution for the expected returns from financial investments.
4. Why was it deemed necessary to devise the FT Actuaries Share indices and the FTSE-100 when the FT 30 already existed?
5. Why did the FT 30 index take the form that it did when it was first devised? Why couldn't a more complex version have been implemented?
6. Explain and critically discuss the contribution that classical utility analysis makes towards our understanding of investor behaviour.
7. To what extent does the Friedman-Savage total utility curve explain the behaviour of investors under different circumstances?
8. What sustainable conclusions does the utility analysis lead to about the behaviour of investors?
9. What is the marginal rate of substitution in the context of the utility analysis of investor behaviour and what does it measure?
10. (a)   If it has been established that on average there are 250 incidences of house fires in a town with 80,000 houses whose average price is £40,000 and that on average the payout ratio is 75%, what is the average premium for house fire insurance before costs and profits are taken into account?
    (b)   If in the following year 10,000 more houses have been added to the housing stock and the average number of fires has increased to 450 while the average price of houses has risen to £50,000 and the average payout ratio has risen to 80% what will the premium be for a house costing twice the average?

3. The operation of the market

Introduction

The basis for any rigorous theoretical and empirical analysis of financial markets is the group of theories known as the 'efficient market' theory or hypothesis. The conclusion is deceptively simple, yet its implications are all-important for the practice and academic analysis of financial investments. This important conclusion is that if markets are efficient then prices will contain enough of the available information about securities so as to make trading systems and traditional security analysis superfluous. If share prices reflect the available information about the underlying companies, then changes must be produced by new information. Thus the analysis of price levels or movements of the recent and not-so-recent past cannot yield a superior investment performance. Similarly, analysis of published information cannot be expected to produce a superior performance as by definition that information has already been reflected in the current price.

A capital market is expected to raise funds for investment, disseminate risk and price financial assets. The last of these is crucial to the achievement of the other two. In order to produce the greatest levels of, and growth in, social welfare, the markets that are at the heart of the free enterprise system must operate as efficiently as possible. Efficiency in any market means that all prices fully reflect all available information and interpretations of that information. Prices may then be described as fair indicators of the market value (it is paradoxical that many of the proponents of free markets believe in their innate inefficiency and unfairness by asserting the value of trading systems).

The primary market exists to raise large amounts of capital for commercial enterprises and governments. This involves an exchange of money for certificates of ownership and/or instruments of debt which have the prospect of a future stream of income. However, the willingness of investors to exchange their money for financial assets is partially dependent on their ability to sell those assets in the market for what they consider to be a 'fair' price. Thus the secondary market which prices financial assets and provides a mechanism for their exchange is essential to the operation of the primary market.

Microeconomic theory gives the study of financial markets a firm basis for rigorous analysis from which testable propositions may be developed. The most appropriate piece of microeconomic theory for this purpose is the perfect competitive market model. It is based on a series of ideal assumptions against which every real market may be measured. In the analyses of the financial markets done by academics, the perfectly competitive model has been the preferred starting point because of the closeness of 'fit' between the theoretical and real worlds in this case.

In the perfectly competitive market model price plays the key role. The price of an asset is both a rationing device and a signal to buyers and sellers. By its very nature in a product or factor market, price will play a rationing role when taken into consideration with the disposable wealth and incomes of consumers. However, it will also act as a signalling device to producers informing them of the state of demand for their products and the state of the competition for sales of those products.

There are 5 principal *a priori* assumptions in the perfect competition model. They are as follows:
1. Both buyers and sellers seek to maximize their gains.
2. The product is homogeneous.
3. Both buyers and sellers are price takers.
4. Freedom of entry and exit into the market for both buyers and sellers.

5. All participants in the market have perfect knowledge.

The first assumption concerning maximization of gains is a reasonable working hypothesis in the case of financial markets if it is amended as follows: the maximization of investors' wealth consistent with the state of their preference (or otherwise) for risk. This broader definition is of more use in finance as it makes no assumption about the distribution of profits between dividends and retained earnings and any risk differential that may be perceived between the two types of reward (see Chapter 8). The second assumption is almost fulfilled by capital markets as financial assets may only be differentiated by the rights and privileges attached to the various types of ownership and debt, and the combination of risk and return that each asset is perceived to have by investors and market intermediaries.

The microeconomic treatment of perfect markets assumes that each and every participant in the market is a price taker. This means that nobody can be large enough to influence the price by manipulating the demand or supply for the financial asset. However, this does not mean that there must be a large number of buyers and sellers (although it helps in reducing the probability of any one participant affecting prices and also in increasing the probability of continuous price setting and reassessment of the risk–return qualities of the share), only that they act upon received prices rather than making their own. In the case of financial markets this assumption may certainly be held where there are a large number of shares being actively traded. Apart from the obvious capital requirements and practice examinations of the various governing bodies and government departments there are no barriers to entry into the financial markets in London for prospective professional market intermediaries. For the private investor the only factors that might effectively bar entry are their own ignorance of the market and their lack of funds.

Operation efficiency

The internal efficiency of financial markets is concerned with the ease or difficulty and the costs, of purchasing and selling securities. Without operational efficiency, pricing efficiency (and hence allocational efficiency) is difficult, if not impossible, to obtain. If there were barriers to entry for prospective market intermediaries, arbitrarily fixed brokerage rates, manipulation of prices by marketmakers without regard to demand and supply, and unreliable information about the assets being traded, it could be confidently stated that the market was likely to be operationally inefficient and would misprice assets and therefore misallocate resources.

Unfortunately there has been very little formal or rigorous work done on this aspect of market efficiency. What has been done has usually been the by-product of research into the pricing efficiency of financial markets. Hence, brokerage commissions and dealers' spreads have been explicitly considered when analysing the profitability of mechanical trading systems. The accuracy of market information has been indirectly assessed when testing the markets' speeds of reaction to new information and the markets' abilities to assess cosmetic changes in share prices.

Undoubtedly, the events of May Day in the NYSE and the Big Bang in the LSE have made considerable differences to the competitive operation of these markets. Memberships have been thrown open to foreign intermediaries and brokerage rates have been cast adrift. That the former situation was not as efficient as it might have been can be seen by the influx of new intermediaries into these markets and the large reductions of brokerage commissions for certain types of business. These events have, and will, lead to improvements in operational efficiency and hence improvements in pricing and allocational efficiency.

However, there will always remain potential souces of operational inefficiency in financial markets in which limited liability has produced a widespread ownership of shares. These potential sources are as follows:

1. Shareholders as silent partners. By remaining quiet and not questioning management, shareholders effectively become silent partners. Management may then proceed unchecked into sloth or recklessness. In the case of the uncomplaining shareholder, management is usually changed by a takeover which is invariably far more costly than if the shareholders had voted management out themselves. The inefficiency produced in this case is allocational, as incompetent management of resources is perpetuated, thus reducing the benefit to shareholders and society as a whole. It is worth bearing in mind that the costs of any acquisition are borne by the shareholders. In the worst scenario the acquirer is an asset stripper who persuades shareholders to part with their assets at a price well below their market worth in the hands of a competent and responsible management. Thus the shareholder pays for his or her inactivity by not receiving the full value for his or her investment.

2. It has often been argued that investor ignorance is a barrier to operational efficiency. This line of criticism is a variation on the well known 'casino' theme. Investors may buy shares on tips or hunches without bothering to find out about the intrinsic merits or otherwise of their proposed investments. This undoubtedly does take place, although on what scale it is impossible to say. However, it should be clear that those who do so purely out of speculative reasons have a high probability of losing their money unless they have an access to genuine inside (unavailable to other investors) information and thus sooner or later leaving the market poorer if not wiser people. Certainly, while the 'punters' luck lasts they will not contribute to the allocational efficiency of the market. The danger of this type of investment is that it may supersede rational investment in value and thereby temporarily disrupt the pricing efficiency of the market. This has undoubtedly happened in the past (South Sea Bubble, etc., see Chapter 1) and will undoubtedly happen in the future unless human nature undergoes a profound change.

3. Retained earnings. Many firms prefer to finance expansion with retained earnings rather than by raising new capital in the market. Not only is such internal financing cheaper than raising new equity but it also enables the management to ignore the firm's market price and hence any market discipline (this will be compounded if investors act as sleeping partners).

Therefore, May Day and Big Bang are a necessary but not sufficient part of operational efficiency. Investor rationality and 'efficiency' are essential to operational efficiency. The more investors thoroughly investigate their investments and the more seriously they take the rights and powers of ownership the more operationally efficient financial markets will be.

Pricing efficiency and research methodology

Research into the efficiency of financial markets has been concentrated on the information content of share prices. This work has not assumed that knowledge is perfect. Rather, it has tried to estimate just how much knowledge has been taken into account in the market price. Perfect knowledge as required by the competitive model includes knowledge of the future. Knowledge of the future carries with it the implicit assumption of certainty. As financial markets are anything but certain this has been abandoned as a theoretical abstraction and attention has been focused on the extent to which past and present information has been included in the price.

No version of the efficient market theory (EMT) is explicitly or implicitly concerned with testing for market equilibrium because the assumption of perfect knowledge is dropped. Rather, the various forms of the EMT are looking at the reaction times of financial markets and the speeds with which they move towards the new equilibria implied by the constant stream of new information reaching the market. It would be misleading to stress the concept of equilibrium in the context of financial markets. Rather, it cannot be overemphasized that these markets are in a constant state of disequilibria as new information about companies, economies and investors reaches the market in a constant stream. Hence, there is a perpetual adjustment and correction of share prices in response to the new information.

The essential characteristic of research into the efficiency of financial markets has been to determine the extent to which future prices are predictable by various means. This also includes tests of the effectiveness of trading rules to produce profits above what a naive buy-and-hold strategy would have achieved. Thus, the research has not directly tested the perfect knowledge proposition of the perfectly competitive model. Rather, it has been content to try and show that the markets and their prices are inherently fair by giving every investor the same change of making profits and losses on their investments.

The alternative positions all involve the assumption that future prices are predictable and that therefore ruling prices do not reflect past and present information. Hence the fundamental analyst assumes that prices may not contain all available information and that through research future prices and returns are predictable. On the other hand, technical analysts (chartists) assume that present prices do not fully take account of past information, and therefore, past price patterns may be used to predict future price changes.

The EMT is concerned with the speed with which markets incorporate information into prices. In 1970, in his seminal article 'Efficient capital markets: a review of theory and empirical work', Eugene Fama[1] proposed the now familiar classification of the states of efficiency in financial markets. The first is called the 'weak form efficiency' in which prices must reflect all historical information. The second is known as the 'semi-strong form efficiency' in which all publicly available information (including all historical information) is taken into account by the current price. The last classification is called the 'strong form efficiency', and includes both of the previous classifications, but in addition assumes that prices will reflect all privately known information.

The rest of this chapter is divided into two sections as follows:
1. Weak form efficiency.
2. Semi-strong form efficiency.

Strong form efficiency and insider trading will be dealt with in Chapter 6. As most of the tests concern the ability of professional fund managers to outperform the market it is felt that it would be more appropriate to deal with this topic when discussing the applications of the market model. Furthermore, it is felt that the weak and semi-strong versions are sufficient at this juncture for the purpose of analysing the operation of the market, and as a basis to develop modern portfolio theory in Chapters 4 and 5. It should be pointed out that some of the tests of the semi-strong version are in fact based on the market model, however, it is not absolutely necessary at this juncture to fully appreciate its development and implications.

Weak form efficiency

The weak form of the efficient markets theory and the associated tests assume the current market prices reflect all past information. If valid, this would imply that all trading systems based on historical price patterns are useless since all past information is fully reflected in the current market price. Most of the theoretical and empirical formulations of the weak form theory use expected returns along the following general lines:

$$E(p_{i,t+1}|\Theta_t) = (1 + E(r_{i,t+1}|\Theta_t))p_{i,t} \tag{3.1}$$

where E is the expected value operator, p is the share price of share i, r is the rate of return on share i, t is a time subscript, and Θ is the body of information fully reflected in the price. The equation states that the value of the expected price in the next period is based solely on the current price plus the expected return for the next period. It also states by implication that the body of information available (which includes all historical information) in the current period is fully reflected in the current price.

The first developments and tests of the 'random walk' model interpreted the proposition that the available body of information was fully reflected in the current price as meaning that successive changes in price were independent. In order to simplify the statistical analysis these studies also assumed that successive price changes (and the associated returns) were normally distributed (see Appendix 1).

It would, however, be unreasonable to expect people to invest their money without an expectation of a positive return, hence:

$$E(r_{i,t+1}|\Theta_t) \geqslant 0 \qquad (3.2)$$

which merely states that the expected return on share i in period $t + 1$ subject to the information set available in period t, is greater than or equal to zero. Therefore, it follows that the expected price of the share in question must also be greater than or equal to zero:

$$E(p_{i,t+1}|\Theta_t) \geqslant 0 \qquad (3.3)$$

The form of Eq. (3.3) describes a stochastic process known as a 'submartingale'. This has the overwhelmingly important implication that no investor, no matter how well informed about the current set of publicly available information, can expect to make a bigger return from 'trading' in the security than from a simple 'buy-and-hold' strategy. However, it must be emphasized at this point that the submartingale process of price movements does not imply that there will never be negative returns. It merely formalizes the common-sense assumption that investors will not buy securities whose prices they expect to fall. Hence, Eq. (3.3) does not preclude the possibility that realized returns will be different from expected returns.

Taken together, Eqs (3.1) to (3.3) constitute the 'fair game' model of market efficiency. Taking the logic of Eq. (3.3) a step further, if the possession of all the current publicly available information does not enable an investor to better a 'buy-and-hold' strategy, this must be the case for all investors, and therefore the market provides an equal opportunity for all and hence constitutes a fair game:

$$x_{i,t+1} = r_{i,t+1} - E(r_{i,t+1}|\Theta_t) \qquad (3.4)$$

and hence:

$$E(x_{i,t+1}|\Theta_{i,t}) = 0 \qquad (3.5)$$

where x is defined as the excess return achieved on share i when the ex-post return r exceeds the ex-ante return $E(r)$. In a fair game this is zero by definition.

The weak form tests

The random nature of share prices and returns has been suspected by various individuals at one time or another for a long time. One of the earliest and most often cited is Louis Bachelier who published his *Théorie de la Spéculation* in 1901. In 1934 an American statistician remarked that both commodity and stock prices behaved in a more or less random fashion. However, the first systematic treatment of the question was by M.G. Kendall[3] in 1953. Kendall analysed the behaviour of weekly changes in the indices of shares on the London stock market and of the prices of cotton and wheat on American commodity markets. Kendall concluded that 'The series looks like a wandering one, almost as if once a week Demon or Chance drew a random number from a symmetrical population of fixed dispersion and added it to the current price to determine next week's price.'[3]

The bulk of the weak form tests have been concerned with examining the serial correlations between successive returns. Serial correlation (or autocorrelation) measures the correlation coefficient between numerical observations in the same time series; i.e. the extent to which each observation is determined by its predecessors. In 1965 Eugene Fama published a paper in which he analysed the serial correlation in the series of prices of the shares that made up the Dow Jones Industrial Average from 1957 to 1962.[4]

Fama's results, presented in Table 3.1, indicate statistically significant serial correlations (*) in 10 out of the 30 shares in the one-day tests, 5 were significant in the four-day tests, 2 in the nine-day tests and only 1 was significant in the sixteen-day test. However, because the tests were based on 1200–1700 observations the statistically significant tests mean that the relationship is only capable of explaining a 0.36 per cent variation in the next price. Even this very small relationship rapidly disappears after a few days. Furthermore, there is no connection between the serial correlations in one test and those in any of the others.

Table 3.1 Fama's 1962 serial correlation study

| Share | Changes in log. price | | | |
	One-day	Four-day	Nine-day	Sixteen-day
Allied Chemical	0.017	0.029	−0.091	−0.118
Alcoa	0.118*	0.095	−0.112	−0.044
American Can	−0.087*	−0.124*	−0.060	0.031
A.T.&T.	−0.039	−0.010	−0.009	−0.003
American Tobacco	0.111*	−0.125*	0.033	0.007
Anaconda	0.067*	−0.069	−0.125	0.202
Bethlehem Steel	0.013	−0.122	−0.148	0.112
Chrysler	0.012	0.060	−0.026	0.040
Du Pont	0.013	0.069	−0.043	−0.055
Eastman Kodak	0.025	−0.006	−0.053	−0.023
General Electric	0.011	0.020	−0.004	0.000
General Foods	0.061*	−0.005	−0.140	−0.098
General Motors	−0.004	−0.128*	0.009	−0.028
Goodyear	−0.123*	0.001	−0.037	0.033
Int. Harvester	−0.017	−0.068	−0.244*	0.116
Int. Nickel	0.096*	0.038	0.124	0.041
Int. Paper	0.046	0.060	−0.004	−0.010
Johns Manville	0.006	−0.068	−0.002	0.002
Owens Illinios	−0.021	−0.006	0.003	−0.022
Proctor & Gamble	0.099	−0.006	0.098	0.076
Sears	0.097*	−0.070	−0.113	0.041
Standard Oil [Cal.]	0.025	−0.143*	−0.046	0.040
Standard Oil [NJ]	0.008	−0.109	−0.082	−0.121
Swift & Co.	−0.004	−0.072	0.118	−0.197
Texaco	0.094*	−0.053	−0.047	−0.178
Union Carbide	0.107*	0.047	−0.101	0.124
United Aircraft	0.014	−0.190*	−0.192*	−0.040
U.S. Steel	0.040	−0.006	−0.056	0.236*
Westinghouse	−0.027	−0.097	−0.137	0.067
Woolworth	0.028	−0.033	−0.112	0.040

First-order serial correlation coefficients for one-, four-, nine-, and sixteen-day.
Source: E. Fama[4].

Similar tests were performed by Bruno Solnik on data drawn from European markets. Similar results were obtained and these are set out in Table 3.2.

Table 3.2   Serial correlation in European stock markets

Country	One day changes	One week changes	One month changes	Number of shares in sample
Belgium	−0.018	−0.088	−0.22	17
France	−0.019	−0.049	0.012	65
Germany	0.078	0.056	0.058	35
Italy	−0.023	0.001	−0.027	30
Netherlands	0.031	0.002	−0.011	24
Sweden	0.056	0.024	0.140	6
Switzerland	0.012	−0.022	−0.017	17
UK	0.072	−0.055	0.020	40
USA	0.026	−0.038	0.009	*

First-order serial correlation coefficients for one day, one week, and one month changes in log-prices adjusted for dividends and splits.
Source: B.H. Solnik[5].
* Solnik used the results for the USA generated by Fama (see Table 3.1) as a basis for comparison.

Solnik concluded that:

all the sample correlation coefficients are quite small although only slightly larger, on average, than their U.S. equivalent; ... For daily returns, violations of the random walk are more apparent than on Wall Street. This could be due to the thinness of the market and the discontinuity in trading. The slow diffusion of relevant information among investors may be important. It would imply that it takes more time for prices to adjust to new information.[5]

In 1970 Dryden reported on a comprehensive range of random walk tests on 15,000 (the minimum sample size needed to have any chance of describing a normal distribution is 1000) daily share prices of 15 shares quoted on the LSE.[6] The first set of tests involved calculating serial correlation coefficients for lags between 1 and 12 days. Of 180 correlation coefficients only 21 were greater than 2 standard errors. Of those that were statistically significant, 12 were found among the coefficients for one- and two-day lags. Although the coefficients had positive signs for the most part, Dryden concluded that there was no significant evidence for any one- or two-day persistence of a price change.

Dryden also tested the efficacy of mechanical rules over simple buy-and-hold strategies. These were standard tests of the proposition that a random series of price changes (with a mean of zero) in any particular share would not allow an investor to construct a profitable mechanical trading rule based on a knowledge of the past. However, if the random walk has a positive mean, it is possible to produce profits because of long-term 'drift'. This is not an unreasonable assumption if one considers the reinvestment of profits and the subsequent growth of the economy; the real value of a company (and hence the equity shares) will increase. To try to take account of this Dryden used the filter system refined by Fama and Blume.[7] This mechanical rule uses a moving base so as to protect the profit accumulated by a positive series of price changes. Therefore, if a share has been bought for 50p, and is followed by a price change of +20p and the filter has been set at 10 per cent, the investor will only sell if the price falls to 63p [70 − (70)(0.1)]. If on the second day the price moves up to 80p, the investor will sell if the price falls below 72p $[80 - (80)(0.1)]$. However, if the price falls by less than the filter, then the base does not change. Thus, if the price fell to 75p the selling price would remain at 72p rather than falling to 67.5p $[75 - (75)(0.1)]$.

Dryden's results showed that the buy-and-hold gave superior returns in all cases except for the two smallest filters (0.2 and 0.6 per cent); the returns on the filters fell as the size decreased and above 2.5 per cent the returns were negative. Dryden concluded that these tests favoured the random walk hypothesis in the LSE. The only exceptions to be found were in the cases of small price changes and some serial dependence over the very short run (one or two days).

The weak form efficiency of the LSE was tested by Girmes and Benjamin.[8] The method of analysis used was to test for serial dependence in closing daily share prices for 543 stocks and shares between October 1968 and April 1971 (some 600 observations). Girmes and Benjamin segregated their results into three classes:
1. Random stocks and shares.
2. Indeterminate stocks and shares.
3. Non-random stocks and shares.

They found that 30 per cent of the sample fell into the first class, 50 per cent into the second class and 20 per cent into the third class. They noted that the random stocks tended to be those which enjoyed heavy trading on the market while those that were not random tended to experience thin markets. The authors also tested the proposition that the larger the capitalization of the company the greater the probability of a random share market. Although their tests tended to be contradictory, Girmes and Benjamin concluded that the balance of evidence suggested that probability of randomness increased with the size of the company.

Several studies since have tried to identify just what makes a market efficient.[9] Attention has been concentrated on factors such as the attention of financial analysts (the smaller the number of analysts that show an interest in a share the greater the probability of mispricing), the number of traders making markets in a security (the smaller the number of traders the greater the probability of inefficient pricing), the numbers of transactions (the smaller the number of transactions in any particular security over a given period the greater the probability of inefficient pricing), and the size of the market (the larger the market the greater the probability that security prices will be efficient).

Two studies published in 1959 compared share prices with randomly generated simulations. Osbourne[10] compared stock market prices with the random movement of microscopic particles suspended in a solution. This is known as Brownian motion in physics (named after the Scottish botanist who first identified the phenomenon in the nineteenth century by observing the movement of pollen grains in water). Although Osbourne's findings were generally consistent with the thesis of weak form efficiency, he noted that daily closing prices tended to be concentrated either at the day's highs or lows. In a later study, Osbourne[11] also noted that reversals (pairs of price changes with opposite directions) tended to be much more common than continuations (prices changes in the same direction). The second study, by Harry Roberts,[12] simulated stock market price changes using independent observations from a normal distribution with a mean of 0.5 and a standard deviation of 5.0. Roberts concluded that although the chance model seemed to be satisfactory in simulating the market in the short run, it would not be sufficient for long-run purposes as it could not take into account long-run economic growth which would have a beneficial effect on stock prices. However, he did suggest that predictive analysis based on past price information alone would be inadequate without a thorough knowledge of economic theory.

Despite the statistical evidence to the contrary, predictive systems based on historical data continue in widespread use in every stock market in the world. For example, moving averages are one of the simpler methods used. Figure 3.1 uses the FTSE 100 index to show 10 week moving averages. The trading rules are simply buy when prices move above the moving average and sell when they fall below the moving average. Apart from there being no obvious rationale for this system to be profitable, there is the problem of choosing the period for the moving average. If the period is too short, too many trades will be initiated and costs will eliminate any profits. If the period is too long too few trades will be made as the moving average will tend to ignore large movements in prices.

If markets are weak form inefficient then historical data could be used to determine profitable trading systems. Consequently, the most common types of tests of weak form efficiency are those that examine the profitability of trading systems. One of the livelier debates concerned the efficacy of the 'relative strength' or 'portfolio upgrading' trading rule. The debate was started in 1966–67 by R. A. Levy[13] who reported significantly better results for two relative strength trading rules over the returns from a simple buy-and-hold strategy. These trading rules were comprehensively tested and refuted by M. C. Jensen and G. A. Bennington in 1970.[14]

The version of the relative strength rule devised and tested by Levy, Jensen and Bennington may be described as follows:

Let $P = (P_t)/n$, where P_t is the closing price for week t and $n = 27$ weeks. Let $R_t = P_t/P$; R is the ratio of the current price to the average of the previous 27 weeks. The higher the value for R the greater the relative strength of the share. Let X be defined as a percentage between 0 and 100 $(0 > X > 100)$ and let K be defined as the cast out rank. Levy reported two trading rules ($X = 10$ per cent, $K = 160$; and $X = 5$ per cent, $K = 140$) to be particularly profitable. These were subsequently tested by Jensen and Bennington for 7 periods between 1930 and 1965 using the securities listed on the NYSE. Two hundred securities were drawn at random for each period and the portfolios were selected and updated using Levy's trading rules. This produced 29 independent samples in which an equal dollar amount was invested in each of the selected securities.

The results, presented in Table 3.3, show that any slight advantage gained by using the relative strength trading rule is dissipated by brokerage costs. The third column shows that the buy-and-hold policy earned 0.18 per cent less than was implied by the portfolio's level of risk. On the other hand the two portfolios selected and updated on the relative strength trading rules underperformed their risk classes by 0.49 per cent and 2.54 per cent respectively. The second and third columns also imply that the trading rules tend to select riskier portfolios than the buy-and-hold strategy.

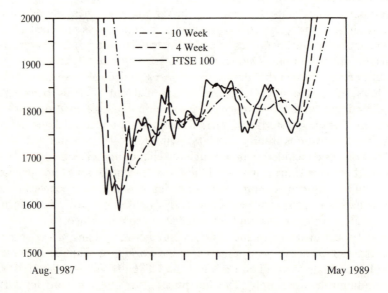

Figure 3.1(a)   4 and 10 week moving averages based on the FTSE 100 1987–89.

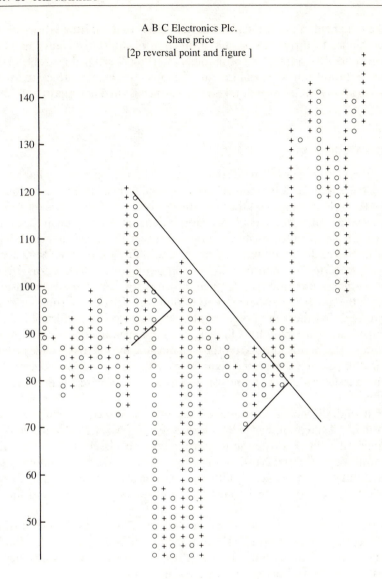

Figure 3.1(b)   Simulated point and figure chart.

Table 3.3   The Jensen and Bennington results

| | Average annual returns | | Average |
Policy	Net of trans. costs.	Gross of trans. costs	performance measure*
Buy and Hold	0.107	0.111	−0.0018
[X = 10%, K = 160]	0.107	0.125	−0.0049
[X = 5%, K = 140]	0.093	0.124	−0.0254

* This measure is Jensen's portfolio performance measure, see Chapter 6.
Source: M.C. Jensen and G.A. Bennington[14].

The evidence presented in this section strongly suggests that charting is a waste of effort. That the practice continues to thrive is not only a function of the statisticians' inability to provide overwhelmingly conclusive proof (i.e. a probability of 1) that charting does not lead to consistently superior investment results, it is also a function of people's permanent desire to foretell the future and the convincing power of the anecdotal evidence which is cited in support of technical analysis.

Semi-strong theory

The semi-strong version of the EMT holds that prices contain all publicly available information. In a market where there were no transactions costs, all publicly available information was free to all participants and everybody agreed on the interpretation of the information, the price of a security would obviously reflect all publicly available information. However, even in the absence of such a frictionless market it is still quite possible for prices to reflect all publicly available information. So long as transaction costs do not inhibit trading on new information, and if 'sufficient' numbers of investors have access to the information, it will not matter if investors disagree on the interpretation of that information as long as no investor can show a consistently superior performance over the rest. All financial markets exhibit these frictions to some degree or other, but it should be stressed that these are potential not actual sources of inefficiency.

The major implication and paradox of this is that fundamental analysis cannot be expected to produce consistently superior profits to those indicated by the risk classes of the securities involved; yet the very existence of such activity helps to make the market efficient. This variant of the EMT has been tested by looking at the way in which the market reacts to the announcement of new information.

The study that set the fashion and technique for most of the subsequent work was done by Fama, Fisher, Jensen and Roll and published in the *International Economic Review* in 1969.[15] The authors set out to examine the NYSE's reaction to stock splits (scrip issues—increasing the number of shares without raising new capital so that a one-for-one scrip issue would double each investors number of shares but without necessarily altering the value of his or her investment). This involved studying the effect of any information implicit in the split on the price before and after the split took place.

Fama et al. took their data from the NYSE between 1927 and 1959. It encompassed 940 splits. The data was adjusted to remove the effects of any changes in capitalization, for dividends, and for market movements immediately before and after the split. For each of the splits they estimated the following equation (ordinary least squares regression):

$$r_{i,t} = a_i + b_i r_{m,t} + e_{i,t} \tag{3.6}$$

where $r_{i,t}$ is the return of the ith firm in month t, a_i is the intercept for firm i, $r_{m,t}$ is the market return in month t, and $e_{i,t}$ is the residual error (the difference between the predicted return and the actual return).

They then aggregated the residuals of all 940 cases and calculated the average value for each month:

$$e_{a,t} = (1/940)\Sigma e_{i,t} \tag{3.7}$$

and then calculated the cumulative average residuals for 30 months before and 30 months after the split (Fig. 3.2).

The authors interpret their results by arguing that stock splits are more likely to occur during 'abnormally' good periods when the companies have performed well relative to the market during a 'boom' in general market prices. Figure 3.2 shows that cumulative average residuals (CARs) rise

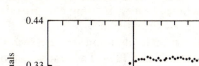

(*a*) Cumulative average residuals – all splits

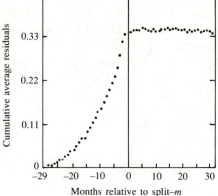

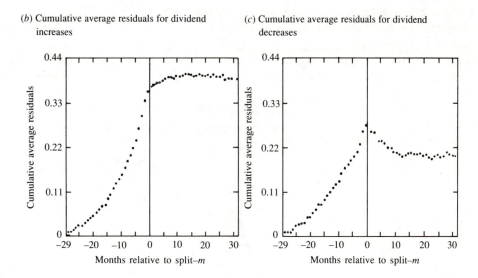

(*b*) Cumulative average residuals for dividend increases

(*c*) Cumulative average residuals for dividend decreases

Figure 3.2   Semi-strong evidence: stock splits. (Source: Fama et al.,[15] pp. 13, 15.)

most in the 3 or 4 months before the split, thereafter exhibiting little or no systematic movement. It is suggested that the market anticipates better performance from the firm and interprets the split as being confirmation. The authors show that the split itself has no effect on the market's evaluation of shares by splitting their sample into those firms which increased dividends and those which cut dividends after the split. The latter sub-sample indicated that when the anticipated dividend increase did not materialize, the market reduced the value of the shares (Fig. 3.2(c)).

Fama et al. also suggest that the evidence indicates that splits cannot be used to generate trading profits by buying on announcement. Those companies which do increase dividends after the split experience no systematic price rises as the improvement has already been anticipated and discounted by the market. In the case of the firms which decrease their dividends after the announcement of the split, the trader who bought on announcement would very likely suffer a capital loss. Therefore, they concluded that their study had provided evidence in support of the proposition that the NYSE was semi-strong efficient.

Firth[16] repeated this study with UK data on scrip issues. The data consisted of 227 capitalization issues made between 1973 and 1974. The sample had no industry bias and, as in the US study, the majority of the sample exhibited above average performance in the market prior to the issue. The most notable difference from the American study was that Firth concentrated on the month prior to and the month after the issue. The results showed a considerable increase in the price in the week prior to the announcement and no systematic movement in the price in the month after the announcement. Hence, Firth concluded that scrip issues had no effect on share prices and that any movements are associated with the anticipation of better company performance and companies not meeting market expectations.

The fundamental issue at stake in the above two studies is whether financial markets can distinguish between real and illusory changes in the position and prospects of the firm. Both studies suggested that markets are not misled by cosmetic changes which in themselves have no bearing on the firms' abilities to generate future cash flows. Stock splits and capitalization issues can be justified by arguing that they increase the marketability of the firms' shares. Whether this is correct or not matters little if corporate financial officers believe it to be the case. However, US corporations also indulge in stock 'reverse splits' or share consolidations. This phenomenon has been examined by Radcliffe and Gillespie who found that the market tended to impute negative information to reverse splits.[17]

Using the methods of Fama et al., Radcliffe and Gillespie examined the price behaviour of the shares of those firms which conducted reverse splits. The sample consisted of 44 shares from the

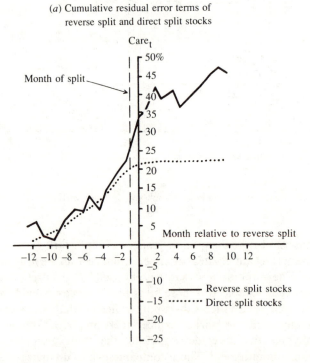

(a) Cumulative residual error terms of
reverse split and direct split stocks

$Care_t$

Month of split

50%
45
40
35
30
25
20
15
10
5

Month relative to reverse split

−12 −10 −8 −6 −4 −2   2 4 6 8 10 12
−5
−10
−15
−20
−25

—— Reverse split stocks
········ Direct split stocks

Figure 3.3 Cumulative average residual error terms for direct and reverse splits. (Source: R. Radcliffe and W. Gillespie.[17])

(*b*) The impact of dividend policy change

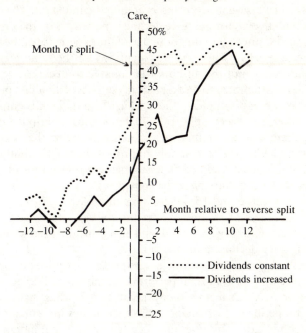

(*c*) Impact by post-split price ranges

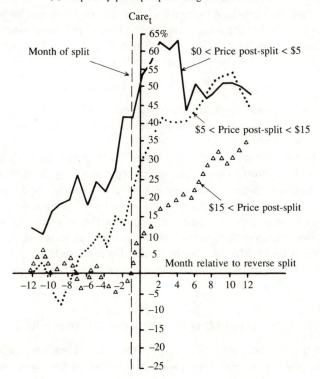

NYSE and the American Stock Exchange over a period of 12 months immediately prior to and after the reverse split. The residuals were aggregated and cumulated. They found that by month (-1) the average cumulative abnormal price decline experienced by the firms in their sample was 21.74 per cent. This turned out to be a mirror image of the experience of the firms in the Fama et al sample where an increase of 21.79 per cent was identified for the same period (although whether this was pure coincidence or not the authors were unable to decide).

Radcliffe and Gillespie attempted to distinguish any impact of dividend policy in their sample by re-running the test on two sub-samples—those which held dividends constant and those which increased dividends after the reverse split. In both cases prices continued their abnormal decline after the split and there was no significant difference between the two groups. Lastly, they attempted to discover whether the reverse split improved the marketability of the shares as some corporate financial officers have claimed. The sample was divided into three groups:
1. those with prices under 5 dollars after the split;
2. those with prices between 5 and 15 dollars after the split;
3. those with prices in excess of 15 dollars after the split.
Again no significant differences were found and firms in all three sub-samples continued to experience abnormal price declines after the split.

An alternative method of analysis used to gauge the semi-strong efficiency of financial markets involves the development of an abnormal performance index (API). The Fama et al. cumulative average residual error (CARE) methodology involves a readjustment of the portfolio under scrutiny with each time period so as to maintain an equal money investment in each share. The API method avoids this complication by assuming merely that an equal money amount is invested in each of the shares in the portfolio at the start of the period under investigation. Thereafter any changes in the weights of investment in each share produced by different directions and rates of price movement are ignored. It has been argued that this approach is intuitively more appealing as it more readily conforms to practice.

The path-breaking work on the API approach was done by Ball and Brown in 1968.[18] Residual error terms were calculated in the same way as in the Fama et al. study (see Eqs (3.6) and (3.7)) but instead of calculating a cumulative average, Ball and Brown treated the term as an abnormal rate of return which could then be compounded as follows:

$$API = (1/N)(1 + e_{i,t}) \tag{3.8}$$

At the beginning of the period to be examined the index will have a value of 1.00. If no abnormal returns are experienced then the index will remain at 1.00, if however the errors are positive then the index will rise and vice versa.

Ball and Brown took a sample of 261 firms over a 20 year period and using the API methodology examined the market reaction to earnings announcements. They divided their sample into those firms which announced earnings above expectations and those which announced earnings below expectations. In the case of those firms reporting better profits than expected, the API showed a 6 per cent increase by the month immediately preceding the announcement. On the other hand, those firms reporting profits inferior to that which had been expected showed a 9 per cent decrease in the API by month (-1). The authors interpreted these results as being consistent with semi-strong efficiency as investors experienced considerable success in forecasting firms' profits.

Anomalies in the semi-strong version of the EMT

There are two major anomalies associated with the semi-strong version of the efficient market theory. The first, using price/earnings ratios as a criterion for share selection and portfolio composition, will be discussed in Chapter 6 when the relevant analytical tool (the capital asset pricing model) has been developed. The second, which concerns the 'weekend effect' has been reported from most major markets (UK, USA, Canada, Japan, Australia). The weekend effect suggests that there is a predictable pattern in share prices and hence that they are not completely random. Fama[4] noticed that the variance of the returns on equities on Mondays showed about 20 per cent greater variance than those on other days. Other more recent studies have also found evidence of negative return for Mondays.[19] However, one striking feature that seems to be emerging is a diminution of this effect over time.[19]

One of the most recent studies, by Board and Sutcliffe,[20] used the 6088 closing values of the FT All Share Index between 30 April 1962 and 30 April 1989. The data was divided into 4 subperiods, 1962–68, 1968–74, 1974–80, 1980–86. Board and Sutcliffe found that mean returns for all 4 periods and the overall period were negative. The results were significant at the 1 per cent level of confidence for the overall period and sub-periods 1 and 3. They also found the returns in every case to be slightly skewed (although not enough to reject the hypothesis that the true population of returns is unskewed) and in varying degrees leptokurtic. It is also worth noting that the last sub-period showed considerably smaller measures of kurtosis (and hence the degree to which the distributions were leptokurtic). However, care should be exercised here as only in the overall period were there enough observations (> 1000) to perform these tests.

One explanation of the weekend effect is that it is only a manifestation of a general closed market effect. Board and Sutcliffe tested this by looking at the impact of weekday bank holidays (sample size 28) on UK share returns. However, this produced no conclusive evidence in favour of the idea (similar conclusions were reached on US data by French).[19] The most commonly advanced explanation for the weekend effect is the market settlement period—or the 'account period' in the London International Stock Market. The account period invariably begins on a Monday and usually lasts for 2 weeks and payment is not required until the second Monday following the end of the account. Hence, the purchaser of shares on the first day of an account has at least 2 weeks in which the cash needed for the investment can earn interest. This interest rate effect must logically lead to an increase in demand for securities—as it is the most advantageous time to buy during the period of the account—and hence should imply an increase in price and a positive return for sellers.

In addition to the interest rate effect, most shares are declared ex-dividend (the purchaser of an ex-dividend share does not have the right to the dividend, it remains with the seller) on the first day of the account period. On going ex-dividend the price of the share drops producing a negative return approximately equal to the size of the lost dividend. Board and Sutcliffe found that the interest rate effect produced positive returns in all periods except for the first thus overturning the negative weekend and ex-dividend effects. Despite the existence of these anomalies, they argue that the existence of transactions costs do not permit the operation of a profitable trading system based on the weekend effect. However, it is worth pointing out that in the absence of trading costs, such anomalies may disappear as an increasing number of investors try to benefit from the same phenomenon. For example, the authors cite the possibility of selling short £1 million worth of shares on a Friday (which is not the end of an account period) and buying them back on the following Monday. They estimate a mean profit of £3000 with a variance of £800. This profit would undoubtedly be wiped out by transactions costs. On the other hand in the absence of dealing costs that profit would be discernable to the investors at large. If they all tried to imitate the operation, prices on Friday would fall and those on the following Monday would rise thus eliminating the profit potential.

Although this section has concentrated on the weekend anomaly in the UK market, similar phenomena have been identified in most other markets.[21]

Conclusions on semi-strong efficiency

There have been a plethora of studies analysing the speed of reaction of US and UK markets to the announcement of information. Direct splits, reverse splits, acquisition and merger announcements, changes in dividend policy announcements and changes in short-term interest rates have all been examined. In the cases of the LSE and the NYSE the unanimous (even if with the odd caveat) conclusion has been that these markets are semi-strong efficient. Prices do embody all publicly known information.

Notes

1. E. Fama, 'Efficient capital markets: a review of theory and empirical work', *Journal of Finance*, Vol. 25, May 1970.
2. R. D. Edwards and J. Magee, *Technical Analysis of Stock Trends*, 4th edn, Magee, Boston, Mass., 1958.
3. M. Kendall, 'The analysis of economic time series, part 1: prices', *Journal of the Royal Statistical Society*, Vol. 116, 1953.
4. E. Fama, 'The Behaviour of stock market prices', *Journal of Business*, Vol. 21, January 1965.
5. B. Solnik, 'Note on the validity of the random walk for European stock prices', *Journal of Finance*, Vol. 28, 1973.
6. M. M. Dryden, 'A statistical study of UK share prices', *Scottish Journal of Political Economy*, Vol. 17, 1970.
7. E. Fama and M. Blume, 'Filter rules and stock market trading', *Journal of Business*, Vol. 22, January 1966.
8. D. H. Girmes and A. E. Benjamin, 'Random walk hypothesis for 543 stocks and shares registered on the Stock Exchange', *Journal of Business Finance and Accounting*, Vol. 1, 1974.
9. A. Arbel S. Carvell and P. Strebel, 'Giraffes, institutions and neglected firms', *Financial Analysts' Journal*, May 1983.
   R. Verrecchia, 'On the theory of market information efficiency', *Journal of Accounting and Economics*, 1979.
   B. Goldman and H. Sosin, 'Information dissemination, market efficiency and the frequency of transactions', *Journal of Financial Economics*, Vol. 7, 1979.
   H. Hong, 'The random walk in stock markets: theory and evidence', *Securities Industry Review*, 1978.
10. F. Osbourne, 'Periodic structure in the Brownian motion of stock prices', *Operations Research*, 1959.
11. F. Osbourne and V. Niederhoffer, 'Market making and reversal on the Stock Exchange', *Journal of the American Statistical Association*, Vol. 61, November 1966.
12. H. Roberts, 'Stock market "patterns" and financial analysis: methodological suggestions', *Journal of Finance*, Vol. 15, 1959.
13. R. Levy, 'Conceptual foundations of technical analysis', *Financial Analysts' Journal*, Vol. 22, May 1966.
   R. Levy, 'Random walks: reality or myth', *Financial Analysts' Journal*, Vol. 23, January 1967.
   M. Jensen, 'Random walks: reality or myth—comment', *Financial Analysts' Journal*, Vol. 23, September 1967.
   R. Levy, 'Random walks: reality or myth—reply', *Financial Analysts' Journal*, Vol. 24, 1968.
14. M. Jensen and G. Bennington, 'Random walks and technical theories: some additional evidence', *Journal of Finance*, Vol. 25, 1970.

15. E. Fama, L. Fisher, M. Jensen and R. Roll, 'The adjustment of stock prices to new information', *International Economic Review*, Vol. 10, February 1969.
16. M. Firth, 'An empirical investigation of the impact of the announcement of capitalisation issues on share prices', *Journal of Business Finance and Accounting*, Vol. 4, 1977.
17. R. Radcliffe and W. Gillespie, 'The price impact of reverse splits', *Financial Analysts' Journal*, Vol. 35, January–February 1979.
18. R. Ball and P. Brown, 'An empirical evaluation of accounting income numbers', *Journal of Accounting Research*, April 1968.
19 F. Cross, 'The Behaviour of stock prices on Friday and Monday', *Financial Analysts' Journal*, Vol. 39, 1983.
   D. W. French, 'Stock returns and the weekend effect', *Journal of Financial Economics*, Vol. 8, 1980.
20. J. Board and C. Sutcliffe, 'The weekend effect in UK stock market returns', *Discussion Paper in Finance and Accounting, No. 6, London School of Economics and the University of Reading*, 1987.
   M. Theobald and V. Price, 'Seasonality estimation in thin markets', *Journal of Finance*, Vol. 39, 1984.
21. For example see the following:
   M. Santesmases, 'An investigation of the Spanish market seasonalities', *Journal of Business Finance and Accounting*, Vol. 13, 1986.
   W. van den Bergh and R. Wessels, 'Stock market seasonality and taxes: an examination of the tax-loss selling hypothesis', *Journal of Business Finance and Accounting*, Vol. 12, 1985.
   For an example of the importance of size:
   S. Dawson, 'The trend toward efficiency for less developed stock exchanges: Hong Kong', *Journal of Business Finance and Accounting*, Vol. 11, 1984.

Questions

1. Does the stock market collapse of October 1987 constitute a rebuttal of the efficient market hypothesis or merely a temporary aberration?
2. Discuss the proposition that the collapse of October 1987 shows the importance of the volume of trade to the price efficiency of the stock market.
3. Explain and critically discuss the irony of market practitioners like chartists and fundamental analysts implicitly assuming the stock market to be inefficient.
4. Critically discuss the proposition that the Big Bang of 1986 has made the market more efficient.
5. Critically discuss the proposition that the hallmark of a well run stock market is the stability of its prices.
6. Explain and critically discuss the rationale underlying technical analysis.
7. Why might the prices of shares quoted on a stock market be described as conforming to the Brownian Law of Motion?
8. Critically discuss the propositions that a stock market misallocates funds and syphons off funds needed for 'real' investment.
9. Distinguish and explain the difference between the random walk and the fair game versions of market efficiency.
10. Of what importance is 'thinness of trading' or 'market liquidity' for market efficiency?

4. Markowitz and modern portfolio theory

Introduction

In Chapter 2 it was established that the normal distribution could be used as a working approximation for the distribution of the returns of a financial asset in spite of it being slightly leptokurtic. Chapter 3 demonstrated that financial markets may be described as being semi-strong efficient and hence constitute a fair game for investors. In addition, Chapter 2 used indifference curve analysis to explain and describe the behaviour of investors. Based on the bedrock of EMT this chapter takes the analytical tools presented in Chapter 2 and develops them into a more rigorous system of analysis of portfolio construction. The chapter title indicates to whom the principal credit for this particular advance in theory should go.[1] Markowitz's first article, published in 1952, appeared at a time when rigorous analysis of investments was not commonplace among the practitioners of investment advice and portfolio management. The article spawned a whole new academic industry concerned with refining the statistical analysis of investments. This approach has been called modern portfolio theory, hereafter referred to as MPT.

Investors and securities

Modern portfolio theory is essentially an application of economic theory and, as in the analysis of the efficiency of financial markets, it rests upon a number of assumptions. It is worth pointing out once again that it matters not how many assumptions there are or how unrealistic they may be, what is important is that the resultant analysis should yield accurate predictions of economic behaviour. MPT follows other economic theories and applications in that once the basic system of analysis has been established, the models have been amenable to modification to reflect various strands of reality in the market under scrutiny.

The assumptions underlying MPT can be summarized as follows:
1. Investors do envisage expected return as a function of a normal distribution of the possible returns and that investors do prefer a greater return to a lesser return; $\partial U/\partial E(r) > 0$.
2. Investors do envisage risk as being a positive function of the size of expected return and that investors do prefer less risk to more risk; $\partial U/\partial \sigma < 0$.
3. Investors do base their investment decisions on the two parameters risk and return, and hence $U = f[E(r), \sigma]$.

Therefore, investors are assumed to be Markowitz efficient. Although assumptions 1 to 3 say nothing about what investors base their estimations of expected returns and associated risks on, it is assumed that they are rational. This means that they base their expectations on the hard evidence of performance of the companies that issued the shares in question. It therefore excludes expectations and investment behaviour that is without firm foundation. The assumptions about the market are as follows:
4. The investors are Markowitz efficient (i.e. they are rational and their behaviour conforms to assumptions 1 to 3).
5. There are homogeneous expectations (an idealized and uniform uncertainty).

6. All investors operate on a one period time horizon.
7. There are no taxes or brokerage.
8. Inflation is fully anticipated (called the Fisher effect).
9. Investments are infinitely divisible (this removes the usual requirement of buying and selling securities in blocks of 100 units).
10. All securities have a variance exceeding zero (all securities have some degree of risk).
11. There are no short sales of securities or gearing of portfolios (there is no provision for borrowing or lending in the money markets or increasing available funds by borrowing and temporarily selling somebody else's shares).
12. The capital market is in equilibrium (this requires that there is no excess supply of, or demand for, all securities and the price for any security at any time has been adjusted to bring about an equality between demand and supply.)[2]

Within the context of these assumptions, the basic market model may be created. The starting point chosen here is the processes and criteria by which securities are selected—the principle of dominance.

Dominance, the opportunity set and the efficient frontier

Chapter 2 established the principle that investors consider not only the expected return but also the variance or standard deviation of the expected return. Suppose an investor has the investments shown in Table 4.1 to consider. These expected returns and risks are plotted on a graph, Fig. 4.1, showing very clearly which of the investments are preferable. First of all, the two investments with the highest risk are Fogarty and Hambros each with standard deviations of 40 per cent. Hambros offers the superior expected return of 24 per cent compared with only 18 per cent from Fogarty. However, Crystalate offers an expected return of 24 per cent with an associated risk of only 33 per cent. Hence, as investments Hambros dominates Fogarty, but is in turn dominated by Crystalate; *ceteris paribus*, the investor should reject both Hambros and Fogarty as Crystalate offers a superior return for a lower risk.

Secondly, there are two investments offering a return of 21 per cent, Brown and Tawse, and Vaux. It is clear that as an investment Vaux offers the better prospects as the expected return of 21 per cent is associated with a risk of only 25 per cent compared with the 33 per cent of Brown and Tawse. It should also be noted that Brown and Tawse is dominated by Crystalate which offers an expected return of 24 per cent for a risk of 33 per cent. Therefore, in this small selection of investments two emerge as dominant; that is to say they offer either the superior expected return for a given level of risk or they offer the lowest risk associated with a given level of expected return.

If this process was extended to every equity and combination of equities on the stock market an opportunity set would be observed as shown in Fig. 4.2.

The opportunity set contains the loci of all the possible equity (and combinations of equities)

Table 4.1 Expected risks and returns

Name	Expected return (%)	Standard deviation (%)
Brown & Tawse	21	33
Vaux	21	25
Crystalate	24	33
Fogarty	18	40
Hambros	24	40

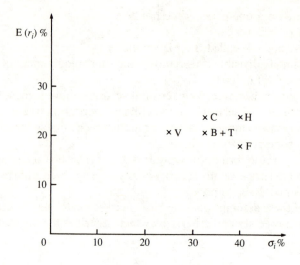

Figure 4.1   Dominance.

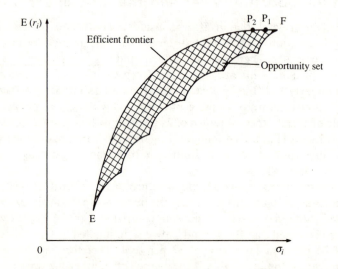

Figure 4.2   The opportunity set and the efficient frontier.

investments on the stock market. The leading edge nearest the vertical axis labelled EF is called the efficient frontier. It marks the loci of all the dominant investments. The curvature of the efficient frontier illustrates what Adam Smith observed in *The Wealth of Nations*, namely that the ordinary rate of profit is affected by the risk or security of an enterprise but that 'the ordinary profit of stock, though it rises with the risk, does not always seem to rise in proportion to it.'[3]

Hirschleifer has shown that this particular curvature is the product of the covariance effect. Moving to obtain higher and higher values of $E(r_i)$ involves the investor in choosing from fewer and fewer securities which progressively impairs his or her ability to reduce the amount of risk associated with higher and higher levels of return. Therefore, the investor will experience diminishing expected returns for each increment of risk that is borne. Conversely, the search for security involves the identification of those securities with the lowest standard deviations of returns. As the target for the risk of the portfolio is progressively reduced so is the number of securities available from which to select a portfolio. Hence, the investor will experience diminishing marginal reductions of risk for each unit of expected return forgone.[3] The implication of this is that points E and F must by definition consist of single share portfolios. As point F indicates the maximum expected return possible it cannot be other than that share which offers the highest return. Any combination must, perforce, be with a share offering an inferior return thus reducing the expected return below the maximum possible. The same reasoning must apply to the minimum risk portfolio. It must consist of the share offering the lowest risk, and any combination with another share will increase the risk.

Although portfolios E and F consist of single securities it would be more correct to consider them as being made up of all the potential shares with zero weights for all except one:

$$w_1 + w_2 + w_3 + \ldots + w_n$$

where $w_1 = 1$ and w_2 to $w_n = 0$.

Each subsequent portfolio along the efficient frontier constitutes the best available combination in terms of return (or risk if moving along EF away from point E). Hence, in Fig. 4.2 portfolio P_1 can be assumed to be the next portfolio along from portfolio F. It is created by combining another share with portfolio F. In this case we have the following condition:

$$w_1, w_2 > 0 \quad \text{and} \quad w_3 \text{ to } w_n = 0$$

and therefore, $w_1 + w_2 = 1$.

The next portfolio, represented by P_2 may be produced by combining a third share with portfolio P_1. Therefore, w_1, w_2, and w_3 are all greater than zero but their sum must be equal to unity.

Markowitz efficient diversification

Up to this point the Markowitz analysis has offered nothing too remarkable. However, this analysis offers the investor a method of diversification which is aimed at producing the dominant portfolio for the risk or return class which has been chosen. In this respect, Markowitz's model really shows itself to be superior to the methods in practice when the original article was published (and, it may be said variants of which are still in use today). This model shows that it is no longer adequate just to spread the risk of the portfolio by investing in different industrial and commercial sectors. Nor is it sufficient merely to pick the best performing shares in each sector. Markowitz pointed out that what really matters is the overall performance, which is to a great extent determined by the covariance between each pair of shares in the portfolio.

Assume that a portfolio is made up from two securities M and F. Further assume that the expected returns of each are normally distributed and have standard deviations σ_m and σ_f respectively. Let r_p, r_m and r_f be the expected returns for the portfolio, security M and security F respectively. Hence, the portfolio's return may be written as follows:

$$r_p = w_m r_m + w_f r_f \tag{4.1}$$

This is of course a specific two-share application of the general proposition that the return of a portfolio is the weighted average returns of the constituent parts:

$$r_p = \sum_{i=1}^{n} w_i r_i \tag{4.2}$$

The risk of the portfolio is a little more involved. The variance of a security's return has previously been defined as the sum of the squares of the probability weighted deviations from the expected mean value. This applies no less to the variance of the portfolio's returns. However, in this form it is difficult to evaluate the effect of each share on the risk–return profile of the portfolio. Using E as the expected value operator to simplify the equations, the variance of the portfolio may be defined as follows:

$$\sigma_p^2 = E[(r_p - \tilde{r}_p)^2] \tag{4.3}$$

This term may be expanded to show the individual returns and weights; r_p is equal to $w_1 r_1 + w_2 r_2$. This produces the following:

$$\sigma_p^2 = E\{[(w_1 r_1 + w_2 r_2) - (w_1 \tilde{r}_1 + w_2 \tilde{r}_2)]^2\} \tag{4.4}$$

where $\tilde{r}_1$ and $\tilde{r}_2$ are the mean expected returns for shares 1 and 2 respectively.
Equation (4.4) simplifies as follows:

$$\sigma_p^2 = E[(w_1 r_1 + w_2 r_2 - w_1 \tilde{r}_1 - w_2 \tilde{r}_2)^2] \tag{4.5}$$

$$\sigma_p^2 = E\{[w_1(r_1 - \tilde{r}_1) + w_2(r_2 - \tilde{r}_2)]^2\} \tag{4.6}$$

$$\sigma_p^2 = w_1^2 E(r_1 - \tilde{r}_1)^2 + w_2^2 E(r_2 - \tilde{r}_2)^2 + 2w_1 w_2 E[(r_1 - \tilde{r}_1)(r_2 - \tilde{r}_2)] \tag{4.7}$$

$$\sigma_p^2 = w_1^2 \sigma_1^2 + w_2^2 \sigma_2^2 + 2w_1 w_2 \sigma_{1,2} \tag{4.8}$$

The last part of the third term of Eq. (4.8) is the covariance of the returns of the two securities. This may be written as $\sigma_1 \sigma_2 \rho_{1,2}$. The last term, $(\rho_{1,2})$ is the correlation coefficient for the two securities in the portfolio. The generalized formula for the determination of portfolio variances may be described as follows:

$$\sigma_p^2 = \sum_{i=1}^{n} w_i^2 r_i^2 + \sum_{i=1}^{n} \sum_{j=1}^{n} w_i w_j \rho_{ij} \tag{4.9}$$

Equation (4.8) may be used to calculate the variance of a two-security portfolio but also the optimal distribution of weights between the two. Furthermore it can be used to illustrate the significance of the covariance term and hence the importance of Markowitz efficient diversification. A numerical example will best illustrate this point. Assume the following expected returns for securities M and F for 10 periods:

Time	r_m	$(1/n)(r_m - \tilde{r}_m)^2$	r_f	$(1/n)(r_r - \tilde{r}_f)^2$	$(1/n)(r_m - \tilde{r}_m)(r_f - \tilde{r}_r)$
1	5	0.1	6	0.9	−0.3
2	5	0.1	−1	1.6	0.4
3	7	0.1	−3	3.6	−0.6
4	4	0.4	−2	2.5	1.0
5	2	1.6	6	0.9	−1.2
6	3	0.9	8	2.5	−1.5
7	9	0.9	3	0.0	0.0
8	9	0.9	9	3.6	1.8
9	9	0.9	8	2.5	1.5
10	7	0.1	−4	4.9	−0.7

$$\Sigma r_m = 60, \quad \tilde{r}_m = 6$$
$$\Sigma r_f = 30, \quad \tilde{r}_f = 3$$
$$\sigma_m^2 = 6.0, \quad \sigma_m = 2.45$$

$$\sigma_f^2 = 23.0, \qquad \sigma_f = 4.79$$
$$\sigma_{m,f} = 0.4, \qquad \rho_{m,r} = 0.034$$

Using Eq. (4.8):

$$\sigma_p^2 = w_m^2 6 + (1 - w_m)^2 23 + 2w_m(1 - w_m)0.4$$

Expanding and collecting the terms:

$$\sigma_p^2 = w_m^2 28.2 - w_m 45.2 + 23$$

Differentiating with respect to w_m and setting the derivative equal to zero:

$$0 = (56.4)w_m - 45.2$$
$$w_m = 45.2/56.4 = 0.8$$
$$w_f = 1 - 0.8 = 0.2$$

Using these weights we may now calculate the expected return and risk of the portfolio:

$$r_p = (0.8)6 + (0.2)3 = 5.4\%$$
$$\sigma_p = [(0.8)^2(6) + (0.2)^2(23) + 2(0.8)(0.2)(0.4)]^{1/2}$$
$$\sigma_p = (4.89)^{1/2}$$
$$\sigma_p = 2.21$$

Not only has the analysis produced the optimum weights (in the sense of minimizing the risk of the portfolio) for investment in the two securities, it has shown that an apparently inferior share such as F can have a valuable place in a portfolio to arrive at some desired risk–return combination. Hence, it has shown that the best portfolios are not necessarily made up of the best-performing shares and that selection is a more complex process than was considered before Markowitz. For example, it is no longer sufficient to diversify by picking the winners from each industrial sector. This analysis can now be used to show the importance of the covariance and correlation coefficients of each pair of securities under consideration.

There are three limiting cases. The first is where ρ is equal to $+1$. In other words the two securities are perfectly correlated, so that as the return of the first increases or decreases by 20 per cent so does that of the second. The second case has ρ equal to zero. In this situation the returns of the two securities are completely uncorrelated and no relationship can be discerned between them. Lastly, ρ has the limiting value of -1. Here there is a perfectly perverse relationship between the returns of the two securities. Thus, as the return of the first increases or decreases by 20 per cent the return of the second does exactly the opposite. The previous numerical example may be used to illustrate the effects of each case:

	W_m	W_f	r_p	σ_p	$\sigma_{m,r}$
Case 1: $\rho = +1$	0.49	0.51	4.47	3.65	11.75
Case 2: $\rho = 0$	0.79	0.21	5.37	2.18	0
Case 3: $\rho = -1$	0.67	0.33	5.0	0	-11.75

The results are shown in graphical form in Fig. 4.3.

The analysis implies that, for the purposes of diversification in which the investor seeks to minimise the level of risk associated with his/her preferred level of expected return, highly correlated securities are not suitable. Ideally, the investor would like to find highly uncorrelated shares but as these are virtually non-existent, the investor must seek out those shares which appear to have no sort of relationship.

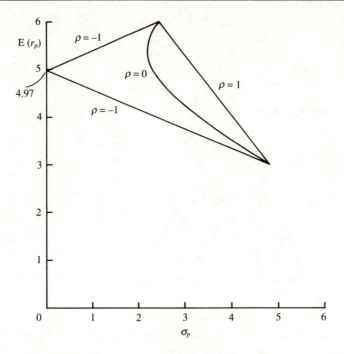

Figure 4.3   Markowitz efficient diversification.

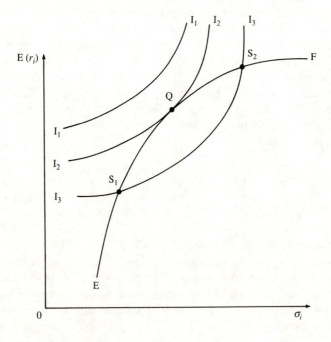

Figure 4.4   Markowitz equilibrium.

Equilibrium in the Markowitz 'model'

The efficient frontier represents all the dominant portfolios. However, this does not indicate which of those portfolios will be chosen by any individual risk-averse investor or whether that choice is optimal or not. This problem is solved by combining the efficient frontier with each investor's 'isoquant map' (isoquants are discussed in Chapter 2, see p. 41).

The point of tangency, Q, in Fig. 4.4 indicates the optimal portfolio for the investor. Any deviation away from Q results in a portfolio which yields an inferior level of utility to the investor. The point of tangency at Q lies on the best possible (in terms of the investor's utility) isoquant. It is impossible to improve on this as there are, by definition, no portfolios to the left (or to the north-west) of the efficient frontier. For example, any movement away from Q puts the investor on an inferior isoquant such as I_3. Therefore, both the portfolios S_1 and S_2 yield a lower level of utility to the investor as they lie on an inferior isoquant even though they are both dominant in their respective risk classes.

This solution has to be repeated for each individual investor. Hence, there will be a multiplicity of preferred portfolios. To obtain a more general solution the basic Markowitz model must be extended.

The risk-free asset

One of Markowitz's key assumptions is that all securities must have a positive variance ($\sigma_i^2 > 0$). Tobin[5] removed this assumption by introducing the 'risk-free asset'. The risk-free assets are assumed to be 3-month treasury bills which are sold at a discount and redeemed at par by a government (see Chapter 9 for a fuller discussion). The probability of any of the governments of any of the developed world becoming insolvent and failing to redeem their short-term debts is so small as to be insignificant. Therefore, short-term government debt can be assumed to be the asset nearest to being totally risk free.

Like Markowitz, Tobin imposed a non-negativity constraint on all risky financial assets. In other words equities cannot be sold short. However, Tobin did allow negative weights for the risk-free asset so that investors can invest in treasury bills and create 'lending' portfolios or they are permitted to borrow capital by selling treasury bills short. Hence, investors are allowed to gear their portfolios. But it should be appreciated that this implies one rate of interest for both borrowers and lenders. This particular assmption will be examined more critically at a later stage in this chapter.

The important result of including a risk-free asset is that it reduces the number of optimal portfolios of risky assets to one for any and every investor. This single portfolio is known as the market portfolio. This result can easily be seen in Fig. 4.5.

The inclusion of the risk-free asset renders all of the opportunity set and all but one of the risky portfolios on the efficient frontier sub-optimal. If a ray pivoted on the risk-free asset is dropped onto the efficient frontier, the point of tangency at M in Fig. 4.5 constitutes the optimal portfolio for every investor. That this is so may be intuitively deduced from the principle of dominance once again. Lending portfolios may be formed by investing in the market portfolio M and the risk-free asset. The risk–return loci of these portfolios will form the line r_f–M. These risk–return combinations are superior to any of those offered by portfolios of risky assets in the opportunity set. If the investor sells the risk-free asset short and invests the proceeds in M, the risk–return locii of the resultant portfolios will extend the line r_f–M to L and beyond depending on how much the investor borrows.

The graphical representation of Fig. 4.5, although intuitively pleasing, does not have the rigour

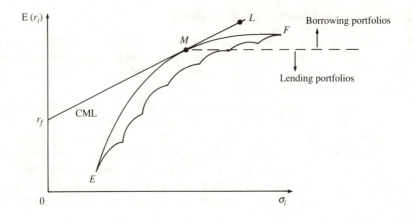

Figure 4.5   Tobin's model and the capital market line (CML).

necessary to give watertight proofs of the results. For this an algebraic exposition is necessary.

$$r_p = w_f r_f + (1 - w_f) r_m \tag{4.10}$$

$$\sigma_p = [w_f^2 \sigma_f^2 + (1 - w_f)^2 \sigma_m^2 + 2 w_f (1 - w_f) \sigma_{f,m}]^{1/2} \tag{4.11}$$

Equations (4.10) and (4.11) are the familiar expressions for the return and risk of the portfolio. However, as the risk-free asset (f) has a zero standard deviation of return Eq. (4.11) simplifies considerably as follows:

$$\text{as } \sigma_f = 0 \text{ and } \sigma_{f,m} = \rho_{f,m} \sigma_r \sigma_m, \ \sigma_{f,m} = 0$$

$$\sigma_p = (1 - w_f) \sigma_m = \sigma_m - \sigma_m w_f \tag{4.12}$$

$$w_f = (\sigma_m - \sigma_p)/\sigma_m \tag{4.13}$$

Substituting for w_f in Eq. (4.10):

$$r_p = ((\sigma_m - \sigma_p)/\sigma_m) r_f + (1 - (\sigma_m - \sigma_p)/\sigma_m) r_m \tag{4.14}$$

$$r_p = r_f (\sigma_m - \sigma_p)/\sigma_m + r_m - r_m (\sigma_m - \sigma_p)/\sigma_m \tag{4.15}$$

By expansion and collection of terms:

$$r_p = r_f + ((r_m - r_f)/\sigma_m) \sigma_p \tag{4.16}$$

Equation (4.16) shows that the expected return on the portfolio is a linear function of the expected risk of the portfolio which itself is dependent on the distribution of investment between the risk-free asset and the market portfolio. This linear function is known as the capital market line (CML) and is shown in Figs. 4.5 and 4.6.

The implications of this analysis were quite revolutionary for the practice of investment. First and foremost it implied that each and every investor could be catered for by just two investments as all risk–return combinations could be achieved by varying the distribution of investment between the market portfolio and the risk-free asset. The market portfolio is approximated by many of the investment trust companies (for more discussion on this point see Chapter 6) on the market and short-term government gilts can be purchased by anybody. This conclusion was and still is highly unpopular among those who make their living selling advice on investments. To put it more prosaically, it implied that the profession of financial investment consultant (the practice of mixing

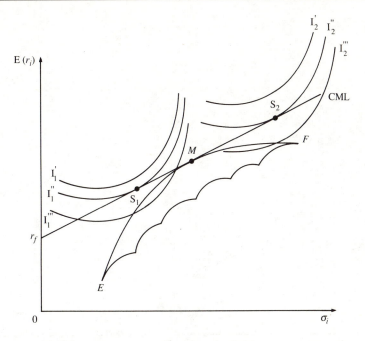

Figure 4.6   Investor equilibrium and the capital market line.

and matching risky assets and gilts to construct portfolios which suited the risk-return characteristics of each individual investor and, as such, has been called 'financial interior decorating') was redundant.

Highly risk-averse investors could be catered for by combining a small investment in the market portfolio with a large quantity of short-term government securities whereas the risk takers could be advised to borrow funds and invest them in the market portfolio as can be seen in Fig. 4.6. Two isoquants are shown each representing an investor with a different attitude towards risk. I_1 shows the investor to be risk averse and suggests a portfolio containing a considerable proportion of short-term government securities; the second isoquant, I_2, illustrates the position of the risk taker who gears his or her investment by borrowing funds and investing in the market portfolio. In either case the appropriate combination of risky assets is the market portfolio regardless of the investor's attitude to risk.

Short selling of risky assets and the Markowitz 'model'

The major constraint on the analysis so far has been the restriction on selling risky assets short (selling what you haven't got and hopefully buying back later at a lower price). Black and others[5] have reformulated the Markowitz analysis to include short selling of risky assets. Black argued that if risk-free borrowing and lending were impossible (as in reality) and short selling (as in the NYSE and technically possible within the period of account in the UK exchange) were possible, the results of Markowitz's model would be slightly modified. The results of this exercise are substantially similar to those of the original model in all respects save one. The removal of this last constraint results in the identification of a minimum variance portfolio which has been used instead of the risk-free asset in some of the studies of the stock market.

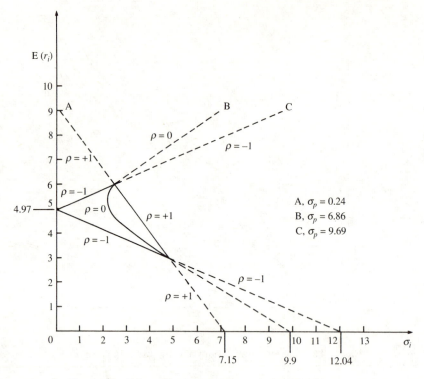

Figure 4.7 Diversification and short selling of risky assets.

The points in Fig. 4.7 were calculated using the numerical example on page 68 and Eqs (4.10) and (4.11). The results may be summarized as follows:

Case	Weights				
	M	F	$\rho_{m,r}$	$E(r_p)$	σ_p
a	2	−1	1.0	9.0	0.24
b	2	−1	0.0	9.0	6.86
c	2	−1	−1.0	9.0	9.69
d	−1	2	1.0	0.0	7.15
e	−1	2	0.0	0.0	9.90
f	−1	2	−1.0	0.0	12.04

In the example used (see page 68) the covariance and correlation coefficient were not significantly different from zero so the results hardly differed from the examples of zero correlation presented here (cases b and e). However the examples illustrate quite well the proposition that going short will only increase the portfolio's return and at the same time lower risk, when the two securities are highly correlated. If the short sale of a risky asset is considered as a loan whose interest rate is equal to the expected return then this proposition becomes clearer. As the cost of funds and the expected returns on the investment are positively and perfectly correlated then increasing costs may be met out of increasing returns. In the situation where the expected return falls so does the cost of funds. Hence, on an intuitive basis it can be seen that a high positive correlation is advantageous when selling short to provide funds for investment. On the other hand if the interest rate is perfectly negatively correlated with the expected return on the investment this will lead to a far more uncertain overall return. As the rate of return on the investment rises we may expect the costs of funds to fall thus giving a far larger net return than in the previous case. But where the investment return falls the cost of funds may be expected to rise, thus cutting the overall return further. These results are in direct contrast to the proposition drawn from the original Markowitz analysis in which diversification was best achieved when the two securities were highly uncorrelated.

The foregoing should be distinguished from the pure speculative short sale in which the transaction is made in the expectation of a capital depreciation of the security which has been sold short.

Black's formulation of the model with short selling also frees investors from the obligation of placing a margin requirement with the broker (necessary on the NYSE where short selling is permitted for ordinary investors). The margin constitutes a deposit of part of the proceeds of the short sale as an insurance against the investor defaulting on the transaction. The opportunity set and efficient frontier in Black's model describes a hyperbola instead of the parabola produced by

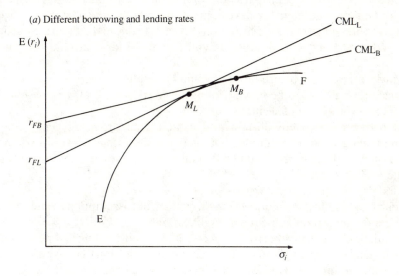

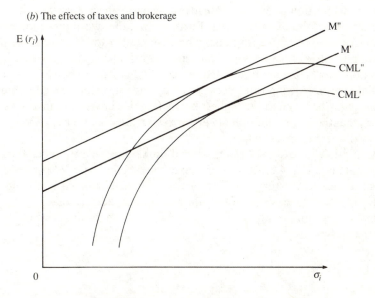

Figure 4.8 The modified Markowitz model.

the Markowitz and Tobin formulations. Despite this difference the model still lends itself to the same sort of results as those produced by the others. The relevant section of the efficient frontier (see Fig. 4.8) allows investors to select dominant portfolios in a particular risk or return class. A tangency between the efficient frontier and the investor's isoquants may still be formed leading to the selection of an optimal portfolio in each individual case.

The second notable result of Black's formulation is that the vertex of the hyperbola identifies a minimum variance portfolio which is used as a substitute for the risk-free asset (see Chapter 6).

Synthesis

The original Markowitz model has undergone considerable adaptation and modification since it first appeared in 1952, yet the principal assumptions remain unchallenged (at least among financial economists). Only two of the many developments have been presented here. It would require a complete text to present all of the variations on this basic theme and that task is outside the scope of this book. What remains is to produce a synthesis of the ideas around the basic risk–return concept.

Before any synthesis may be produced it would be helpful to make a short re-statement of the assumptions on which it is to be based. Following Markowitz it may be assumed that:

1. Investors are Markowitz efficient.
2. Capital markets are in equilibrium and exhibit semi-strong efficiency (fully anticipated inflation, homogeneous expectations, infinitely divisible securities, no taxes, no brokerage).
3. Investors may lend and borrow but at different rates of interest (i.e. the borrowing rate is higher than the lending rate).
4. Investors may sell short any risky assets.

Assumptions 1 and 2 follow the basic Markowitz model, but assumptions 3 and 4 take into account some of the more important subsequent modifications.

This formulation[6] (see Fig. 4.8(a)) of the model allows short selling and permits the existence of the risk-free asset. However, it also takes into account the objection that investors cannot borrow at the risk-free rate of interest. However, the inclusion of a separate and higher borrowing rate produces two market portfolios, M_L for those investing in sort-term government securities and M_B for those gearing a portfolio of risky assets. Furthermore, the two rates of interest introduce an element of indeterminacy for those investors who wish neither to invest in government securities nor to gear their portfolios of risky assets. The market portfolio may lie anywhere between M_L and M_B. This situation may be made more indeterminate by taking into consideration the inevitable profusion of different borrowing rates occasioned by each investor's personal financial circumstances. Thus r_{FB} may be taken as the highest borrowing rate charged to investors. In addition, it may be assumed that there are a multiplicity of borrowing rates between r_{FB} and r_{FL} corresponding to the credit worthiness of investors.

Lastly, if assumption 7 is dropped and taxes and brokerage are introduced the model becomes more indeterminate (see Fig. 4.8(b)). For example, the different rates of personal and corporate taxes applying to different investors, and in some cases different financial assets and different media of investment, will make the position of the efficient frontier indeterminate. The after-tax returns will now depend not only on the individual securities but also on the financial and legal positions of the investors themselves.

Conclusions

In this chapter the foundations of modern portfolio theory have been laid. The principle of risk and return as a basis for investment decisions has been laid and although the inclusion of real world criteria tend to weaken the determinacy of the model, the fundmantal principle remains sound. All of the examples and expositions used in this chapter have so far involved only two securities. It only remains to demonstrate why the single index models discussed in the next chapter were thought necessary. This may be done by looking at a three-security portfolio.

The risk of a two-security portfolio was developed in Eqs (4.3) to (4.8) and generalized in Eq. (4.9). The terms for a three-security portfolio and any other size portfolio may be worked out using the following expansion table:

Securities		[1] $w_1\sigma_1$	[2] $w_2\sigma_2$	[3] $w_3\sigma_3$	...	[n] $w_n\sigma_n$
[1]	$w_1\sigma_1$	$w_2^2\sigma_1^2$	$w_1w_2\sigma_{1,2}$	$w_1w_3\sigma_{1,3}$	...	$w_1w_n\sigma_{1,n}$
[2]	$w_2\sigma_2$	$w_1w_2\sigma_{1,2}$	$w_2^2\sigma_2^2$	$w_2w_3\sigma_{2,3}$	...	$w_2w_n\sigma_{2,n}$
[3]	$w_3\sigma_3$	$w_1w_2\sigma_{1,3}$	$w_2w_3\sigma_{2,3}$	$w_3^2\sigma_3^2$	...	$w_2w_n\sigma_{3,n}$
.	.	.	.	.	...	.
.	.	.	.	.	...	.
.	.	.	.	.	...	.
[n]	$w_n\sigma_n$	$w_1w_n\sigma_{1,n}$	$w_2w_n\sigma_{2,n}$	$w_3w_n\sigma_{3,n}$	...	$w_n^2\sigma_n^2$

$$\sigma_p^2 = w_1^2\sigma_1^2 + w_2^2\sigma_2^2 + w_3^2\sigma_3^2 + 2w_1w_2\sigma_{1,2} + 2w_1w_3\sigma_{1,3} + 2w_2w_3\sigma_{2,3} \tag{4.17}$$

$$\sigma_p^2 = w_1^2\sigma_1^2 + w_2^2\sigma_2^2 + (1-w_1-w_2)^2\sigma_3^2 + 2w_1w_2\sigma_{1,2} + 2w_1(1-w_1-w_2)\sigma_{1,3}$$
$$+ 2w_2(1-w_1-w_2)\sigma_{2,3} \tag{4.18}$$

$$\sigma_p^2 = w_1^2(\sigma_1^2 + \sigma_3^2 - 2\sigma_{1,3}) + w_2^2(\sigma_2^2 + \sigma_3^2 - 2\sigma_{2,3}) + 2w_1w_2(\sigma_3^2 + \sigma_{1,2} - \sigma_{1,3} - \sigma_{2,3})$$
$$+ 2w_1(\sigma_{1,3} - \sigma_3^2) + 2w_2(\sigma_{2,3} - \sigma_3^2) + \sigma_3^2 \tag{4.19}$$

$$\partial\sigma_p^2/\partial w_1 = 2w_1(\sigma_1^2 + \sigma_3^2 - 2\sigma_{1,3}) + 2w_2(\sigma_3^2 + \sigma_{1,2} - \sigma_{1,3} - \sigma_{2,3})$$
$$+ 2(\sigma_{1,3} - \sigma_3^2) = 0 \tag{4.20}$$

$$\partial\sigma_p^2/\partial w_2 = 2w_1(\sigma_3^2 + \sigma_{1,2} - \sigma_{1,3} - \sigma_{2,3}) + 2w_2(\sigma_2^2 + \sigma_3^2 - \sigma_{2,3}) + 2(\sigma_{2,3} - \sigma_3^2) = 0 \tag{4.21}$$

$\Sigma\tilde{r}_i = 41$ $\qquad\qquad \sigma_i^2 = 10.09$ $\qquad\qquad \sigma_{m,i} = 0.2$ $\qquad\qquad \sigma_{f,i} = 4.5$

$E(\tilde{r}_i) = 4.1$ $\qquad\qquad \sigma_i = 3.176$ $\qquad\qquad \rho_{m,i} = 0.03$ $\qquad\qquad \rho_{r,i} = 0.3$

$$\partial\sigma_p^2/\partial w_m = 2w_m(6 + 10.09 - 0.4) + 2w_r(10.09 + 0.4 - 0.2 - 4.5) + 2(0.2 - 10.09) = 0$$

$$\partial\sigma_p^2/\partial w_r = 2w_m(10.09 + 0.4 - 0.2 - 4.5) + 2w_r(23 + 10.09 - 9) + 2(4.5 - 10.09) = 0$$

The weights work out as follows:

weight $M = 0.6$; weight $F = 0.09$; weight $I = 0.31$.

The expansion table gives the variables necessary to work out the variance of a portfolio. A single-security portfolio's variance will be found in the cell bound by column [1] and row [1]; i.e. $w_1^2\sigma_1^2$. The terms needed to calculate the variance of a two-security portfolio are found in the cells bounded by column [2] and row [2]; i.e. $w_1^2\sigma_1^2 + w_2^2\sigma_2^2 + 2w_1w_2\sigma_{1,2}$. In the case of a three-security portfolio the terms are found in the cells bounded by column [3] and row [3] and after collection will be as follows:

$$\sigma_p^2 = w_1^2\sigma_1^2 + w_2^2\sigma_2^2 + w_3^2\sigma_3^3 + 2w_1w_2\sigma_{1,2} + 2w_1w_3\sigma_{1,3} + 2w_2w_3\sigma_{2,3} \tag{4.17}$$

As this equation stands there is one too many unknowns to obtain a solution which minimizes the risk of the portfolio. This problem is solved by defining one of the weights as a function of the other two. The combined weights must add up to 1 so w_3 may be redefined as $1-w_1-w_2$. Equation (4.17) becomes:

$$\sigma_p^2 = w_1^2\sigma_1^2 + (1-w_1-w_2)^2\sigma_2^3 + 2w_1w_2\sigma_{1,2} + 2w_1(1-w_1-w_2)\sigma_{1,3}$$
$$+ 2w_2(1-w_1-w_2)\sigma_{2,3} \tag{4.18}$$

When the brackets are expanded and the like terms collected together Eq. (4.13) reduces to:

$$\sigma_p^2 = w_1^2(\sigma_1^2 + \sigma_3^2 - 2\sigma_{1,3}) + w_2^2(\sigma_2^2 + \sigma_3^2 - 2\sigma_{2,3}) + 2w_1w_2(\sigma_3^2 + \sigma_{1,2} - \sigma_{1,3} - \sigma_{2,3})$$

$$+ 2w_1(\sigma_{1,3} - \sigma_3^2) + 2w_2(\sigma_{2,3} - \sigma_3^2) + \sigma_3^2 \tag{4.19}$$

Two equations may be obtained by partially differentiating with respect to w_1 and w_2, and then setting each result equal to zero. The problem of minimizing the risk of the portfolio has been reduced to solving for two unknowns in two equations of identical form. Hence, this has become an application of the solution to simultaneous equations.

$$\partial\sigma_p^2/\partial w_1 = 2w_1(\sigma_1^2 + \sigma_3^2 - 2\sigma_{1,3}) + 2w_2(\sigma_3^2 + \sigma_{1,2} - \sigma_{1,3} - \sigma_{2,3}) + 2(\sigma_{1,3} - \sigma_3^2) = 0 \tag{4.20}$$

$$\partial\sigma_p^2/\partial w_2 = 2w_1(\sigma_3^2 + \sigma_{1,2} - \sigma_{1,3} - \sigma_{2,3}) + 2w_2(\sigma_2^2 + \sigma_3^2 - \sigma_{2,3}) + 2(\sigma_{2,3} - \sigma_3^2) = 0 \tag{4.21}$$

By adding a third share to the example used earlier in this chapter (see page 68) a three-security portfolio may be created:

Share I Returns	$(1/n)[r_i - E(\tilde{r}_i)]^2$
1	0.961
1	0.961
0	1.681
5	0.081
6	0.361
5	0.081
0	1.681
9	2.401
6	0.361
8	1.521

$\Sigma r_i = 41$	$\sigma_i^2 = 10.09$	$\sigma_{m,i} = 0.2$	$\sigma_{f,i} = 4.5$
$E(\tilde{r}_i) = 4.1$	$\sigma_i = 3.176$	$\rho_{m,i} = 0.03$	$\rho_{f,i} = 0.3$

$$\partial\sigma_p^2/\partial w_m = 2w_m(6 + 10.09 - 0.4) + 2w_f(10.09 + 0.4 - 0.2 - 4.5) + 2(0.2 - 10.09) = 0$$

$$\partial\sigma_p^2/\partial w_f = 2w_m(10.09 + 0.4 - 0.2 - 4.5) + 2w_f(23 + 10.09 - 9) + 2(4.5 - 10.09) = 0.$$

The weights work out as follows:

weight $M = 0.6$; weight $F = 0.09$; weight $I = 0.31$.

The variance of the portfolio is 3.7 per cent, the standard deviation is 1.92 per cent and the expected return is 5.0 per cent. Although the return on the *MFI* portfolio is slightly inferior to that of the earlier *MF* portfolio the risk has been lowered. In fact the three-security portfolio has a lower risk than any of the possible two- and one-security portfolios. The results may be summarized as follows:

Portfolio	Return (%)	Risk (%)
MFI	5.07	1.92
MF	5.40	2.21
MI	5.87	2.29
FI	3.78	2.98
M	6.00	2.45
F	3.00	4.80
I	4.10	3.18

The calculations required for a three-security portfolio, although not onerous, are twice those required for a two-security portfolio. For a portfolio of n securities there are n variances and $(n^2 - n)/2$ covariances to be calculated. Therefore, a ten-security portfolio will require the calculation of 55 covariances and variances. A portfolio comprising all the shares in the FTSE100 will involve the calculation of 5,150 separate terms. Thus, for large portfolios the above system of analysis becomes very time consuming. The computational problems inherent in using the Markowitz system of analysis are not insuperable in the nineties with the availability of cheap computing power, but during the fifties and sixties when such facilities were not widely available there was an obvious need for a simplification of the process of minimizing the risk of a portfolio.

The requirement for a simplified system of risk–return analysis was supplied by the single index models independently developed by Sharpe and Lintner during the early sixties. These developments are discussed in Chapter 5.

Notes

1. H. M. Markowitz, 'Portfolio Selection', *Journal of Finance*, Vol. 7, March 1952.
   Portfolio Selection, Wiley, 1959.
   'Markowitz revisited', *Financial Analysts' Journal*, Vol. 32, September 1976.
2. Given the incessant activity within stock markets concerned with the more popular shares (e.g. the 'alpha' stocks quoted on the London International Stock Exchange's system, SEAQS) it is possible that the Austrian school of economics might have some helpful contribution to make. Essentially, the Austrians do not think of markets ever being in equilibrium, rather they conceive of markets being in a permanent state of disequilibrium in which there is a perpetual state of search, learning and correction. Thus in an Austrian analysis of the stock markets no prices would ever be in equilibrium; prices are always in disequilibrium because they are always in error, being behind the latest piece of information. Equilibrium is reduced to the status of that of the pot of gold at the end of the rainbow. However, it is a pot of gold towards which the market always strives and yet can never obtain as its position changes with the advent of every new piece of information coming to the market. Hence, the Austrian view of the stock market would be that it is very efficient exactly because of the level of activity and the permanent process of price adaption. It tends to be frenetic because the information systems are so much better than

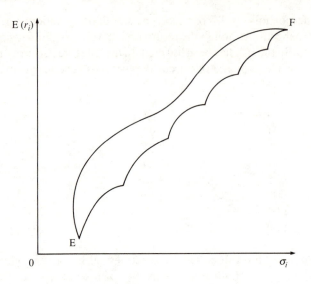

Figure 4.9   Concavity of the efficient frontier.

in other more apparently stable markets. For more detailed explorations of these ideas see *Competition and Entrepreneurship*, by I. Kirzner, University of Chicago Press, 1973.

3. A. Smith, *The Wealth of Nations*, Pelican Classics Edition, 1970, p. 214.

4. Dybvig and Ross have shown that under certain circumstances such as non-normality of the distributions of returns the efficient frontier need not be convex as shown in Fig. 4.2. Under normal conditions of normalcy such non-concavity can be shown to be impossible. Any convexity in the efficient frontier (see Fig. 4.9) is bound to produce two or more market portfolios which, when combined, will offer a superior risk–return relationship to that of the constituent parts. In the worst case where the covariance is equal to 1, the third portfolio will lie somewhere on a straight line between the first two portfolios. Any value less than 1 for the covariance will produce an even better range of risk–return combinations for the third portfolio. Thus, the non-convex efficient frontier is suboptimal.

   P. H. Dybvig and S. A. Ross, 'Portfolio efficient sets', *Econometrica*, Vol. 50, 1982.

   J. Hirschleifer, 'Efficient allocation of capital in an uncertain world', *American Economic Review*, Vol. 54, 1964.

5. J. Tobin, 'The Theory of portfolio selection', in *The Theory of Interest Rates*, F. H. Hahn and F. Brechling (eds), Macmillan, 1965.

   F. Black, 'Capital market equilibrium with restricted borrowing', *Journal of Business*, Vol. 45, 1972.

6. M. Brennan, 'Capital market equilibrium with divergent borrowing and lending rates, *Journal of Financial and Quantitative Analysis*, Vol. 6, 1971.

Questions

1. If a risk-averse investor desires to hold a portfolio of only two of the securities below, which pair would you advise and what would be the expected return and standard deviation of the portfolio you have chosen?

Share	Variance %	Return %	Covariance Matrix			
			A	B	C	D
A	9.0	4.0	1.0	3.0	3.6	1.2
B	4.0	5.0		1.0	0.8	4.8
C	16.0	3.0			1.0	11.2
D	16.0	4.0				1.0

2. If you were allowed to sell any of the above securities short would your answer to question 1 change and if so, why and how?
3. Should the capital market line and the efficient frontier be drawn with the 'broad side of the chalk' and if so why?
4. What is a financial interior decorator?
5. What are the assumptions underlying Markowitz's analysis and how can they be justified?
6. Why cannot the principle of dominance be used as a tool for the selection of shares to be included in a portfolio?
7. What implications does the capital market line have for portfolio management?
8. Given the following information about the returns on two investments (A, B) calculate characteristics of the risk-minimizing portfolio:

Period	1	2	3	4	5	6	7	8	9	10
A	11	6	9	12	2	6	9	−5	−8	8
B	7	−1	−3	−3	8	9	6	7	7	3

9. Using the results from question 8 above and assuming that either of the investments could be sold short, which of them would you sell short (investing the proceeds in the other) and why?
10. What are the practical difficulties of implementing an investment strategy based on the implications of the CML?

5. Capital market theory

Introduction

Chapter 4 showed the basic principles of the analysis of securities and portfolios initially developed by Markowitz, and the embellishments added by Black, Tobin, etc. Markowitz's two-parameter model spawned an academic industry engaged in exploring the ramifications of the investor behaviour implied in the original formulation. Capital market theory is not a single theory, rather it is a collection of theories which try to explain and predict market behaviour. The two basic variants presented in this chapter are the capital asset pricing model and what has become known as the market model, developed by Sharpe[1] and Lintner.[2] In Chapter 6 the variant known as the arbitrage pricing model will be presented.

The original formulation of the theory by Sharpe and Lintner made the following assmptions:
1. Investors are risk averse and maximize their return (as measured by the rate of return) over a one period time horizon.
2. Investors are rational price takers who make their selection of wealth-producing assets using risks (standard deviation of expected returns) and the expected returns.
3. Wealth-producing assets are assumed to be infinitely divisible and taxes and transactions costs are both zero.

Investors conforming to the above assumptions will be Markowitz efficient and will prefer efficient portfolios (i.e. those portfolios dominant in their risk or their return classes) to all other portfolios. In addition, Sharpe and Lintner made certain assumptions about the nature of the market:
4. There is a risk-free borrowing and a risk-free lending rate which are equal and available to all investors whatever their status.
5. All capital assets can be bought and sold (long or short without restriction), including human capital (i.e. investment in education and skills).
6. Capital markets are perfect in that there are no barriers to exit or entry and information is freely available to all.
7. A one period time horizon and homogeneous expectations on the part of investors—all investors have the same perceptions of expected returns, risks (standard deviations), and covariances.

These 7 assumptions are similar to those that underpin the analysis of Markowitz presented in Chapter 4 but they also make important extensions—principally assumptions 4 and 7. Although these assumptions may seem too numerous and overly restrictive it is worth restating that this is essentially a deductive economic model which abstracts from reality. This process of abstraction is intended to focus on those elements which are the most important in explaining what happens in the real world. In one sense it is a simplification, but also it is a clarification which is intended to provide understanding and prediction. The alternatives to this approach fall into two distinct and equally unsatisfactory categories:
1. Anecdotal evidence, interpretation and prediction. It might be said that this constitutes the bulk of market lore and wisdom. It is an unstructured corpus of independent observations which rarely go beyond what seems to have happened in the past. Each component forms an independent contribution and nowhere are these drawn together to explain the operation of the market in any overall sense. Hence, prediction is reduced to a repetition of what has occurred before in similar circumstances.

2. Statistical experimentation, observation and interpretation. The ubiquitous tools of this form of inquiry are a multiple regression computer program and a data bank of all variables that might be relevant. The process is simply to find the combination of variables which gave the best fit in the past and then to extrapolate the equation to make predictions. This has been called 'econometric strip mining' and again contributes very little to our understanding of how markets actually work. This is not to say that profitable trading strategies have not been devised using this method. However, it is axiomatic that if such successful strategies have been so developed they have not been published and therefore cannot be commented upon here or in any other similar text. Sharpe has summed this up succinctly as follows:

> Capital market theory is an exercise in positive economics. Assuming that people act in certain ways, what is implied about prices, quantities held, etc? ... the realism of the assumptions matters little. If the implications are reasonably consistent with observed phenomena, the theory can be said to 'explain' reality. More important, it may provide useful predictions.[3]

The starting point dictated by the foregoing assumptions is that all investors envisage the same opportunity set, efficient frontier, capital market line and market portfolio (the Tobin position described in Chapter 4). Given different investor preferences they will all obtain maximum utility somewhere along the CML. They will have varying proportions of the market portfolio and the risk-free asset to the extent that there will be lending and borrowing portfolios (see Fig. 4.5). However, the main conclusion is that each investor, whatever his or her preferences as to risk aversion (or otherwise), will have an investment in the market portfolio. This implies that the problem of the selection of the risky securities to include in the investor's portfolio has been solved and the only question to be answered is whether to lend or borrow, and how much to lend or borrow. Therefore, it is appropriate to start at the market portfolio and consider it in some depth.

The market portfolio

The specific portfolio chosen by an investor will depend on his or her particular risk–return preferences. However, if homogeneous expectations and portfolio opportunities are assumed there will be only one optimum portfolio when the market is in equilibrium. It must be stressed that this equilibrium involves no excess demand or supply of any investment asset. Therefore it follows that the optimum portfolio (which is called the 'market' portfolio) will consist of all investment assets in the market and that each asset will be held in proportion to the ratio of its own market value to the total market value:

$$w_i = \text{total value of the } i\text{th asset/total market value of all assets.}$$

where w_i is the weight of asset i in the market portfolio.

The assumptions made earlier in this chapter may be used to derive what has become known as the 'separation theorem' which underpins the foregoing conclusion. Assuming a risk-free borrowing and lending rate, that all investment assets are marketable, that capital markets are perfect and that investors have homogeneous expectations, all investors will envisage the same efficient investment opportunities as described by the efficient frontier. Initially, they will all choose different efficient portfolios on the frontier according to their risk–return preferences. However, when the risk-free asset is introduced to this situation investors will all either borrow or lend at the risk-free rate. By seeking to maximise their expected utility from their investments, investors will, perforce, select the one portfolio of risky assets. Thus, the separation theorem holds that there are only two portfolios in equilibrium; the first composed of n risky assets and the second composed of the risk-free asset. Hence, all investors will hold a proportion of their investment in the risky portfolio, M, and adjust their risk–return combination by going either long or short in the risk-free asset (in equilibrium there will be no net borrowing or lending for the market as a whole).

This proposition may be illustrated by considering a situation in which an investor creates a portfolio consisting of share I and the market portfolio M. If the proportion invested in I is defined as w_i (in effect w_i measures the excess demand for asset I when positive and excess supply of asset I when negative; when w_i is zero then the capital market is in equilibrium as there is neither excess demand nor excess supply of asset I) and the proportion invested in M as $(1-w_i)$, an infinite number of portfolios may be created where the weights for I may vary between $+1$ and -1. The loci of these suboptimal portfolios may be represented by the curve IMI* in Fig. 5.1. IMI* is depicted as lying below the efficient frontier EMF as the investor is engaged in the construction of a series of suboptimal portfolios by the definition of the efficient frontier itself. Position I indicates a weight w_i of $+1$ in which the investor has placed all of his investment in security I. At position M the weight of investment in security I is zero (i.e. $w_i=0$) and the investor has concentrated his investment solely in the market portfolio (where the investor has only invested in I to the extent of the share's capitalization compared to that of the market as a whole). Moving from M towards I* the investor is engaged in selling I short and reinvesting the proceeds in M; therefore $w_i<0$. Given the above assumptions none of these portfolios apart from M can exist as they are all suboptimal, being dominated not only by combinations of M and the risk-free asset but also by other portfolios on the efficient frontier itself.

When the market is in equilibrium there can be no excess demand for, or excess supply of, any investment asset. This implies that for any investment asset the marginal rate of exchange between the expected return and the risk (standard deviation) of that asset must be equal to the marginal rate of exchange for the market as a whole. Hence, equilibrium is uniquely achieved in the above case when the slope of the curve IMI* is equal to the slope of the capital market line at position M (when w_i is equal to zero). This may be demonstrated algebraically as follows:

let the slope of the CML be defined as:

$$(E(\tilde{r}_m)-r_f)/\sigma_m \tag{5.1}$$

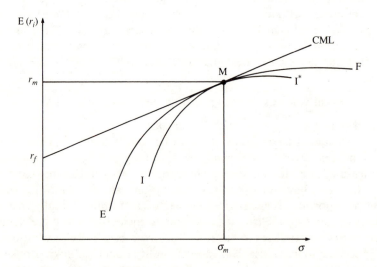

Figure 5.1 Inefficient portfolios and the CML.

let the slope of IMI^{*4} at point M (where the market is in equilibrium and there is no excess demand for, or excess supply of I; i.e. $w_i = 0$) be defined as follows:

$$\sigma_m(E(\tilde{r}_i) - E(\tilde{r}_m))/(\sigma_{m,i} - \sigma_m^2) \qquad (5.2)$$

therefore in equilibrium Eq. (5.1) is equal to Eq. (5.2):

$$\sigma_m(E(\tilde{r}_i) - E(\tilde{r}_m))/(\sigma_{m,i} - \sigma_m^2) = (E(\tilde{r}_m) - r_f)/\sigma_m \qquad (5.3)$$

cross multiplying:

$$\sigma_m^2(E(\tilde{r}_i) - E(\tilde{r}_m)) = (E(\tilde{r}_m) - r_f)(\sigma_{i,m} - \sigma_m^2) \qquad (5.4)$$

dividing both sides by σ_m^2 and rearranging the results:

$$E(\tilde{r}_i) - E(\tilde{r}_m) = (E(\tilde{r}_m) - r_f)[(\sigma_{i,m}/\sigma_m^2) - 1] \qquad (5.5)$$

Adding $E(\tilde{r}_m)$ to both sides and redefining $\sigma_{i,m}/\sigma_m^2$ as β_i, and solving Eq. (5.5) for $E(\tilde{r}_i)$:

$$E(\tilde{r}_i) = (E(\tilde{r}_m) - r_f)(\beta_i - 1) + E(\tilde{r}_m) \qquad (5.6)$$

Multiplying out the brackets on the right-hand side and rearranging:

$$E(\tilde{r}_i) = r_f + \beta_i(E(\tilde{r}_m) - r_f) \qquad (5.7)$$

Equation (5.7) is the capital asset pricing model. It states that the expected mean return of security I is equal to the risk-free rate of return plus a weighted market risk premium. The market return minus the risk-free return is the risk premium that investors expect for investing in the market portfolio. Equation (5.7) merely states that the risk premium that holders of security I should expect is a function (β_i) of the market risk premium. To show this more clearly, subtract r_f from both sides of Eq. (5.7):

$$E(r_i) - r_f = \beta_i(E(r_m) - r_f) \qquad (5.8)$$

The process of development between Eqs (5.1) and (5.8) have transformed the Markowitz–Tobin model, and the expected return of a security can now be thought of solely in terms of its relationship with the expected market rate of return. Therefore, it is now time to look at the concept of beta (β) a little more closely. In Eq. (5.6) beta was defined as the ratio of the covariance between security I and the market, and the variance of the market:

$$\beta_i = \sigma_{i,m}/\sigma_m^2 \qquad (5.9)$$

It should be recalled that the covariance may be defined as follows:

$$\sigma_{i,m} = \rho_{i,m}\sigma_i\sigma_m \qquad (5.10)$$

Hence, Eq. (5.9) may be rewritten thus:

$$\beta_i = \rho_{i,m}\sigma_i\sigma_m/\sigma_m\sigma_m \qquad (5.11)$$

and when simplified:

$$\beta_i = \rho_{i,m}\sigma_i/\sigma_m \qquad (5.12)$$

So beta merely uses the correlation coefficient to weight the ratio of the risks of the security and the market. As such it gauges the extent to which the expected return of the security is affected by the expected return of the market itself.

Equations (5.7) and (5.8) may be depicted on a graph (see Fig. 5.2). As such they have been called the 'securities market line'.

The first thing to notice about Figs. 5.2(a) and 5.2(b) is that the value of beta for the market in

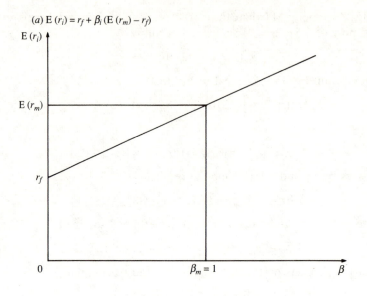

$(a)\ \mathrm{E}\,(r_i) = r_f + \beta_i\,(\mathrm{E}\,(r_m) - r_f)$

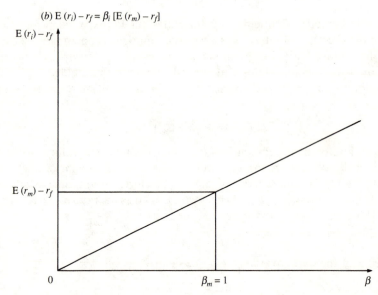

$(b)\ \mathrm{E}\,(r_i) - r_f = \beta_i\,[\mathrm{E}\,(r_m) - r_f]$

Figure 5.2   The securities market line (SML).

each case is shown as 1. This follows directly from the definition of beta as the covariance of the security with the market divided by the variance of the market. In the case of the covariance of the market with itself, it is going to be equal to the market variance ($\sigma_{m,m} = \rho_{m,m}\sigma_m\sigma_m$ where $\rho_{m,m} = 1$ by definition). The horizontal axis is now calibrated in units of beta rather than the standard deviation of expected returns. Instead of all the securities forming an opportunity set they are now ranged along the security market line according to their individual beta values. Securities with betas less than 1 are called defensive shares as a 1 per cent increase in the expected market rate of return is likely to yield a less than 1 per cent increase in the expected rate of return of the security. However, in the event of a 1 per cent fall in the market rate, the return of the security is expected to decrease by less than 1 per cent. Hence, the investor is partially shielded from the full force of any general market decline.

On the other hand, those securities with betas which are greater than 1 are called aggressive shares. In these cases a 1 per cent increase (fall) in the expected market rate of return is accompanied by an increase (fall) in the security's expected return of greater than 1 per cent. Consequently, aggressive shares have a higher expected rate of return than the market during a general increase but the return falls equally sharply when the market turns. These relationships may be clearly seen if betas are considered as proxy measures of security volatility relative to that of the market. Diagrammatically, these relationships may be plotted as 'characteristic' lines (Fig. 5.3). Included in Fig. 5.3 is a beta equal to -0.5. This is merely a hypothetical possibility as in practice there are few if any securities with negative betas. A negative beta implies a company which does well when the rest of the market is doing badly. What is more, it implies that the worse the market does the better is the performance of the underlying company.

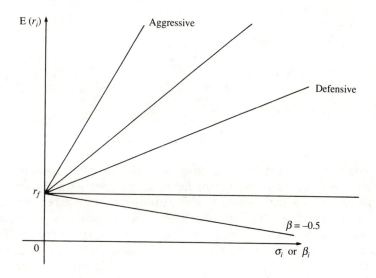

Figure 5.3 Security characteristic lines.

The market model

Sharpe's 1963 article[1] put forward the idea that the return of any security could be related to the return of the market. He specified the relationship as a simple least squares regression as follows:

$$r_{i,t} = a_i + b_i r_{m,t} + e_{i,t} \tag{5.13}$$

where $r_{i,t}$ = return for firm i in period t

   a_i = intercept with the vertical axis and is constant

   b_i = slope of the regression line and is constant

   $e_{i,t}$ = error term for the return of firm in period t

In Eq. (5.13) a_i may be interpreted as an estimation of $r_f(1 - \beta_i)$ and b_i an estimation of β_i. The last term e_{it} is the error term of the equation and in the case that the equation has been specified correctly and is unbiased then the sum of the error terms should be zero which would reduce Eq. (5.13) to an empirical (ex-post) version of the CAPM given the above interpretions of a_i and b_i.[5] It is also assumed that the variance of the error term is constant and that the error terms themselves are uncorrelated with any other firm's error term (cov. $e_{i,t}e_{j,t}=0$) and uncorrelated with the independent variable, $r_{m,t}$ (cov. $e_{i,t}r_{m,t}=0$).

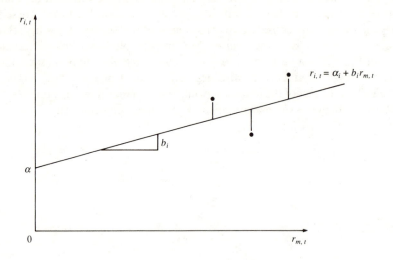

Figure 5.4   The market model.

The market model permits a practical implementation of the CAPM. As noted above, the two models are very similar to the extent that the market model may be regarded as the ex-post version of the CAPM. This means that there is data available to estimate betas, expected returns and risks. However, it should be stressed that this implementation requires the assumption that the distribution of returns in the past is stable and an accurate proxy for future returns.

The precise definition of Eq. (5.13) has important implications for the risk of a security's returns. In Chapter 4 the standard deviation of returns is a total risk proxy. However, beta is a measurement of the volatility of a firm's returns compared with that of the market. As other factors may influence company returns it may be assumed that beta is not a measure of total risk. Rather, it is *market* risk as opposed to *non-market* risk. Taken together market and non-market risk must equal total risk. As it stands the CAPM does not allow the estimation of total risk, but the market model does:

$$\sigma_i^2 = E\{[(a_i+b_ir_m+e_i)-E(a_i+b_ir_m+e_i)]^2\} \tag{5.14}$$

i.e. the sum of the squares of the observations minus the mean expected value.

$$\sigma_i^2 = b_i^2 E[(r_m-\tilde{r}_m)^2]+E(e_i^2) \tag{5.15}$$

$$\sigma_i^2 = b_i^2\sigma_m^2+\sigma_{e_i}^2 \tag{5.16}$$

Hence, the total risk of the security is the sum of market (or non-diversifiable) risk, $b_i^2\sigma_m^2$ and non-market (or diversifiable) risk, σ_{ei}^2.[6] Put another way, market risk is the portion of total variance explained by the specification of the model; i.e. the variance of the distribution of r_i explained by the independent variable r_m. The non-market risk is the portion of total variance left unexplained by the model and is the variance of the error term.

The covariance between the returns of two different securities may be estimated in a similar manner:

$$\sigma_{i,j} = E[(r_i - \tilde{r}_i)(r_j - \tilde{r}_j)] \tag{5.17}$$

$$\sigma_{i,j} = b_i b_j \sigma_m^2 \tag{5.18}$$

Using ex-post data the job of the financial analyst is now considerably easier than using the full mean–variance model presented in Chapter 4. It will be recalled that for n securities, the total number of calculations was $(n^2 - n)/2$. For example the number of calculations that should be made to analyse portfolios from 10 securities is 45, and for 100 securities, 4,950. Using the market model, only a_i, b_i and σ_i^2 have to be calculated as well as the market return and the market risk. Therefore, only $3n + 2$ have to be calculated. For example, in the case of 10 securities only 32 calculations have to be made and in the case of 100 securities, only 302 calculations.

The market model gives a considerable simplification in the analysis of portfolios—whatever the number of securities contained therein. The return of the portfolio is a weighted average of the constituent security returns, the weights used being the proportions of the total investment made in each security:

$$r_p = \sum_{i=1}^{n} w_i r_i \tag{5.19}$$

The portfolio beta is calculated in a similar fashion:

$$\beta_p = \sum_{i=1}^{n} w_i \beta_i \tag{5.20}$$

The systematic or market or non-diversifiable risk of the portfolio is calculated in a similar way to that of an individual security (see Eq. 5.16)):

$$\text{variance due to the market} = \beta_p^2 \sigma_m^2 \tag{5.21}$$

The unsystematic or non-market or diversifiable risk is calculated as follows:

$$\text{non-market variance} = \sum_{i=1}^{n} w_i^2 \sigma_{e_i}^2 \tag{5.22}$$

Therefore, following Eq. (5.16) once more, the total variance of the portfolio's returns is the sum of the two types of risk:

$$\text{total portfolio variance} = \text{market variance} + \text{non-market variance}$$

$$\sigma_p^2 = \beta_p^2 \sigma_m^2 + \sum_{i=1}^{n} w_i^2 \sigma_{e_i}^2 \tag{5.23}$$

To get back to Markowitz's original proxy for the risk of a portfolio (or for that matter an individual security), the standard deviation of the returns, one only has to find the square root of the total portfolio variance.

Using the market model

It was emphasized above that the market model is essentially an ex-post version of the CAPM. As such the statistical inputs needed to evaluate securities and portfolios are readily available. However, the work involved in generating enough statistical observations to produce a reasonable sample size for an examination of 10 potential shares is still considerable and beyond the means and inclination of most private investors and quite a few professonal investors/fund managers. As modern portfolio theory has become widely accepted the necessary inputs are generated in the UK by the London Business School (LBS) on a commercial basis. The LBS produces a quarterly publication called the '*Risk Management Service*' (RMS) which provides all the necessary inputs for all the shares with a full listing on the London International Stock Market and for those currently being traded on the USM.

For the majority of the RMS estimates the sample size is 60 observations consisting of 5 years worth of monthly returns. The betas themselves are the products of simple linear regression calculations as first suggested by Sharpe (see Eq. (5.13)). A typical quotation from the RMS would be as follows:

Sedol	Name		FTA Ind	Mkt Cap	Mkt-ability	Beta	Variability
214209	Commercial Union		INS.COMP	1106	0TF	1.04	29

Spec Risk	Std Error	R Sq-rd	Qly Ab Return	Ann Ab Return	Ann Act Return	Gross Yield	P/E Ratio	Price 30.9.86
25	0.17	25	−6	−1	28	6.5	0.0	268

Source: RMS October–December 1986.

1. Sedol; Stock Exchange daily official list number.
2. Name; the RMS lists companies in alphabetical order.
3. FTA Ind; this is the FT Actuaries industry classification which in this case is insurance composite. This enables investors to compare the performance and characteristic data of the security under scrutiny with that of the industry to which it belongs. The mean beta of the insurance composite sector is 0.91 with a standard deviation of returns of 20 per cent. The actual return earned by this sector in the previous 12 months was 31 per cent. Hence, the investor might conclude that Commercial Union was slightly more volatile than comparable firms and earned slightly less than the average for the sector.
4. Mkt Cap; this is the market capitalization of the share in question which in this case is £1106 million.
5. Mkt-ability; the number at the beginning of this code is the number of days that are likely between transactions. A value of zero as in the case of Commercial Union means that the share is continuously traded. The first letter, which is T in the quote, denotes that the company has trustee status. The second letter, which can be either A or F, indicates whether the share forms part of the FT All Share Index (A) and if the company is also a constituent of the FTSE 100 (F).
6. Beta.
7. Variability; the standard deviation, in percentage terms, of the security's returns.
8. Spec Risk; specific risk (per cent), this is the standard deviation of the non-market risk of the security (σ_{e_i}).
9. Std Error; this is the standard error of the beta estimate and the lower this figure is the better the estimate of beta.
10. R Sq-rd; R-squared (per cent), this is a measure of the extent to which the market model as used by the RMS has explained the security's returns. For Commercial Union the market model explained 25 per cent of the variability of its returns. This particular measure is the square of the correlation coefficient which has been used throughout Chapters 4 and 5. Therefore, taking the square root of this measure we get the correlation coefficient; i.e. $\sqrt{0.25} = 0.5$.
11. Qly Ab Return; quarterly abnormal return (per cent), this represents the difference between what the share might have been expected to earn over the previous quarter given its beta value

and the risk free rate of return, and the return of the market over the same period (ab ret = act ret − exp ret; where the expected return is equal to $r_f(1 - \beta_i) + \beta_i r_m$).

12. Ann Ab Return; annual abnormal return (per cent), this is calculated in the same way as the last measurement, the only difference being the time period under consideration.
13. Ann Act Return; annual actual return (per cent), this is the actual return earned over the past year and includes both capital appreciation (depreciation) and any dividend paid $((P_{i,t} - P_{i,t-1} + d_t)/P_{i,t-1})$.
14. P/E Ratio: price/earnings ratio.
15. Price 30.9.86; the price in pence of the shares on the date specified. This last datum may be accompanied by one of the following letters: S = the company's shares have been suspended, A = company has been acquired, L = company has been liquidated, e = non-voting shares have been enfranchised for some reason, and lastly F = the shares have been withdrawn from the official list for some other reason than those already mentioned.

Using the above information for Commercial Union we may calculate both betas and covariances from first principles. For example, using Eq. (5.12) we may estimate the beta of Commercial Union:

$$\beta_{cu} = (\sqrt{\text{`R-Squared'}})(\text{Variability/standard deviation of the market})$$

The usual proxy for the market in the UK is the FT All Share Index and this may also be found in the RMS. For October–December 1986 the return on the market was 28 per cent and the standard deviation of this was 14 per cent.

$$\beta_{cu} = \sqrt{0.25}(29/14) = 1.0357$$

Given a standard error of 0.17 for the market model's estimate of beta in this case the 'true' value is likely to lie between 1.21 and 0.87. This process does not work so well in all examples. Using the quotation for British Petroleum in the same issue of the RMS we observe a market model estimate of beta of 1.05, an R^2 of 19 per cent and a standard deviation of 35 per cent, and using this data a beta of 1.0897 is estimated, a small difference and well within the standard error limits of ± 0.2.

Using the equations for the expected return (5.7), actual return (5.19), beta (5.20), variance due to the market (5.21), non-market variance (5.22), and total variance (5.23) we may construct and analyse any portfolio of equities. For example, consider a portfolio composed of the shares making up the FT 30 using data from the RMS of October–December 1986 (see Table 5.1).

Total capitalization = £88,774 million
Portfolio beta, $\Sigma w_i \beta_i = 1.026$
Market portfolio risk $\sigma_m = 14\%$
Market portfolio return = 28%
Risk-free rate = 10%
Variance due to the market $(\beta_p^2 \sigma_m^2) = 0.020,618$ (2.06%)
Non-market variance $\sum_{i=1}^{n} [w_i^2 (\text{sp}/100)^2] = 0.002,868$ (0.29%)
Total portfolio variance $= 0.020,618 + 0.002,868 = 0.023,486$ (2.35%)
Portfolio risk (standard deviation of returns) $= \sqrt{0.023,486}$
$\qquad\qquad\qquad\qquad\qquad\qquad = 0.153,251$ (15.33%)
Coefficient of diversification, (non-market variance/total variance) $= (0.002,868/0.023,486)100$
$\qquad\qquad\qquad\qquad\qquad\qquad\qquad\qquad\qquad = 12.21\%$

Actual return, $(w_i r_i) = 25.87\%$
Expected return, $(r_f + \beta_p(E(r_m) - r_f) = 28.46\%$
Abnormal return, (actual − expected) = 25.87 − 28.46 = −2.59

Table 5.1   The FT 30 portfolio

Company	Capital-ization (£million)	Weight	Beta	Specific risk (%)	Actual ret. (%)	Security risk (%)	Ann. Ab. ret. (%)
Allied Lyons	2 037	0.023	0.82	24	7	26	−17
ASDA-MFI	1 685	0.019	0.9	23	14	26	−12
Beecham	2 941	0.033	0.96	20	27	24	0
BICC	497	0.006	1.21	22	16	28	−15
Blue Circle	717	0.008	0.9	21	13	24	−13
BOC	1 388	0.016	1.13	22	23	27	−7
Boots	1 993	0.022	0.69	24	14	25	−8
BP	12 170	0.137	0.97	23	33	27	5
BT	10 818	0.122	1.11	18	−19	25	−50
BTR	4 773	0.054	1.07	15	27	21	− 2
Cadbury-Schw.	959	0.011	1.03	19	35	24	6
Courtaulds	1 055	0.012	1.23	30	89	35	56
Gen. Electric	4 427	0.05	1.11	22	10	27	−20
GKN	608	0.007	1.05	28	18	32	−11
Glaxo	6 906	0.078	1.07	22	47	27	17
Grand Met.	3 549	0.04	0.96	18	41	23	13
Guinness	2 575	0.029	1.19	24	19	29	−12
Hanson	4 849	0.055	0.99	23	27	27	0
Hawker-Sid.	849	0.01	1.05	18	18	23	−11
ICI	6 970	0.079	0.98	18	68	22	40
Lucas	598	0.007	1.2	31	35	35	3
Marks & Sp.	5 088	0.057	0.99	20	21	25	−6
NatWest	3 717	0.042	1.11	21	36	26	5
Plessey	1 248	0.014	1.01	31	28	35	0
P & O	1 634	0.018	0.95	28	28	31	0
Royal Ins.	1 799	0.02	0.92	21	21	24	−5
Tate & Lyle	402	0.005	1.04	21	31	26	2
Thorn EMI	977	0.011	1.14	27	31	32	0
Trusthouse	1 194	0.013	1.19	19	17	25	−14
Vickers	351	0.004	1.16	30	35	34	3
		1.000					

Source: Risk Management Service.

There are several points to note about the above portfolio analysis:
1. The portfolio's estimated risk (i.e. the standard deviation of returns) is lower than any of the constituent securities. At just over 15 per cent it is 6 per cent lower than the least variable of the constituent shares (BTR).
2. Over the previous 12 months the portfolio underperformed its expected rate of return by just over 2.5 per cent. From the data above this can be mainly ascribed to the returns of British Telecom (BT) which had an abnormal return of −50 per cent. However, this does not imply that BT will underperform during the next 12 months or that those shares which overperformed (e.g. ICI with an abnormal return of +40 per cent) will repeat their past performance.
3. These calculations can be easily set up on a computer spreadsheet and variations may be performed to determine the best-looking selection according to the investor's risk–return preferences. For example, the above portfolio was re-evaluated using equal weightings instead of capitalization-based weightings and the following results were obtained:
   Portfolio beta = 1.088
   Non-market variance = 0.18%

Market variance = 2.11%
Total variance = 2.29%
Portfolio risk = 15.13%
Actual return = 27%
Expected return = 28.68%
Abnormal return = −1.68%
Coefficient of diversification = 7.8%

4. The coefficient of diversification measures the extent to which the portfolio has been diversified. In modern portfolio theory this is defined as the extent to which the construction of the portfolio has eliminated non-market risk. As such it is measured by the ratio of the variance of non-market risk to the total variance and expressed as a percentage. In the above example using capitalization-based weights, the coefficient of diversification is 12.21 per cent. In other words just over 12 per cent of the total variance is still accounted for by non-market factors.

Diversification

The coefficient of diversification used in the above analysis reintroduces the concept of security selection for portfolios. Two of the most important implications of the Markowitz analysis and the Tobin–Markowitz model presented in Chapter 4 were that:

1. In the absence of the risk-free asset, efficient diversification depended on the covariances between securities and 'financial interior decorating' was no longer sufficient to create a portfolio with the requisite risk–return characteristics.
2. In the presence of the risk-free asset the market portfolio may be identified and diversification was reduced to a process of investment in the market portfolio and the risk-free assets to derive the required risk–return attributes.

However, given the practical difficulties of identifying the risk free asset and identifying the market portfolio with the existence of brokerage and taxation, security selection and portfolio construction remains important. Therefore, it remains to draw the relevant lessons about such practices in the light of the CAPM and the market model. The first implication to draw from these models is that diversification within a national market cannot eliminate the risk due to the market. Although defensive (low beta) securities may be chosen, the market risk will still be present to some degree unless the investor decides to move his or her capital into another form of investment in which case he or she will be faced with another set of risks. Assuming the investor does decide to remain within the equity market then the second implication of MPT is that the process of diversification is essentially an effort to combine shares in such a way as to eradicate non-market risk. That is to say, all those specific causes of fluctuations in returns should offset each other leaving the majority of risk inherent in the portfolio's return being solely due to the market.

In a study by Evans and Archer[7] it was shown that random selection of securities would eliminate most of the non-market risk once the number of securities in the portfolio had reached 10–15 shares. Random diversification allows the reduction of non-market risk because the error terms from the market model's estimation of each security will tend to cancel each other out and sum to zero because they are uncorrelated. For each portfolio size (in terms of the number of constituent securities) Evans and Archer took the average portfolio risk of 60 randomly generated sets. As beta values were also randomly assigned to portfolios it was assumed that in each case the average beta value would approach unity. Therefore, as the number of securities increased the portfolios would increasingly approximate the market portfolio and the total level of risk would asymptotically approach the market level. This was indeed observed and the results are plotted in Fig. 5.5. However, other research has shown that in addition to the mean level of risk observed

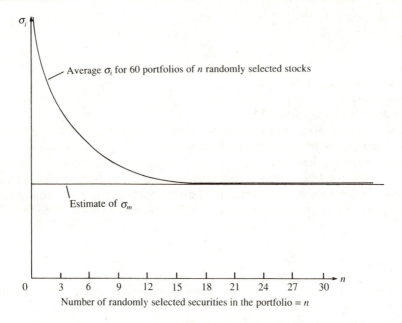

Figure 5.5   Random diversification.

from a sample of portfolios containing the same number of randomly selected shares, the standard deviation also has to be taken into account. By allowing for the distribution of results in random diversification, reductions in the overall risk of a randomly selected portfolio of shares may continue until the number of constituent securities reaches about thirty. This study also suggested that the maximum number of shares suggested by Evans and Archer should in fact be regarded as the minimum.

The effects of random diversification may be further illustrated by using the data presented in Table 5.1. The characteristics of two, 30-share portfolios were presented earlier. If the list of shares in the portfolio was progressively reduced by 1 then 29 multiple security portfolios could be observed. This was done by first starting at the top of the list with Allied Lyons and working down the list. The process was repeated by starting at the bottom and working upwards. In each case the coefficient of diversification was taken to illustrate the effect of size on the reduction of non-market risk. Even with such a small number of observations and an inherently biased sample such as the FT 30, the results are quite plain to see (Fig. 5.6).

The small number of observations and the biased nature of the sample did not produce average betas of unity and the effect on the overall portfolio risk was less dramatic, the lowest being 15 per cent for one of the 27-share portfolios and the highest being just under 26 per cent for one of the 2-share portfolios.[9]

Despite the above, it still remains valid that the importance of the covariances between the returns of securities is the mot effective method of reducing risk where the number of shares in a portfolio is necessarily limited.

So far we have only considered diversification within a national market where the stock market and the shares listed therein are going to be affected by the same macro- and microeconomic forces and developments. This limitation forces the investor to accept the level of market risk and the only ways in which this can be avoided are to select defensive (low beta) securities or to move out of the equities market into alternative investments or to reduce the market influence by combining equities with the risk-free asset.

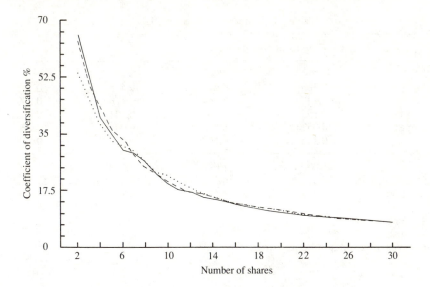

Figure 5.6   The effect of portfolio size on the coefficient of diversification.

However, if the national limitation is removed and the investor can invest in foreign securities there arises the possibility that market risk itself may be effectively reduced. Of course this possibility is dependent on national markets being 'segmented' or uncorrelated with each other. Much is heard and read in the media of essentially anecdotal evidence about the apparent interdependence of markets and the existence of a global securities market. But is this the case? The activities of fund managers would suggest otherwise. Since the liberalization of exchange controls in 1979 a considerable proportion of their capital has found its way abroad (see Table 1.1) to other national stock markets. This may be in part a search for higher returns but it must also be a function of the desire to diversify away from the risk of the domestic market.

The principal additional complication inherent in international equities investment is the exchange rate risk—that the returns of the investments made on the NYSE by British fund managers will be subject not only to the vagaries of the securities involved but also to the uncertain movements of the exchange rate between the US dollar and sterling. However, it is possible to construct hedges (completely in theory but only partially in practice) against most exchange risks by using the futures markets. An international version of the CAPM has been developed by Solnik using the assumption of complete hedging against exchange rate risk.[10]

One of the first attempts to use MPT to assess the potential of international investment was published by Levy and Sarnat in 1970.[11] They converted the annual stock market returns for 20 countries into US dollars. These observations were used to generate an international efficient frontier (with no short selling) and the market portfolios were identified by using risk-free rates of returns of 2, 3, 4 and 6 per cent. The weights, mean rates of return and standard deviations were as shown in Table 5.2.

Levy and Sarrat argued that as the US market index had a mean return of 12.1 per cent and a standard deviation of 12.1 per cent, international diversification improved portfolio characteristics by reducing risk.

In 1974 Solnik published results of study similar to that done by Evans and Archer, in which he measured the risks of different-sized randomly selected portfolios consisting of (a) US stocks and (b) US and other national stocks.[12] (The results are shown in Fig. 5.7.)

Table 5.2 International diversification

Areas	Weights at risk-free rates			
	2%	3%	4%	6%
USA	0.366	0.41	0.428	0.511
Japan	0.147	0.167	0.176	0.209
Latin and S. America*	0.195	0.16	0.141	0.032
Western Europe†	0.057	0.07	0.09	0.12
Others**	0.235	0.193	0.165	0.128
	1.000	1.000	1.000	1.000
Mean portfolio return	9.5%	10.5%	11.0%	12.5%
Standard deviation	5.7%	6.4%	6.8%	8.4%

* primarily Venezuela
† primarily Austria
** primarily New Zealand and South Africa

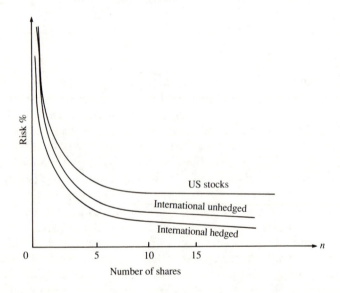

Figure 5.7 International diversification. (Source: B. Solnik,[12] p. 51.)

It is noteworthy that this study not only found internationally diversified portfolios less risky than domestically diversified portfolios but also that the gains from hedging against exchange rate risk were minimal.

Conclusions

In their distinctly separate ways both the market model and the CAPM have taken the rather cumbersome analysis developed by Markowitz and the CML model developed by Tobin to a point which is of practical use for professional portfolio management. In addition, they have extended our understanding of the nature of portfolio risk and exactly what is achieved by diversification.

In Chapter 6, MPT is extended further to include the practical difficulties of implementation, testing portfolios, its implications for market efficiency and finally the lastest development— arbitrage pricing theory.

Appendix A: Complete algebraic derivation of the CAPM

The explanation of Fig. 5.1 and of the derivation of the CAPM was shortened in order to avoid unnecessary difficulties. This appendix now presents the complete development of the model from first principles. The return on the portfolio consisting of security I and the market portfolio may be expressed as,

$$E(\tilde{r}_p) = w_i E(\tilde{r}_i) + (1 - w_i)E(\tilde{r}_m) \tag{5A.1}$$

and the risk of the portfolio return as,

$$\sigma_{\tilde{r}_p} = [w_1^2 \sigma_{\tilde{r}_i}^2 + (1 - w_i)^2 \sigma_{\tilde{r}_m}^2 + 2w_i(1 - w_i)\rho_{i,m}\sigma_{\tilde{r}_i}\sigma_{\tilde{r}_m}]^{1/2} \tag{5A.2}$$

The slope of IMI* may be defined as follows:

$$\partial E(\tilde{r}_p)/\partial \sigma_{\tilde{r}_p} \tag{5A.3}$$

However, this may be expanded as follows:

$$\partial E(\tilde{r}_p)/\partial \sigma_{\tilde{r}_p} = [\partial E(\tilde{r}_p)/\partial w_i]/(\partial \sigma_{\tilde{r}_p}/\partial w_i) \tag{5A.4}$$

and,

$$\partial E(\tilde{r}_p)/\partial w_i = E(\tilde{r}_i) - E(\tilde{r}_m) \tag{5A.5}$$

and,

$$\partial \sigma_{\tilde{r}_p}/\partial w_i = \frac{\frac{1}{2}(2w_i\sigma_{\tilde{r}_i}^2 - 2\sigma_{\tilde{r}_m}^2 + 2w_i\sigma_{\tilde{r}_m}^2 + 2\rho_{i,m}\sigma_{\tilde{r}_i}\sigma_{r_m} - 4w_i\rho_{i,m}\sigma_{\tilde{r}_i}\sigma_{\tilde{r}_m})}{[w_i^2 \sigma_{\tilde{r}_i}^2 + (1 - w_i)^2 \sigma_{\tilde{r}_m}^2 + 2w_i(1 - w_i)\rho_{i,m}\sigma_{\tilde{r}_i}\sigma_{\tilde{r}_m}]^{1/2}} \tag{5A.6}$$

If $w_i = 0$, equation (5A.6) simplifies to:

$$\partial \sigma_{\tilde{r}_p}/\partial w_i = (\rho_{i,m}\sigma_{\tilde{r}_i}\sigma_{\tilde{r}_m} - \sigma_{\tilde{r}_m}^2)/\sigma_{\tilde{r}_m} \tag{5A.7}$$

Assuming $w_i = 0$, we may now substitute equations (5A.6) and (5A.7) into (5A.4),

$$\partial E(r_p)/\partial \sigma_{\tilde{r}_p} = \frac{[E(\tilde{r}_i) - E(\tilde{r}_m)]}{(\rho_{i,m}\sigma_{\tilde{r}_i}\sigma_{\tilde{r}_m} - \sigma_{\tilde{r}_m}^2)/\sigma_{\tilde{r}_m}} \tag{5A.8}$$

and hence

$$\partial E(\tilde{r}_p)/\partial \sigma_{\tilde{r}_p} = \frac{\sigma_{\tilde{r}_m}[E(\tilde{r}_i) - E(\tilde{r}_m)]}{(\rho_{i,m}\sigma_{\tilde{r}_i}\sigma_{\tilde{r}_m} - \sigma_{\tilde{r}_m}^2)} \tag{5A.9}$$

If $w_i = 0$, then we must be at point M in Fig. 6.1. Therefore, the slope of IMI* is now equal to the slope of the CML which may be defined as,

$$\text{Slope of CML} = [E(\tilde{r}_m) - r_f]/\sigma_{\tilde{r}_m} \tag{5A.10}$$

Hence, at M we have

$$\frac{[E(\tilde{r}_m) - r_f]}{\sigma_{\tilde{r}_m}} = \frac{\sigma_{\tilde{r}_m}[E(\tilde{r}_i) - E(\tilde{r}_m)]}{(\rho_{i,m}\sigma_{\tilde{r}_i}\sigma_{\tilde{r}_m} - \sigma_{\tilde{r}_m}^2)} \tag{5A.11}$$

Cross-multiplying,

$$[E(\tilde{r}_m) - r_f](\rho_{i,m}\sigma_{\tilde{r}_i}\sigma_{\tilde{r}_m} - \sigma_{\tilde{r}_m}^2) = \sigma_{\tilde{r}_m}^2[E(\tilde{r}_i) - E(\tilde{r}_m)] \tag{5A.12}$$

dividing both sides by $\sigma_{\tilde{r}_m}^2$,

$$[E(\tilde{r}_m) - r_f]\left[\frac{\rho_{i,m}\sigma_{\tilde{r}_i}\sigma_{\tilde{r}_m}}{\sigma_{\tilde{r}_m}^2} - \frac{\sigma_{\tilde{r}_m}^2}{\sigma_{\tilde{r}_m}^2}\right] = E(\tilde{r}_i) - E(\tilde{r}_m) \tag{5A.13}$$

adding $E(\tilde{r}_m)$ to both sides in order to isolate $E(\tilde{r}_i)$,

$$[E(\tilde{r}_m) - r_f]\left[\frac{\rho_{i,m}\sigma_{\tilde{r}_i}\sigma_{\tilde{r}_m}}{\sigma_{\tilde{r}_m}^2} - 1\right] = E(\tilde{r}_m) - E(\tilde{r}_i) \tag{5A.14}$$

and defining $[\rho_{i,m}\sigma_{\tilde{r}_i}\sigma_{\tilde{r}_m}/\sigma_{\tilde{r}_m}^2]$ as β_i we have,

$$[E(\tilde{r}_m) - r_f](\beta_i - 1) - E(\tilde{r}_m) = E(\tilde{r}_i) \tag{5A.15}$$

multiplying out the bracket,

$$\beta_i E(\tilde{r}_m) - \beta_i r_f - E(\tilde{r}_m) + r_f + E(\tilde{r}_m) = E(\tilde{r}_i) \tag{5A.16}$$

therefore

$$r_f + \beta_i(E(\tilde{r}_m) - r_f) = E(\tilde{r}_i) \tag{5A.17}$$

Equation (5A.17) is the capital asset pricing model.

Notes

1. W.F. Sharpe, 'A simplified model for portfolio analysis', *Management Science*, Vol. 9, 1963. W.F. Sharpe, 'Capital asset prices: a theory of market equilibrium under conditions of risk, *Journal of Finance*, Vol. 19, September 1964.
2. J. Lintner, 'The valuation of risky assets and the selection of risky investments in stock and capital budgets, *Review of Economics and Statistics*, Vol. 47, 1965.
3. W.F. Sharpe, *Portfolio Theory and Capital Markets*, McGraw-Hill, 1970, p. 77.
4. Some steps have been missed out at this point. The slope of IMI* is the rate of change in the portfolio return divided by the rate of change in the portfolio risk:

$$\text{The slope of IMI*} = \partial E(\tilde{r}_p)/\partial\sigma_p \tag{5a}$$

However, in both the numerator and the denominator the rate of change is produced by redistributing investment between I and M. Therefore, 5a may be rewritten as follows:

$$\partial E(\tilde{r}_p)/\partial\sigma_p = [\partial E(\tilde{r}_p/\partial w_i)/(\partial\sigma_p/\partial w_i) \tag{5b}$$

and

$$\partial E(\tilde{r}_p)/\partial w_i = E(\tilde{r}_i) - E(\tilde{r}_m) \tag{5c}$$

and

$$\partial\sigma_p/\partial w_i = \frac{\frac{1}{2}(2w_i\sigma_i^2 - 2\sigma_m^2 + 2w_i\sigma_m^2 + 2\sigma_{i,m} - 4w_i\sigma_{i,m})}{[w_i^2\sigma_i^2 + (1-w_i)^2\sigma_m^2 + 2w_i(1-w_i)\sigma_{i,m}]} \tag{5d}$$

At point M in Fig. 5.1 w_i is equal to zero and Eq. (5d) simplifies considerably as most of the terms contain w_i and thus disappear:

$$\partial\sigma_p/\partial w_i = (\sigma_{i,m} - \sigma_m^2)/\sigma_m \tag{5e}$$

Therefore

$$\partial E(r_p)/\sigma_p = \sigma_m(E(\tilde{r}_i) - E(\tilde{r}_m))/(\sigma_{i,m} - \sigma_m^2) \tag{5f}$$

which is Eq. (5.2).

It should also be noted that the exact curvature on the line IMI* shown in Fig. 5.1 is dependent on the value of $\rho_{i,m}$. As long as this has a value lower than unity, the function IMI* will have a curvature as shown in Fig. 5.1.

5. It must be stressed at this point that the CAPM is an *ex-ante* model which deals with expected returns rather than past returns.
6. The variance of the error term may be defined as $E(e_i^2)$ because the sum of the error terms is equal to zero and hence the mean error term is also equal to zero.
7. J. Evans and S. Archer, 'Diversification and the reduction of dispersion: an empirical analysis', *Journal of Finance*, Vol. 23, December 1968.
8. R. Upson, P. Jessup and K. Matsumoto, 'Portfolio diversification strategies', *Financial Analysts' Journal*, Vol. 31, May 1975.
9. The data for Fig. 5.6 are as follows:

		Coefficient of diversification (%)					
Number of shares	Down	Up	Random	Number of shares	Down	Up	Random
30	7.8	7.8	7.8	15	14.7	14.3	14.6
29	7.9	7.9	8.0	14	15.8	15.3	15.7
28	8.1	8.4	8.4	13	17.1	15.7	16.7
27	8.4	8.6	8.6	12	18.2	17.1	17.0
26	8.8	9.0	8.8	11	20.1	17.8	18.5
25	9.1	9.3	8.9	10	22.2	19.7	20.2
24	9.6	9.4	9.3	9	23.5	22.7	22.7
23	9.7	9.4	9.9	8	26.2	26.3	24.7
22	10.0	9.9	10.4	7	30.0	29.0	28.5
21	10.6	10.4	11.0	6	31.3	30.0	33.7
20	11.4	10.6	11.6	5	33.0	35.1	36.4
19	12.1	11.2	12.0	4	37.7	40.1	43.1
18	12.5	12.0	12.3	3	45.5	51.7	50.1
17	13.3	12.5	13.1	2	53.8	65.6	63.8
16	13.8	13.3	13.7				

10. B. Solnik, 'An equilibrium model of the international capital market', *Journal of Economic Theory*, Vol. 8, August 1874.
11. H. Levy and M. Sarnat, 'International diversification of investment portfolios', *American Economic Review*, Vol. 60, September 1970.
12. B. Solnik, 'Why not diversify internationally rather than domestically?', *Financial Analysts' Journal*, Vol. 30, July 1974.

Questions

1. What is superfluous diversification and explain what problems can often result from it.
2. Evaluate the following portfolio using equal weights.

Share	Mkt Cap (m)	Beta	St Dev (%)	Sp Risk (%)	Act Ret (%)
Electric Tram Co	64	0.71	30	26	37
Fleet Motors Ltd	227	0.9	30	23	31
Sam's Supermarkets	298	0.78	28	22	21
Northern TV Plc	181	0.89	36	30	−7

The risk-free rate of return is 13% and the return on and risk of the market are estimated at 19% and 21% respectively.

3. Re-evaluate the above portfolio using weights based on relative capitalization. Which version appears to be preferable and why?
4. Compare and contrast the CML with the SML.
5. Are the CML and the SML substitutes or complements to each other?
6. Why should the export of capital from the UK after 1979 have been expected?
7. What are the non-market factors which may increase the risk of an investment and how may they be minimized if not eradicated?
8. Demonstrate that a non-convex efficient frontier is both sub-optimal and a transient phenomenon.
9. Critically discuss the concept of the coefficient of diversification and show how it might be argued that it is in direct contradiction to the theoretical conclusions of the CML.
10. What are the implications for the CAPM if the market could not be assumed to be perfect?

6. CAPM extensions

Introduction

Chapters 4 and 5 described the foundations of modern portfolio theory which are underwritten by the efficient market hypothesis presented in Chapter 3. In Chapter 6 we will look at the following related topics:

1. A selection of the empirical research on the validity of the CAPM.
2. Strong form market efficiency and the performance of professionally managed portfolios. In this section we will consider the possibility of being able to 'beat the market' using professional advice.
3. Finally, the possible successor to the CAPM and the market model, the arbitrage pricing theory (APT), will be presented.

Testing the market model

Although we have already made use of the market model in the construction and evaluation of portfolios, we have not evaluated the model itself. How much of the variation in a security's returns does it actually explain? How reliable are its estimates of security betas? A complete and rigorous example of testing the results of the market model is given by Fama.[1] Taking the monthly data for IBM between July 1963 and June 1968 (inclusive), Fama proceeds first to calculate the market model equation as follows (see Fig. 6.1):

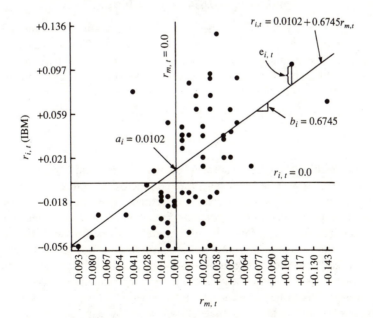

Figure 6.1 Plot of sample points and estimated market model regression function for IBM for July 1963–June 1968. (Source: E. Fama,[1] 1977.)

$$r_{i,t} = a_i + b_i r_{m,t} + e_{i,t} = 0.0102 + 0.6745 r_{m,t} + e_{i,t} \qquad (6.1)$$

During the period under consideration, the mean monthly returns for IBM and the market were 0.0212 and 0.0162 respectively (2.12 and 1.62 per cent). The sample variances of the returns for IBM and the market were 0.002,25 and 0.001,52 respectively and the variance of the error term was 0.001,58. The explanatory power of the model in this case may be estimated by expressing the unexplained variance (σ_{ei}^2) as a proportion of the total variance in IBM's returns (σ_{IBM}^2):

$$0.001\,58/0.002\,25 = 0.702 \ (70.2 \text{ per cent})$$

Hence the equation leaves unexplained just over 70 per cent of the total variance, or conversely it explains just under 30 per cent of the variance $[(1-0.702)100 = 29.8$ per cent$]$.

From the equation of the market model for IBM we can see that the estimation of β_{IBM} is 0.67. However, it should be borne in mind that this is the estimate derived from one random sample of a true but unknown population. Therefore, it is necessary to have some sort of measure to gauge the quality of the estimate. The standard statistical technique is to calculate the standard deviation of the estimate (standard error) and use the cumulative normal frequency distribution to set confidence limits. The standard deviation of the estimate of β is calculated as follows:

$$\sigma_b^2 = \sigma_{e}^2/(t-1)\sigma_m^2 = 0.001\,58/(59)(0.001\,52) = 0.017\,618 \qquad (6.2)$$

therefore, the standard deviation is:

$$\sqrt{0.017\,618} = 0.1327$$

Using the unit cumulative normal frequency distribution we may compute confidence limits for our estimate of beta. For example, we may estimate the values of beta at the limits of the expected value plus and minus one standard deviation,

$$E(b_i) + \sigma_{bi} = 0.674 + 0.133 = 0.541$$

$$E(b_i) - \sigma_{bi} = 0.674 - 0.133 = 0.807$$

Therefore, there is a probability of 0.68 that the true value of beta will lie between 0.541 and 0.807. We may go further and specify confidence limits such as 95 per cent. That is to say, the range within which the true value will lie with a probability of 0.95. Using the cumulative normal distribution table, we know that this range will be within plus/minus 1.96 standard deviations of the expected mean. Hence,

$$E(b_i) + 1.96\sigma_{bi} = 0.674 + (1.96)(0.133) = 0.935$$

$$E(b_i) - 1.96\sigma_{bi} = 0.674 - (1.96)(0.133) = 0.413$$

Fama notes that this result is typical for samples consisting of 60 monthly returns. Fama carried out similar tests for 30 randomly selected firms quoted on the NYSE. On average he found that the model explained 27 per cent of the total variance of returns. The best results were for the Ford Motor and the Dana corporations which predicted 45 per cent of the total variance of returns. The worst case was Canadian Breweries for which the model explained none of the variance of the returns. Fama also tested for changes in the model's explanatory power over time. Thus, for 19 randomly selected larger firms the average amount of the variance of the returns explained was 52 per cent (for 16 smaller firms over the same period the degree of explanation was 56 per cent) for the period January 1934 to December 1938, significantly higher than in the post-war period. The CAPM specifies a relationship between market risk and the expected return on a security. However, expected returns cannot be observed. Hence, tests of this relationship have had to use historical data and have had to assume that the distribution of returns has remained stable over time. The second piece of work presented here relies on this assumption. It was done in 1972 by Black, Jensen and Scholes,[2] who took a random sample of shares quoted on the NYSE and calculated the betas from 60 consecutive monthly returns. They repeated this process for 35 overlapping 5-year periods from 1926 to 1964. For this process they used the risk-premium version of the CAPM:

$$r_{i,t} - r_f = a_i + b_i(r_{m,t} - r_f) + e_{i,t} \tag{6.3}$$

This equation may be respecified to define a_i,

$$a_i = (r_{i,t} - r_f) - b_i(r_{m,t} - r_f) - e_{i,t} \tag{6.4}$$

If the CAPM is valid, then a_i must not be significantly different from zero. However, the authors rejected this possibility of testing the CAPM as the data could produce biased estimators in certain cases.[3] Having estimated the security betas, they then proceeded to construct 10 portfolios in various risk classes ranging from the highest with a value of 1.56 to the lowest with 0.5. In order to avoid any bias resulting from the selection process (originating from measurement errors which may tend to put shares which had positive discrepancies into the high beta portfolios and vice versa) the return was calculated using the data from the sixth year following the beginning of the period in which the betas had been estimated and chosen. Thus, betas were calculated for the period 1926–31 and portfolios selected from these results; then the returns were estimated for these portfolios using data from the period 1932. This was repeated for 10 portfolios over the 420 months between 1931 and 1965. These results were then subjected to both time series and cross-section tests. The time series tests showed that apart from the period 1931–39, the high beta portfolios tended to earn less than expected and the low beta portfolios more than expected.

The cross-sectional test took the form of the following equation:

$$r_i - r_f = y_o + y_i \beta_i + e_i \tag{6.5}$$

The term on the left-hand side of the equation is the risk premium of the portfolio which is described as a linear function of beta where y_o and y_i are the intercept and slope of the regression line respectively. The cross-sectional results are summarized in Table 6.1.

Table 6.1   The cross-sectional results

Period	y_o	y_i	$r_m - r_f$
1/1931–12/65	0.0036	0.0108	0.0142
1/1931–9/39	−0.008	0.0304	0.022
10/1939–6/48	0.0044	0.0107	0.0149
7/1948–3/57	0.0078	0.0033	0.0112
4/1957–12/65	0.0102	−0.0012	0.0088

Note: All of the y_o values are significantly different from zero at the 5 per cent level.
Source: F. Black et al.,[2] pp. 79–121.

All the intercepts are significantly greater than zero except for the first sub-period when it is significantly lower than zero. In addition the estimate for the slope (substituting 1 for β_i in Eq. (6.5)) was found to be less than the market risk premium $(r_m - r_f)$. These results confirm those of the time series test in which high and low beta portfolios earned less than expected and more than expected respectively. The authors interpret these results as supporting the zero-beta version of the CAPM. In this variant the risk-free asset is replaced by the zero-beta portfolio. Hence, y_o should be equal to $r_z - r_f$ and y_i (the estimated value after substituting the value of 1 for β_i in Eq. (6.5)) should be equal to $r_m - r_z$. However, Black et al. did not follow this interpretation of their results with more

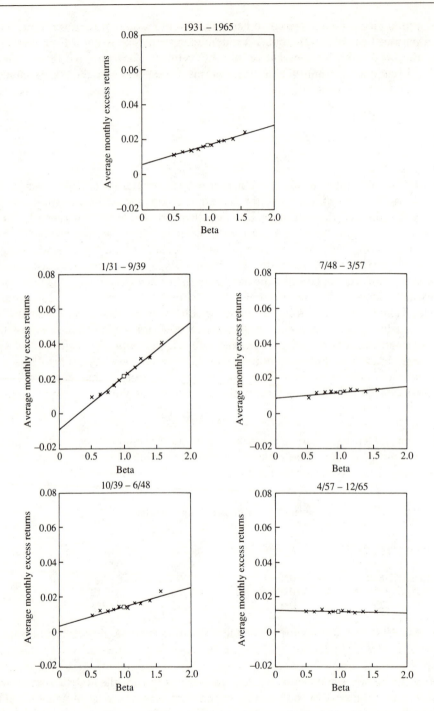

Figure 6.2   Estimates of the SML. (Source: F. Black et al.[2])

empirical testing. In addition to suggesting the validity of the zero-beta version of the CAPM, their results also showed the model (both versions) to be unstable over time. This can most easily be appreciated from Fig. 6.2.

A similar test of the CAPM was conducted in 1973 by Fama and MacBeth[4] who constructed 20 portfolios from NYSE listed stocks over the period January 1926 to June 1968. Betas and returns were estimated using methods which were similar but not identical to those used by Black, Jensen and Scholes. The data was fed into a cross-sectional model with the following specification:

$$r_{i,t} = y_{o,t} + y_{1,t}\beta_{i,t-1} + y_{2,t}\beta_{i,t-1}^2 + y_{3,t}\sigma_{i,t-1} + n_{i,t} \tag{6.6}$$

where: $r_{i,t}$ = return on portfolio i in month t

$y_{o,t}$ = intercept

$\beta_{i,t-1}$ = estimated beta for portfolio i in month $t-1$

$\sigma_{i,t-1}$ = estimated non-market risk (specified as a standard deviation)
            for portfolio i in month $t-1$

$n_{i,t}$ = unexplained residual return on portfolio i in month t

Fama and MacBeth proposed three hypotheses which could be tested by the model:
1. If the relationship between risk and return is linear then the value of $y_{2,t}$ should not be significantly different from zero.
2. If beta is the relevant measure of portfolio risk then the value of $y_{3,t}$ should not be significantly different from zero.
3. If the acceptance of increased risk is rewarded by a greater return as predicted by the model then $y_{1,t}$ should be positive.

The results are summarized in Table 6.2.

Table 6.2   The cross-sectional results (Fama and MacBeth)

Period	y_o	y_1	y_2	y_3
1/1935–6/68	0.002	0.0114*	−0.0026	0.0516
1/1935–12/45	0.0011	0.0118	−0.0009	0.0817
1/1946–12/55	0.0017	0.0209*	−0.0076	−0.0378
1/1956–6/68	0.0031	0.0034	0.0000	0.0966

* significant at the 5% level
Source: E. Fama & J. MacBeth,[4] pp. 607–636.

Fama and MacBeth also found that the intercept (y_o) was significantly different from the risk-free rate for the entire period and for the first of the sub-periods, which tends to lend support to the zero-beta version of the CAPM rather than the risk-free rate variant. They also found that the average value of $r_m - r_f$ was significantly different from y_1 which implies that the empirical version of the CAPM had a smaller slope than that predicted by the risk-free rate version of the CAPM.

Despite these discrepancies between the theoretical and empirical versions of the CAPM, the lack of significance of any of the coefficients except those for y_1 means that none of the hypotheses can be rejected. Hence, there is a positive and linear relationship between risk and return and the relevant measure of risk is shown to be systematic rather than unsystematic.

In 1977 Richard Roll[5] published an article which cast doubt on the validity and methodology of the CAPM tests which had been done up to that time. Roll argued that the true market portfolio is

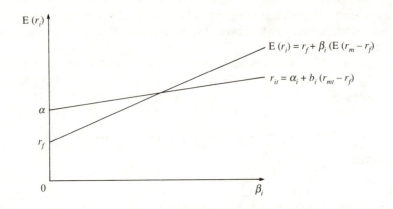

Figure 6.3   Theoretical and empirical SMLs.

a mean–variance efficient portfolio and cannot be observed. This is because it must include all assets which might be acquired for investment purposes. Hence, it must include such assets as property, objets d'art, shares, debentures and other physical investment assets and collectables. As the risk and returns of most of the assets cannot be observed the tests hitherto had been biased. In other words, by restricting tests to just one equity market, the tests had built into them a bias which meant that they were not valid tests of the CAPM. In effect, Roll argued that the tests reduced the CAPM to a model of partial equilibrium in which all other factors, such as the returns on other investment assets, must be held constant before its prescriptions can be applied. Moreover, as most of these tests have been conducted on a single national market, they impose an arbitrary segmentation on the model in which the effects of even other equity markets are arbitrarily ignored.

However, if the above criticism of the partial equilibrium model is put to one side, the implication of Roll's work is that the only valid test is one in which the various market indices, which are used as proxies for the market portfolio, are examined to see if they are mean–variance efficient. Taken to its logical extent, this point implies that even such indirect tests as those previously described are invalid.

Roll pointed out that tests which used a market index as a proxy for the market portfolio could suffer from two types of error:
1. The proxy might be efficient when the market portfolio is inefficient.
2. The proxy might be inefficient when the market portfolio is efficient.

Most market indices are highly correlated with each other, for example, the FT 30, the FTSE 100 and the FT All Share Indices.[6] However, this does not mean that it does not matter which of the indices is used as the proxy in estimating the CAPM. Roll showed that if Black et al. had selected another proxy for their tests, the results would have supported the traditional risk-free rate version of the CAPM rather than the zero-beta variant.

It is important to appreciate that Roll's critique does not reject the theoretical model. It merely argues that the CAPM is untestable. In addition, it is worth noting that Markowitz has argued that the inconclusive nature of the empirical research does not mean that the CAPM cannot be sensibly used for portfolio analysis and assessment.

Using the market model to evaluate portfolio performance

In Chapter 1 we saw how institutional investors have come to dominate shareholding in the International Stock Exchange. Some 60 per cent of UK securities are held in professionally managed portfolios. The CAPM and the market model provide a means to test the performance of these portfolios and in doing so have given indications of the extent to which the market is strong form efficient in assessing the ability of managers to consistently beat the market.

There are four basic types of fund managers in the UK financial serives market:

Pension funds

These may be self-administered by employees or corporate trustees. They may also be independent funds managed by insurance companies. For example, at the end of 1986 a small fund owned and administered by a group of workers in a nationalized industry which we shall call 'The General Sickness and Funeral Fund' had the following investments:

Fixed interest	Total cost (£)	Market value (£)	Income (£)	Gross yield (%)
Gilts	1 388 800	1 442 250	164 750	11.42
UK Debs	64 300	82 450	8 300	10.08
Total Debt	1 453 100	1 524 700	173 050	11.35
Equities				
Building	5 100	21 250	550	2.65
Other	35 950	44 200	2 950	6.66
Food	14 900	22 250	1 300	5.77
Packaging	22 800	57 000	2 250	3.98
Textiles	17 650	18 550	1 000	5.60
Property	13 600	24 800	1 100	4.51
Utilities	23 550	46 200	1 000	2.16
Total Equities	133 550	234 250	10 150	4.36
Grand Total	1 586 700	1 759 000	183 300	10.42

Notes: The figures for the gross yield on equities takes into account the time over which the investment has been held (unstated) and cannot be used as a holding period return for CAPM as the periods are unequal.

This fund was set up during the 1880s as a means of providing sickness benefit for employees. Since the advent of the Welfare State the members, through their trustees, have decided to freeze the sickness benefit and concentrate on a terminal benefit at retirement.

Source: Stockbroker's Report.

Insurance companies

These companies through their business of providing life assurance have to create and manage portfolios of financial assets. Indeed, the investment of the premiums from their general insurance business has made significant contributions to their overall profitability. In those years in which claims have exceeded premium income, the profits on the investment of premiums have been sufficient to produce an overall profit.

Investment trusts (US terminology 'closed-end funds')

These are public limited companies whose sole purpose is to invest their shareholders' funds in the shares of other companies. It is a distinctive feature of these companies that their shares usually trade on the stock market at a discount to their net asset values. Being public limited companies, the investment trusts can raise debt capital and gear their portfolios.

Unit trusts (US terminology 'open-end funds.)

Unlike the investment trust, the unit trust is not a company. It is merely a fund which is managed by a company. The management company may be dedicated to the purpose or this activity may be just one of a number of related activities. Hence, unit trusts are offered by specialist companies such as M & G or Save & Prosper, or the high street banks like Barclays, Lloyds, the Midland and the NatWest. The management company makes an initial investment charge when it sells a unit to an investor and makes an annual charge on the value of the fund. Unlike the investment trust, the unit trust cannot raise capital by selling debt, its capital rises (falls) with the sale (redemption) of units to the public.

Because the capital of unit trusts can vary constantly with the sale or redemption of units, the actual size of the fund is not an accurate indicator of investment performance. It has to be adjusted for cash flows before any analysis is done. On the other hand, the units themselves are subject to market prices as they each represent a share of the fund's net asset value. The unit prices are published daily in the form of an offer–bid spread (the price at which units are offered to the public and the price bid by the management for redemption which differ by around 6%). Typical unit trust quotes are shown at Table 6.3.

Table 6.3   Unit trust quotes

Name	Init. charge	Canc. price	Bid price	Offer price	+ or −	Gross yield
Management: *Framlington Group H*						
Extra Income	5	236.0	241.6	255.6	+0.3	4.88
Europe	5	60.1	60.1	63.6	−0.25	1.00
Management: *Midland Bank F*						
Name						
British Trust	5.25	48.0	48.2	51.3	−0.17	3.79
European Growth	5	109.7	109.8	115.8	−1.0	1.02

Notes:
(1) Cancellation price. The maximum spread between the bid and offer prices is fixed by a government formula. It is usual practice for the management of the trust to set the bid price above the limit set by the formula. Hence, the cancellation price represents the minimum price which the management must offer to repurchase the units. When the demand for units is strong the management has no need to destroy units as they may be sold within a short period. However, when demand is slack and there is an excess of supply over the demand for units, the bid price may equal the cancellation price.
(2) H. This stands for historic pricing and indicates that unless there has been an intervening revaluation investors may deal at the prices quoted in the newspaper on that day (which were set at the closing levels of the previous day).
(3) F. This stands for forward pricing and indicates that investors can be given no firm price before the transaction takes place.
(4) The gross yield is calculated having taken all costs into consideration.
Source: *Financial Times*, 21 October 1988

The return to the unit holder may be calculated by taking into account the three basic income streams:

1. Dividends or interest payments (d).
2. Cash disbursements from capital gains (c).
3. The selling price, based on the net asset value per unit (bid price).

This is then compared with the purchase or offer price (which includes the initial management fee),

$$1 + r = (d + c + B_{t+1})/O_t$$

By concentrating on the return to the unit holder the problems of adjusting the net asset value of the fund for capital inflows and outflows may be avoided.

The performance and performance resting of selected unit trusts are shown in Tables 6.4 and 6.5.

Table 6.4 UK unit trust performance

Type of fund	Number of funds	Average size (£ million)	Average (–) 6 months	Offer/bid 12 months	Performance 36 months
UK General	106	46	3	21	89
UK Growth	113	22	2	19	81
UK Equity Inc	99	27	2	23	106
UK Mixed Inc	19	17	1	18	83
G & FI Growth[1]	28	11	0	4	29
G & FI Income[1]	40	8	–1	3	23
Investment UTs	8	12	3	14	91
F & P Shares[2]	15	29	1	26	105
Int Growth	93	18	3	4	61
North America	96	16	4	0	35
Europe	43	21	5	35	150
Australia	18	6	–8	–24	10
Japan	52	24	2	–3	98
Far Eastern	55	11	–1	–6	63
Comm & Energy	37	7	–1	–18	–15
Int Income	26	9	1	1	36
Managed Funds	3	N/A	N/A	N/A	N/A
FT 30 Index			14	25	131
FT All Share			10	24	86

Notes:
(1) Gilt and fixed interest.
(2) Financial and property shares.
Source: *Unit Trust Management*, January 1986.

The returns published in Tables 6.4 and 6.5 are inadequate without the associated measures of risk. The mean-variance analysis and the CAPM provide the means to make risk-adjusted assessment of fund performance. In doing so they also indirectly test the strong form efficiency of the stock market by measuring the ability of the market professionals to consistently make excess profits (on a risk-adjusted basis). Three tests have been developed to estimate the risk-adjusted performance of portfolios:

Table 6.5   Unit trusts performance league tables

Percentage change in price offer to bid.
Best results 12 months to 1 December 1985

FS Balanced Growth	83.2
Simon & Coates	60.3
TR Special Opps	58.6
BG Income Growth	56.7
Oppenheimer Euro.	56.4
Vanguard Special Sits	47.4
County Bank Financial	46.1
TR Smaller Co's	45.7
Murray European	45.5
Govett European	44.4
Mercury European	44.0
Oppenheimer UK Growth	43.4

Best results 60 months to 1 December 1985

Barrington European	307.9
Vanguard Special Sits	281.4
MLA General	267.7
Henderson Inc & Growth	266.8
EFM Tokyo	265.5
Henderson European	265.0
Capel Income	256.7
Oppenheimer Int Growth	259.7
Perpetual Income	253.4
M&G Midland	247.9
Gartmore Income	243.4
Prolific High Inc	241.7

Source: *Unit Trust Management*, January 1986.

Sharpe's risk premium/standard deviation ratio (S)

Sharpe[7] analysed the performance of 34 mutual funds between the years 1954 and 1963 (inclusive). His measure consisted of the risk premium divided by the funds' standard deviation of returns. This may be derived from the CML. The total risk on a security or portfolio may be described as follows:

$$E(r_i) = r_f + \sigma_i(E(r_m) - r_f)/\sigma_m$$

If ex-post and ex-ante returns are equal, then we may rewrite this equation as follows,

$$\bar{r}_i = \bar{r}_f + \sigma_i(\bar{r}_m - \bar{r}_f)/\sigma_m$$

where σ_i and σ_m are the ex-post measures of the standard deviations of the portfolio and market returns. This may be manipulated by subtracting the riskless rate from both sides and dividing the result by the standard deviation of the portfolio's returns to obtain,

$$(\bar{r}_i - \bar{r}_f)/\sigma_i = (\bar{r}_m - \bar{r}_f)/\sigma_m$$

This may be interpreted as saying that, in equilibrium, the ex-post risk premiums per unit of risk on well-diversified portfolios should be the same as the risk premium per unit of risk for the market portfolio. The left-hand side of this equation is Sharpe's measure of performance (see Fig. 6.4),

$$S_1 = (\bar{r}_i + \bar{r}_f)/\sigma_i$$

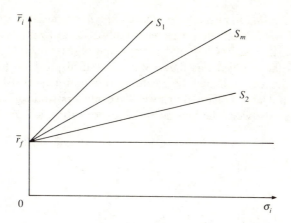

Figure 6.4   Sharpe's ranking technique. Notes: (a) S_m is the Sharpe score for the market, and S_1 and S_2 are the scores for two portfolios. (b) As $S_1 > S_m$, portfolio has a higher risk-premium per unit of risk and can be said to be out-performing the market. As $S_2 < S_m$, it is under-performing the market.

The right-hand side provides a benchmark against which all portfolios may be assessed. Sharpe calculated a benchmark ratio using the Dow Jones Industrial Average as a proxy for the market portfolio. This gives the slope of the CML and hence the measure could be used to position portfolio performance in the risk–return space.

The ratio for the Dow Jones Industrial Index was 0.6673 while the average for the 34 funds was 0.633 and only 11 of the funds had ratios higher than that of the index. The highest fund ratio was 0.7784 and the lowest 0.4311. If the sales commissions (averaging 8 per cent) had been included in the calculation the results for the funds would have been concomitantly worse when compared to a buy-and-hold strategy.

Treynor's risk premium/beta ratio (T)

Sharpe's measure was a ratio which compared the risk premium with the total variability of the portfolio's return. Treynor[8] used the CAPM to devise a ratio which measured the risk premium against the portfolio's systematic risk,

$$E(r_i) = r_f + \beta_i (E(r_m) - r_r)$$

This may be manipulated by subtracting the risk-free rate from both sides and dividing by the portfolio beta to obtain,

$$(E(r_i) - r_f)/\beta_i = (E(r_m) - r_f)$$

and as $\beta_m = 1$, we may rewrite this equation as,

$$(E(r_i) - r_f)/\beta_i = (E(r_m) - r_r)/\beta_m$$

As in the case of the Sharpe measure, the right-hand side provides the benchmark risk premium and the left-hand side is the ex-ante measure of the portfolio risk premium per unit of systematic risk. All that remains is to assume an equilibrium in which investors' expectations are realized on average and we have the ex-post version of Treynor's measure,

$$T_i = (r_i - r_f)/b_i$$

Instead of plotting the ratios in risk–return space, Treynor's measure is plotted in a return–systematic space. Intuitively, we should not expect widely differing results from these two measures in the assessment of portfolios. In Chapter 5 the concept of diversification was discussed in the CAPM framework. What emerged was that a well-diversified portfolio (or in this case a well-diversified fund) should have eliminated the greater part of non-market risk. Therefore, total and systematic risk should not be too different in a well-diversified portfolio. This result was observed by Sharpe.[7] Comparison between the Sharpe and Treynor ratios is shown in graphical form in Fig. 6.5.

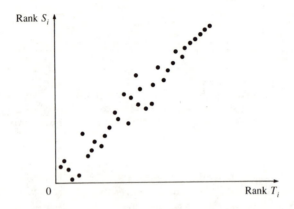

Figure 6.5 Comparing the rankings of the Sharpe and Treynor ratios. (Source: W. Sharpe,[7] p. 129.)

Both measures use the risk-free rate to obtain the risk premiums for the funds under analysis. The implicit assumption is that investors can borrow and lend at the riskless rate of interest. Friend and Blume have shown that this assumption is critical to the rankings produced by both measures.[9]

Jensen's differential return measure

Jensen[10] has developed an absolute measure of portfolio performance based on the risk premium version of the CAPM:

$$E(r_i) - r_f = \beta_i(E(r_m) - r_r)$$

This may be estimated by an ex-post linear regression,

$$r_{i,t} - r_{f,t} = \alpha_1 + b_i(r_{m,t} - r_f) + e_{i,t}$$

where the sum of the error terms is expected to be zero. Jensen's measure may now be defined as,

$$J_i = (\bar{r}_i - r_r) - (\bar{r}_m - r_f)b_i$$

Essentially, it is an estimate of the difference between the actual risk premiums and the premiums predicted by the ex-post CAPM and may be interpreted as an abnormal return.

The Jensen measures J_1 and J_2 in Fig. 6.6 measure the vertical displacement from the ex-post CAPM. Hence, in the figure, portfolio P_1 has a positive value for J ($J_1 > 0$) and portfolio P_2 has a negative value for J ($J_2 < 0$). As the Jensen measure is an absolute measure it is not as appropriate as the Sharpe and Treynor measures for the relative comparison of portfolios with different levels of risk.

Table 6.6(a)   Realized portfolio returns and the evaluation methods

(Risk-free rate 0.8% pm)

Month	P_1	P_2	P_3	P_4	P_5
1	−3.00	−1.00	4.00	0.00	3.00
2	4.00	−2.00	12.00	4.00	5.00
3	2.00	0.00	−5.00	8.00	3.00
4	8.00	3.00	−8.00	3.00	0.00
5	−2.00	3.00	0.00	12.00	0.00
6	0.00	7.00	3.00	−6.00	2.00
7	5.00	2.00	6.00	5.00	7.00
8	5.00	3.00	0.00	4.00	5.00
9	−4.00	6.00	−8.00	6.00	0.00
10	2.00	−6.00	7.00	−9.00	2.00
11	−6.00	−5.00	−9.00	6.00	1.00
12	6.00	−3.00	8.00	4.00	7.00
13	6.00	−4.00	5.00	−2.00	−2.00
14	4.00	−2.00	3.00	0.00	−1.00
15	5.00	5.00	4.00	0.00	3.00
16	5.00	7.00	2.00	4.00	1.00
17	−4.00	8.00	5.00	2.00	−3.00
18	4.00	2.00	8.00	−8.00	−2.00
19	5.00	1.00	18.00	3.00	−1.00
20	2.00	6.00	2.00	10.00	2.00
21	−3.00	7.00	1.00	5.00	2.00
22	−2.00	3.00	12.00	5.00	1.00
23	3.00	3.00	2.00	2.00	2.00
24	3.00	−3.00	0.00	0.00	−1.00
Average	1.88	1.67	3.00	2.42	1.50
Std Dev	3.89	4.17	6.83	5.06	2.67
$\rho_{i,m}$	0.80	0.70	0.85	0.90	0.65
Beta	0.62	0.58	1.16	0.91	0.35

(Market return 3% pm, market risk 5%)   *Market*

	P_1	P_2	P_3	P_4	P_5	Market
Sharpe	0.28	0.21	0.32	0.32	0.26	0.44
Rank	(3)	(5)	(1=)	(1=)	(4)	
Treynor	1.73	1.49	1.89	1.77	2.02	2.2
Rank	(4)	(5)	(2)	(3)	(1)	
Jensen	−0.30	−0.42	−0.35	−0.39	−0.06	0
Rank	(2)	(5)	(4)	(3)	(1)	

(Riskless rate 1% pm)   *Market*

	P_1	P_2	P_3	P_4	P_5	Market
Sharpe	0.22	0.16	0.29	0.28	0.19	0.4
Rank	(3)	(5)	(1)	(2)	(4)	
Treynor	1.42	1.16	1.72	1.56	1.43	2
Rank	(4)	(5)	(1)	(2)	(3)	
Jensen	−0.36	−0.49	−0.32	−0.40	−0.20	0
Rank	(3)	(5)	(2)	(4)	(1)	

(Riskless rate 0.5% pm)

	P_1	P_2	P_3	P_4	P_5	Market
Sharpe	0.35	0.28	0.37	0.38	0.37	0.5
Rank	(4)	(5)	(2=)	(1)	(2=)	
Treynor	2.23	2.02	2.16	2.11	2.86	2.5
Rank	(2)	(5)	(3)	(4)	(1)	
Jensen	−0.18	−0.29	−0.40	−0.36	0.13	0
Rank	(2)	(3)	(5)	(4)	(1)	

Table 6.6(b)   The effect of diversification of the measures of portfolio performance

Risk-free rate 0.8% pm, market risk 5%, market return 3%

Fund	Rp	Sp	$\rho_{p,m}$	$\beta(p)$	Sharpe	Rank	Treynor	Rank	Jensen	Rank	CD*
Market	3.0	5.0	1.00	1.00	0.44		2.2		0.0		
P_1	1.88	3.89	0.8	0.62	0.28	(3)	1.74	(4)	−0.29	(2)	0.36
P_2	1.67	4.17	0.7	0.58	0.21	(5)	1.49	(5)	−0.41	(5)	0.51
P_3	3.0	6.83	0.85	1.16	0.32	(1=)	1.89	(2)	−0.35	(3)	0.28
P_4	2.42	5.06	0.9	0.91	0.32	(1=)	1.78	(3)	−0.38	(4)	0.19
P_5	1.5	2.67	0.65	0.35	0.26	(4)	2.02	(1)	−0.06	(1)	0.58
P_{1a}	1.88	3.89	0.98	0.76	0.28	(3)	1.42	(4)	−0.60	(3)	0.04
P_{2a}	1.67	4.17	0.96	0.80	0.21	(5)	1.09	(5)	−0.89	(5)	0.08
P_{3a}	3.0	6.83	0.94	1.28	0.32	(1=)	1.71	(2)	−0.62	(4)	0.12
P_{4a}	2.42	5.06	0.92	0.93	0.32	(1=)	1.74	(1)	−0.43	(2)	0.15
P_{5a}	1.5	2.67	0.9	0.48	0.26	(4)	1.46	(3)	−0.36	(1)	0.19
P_{1b}	1.88	3.89	0.94	0.73	0.28	(3)	1.48	(3)	−0.53	(4)	0.12
P_{2b}	1.67	4.17	0.92	0.77	0.21	(5)	1.13	(5)	−0.82	(5)	0.15
P_{3b}	3.0	6.83	0.9	1.23	0.32	(1=)	1.79	(1)	−0.50	(3)	0.19
P_{4b}	2.42	5.06	0.93	0.94	0.32	(1=)	1.72	(2)	−0.45	(2)	0.14
P_{5b}	1.5	2.67	0.96	0.51	0.26	(4)	1.37	(4)	−0.43	(1)	0.08

* CD is coefficient of diversification.

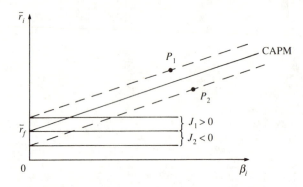

Figure 6.6   Jensen's differential return measure.

Table 6.6 is an illustration of the three measures in practice and illustrates the differences in rankings between them. Some of the discrepancies between the three measures can be ascribed to the use of random hypothetical data which has not produced well-diversified portfolios. The best is P_4 with a coefficient of diversification of 0.19 while the worst is P_5 with a coefficient of 0.57. We would expect these figures to be much lower for a randomly diversified portfolio with more than 10–15 shares (see Chapter 5). Table 6.6 includes 3 different risk-free rates to illustrate the point made by Friend and Blume that these measures are sensitive to the rate of return on the risk-free asset. In the second part of Table 6.6, slight adjustments have been made to the portfolios to reduce the levels of non-market risk in order to illustrate the effect of diversification on the evaluation measures.

In part (a) of Table 6.6, five hypothetical portfolios (P_1 to P_5) are compared using the three principal yardsticks. It is clear that in all three measures, changes in rank can be induced by altering the riskless rate of return. It is also clear that due to the differences in construction, the measures do not provide the same ranking. In the second part of Table 6.6(b) all of the variables have been held constant except for ρ, the correlation coefficient between the various portfolios and the market. The first 5 portfolios (P_1 to P_5) use the data from the first part of Table 6.6(a). Portfolios P_{1a} to P_{5a} are varied by making changes in the correlation coefficients. The general result is that the higher the correlation coefficient the lower the CD score and the better the diversification of risk. This will naturally change the Sharpe, Treynor, and Jensen scores and rankings.

All three measures were used in a study of the performance of 123 mutual funds between 1960 and 1969 by McDonald.[11] The yields on high grade commercial paper were used as a proxy for the risk-free rate of interest and the funds were divided into groups by their investment objectives. The results obtained are summarized in Table 6.7.

In 1976 Ward and Saunders published the results of their application of MPT-based performance measures on UK unit trusts.[12] They calculated the continuously compounded annual rates of return for 49 unit trusts between 1 January 1964 and 31 December 1974. They used the 12 month deposit rate for local authorities as their estimate of the riskless rate of return and the FT 650 index as a proxy for the market portfolio. The results of applying the market model to these data are shown in Fig. 6.7, where the ex-post returns have been plotted against betas which have

Table 6.7   Comparison of the Sharpe, Treynor and Jensen measures of portfolio performance

Fund objective	Beta	St Dev (%)	Excess return (%)	Sharpe	Treynor	Jensen
Capital Gain	1.22	5.90	0.693	0.117	0.568	0.122
Growth	1.01	4.57	0.565	0.124	0.560	0.099
Growth–Income	0.90	3.93	0.476	0.121	0.529	0.058
Income–Growth	0.86	3.80	0.398	0.105	0.463	0.004
Balanced	0.68	3.05	0.214	0.070	0.314	−0.099
Income	0.55	2.67	0.252	0.094	0.458	−0.002
Sample Means	0.92	4.17	0.477	0.112	0.518	0.051
NYSE Index	1.00	3.83	0.510	0.133	0.510	0.000

Source: J. McDonald,[11] Table 1, p. 319.

been adjusted for the changes in the cash holdings of the unit trusts: Ward and Saunders argue that these managerial decisions are particularly important in determining unit trust performance. They found that on average the unit trusts had increased their investments in short-term assets from 9 per cent in 1972 to 27.9 per cent in 1974. The authors provide three possible explanations:

1. Despite the adjustment there are 40 trusts performing better than expected. The interpretation they suggest is that the compositions of the trusts were changing too quickly for the adjustment procedure.
2. They also suggest that their choice of index was incorrect but justify it by pointing out that it included both industrial and financial sectors and so could not have any undue bias.
3. Lastly, they point out that although transactions costs are taken into account when unit trusts returns are calculated, they are omitted when estimating the returns on the market portfolio. They also point out that when the SML has a negative slope it is quite conceivable that inefficiently diversified trusts could outperform the market portfolio.

The performance ranking of a selection of unit trusts is shown in Table 6.8.

Table 6.8   Ranking of unit trusts' performances

Name	Type	Beta	J_1	J_2	T	S
Allied Cap	C	0.94	12	11	12	11
Allied First	B	0.89	23	23	23	21
Allied G. Inc	B	0.91	9	9	9	8
B.I.F.	B	0.86	7	7	7	4
B. Life	B	0.8	39	37	40	38
Crescent High	I	0.86	26	28	29	24
Crescent Reserve	B	0.87	40	39	39	39
Discretionary	B	0.93	6	6	6	3
Elec & Ind	B	0.9	18	19	17	17
H.S. Brit	B	0.89	36	35	35	34
H.S. Cap	C	0.99	11	13	11	14
H.S. Inc	I	0.85	37	36	38	36
H.S. Int	G	0.79	32	25	33	35
J.-L. Cons	G	0.67	49	49	48	47
Jessel Global	G	1.09	35	38	31	33
Jessel New Iss	S	1.09	30	34	24	30
M&G Gen	B	0.94	13	12	13	12
M&G Midland	B	1.01	8	8	8	9
M&G 2nd Gen	G	0.93	2	2	2	2
M&G Trustees	B	0.97	5	5	5	6
Metals	S	0.78	33	31	37	37
Mutual Sec	B	0.88	22	22	21	15
Nat Bif	C	0.83	20	21	18	20
Nat Dom	B	0.91	17	15	20	13
Nat Scot	B	0.8	34	33	36	32
Nat Sec 1st	B	0.77	41	41	42	42
Nat Shield	G	0.75	31	27	34	31
Ocean Gen	B	0.87	47	46	47	46
Practical	S	0.88	10	10	10	10
S&P Cap	G	0.85	28	26	30	29
S&P Fin	S	0.81	4	4	4	1
S&P Inc	I	0.8	44	43	45	48
S&P I.T.	C	1.07	38	40	32	40
Scot Bits	B	0.87	19	18	19	25
Scot Shares	B	0.92	25	29	26	23
Stockholders	G	0.82	3	3	3	3
Target Cons	B	1.14	45	45	41	41
Target Fin	S	1.02	1	1	1	7
Target Prof	I	0.37	48	47	49	49
Trade Union	B	0.79	21	17	25	16
Tyndall Cap	B	0.95	15	14	14	22
Tyndall Inc	I	0.89	27	30	28	26
Unicorn Cap	B	0.99	29	32	27	27
Unicorn Gen	B	0.89	16	16	16	19
Unicorn Trust	B	0.97	14	20	15	18
Vav. Cap	C	0.97	46	48	46	45
Vav. Int	B	0.94	24	24	22	28
Vav. Inc	G	0.81	43	44	44	44
Ulster	B	0.74	42	42	43	43

Source: C. Ward and A. Saunders,[12] Appendices I and II.

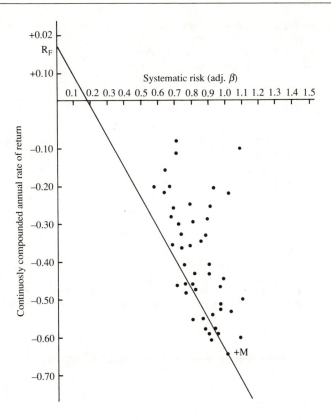

Figure 6.7 Scatter diagram of adjusted risk (β) and return for 49 unit trusts in 1974. (Source: C. Ward and A. Saunders,[12] p. 92.)

Ward and Saunders conclude:

If Unit Trust Managers maintained the level of risk (ρ) then investors might reasonably use Unit Trusts as a mechanism for buying into an effectively diversified portfolio. If, as we found during 1973 and 1974, the risk characteristics were changing, then the 'usefulness' of the Trusts would be diminished, unless of course managers have a more accurate forecasting ability than the market price makers. In the light of 1964–72 empirical results this view appears insupportable.[13]

These conclusions were echoed by Moles[14] in a study of unit trust performance between 1966 and 1975. He noted that unit trust managements were unable to consistently outperform the market on a risk-adjusted basis. However, Moles suggested that unit trusts were a useful and cost-efficient method for private investors to acquire a well-diversified portfolio.

The foregoing conclusions regarding the inability of the professional participant in the stock market to consistently produce excess returns is at variance with some of the work on the performance of brokers' advisory services. Dimson and Marsh[15] summarized these various studies in an article published in 1981 (see Table 6.9).

Dimson and Marsh analysed the recommendations made by a UK stockbroker during 1983. Using cumulative average residual methodology, they found that a portfolio of the recommendations showed a 0.7 per cent abnormal return during the first week after recommendation, and

Table 6.9   Performance of brokers, and advisory services' recommendations

Author	Date	Country	Number of services	Number of recommen- dations	(%) Return PD	PD+1	PD+7	LT
Cowles (a)	1933	USA	45	7 500				−1.4
Cowles (b)	1944	USA	11	6 904				0.2
Ferber	1958	USA	4	345	0.5		1.1	0.7
Ruff	1963	USA	1	31			4.0	
Colker	1963	USA	1	1 054				3.6
Stoffels	1966	USA	3	264	0.7	1.0	1.5	1.4
Cheney	1969	USA	4	n/a				2.0
Brealey	1971	UK	1	360				4.1
Diefenbach	1972	USA	24	1 209				2.7
Firth	1972	UK	4	1 100			−1.0	−3.0
Black	1973	USA	1	500				10.0
Fitzgerald (c)	1975	UK	35	635	0.5	1.0	1.5	0.5
Davies	1978	USA	8	785	1.3	1.6	1.7	
Fitzgerald (b)	1978	UK	11	467	3.1	3.2	3.5	1.0
Groth et al.	1979	USA	1	6 014			1.8	2.6

Source: E. Dimson and P. Marsh [15] 'New approaches to measuring share selection skills', *Investment Analyst*, April 1981, Table 2, p. 26.

Table 6.10   Estimates of forcasting correlations

Author	Date	Country	No. of organizations	No. of recommendations	Correlation
Malkiel	1970	USA	17	178	0.06
Hodges	1972	UK	1	550	0.15
Ambachtsheer	1972	USA	1	250	0.16
Ambachtsheer	1974	USA	16	6 800	0.16
Ambachtsheer	1979	USA	2	1 200	0.07
Dimson	1984	UK	35	4 000	0.08

Source: E. Dimson and P. Marsh[17] Table 3, p. 28; E. Dimson and P. Marsh, 'An analysis of brokers' and analysts' unpublished forecasts of UK stock returns', *Journal of Finance*, 1984.

−0.8 per cent after 26 weeks (with a standard error of 0.97 per cent). It is worth noting that the correlation coefficient between realized and forecast returns for this broker was 0.12 which is unexceptional by the standard of other studies[16] (see Table 6.10).

The evidence of Table 6.10 strongly supports the case that in a competitive and semi-strong form market, few investment advisors can be consistently successful.

Arbitrage pricing theory (APT)

The arbitrage pricing theory was developed in 1976 by Stephen Ross as an alternative to the CAPM and the market model.[18] Ross argued that an asset's average long-term return is dependent on its sensitivity to *unanticipated* changes in a few economic variables. These were later identified by Roll and Ross[19] as:
1. unanticipated changes in inflation;

2. unanticipated changes in the growth of industrial production;
3. unanticipated changes in the risk premium;
4. unanticipated changes in the slope of the term structure of interest rates.

These four factors may be justified intuitively by putting them in the context of the discounted cash flow (DCF) valuation model. The first two are determinants of the numerator in the DCF model. The growth in industrial production may be seen as a proxy for the real growth in cash flows from an investment in a financial asset. The rate of inflation is included as the growth rates of nominal cash flows are not necessarily equal to the rate of change in retail prices. The last two factors refer to the denominator in the DCF model. Given that an investment in a financial asset is expected to yield a stream of cash flows into the future, the term structure of interest rates enters the APT equation because it describes the relationship between the cost of money and the period in which cash flows are expected. However, the investment in all assets except for short-term government debt involves some degree of risk. This is reflected by the inclusion of the risk premium factor.

The APT makes fewer assumptions than does the CAPM. Like the CAPM it assumes that investors prefer more wealth to less, less risk to more risk, and that they are rational decision makers. Similarly, it assumes a perfect capital market in which there are no barriers to entry or exit, free information available to all investors, an absence of both transactions costs and taxes, and homogeneous expectations on the part of investors. However, the APT is not restricted to
1. a one period time horizon;
2. the requirement that returns conform to a normal distribution;
3. the necessity of a uniquely desirable portfolio;
4. the requirement for a riskless asset which may be used to set equal lending and borrowing rates.

However, the APT does make the rather unrealistic assumption that portfolios of desirable assets are financed by short selling of undesirable assets.

Despite its apparent lack of reality, this last assumption raises the possibility of an investor making a risk-free return in a market in disequilibrium without having to lay out any of his personal capital. A perfect market in equilibrium will not allow two prices for identical assets to coexist. In this case the identical assets are defined by their risk–return characteristics. Therefore, any pair of securities having the same level of risk cannot have two different levels of expected long-term return when a perfect capital market is in equilibrium. Arbitrage between the two assets will ensure that equilibrium is maintained. If two assets have the same risk but one of them has a lower return than the other, then it is sold and the proceeds are invested in the other. This will have the effect of raising the demand and, *ceteris paribus*, the price of the high return security. On the other hand the short sales will have the effect of increasing the supply of the low return asset and, *ceteris paribus*, cutting the price and increasing the expected return.[19a]

Risk sensitivity factors

In the CAPM the returns on an individual security are related to a single index, the performance of the market portfolio. The model is couched in ex-ante terms as it specifies expected security returns as a function of the expected return on the market portfolio. Furthermore, the model can be adapted so that it can express the risk premium (expected return less the riskless rate of return) of the security as a function of the risk premium of the market portfolio. The APT takes this principle a stage further and enables us to define the expected risk premium of the security as a function of the risk premium of any index.

The total return from a security in a future time period is dependent on a series of anticipated and unanticipated events. Those anticipated by the market will form its expectation of return and be incorporated into the market price of the security. Investors realize that it is highly improbable that

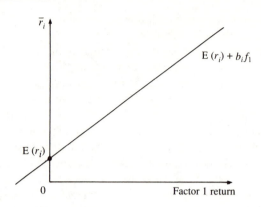

Figure 6.8   Returns and factor one.

events will turn out as expected. However, even though the unexpected is likely to happen, the APT maintains that it is possible for investors to estimate the sensitivity of assets to the likely variety of events that may take place.

As is the case with the CAPM, the APT does not claim to explain all of the variance of a security's return. There are still idiosyncratic factors which are specific to both industries and firms. However, as in the CAPM, the APT argues that these idiosyncratic influences can be minimized, if not entirely eliminated, through a process of creating a diversified portfolio. Figure 6.8 shows the effect of holding systematic factors 2, 3 and 4 at zero. The vertical axis measures the actual return from the security and the horizontal axis measures the return on the first systematic factor. The intercept is the expected return on the security which implies that even if the return on this factor was zero (as in the case of the other three), the actual return would be equal to that expected, there have been no deviations in reality from what had been expected. Therefore the value of f_1 represents the deviation of the factor's return from what was expected. The return on any security may be expressed as follows:

$$r_{i,t} = E(r_{i,t}) + b_i f_{i,t} + e_{i,t} \tag{6.7}$$

where $r_{i,t}$ = actual return on security i in period t

   $E(r_{i,t})$ = expected return on security i in period t

   b_i = security's sensitivity to any change in the systematic factor

   $f_{i,t}$ = systematic factor which affects the asset's return and which has an expected value of zero in period t

   $e_{i,t}$ = random unexplained residual return to the security's idiosyncratic factors (or, in terms of the market model, the unexplained return) which have an expected value of zero.

This equation merely states that the actual return is the sum of the expected return, the response of the security to any change in the return on the systematic factor, and any idiosyncratic return.

Figure 6.9 shows the relationship between the expected return on the asset and its sensitivity to factor 1. The risk-free rate of return has been set at 9 per cent and two security returns (14 and 21 per cent) have been indicated on the line representing the relationship between expected return and sensitivity. The locus of Z is mid-way between r_f and Y and shows the sensitivity–return combination of a portfolio constructed by investing one-third of the investor's capital in the risk-free asset and two-thirds in the risky security Y. The portfolio expected return and sensitivity may be calculated as follows:

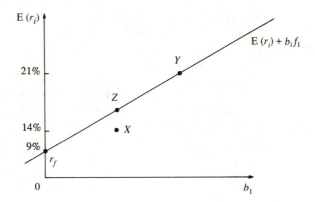

Figure 6.9 Expected return and factor sensitivity.

$$E(r_p) = (1/3)r_f + (2/3)E(r_y)$$
$$= (1/3)9 + (2/3)21 = 17$$
$$b_{1,p} = (1/3)b_{1,rf} + (2/3)b_{1,y}$$
$$= (1/3)0 + (2/3)1.5 = 1$$

The position of the portfolio Z dominates (in the terminology of Chapter 4) the sensitivity–return combination of security X. Furthermore, this dominance will persist whatever the value of the expected return on systematic factor 1. It is a disequilibrium situation which cannot survive as it offers investors a profitable arbitrage opportunity. By selling security X short and investing the proceeds in a portfolio made up of the risk-free asset and security Y, a riskless return may be obtained. The arbitrage process will ensure that the supply of security X and the demand for security Y will both be increased, thus reducing the return on Y and increasing it on X. The process will continue until there are no more profitable arbitrage opportunities.

On its own the APT does not specify either the number or the nature of the determinant factors. Although Roll and Ross have subsequently identified 4 factors,[19] it is more convenient for the purposes of exposition to assume that there are only 2 as follows:

$$r_{i,t} = E(r_{i,t}) + b_{i,1}f_{1,t} + b_{i2}f_{2t} + e_{i,t} \qquad (6.8)$$

Two additional conditions must be noted for this multi-factor return generating process. First, the unexplained residual returns between all assets must be independent of each other and second, the factors and assets must be independent; i.e. $\text{cov}(f_i, e_1) = 0$.

The APT may now be derived from the above return generating processes. Using Eq. (6.8) we can develop the APT by assuming the creation of a portfolio of n assets which must exceed the number of determinant factors. The portfolio return may be defined as

$$r_{p,t} = \Sigma w_i r_1$$
$$= \Sigma w_i E(r_{i,t}) + \Sigma w_i b_{i1}f_{1t} + \Sigma w_i b_{i2}f_{2t} + \Sigma w_i e_i \qquad (6.9)$$

where $\Sigma w_i = 1$ and in a well-diversified portfolio $\Sigma w_1 e_1 = 0$. Equation (6.9) now simplifies to

$$r_{i,t} = \Sigma w_i E(r_{i,t}) + \Sigma w_i b_{i,1}f_{1,t} + \Sigma w_i b_{i,2}f_{2,t} \qquad (6.9a)$$

The systematic or explained risk is $\Sigma w_i b_{i,1}$ and $\Sigma w_i b_{1,2}$.

This may be transformed into the formal APT model as follows:

$$E(r_i) = \lambda_0 + \lambda_1 b_{i,1} + \lambda_2 b_{i,2} \qquad (6.10)$$

where λ_0 is a constant which will have a positive value if there is a risk-free asset and λ_i are the factor risk premiums. Hence, from Eq. (6.10) it may be seen that the risk premium for any asset is the sum of the risk factor premiums weighted by that asset's sensitivity to each of the determinant factors.

Figure 6.10 plots the arbitrage pricing line (APL) which shows the position of the market equilibrium. If the returns of all securities lay on this line there would be no opportunities for profitable arbitrage. The opportunity to create a zero-investment, perfect hedge is shown by the two disequilibrium returns X and Y. The two securities have the same risk; i.e. the same level of sensitivity to factor f_1, and equilibrium should lie on the APL at point Z. The return on security X is higher than that of Z implying that X is underpriced and Y is overpriced. Y may be sold short and the proceeds invested in X yielding a riskless return for no investment.

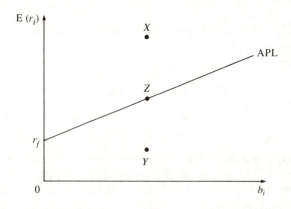

Figure 6.10   The arbitrage pricing line (APL).

Arbitrage

Suppose that there are 3 portfolios of n assets each with the following returns and factor loadings in a two-factor APT model as follows:

Returns vector (R)		Factor loadings matrix (F)	
10	1.0	0.7	0.6
13	1.0	0.6	0.8
15	1.0	0.8	1.0

From Eq. (6.10) we know that there will also be a vector of factor premiums (λ, where λ_0 is the model's estimate of the risk-free rate of return). Using matrix algebra we may arrive at a numerical solution for the factor premiums,

$$\text{if } R = F\lambda$$

$$\text{then } \lambda = R(F^{-1})$$

where F^{-1} is the inverse matrix of F,

$$F^{-1} = \begin{array}{ccc} 0.67 & 3.67 & -3.33 \\ 3.33 & -6.67 & 3.33 \\ -3.33 & 1.67 & 1.67 \end{array} \times R \ 10 = \begin{array}{cc} 4.33 \\ 13 & -3.33 \\ 15 & 13.33 \end{array}$$

These results may be checked by putting the values into the right-hand side of Eq. (6.10). Thus for the first portfolio we have

$$r_1 = 4.33 + 0.7(-3.33) + 0.6(13.33) = 10$$

$$r_2 = 4.33 + 0.6(-3.33) + 0.8(13.33) = 13$$

$$r_3 = 4.33 + 0.8(-3.33) + 1.0(13.33) = 15$$

If a portfolio were constructed from the above investments with weights of $w_1 = 0.3$, $w_2 = 0.3$ and $w_3 = 0.4$ the return and factor weightings would be as follows:

$$r_p = (0.3)10 + (0.3)13 + (0.4)15 = 12.9$$

$$b_{p2} = (0.3)(0.7) + (0.3)(0.6) + (0.4)(0.8) = 0.71$$

$$b_{p3} = (0.3)(0.6) + (0.3)(0.8) + (0.4)1.0 = 0.82$$

By constructing a portfolio of efficiently priced assets, the investor can create opportunities for profitable arbitrage if there are assets or portfolios that have been underpriced or overpriced. In the situation where the investor has spotted an asset with factor loadings of 0.71 and 0.82 which has a return of less than 12.9 per cent, an arbitrage portfolio may be created by short selling the overpriced asset and investing the proceeds in the above efficient portfolio. On the other hand if the investor has spotted an underpriced asset with the same factor loadings as the above portfolio, the portfolio may be short sold and the revenue invested in the underpriced asset to obtain a risk-free return without the investor having to use his own capital.

Testing the APT

The first major test of the APT was carried out by Roll and Ross[20] and published in 1980. They used a two-stage process to test the APT. The first consisted of estimating expected returns and factor scores (b_i) from historical data. This process analysed a matrix of the returns of n assets for $t+1$ periods. This first stage produced a smaller matrix $[k(t+1)]$ of explanatory factors which were analogous to the beta of the CAPM. The second step used these estimates to test Eq. (6.10). This second stage yielded a set of (λ) which were the factor risk premiums.

Daily returns were used from 1260 securities over the period July 1962 to December 1972. This data was divided into 42 groups of 30 securities each. The results are summarized in Table 6.11.

Roll and Ross concluded that at least 3 factors were significant and that no more than 4 were significant. Regarding Part I of Table 6.11 they concluded, 'As can be seen, all factors are significantly greater than the chance level (5%) with particularly heavy weight on the first two. The remaining three are significant, but this may be more a consequence of mixing the order of factors across the groups than of anything important.'[21] However, they went on to comment that the assumed riskless rate of 6 per cent in Part I of the results may have been an over estimate, as Part II shows only the first 2 factors to be significant while the fifth factor lost all explanatory power. The explanatory power (coefficient of multiple determination R^2) of this test was found to be 0.743 on average over the 42 groups.

Burmeister and Wall[22] have identified 5 significant macroeconomic factors,

1. Risk of unexpected changes in default premium. This is measured by the difference between the yields on twenty-year government and corporate debt.

Table 6.11   The Roll and Ross results showing the number of groups with factors significant at the 95% level

Factors	Number of groups	% of 42 groups	Expected % due to chance
Part I $[E(r_i)-r_f]=\lambda_1 b_{i,1}+\lambda_2 b_{i,2}+ \dots +\lambda_k b_{i,k}$			
1 factor	37	88.1	22.6
2 factors	24	57.1	2.6
3 factors	14	33.3	0.115
4 factors	7	16.7	0.003
5 factors	2	4.8	0.000 03
Part II $E(r_i)=\lambda_0+\lambda_1 b_{i,1}+\lambda_1 b_{i,2}+ \dots +\lambda_k b_{i,k}$			
1 factor	29	69.0	22.6
2 factors	20	47.6	2.6
3 factors	3	7.1	0.115
4 factors	2	4.8	0.003
5 factors	0	0.0	0.000 03

Source: R. Roll and S. Ross,[20] Table III, p. 1092.

2. Risk of unanticipated changes in the term structure of interest rates. This is measured by the total monthly spread between government debt and treasury bills.
3. Risk of unanticipated price changes.
4. Risk of change in the expected rate of long-term growth of the economy. This is measured by the difference between the expected long-term rates of growth in real sales at the beginning and end of each month and is used as a proxy for porfits.
5. That part of the Standard and Poor 500 market index not explained by the first 4 factors.

In a second article Burmeister, McElroy and Berry[23] used these factors to test the APT. The first test consisted of setting up portfolios of equally-weighted stocks in the seven main macroeconomic sectors in the American economy. The coefficient of multiple determination (adjusted R^2) varied between 0.5 for the oil sector and 0.84 for the 'growth' sector. It was found that the financial, growth and transportation sectors were especially sensitive to the default factor because the firms in these sectors tend to be highly geared. On the other hand, utilities were found to be insensitive to both unanticipated inflation and the unanticipated changes in the expected real long-term rate of growth of sales because this sector is highly regulated. Lastly, the authors noted that, as expected, the growth and transportation sectors were both highly sensitive to unanticipated inflation and changes in the expected real long-term rate of growth of sales.

The authors concluded, 'APT provides effective means for managing the different types of risk to which investors are exposed. Its use in the investment community is certain to increase as managers become more familiar with the new strategic investment opportunities it offers.'[24]

The APT has been applied to British data by Diacogiannis,[25] who used 302 monthly observations for 200 securities between November 1956 and December 1981. Five master groups of 40 securities each were randomly chosen and the observations were split into 5 sub-periods, 3 with 100 observations each and 2 with 150 each (11/1956–2/65, 3/1965–6/73, 7/1973–12/81, 11/1956–5/69, and 6/1969–12/81). The power of the tests was increased by generating 7 sub-groups (containing 5, 10, 15, 20, 25, 30, 35 securities) from each master group. The results, shown in Table 6.12, may be summarized as follows:

1. In 93 out of 100 cases the number of relevant factors increased with the size of the sub-group.
2. The number of relevant factors and their explanatory power changed between sub-periods.

Diacogiannis points out that the APT specifies neither the number nor the identity of the explanatory factors and that this problem is not solved by the use of the factor analysis methodology and therefore:

Table 6.12 **The number of relevant factors in the application of the APT to UK data**

Group size	Average cumulative (%) variance explained
1	52.5
2	56.5
3	60.1
4	57.9
5	59.1
6	61.6
7	62.4
9	62.8

Source: G. Diacogiannis,[25] Table 1, p. 495.

1. it is difficult to determine the appropriate group size for analysis, and therefore
2. the unique return generating model of the APT is unobservable.

These implications were first raised by Shanken:[26]

> Roll argues that the empirical investigations of the CAPM which use proxies for the true market portfolio are really tests of the mean-variance efficiency of those proxies, not tests of the CAPM. The CAPM implies that a particular portfolio, the market portfolio, is efficient. The theory is not testable unless **that** portfolio is observable and used in the tests.
>
> Similarly, it is argued here that factor-analytic empirical investigations of the APT are not necessarily tests of that theory. In the case of the APT, we are confronted with the task of identifying the relevant factor structure, rather than the true market portfolio. Whereas we have a reasonably clear notion of what is meant by 'the true market portfolio' it is not clear in what sense, if any, a uniquely 'relevant factor structure' exists.[27]

Shanken goes on to argue that the factor analysis methodology may be manipulated by merely recombining a given set of securities and that therefore on its own the factor model is inadequate as it is incapable of economic interpretation.

A second study of the APT using UK data was published in 1987 by Abeysekera and Mahajan.[28] They used monthly returns on individual securities with a continuous listing on the London Stock Exchange between January 1971 and December 1982. The 90 day treasury bill rate was used as a proxy for the risk-free rate of interest. Seven portfolios were constructed, each consisting of 40 randomly selected securities. They found that they were unable to specify a unique number of determinant factors across the 7 portfolios. However, they did find that the APT correctly predicted the risk-free rate in 6 out of the 7 portfolios. However, their tests found only 2 out of the 183 possible risk premiums to be significantly different from zero.

Conclusion: the APT and the CAPM

The CAPM measures risk with one variable, the market index. The APT allows any number of explanatory variables. Roll and Ross have produced a diagram (Fig. 6.11) which admirably illustrates the difference between the two theories.

The CAPM beta is measured along the ray from the origin OZ. The axes represent the factor loadings (or betas) of the APT. In this case two have been chosen arbitrarily, inflation and productivity. The diagonal represents a value of 1 for the CAPM beta. Portfolio M is the market and has a value of 1.0 and is situated on the ray OZ by definition. However portfolios A, B and C

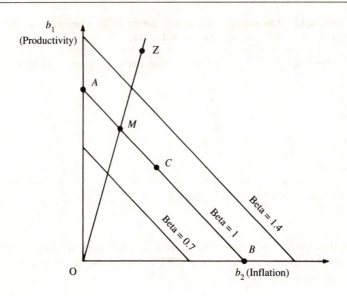

Figure 6.11 CAPM and APT betas. (Source: R. Rolland and S. Ross,[19] p. 23.)

also have CAPM betas of 1 but do not lie on the ray OZ. Roll and Ross argue that these portfolios may have desirable qualities for the potential investor. For example, portfolio B being more sensitive to inflation than to production may be desirable to certain investors while portfolio A has the opposite qualities. It may be that these portfolios both have the same level of expected return but the APT points out they are subject to very different types of risk. Roll and Ross state that 'To argue that there is one best strategy for everyone—such as "buying the market"—is simply wrong.'[29]

However, Jarrow and Rudd[30] have shown that if $\lambda_0 = r_f$ and where $b_{i,1} = 1$ while b_{i2} to $b_{i,k} = 0$, the APT may be reduced to the CAPM,

$$E(r_i) - r_f = \lambda_1 b_{i,1}$$

where $\lambda_i = E(r_m) - r_f$

Hence, in this interpretation, the CAPM is merely a special case of the APT. Even so, there is one essential difference which is that the determinant factor is specified in advance of testing by economic theory. In the case of the APT, the approach is diametrically opposite in that although it derives a causal relationship, it does not identify the determinant factors. These are discovered in the empirical tests and economic interpretation and justification is supplied afterwards. The APT is a relatively new model and is still subject to considerable investigation which will undoubtedly yield greater insights into the pricing of investment assets in the future.

Notes

1. E. Fama, *Foundations of Finance*, Blackwell, 1977, pp. 99–132.
2. F. Black, M. Jensen and M. Scholes, 'The capital asset pricing model: some empirical tests' in *Studies in the Theory of Capital Markets*, M. Jensen (ed.), Praeger Publishers Inc., 1972.
3. This was demonstrated by B. King, 'Market and industry factors in stock price behaviour', *Journal of Business*, Vol. 22, 1966.

4. E. Fama and J. MacBeth, 'Risk, return, and equilibrium: empirical tests', *Journal of Political Economy*, Vol. 81, May 1973.

5. R. Roll, 'A critique of the asset pricing theory's tests; part I. On past and potential testability of the theory', *Journal of Financial Economics*, Vol. 5, March 1977.

6. Using weekly data over the same period, the correlation coefficient between the FT All Share Index and the FT-ST 100 was 0.9887.

7. W. Sharpe, 'Mutual fund performance', *Journal of Business*, Vol. 22, January 1966.

8. J. Treynor, 'How to rate management of investment funds', *Harvard Business Review*, January–February 1965.

9. Friend, I. and M. Blume, 'Measurement of portfolio performance under uncertainty', *American Economic Review*, Vol. 60, September 1970.

10. M. Jensen, 'The performance of mutual funds in the period 1945–1964', *Journal of Finance*, Vol. 23, May 1968.

11. J. McDonald, 'Objectives and performance of mutual funds', *Journal of Financial and Quantitative Analysis*, Vol. 9, June 1974.

12. C. Ward and A. Saunders, 'Unit trust performance 1964–74', *Journal of Business Finance and Accounting*, Vol. 3, 1976.

13. Ibid. p. 95.

14. P. Moles, 'Components of unit trust performance 1966–1975', *Investment Analyst*, Vol. 37, March 1981.

15. The data presented in Table 6.9 was compiled from the following publications:

A. Cowles, 'Can stock market forecasters forecast?', *Econometrica*, Vol. 2, 1933.

A. Cowles, 'Stock market forecasting', *Econometrica*, Vol. 13, 1944.

F. Ferber, 'Short run effects of stock market services on stock prices', *Journal of Finance*, Vol. 13, 1958.

R. Ruff, 'Effect of a selection and recommendation of a 'stock of the month'' ', *Financial Analysts' Journal*, Vol. 19, May 1963.

S. Colker, 'An analysis of security recommendations by brokerage houses', *Quarterly Review of Economics*, Vol. 77, 1963.

J. Stoffels, 'Stock recommendations by investment advisory services: immediate effects on market pricing', *Financial Analysts' Journal*, Vol. 22, May 1966.

H. Cheney, 'How good are subscription investment advisory services?', *Financial Executive*, 1969.

H. Brealey, *Security Prices in a Competitive Market*, MIT Press, 1971.

R. Diefenbach, 'How good is institutional brokerage research?', *Financial Analysts' Journal*, Vol. 28, May 1972.

M. Firth, 'The performance of share recommendations made by investment analysts and the effects on market efficiency', *Journal of Business and Finance*, Vol. 4, 1972.

F. Black, 'Yes Virginia, there is hope: tests of the value line ranking system', *Financial Analysts' Journal*, Vol. 29, March 1973.

M. Fitzgerald, 'A proposed characterisation of UK brokerage firms and their effects on market prices and returns' in J. Elton and M. Gruber (eds), *International Capital Markets*, North-Holland, 1975.

P. Davies and M. Cannes, 'Stock prices and the publication of second hand information', *Journal of Business*, Vol. 34, 1978.

M. Fitzgerald, 'Media Investment Advisory Service Recommendations and Market Efficiency', *Saloman Brothers Center for the Study of Financial Institutions Working Paper No. 159*, New York University, 1978.

J. Groth, W. Lewellen, G. Schlarbaum and R. Leas, 'An analysis of brokerage house recommendations', *Financial Analysts' Journal*, Vol. 35, January 1979.

16. E. Dimson and P. Fraletti, 'Brokers' recommendations: the value of a telephone tip', *Economic Journal*, Vol. 96, 1986.

17. The data presented in Table 6.10 was compiled from the following publications:

    E. Dimson and P. Marsh, 'New approaches to measuring share selection skills', *Investment Analyst*, April 1981.

    B. Malkiel and J. Cragg, 'Expectations and the structure of share prices', *American Economic Review*, Vol. 60, 1970.

    S. Hodges and M. Brealey, 'Portfolio selection in a dynamic and uncertain world', *Financial Analysts' Journal*, Vol. 29, April 1973.

    K. Amsbachtscheer, 'Portfolio theory and the security analyst', *Financial Analysts' Journal*, Vol. 28, November 1972.

    K. Amsbachtsheer, 'Profit potential in an "almost efficient market"', *Journal of Portfolio Management*, 1974.

    K. Amsbachtsheer and J. Farrel, 'Can active management add value?', *Financial Analysts' Journal*, Vol. 35, January 1979.

18. S. Ross, 'The arbitrage theory of capital asset pricing', *Journal of Economic Theory*, Vol. 13, December 1976.

19. R. Roll and S. Ross, 'The arbitrage pricing theory approach to strategic portfolio planning', *Financial Analysts' Journal*, Vol. 40, May–June, 1984.

19a. The coexistence of provincial markets in the UK during the nineteenth century resulted in the temporary existence of different prices for the same shares. These anomalies were removed by the arbitraging activities of individuals known as 'shunters' who bought cheaply in one market and sold for a profit in another provincial market.

20. R. Roll and S. Ross, 'An empirical investigation of the arbitrage pricing theory', *Journal of Finance*, Vol. 35, December 1980.

21. Ibid. p. 1092.

22. E. Burmeister and K. Wall, 'The arbitrage pricing theory and macroeconomic factors measures', *The Financial Review*, February 1986.

23. M. Berry, E. Burmeister and M. McElroy, 'Sorting out risks using known APT factors', *Financial Analysts' Journal*, Vol. 44, March 1988.

24. Ibid. p. 41.

25. G. Diacogiannis, 'Arbitrage pricing model: a critical examination of its empirical applicability for the London Stock Exchange', *Journal of Business Finance and Accounting*, Vol. 13, 1986.

26. J. Shanken, 'The arbitrage pricing theory: is it testable?', *Journal of Finance*, Vol. 37, 1982.

27. Ibid. pp. 1135–1136.

28. S. Abeysekera and A. Mahajan, 'A test of the APT in pricing UK stocks', *Journal of Accounting and Finance*, Vol. 17, 1987.

29. R. Roll and S. Ross, 'The arbitrage pricing theory approach to strategic portfolio planning', *Financial Analysts' Journal*, Vol. 40, March 1984, p. 24.

30. R. Jarrow and A. Rudd, 'A comparison of the APT and the CAPM', *Journal of Banking and Finance*, June 1983.

Questions

1. Is the stability over time of a portfolio beta affected by the number of constituent securities and if so why?
2. Why might it be claimed that of all the criticisms of the CAPM, only that of Roll constitutes a serious theoretical attack?
3. Explain why you might expect security betas to change over time.

4. Given the following information about the quality of estimators used in questions 5.2 and 5.3 in the previous chapter,

Share	Std. error	R. sqrd
Electric Tram Co	0.14	26
Fleet Motors Ltd	0.13	40
Sam's Supermarkets	0.12	36
Northern TV Plc	0.16	28

would your assessments of the portfolio remain the same?

5. How has modern portfolio theory been used to evaluate portfolio performance and show how and why you might expect to find different performance rankings from the different measures.

6. Explain and critically discuss cumulative average residual methodology and explain how it has been used to test a whole range of market phenomena from semi-strong efficiency theory to the efficacy of stockbrokers' tips.

7. Show how the CAPM can be regarded as being a special and restrictive case of the arbitrage pricing theory.

8. Critically discuss Shanken's argument that factor analysis methodology is open to manipulation and is not amenable to economic interpretation.

9. Suppose we have data for the expected returns for three portfolios and the factor loadings in a two-factor APT model as follows:

Security	Return vector	Factor loadings		
1	12	1	0.8	0.5
2	10	1	0.4	0.7
3	15	1	0.7	0.9

(a) If a portfolio is constructed from the three above securities with weights of $w_1 = 0.3$, $w_2 = 0.3$, and $w_3 = 0.4$, what would the factor weightings be and what would be the expected return?

(b) How would you interpret your findings?

10. Critically discuss the apparent inability of academics to arrive at a universal set of determinant factors for the APT.

7. Options

Introduction

Options are rights rather than assets or claims on assets. An option may give the holder either the right to buy or sell a share at a predetermined price from or to the issuer of the option, which is another individual rather than the firm underlying the security. A warrant, which is usually a long-term version of an option, confers on the holder the right to buy a share directly from the issuing company at a price calculated with a previously agreed formula. The essential difference between these two types of rights is that options are short-term, having lives of up to 9 months in the case of traded options and 3 months in the case of non-traded options. On the other hand warrants invariably start out with much longer lives and are exercised on dates predetermined by the issuing company.

The first part of this chapter will be devoted to a description of the modern Traded Options Market (TOM) in the London International Stock Market and a general discussion of the factors which influence option prices. The second part is an overview of the trading strategies which may be created using traded options. The last part describes the binomial and Black and Scholes models of option pricing.

Options

The modern theory of option valuation began with the publication of an article by Black and Scholes[1] in 1973. The model which they developed has become a valued tool of analysis in both academic and professional circles. Although only a recent feature of modern financial systems, options have existed at various times in the past. They were certainly known during the European markets of the seventeenth century but came into disrepute in England with the collapse of the South Sea Bubble (see Chapter 1) in 1720. They were subsequently banned by law from 1734 until 1860; they were also banned between 1939 and 1958 as part of the measures deemed necessary for the prosecution of the Second World War. Between 1958 and 1978, traditional non-traded options were available in the London Stock Exchange.

Traditional options were and still are offered in three forms:
1. *Calls*. Rights to buy a share at a specified price within a specified time (usually 3 months).
2. *Buts*. Rights to sell a share at a specified price within a specified time (3 months).
3. *Doubles*. Rights to either buy or sell at a specified price within a specified period (3 months).
In the case of traditional options the commission charges are based on the value of the underlying shares rather than the option price itself. Hence, if 10,000 call options are bought for 10p each on Hanson shares which are priced by the market at 200p each, the total cost of the options will be 10,000 (£0.1) = £1,000 and the commission (at a rate of 1 per cent) will be (10,000) (£2) (0.01) = £200 (rather than 1 per cent of the value of the options; i.e. £10). However, should the purchaser of the option exercise and buy the shares at the preset price the commission on the transaction will have already been paid. On the other hand, if the option is not exercised, the purchaser not only loses the initial value paid for the options themselves but also the commission paid on the shares he or she did not buy. Having paid the commission on the shares at the time when the options were bought, the investor is deemed to be the 'retrospective' owner of the shares so that no further commission is due.

EUROPEAN OPTIONS EXCHANGE

Series		Nov. 88		Feb. 89		May 89		Stock
		Vol	Last	Vol	Last	Vol	Last	
GOLD C	$ 420	24	19.50	–	–	17	40.50	$ 429.60
GOLD C	$ 460	5	3.10	–	–	11	17.50	$ 429.60
GOLD P	$ 420	–	–	20	8.30	–	–	$ 429.60
		Sep. 88		Oct. 88		Nov. 88		
EOE Index C	Fl. 220	40	13	–	–	–	–	Fl. 232.77
EOE Index C	Fl. 225	22	8.70	–	–	2	13.50	Fl. 232.77
EOE Index C	Fl. 230	157	4.50	71	9	7	10.70	Fl. 232.77
EOE Index C	Fl. 235	137	2.10	10	6.50	–	–	Fl. 232.77
EOE Index C	Fl. 240	123	0.80	68	4.40	60	6	Fl. 232.77
EOE Index C	Fl. 250	38	0.20	–	–	–	–	Fl. 232.77
EOE Index P	Fl. 210	–	–	14	2.10	–	–	Fl. 232.77
EOE Index P	Fl. 220	29	0.60	12	3	5	5	Fl. 232.77
EOE Index P	Fl. 225	68	1	136	4	–	–	Fl. 232.77
EOE Index P	Fl. 230	81	2.50	74	6.60	14	8.70	Fl. 232.77
EOE Index P	Fl. 235	37	4.50	13	8.80	1	11.50	Fl. 232.77
EOE Index P	Fl. 240	159	8	–	–	–	–	Fl. 232.77
EOE Index P	Fl. 245	14	12.40	–	–	22	18	Fl. 232.77
		Nov. 88		Feb. 89		May 89		
OBL Index P	Fl. 100	142	0.70	–	–	–	–	Fl. 99.94
		Sep. 88		Oct. 88		Nov. 88		
$/FI C	Fl. 200	13	8.20	–	–	–	–	Fl. 208.80
$/FI C	Fl. 205	18	3.70	13	5.20	10	5.80 B	Fl. 208.80
$/FI C	Fl. 210	78	0.70	27	2.40	2	3.30 B	Fl. 208.80
$/FI C	Fl. 215	4	0.20	20	0.90	15	1.50	Fl. 208.80
$/FI P	Fl. 210	15	2.50	5	4.50	–	–	Fl. 208.80
		Oct. 88		Jan. 89		Apr. 89		
ABN C	Fl. 45	30	0.70	320	2.10	8	3.20	Fl. 42.40
ABN P	Fl. 40	39	0.80	3	1.30	–	–	Fl. 42.40
AEGON C	Fl. 90	36	1.10	142	3.40	3	5.20	Fl. 84.50
AEGON P	Fl. 85	6	3	3	5	25	5.30	Fl. 84.50
AHOLD C	Fl. 85	–	–	35	4.50	–	–	Fl. 82.30
AKZO C	Fl. 150	218	2.30	92	6.50 A	13	9.70	Fl. 141.70
AKZO P	Fl. 120	15	0.60	137	2.20	–	–	Fl. 141.70
AMEV C	Fl. 50	104	2	43	4	1	4.60	Fl. 50.10
AMRO C	Fl. 85	2	0.30	372	1.10	1	2	Fl. 73.50
AMRO P	Fl. 75	–	–	202	4.30	–	–	Fl. 73.50
BUHRMANN-T C	Fl. 50	22	4	–	–	–	–	Fl. 53.10
ELSEVIER C	Fl. 60	102	1.80	8	3.90	–	–	Fl. 59
ELSEVIER P	Fl. 55	32	0.70	–	–	4	3.70	Fl. 59
GIST-BROC. C	Fl. 40	44	0.80	20	2	14	3.20	Fl. 35.90
GIST-BROC. P	Fl. 35	94	1	–	–	4	3	Fl. 35.90
HEINEKEN C	Fl. 160	37	0.50	95	2.10	–	–	Fl. 137
HOOGOVENS C	Fl. 50	144	12	20	13.20	–	–	Fl. 61.20
HOOGOVENS P	Fl. 50	10	0.50	30	1.70	–	–	Fl. 61.20
KLM C	Fl. 40	15	0.40	152	1.50	4	2.30	Fl. 34.80
KLM P	Fl. 35	227	1.50	57	2.50	–	–	Fl. 34.80
KNP C	Fl. 190	2	0.40	90	3.70	50	7.20 A	Fl. 168
KNP P	Fl. 160	76	2.40	26	4.80	–	–	Fl. 168
NEDLLOYD C	Fl. 230	22	4.70	–	–	–	–	Fl. 221
NEDLLOYD P	Fl. 220	22	7.50	2	13.40 A	–	–	Fl. 221
NAT.NED. C	Fl. 65	89	1.10	–	–	–	–	Fl. 62.40
NAT.NED. P	Fl. 60	15	1.10	2	2.20	–	–	Fl. 62.40
PHILIPS C	Fl. 35	37	0.40	109	1.30	33	2.30	Fl. 31.90
PHILIPS P	Fl. 30	5	0.60 B	15	1.70	90	2.50 B	Fl. 31.90
ROYAL DUTCH C	Fl. 240	67	0.80	243	3.90	38	6.10	Fl. 223.60
ROYAL DUTCH P	Fl. 220	217	5	32	7.90	10	9	Fl. 223.60
ROBECO C	Fl. 90	63	3	2	5.30	–	–	Fl. 92
ROBECO P	Fl. 90	50	1	–	–	–	–	Fl. 92
UNILEVER C	Fl. 120	610	1.30	114	4	15	6.60	Fl. 112.30
UNILEVER P	Fl. 100	314	0.70	7	2.30	–	–	Fl. 112.30
WESSANEN C	Fl. 85	20	0.70	–	–	–	–	Fl. 75.70
WESSANEN P	Fl. 75	–	–	–	–	50	5.50	Fl. 75.70

TOTAL VOLUME IN CONTRACTS : 14,588

A = Ask   B = Bid   C = Call   P = Put

Figure 7.1 European options exchange, closing prices, 9 September 1988. (Source: *Financial Times* 10 September 1988.)

LONDON TRADED OPTIONS

Option		CALLS Oct	CALLS Jan	CALLS Apr	PUTS Oct	PUTS Jan	PUTS Apr
Allied Lyons	360	40	–	–	3	–	–
(°392)	390	17	28	36	11	18	21
	420	5	15	22	33	38	40
Brit. Airways	140	15	19	23	2	5	7½
(°151)	160	4	9	14	13	17	20
	180	1	3	–	30	33	–
Brit. & Comm.	220	10	18	23	11	15	17
(°222)	240	4	8	12	27	28	30
	260	2	4	7	45	45	47
B.P.	220	20	29	31½	2	4	8¾
(°237)	240	7	15	18	8½	11	17
	260	[illegible]½	7	9½	24	24	31
Bass	700	50	65	75	8	18	23
(°738)	750	18	33	45	23	42	47
	800	4	15	25	65	75	80
Cable & Wire	330	40	50	60	3	8	13
(°363)	360	17	30	40	8½	20	25
	390	5	17	25	32	35	40
Cons. Gold	950	118	160	190	24	43	57
(°1039)	1000	82	127	160	45	67	82
	1100	40	84	105	105	120	135
Courtaulds	300	14	24	32	11	17	19
(°299)	330	4	10	18	33	37	38
	360	1	5	9	63	63	63
Com. Union	300	32	44	–	5	9	–
(°325)	330	14	26	30	15	20	27
	360	5	14	18	38	40	46
G.E.C.	140	20	24	27	1	3½	6
(°155)	160	5	10	14	6	9½	13
	180	1	3	7	25	25	27
G.K.N.	300	20	30	37	4	9	15
(°311)	330	6	15	19	22	25	30
	360	1	6½	9	52	53	54
Grand Met.	460	32	45	53	7	13	18
(°478)	500	10	23	32	28	33	38
	550	1½	9	14	75	77	80
I.C.I.	950	67	100	112	10	20	37
(°997)	1000	33	67	80	27	38	60
	1100	4½	25	36	110	110	122
Jaguar	220	27	38	–	2	7	–
(°241)	240	12	24	32	8	14	19
	260	4½	14	19	22	26	34
Land Securities	500	58	70	83	2½	8	14
(°552)	550	20	35	48	16	24	28
	600	4	15	25	52	55	58
Marks & Spencer	140	17	21	26	1½	3	4½
(°153)	160	3½	8½	14	11	13	12
	180	1	3½	7	28	28	30
Britoil	420	–	–	–	1	–	–
(°500)	460	–	–	–	5	–	–
	500	–	–	–	14	–	–
Rolls-Royce	120	12	16	20	2½	5	7
(°130)	130	5½	9½	14	6½	8½	11
	140	2	6	9	14	15	18
STC	220	35	42	–	1	4	–
(°251)	240	19	27	32	5	9	12
	260	7	16	22	14	18	22
Sainsbury	200	12	18	25	4	8	10
(°206)	220	3	7	12	15	18	21
	240	1	3½	–	35	35	–
Shell Trans.	950	33	67	83	28	37	55
(°971)	1000	13	42	57	58	63	90
	1100	2	13	22	157	157	172
Storehouse	180	17	24	28	7	10	15
(°187)	200	7	14	19	20	23	24
	220	2	8	11	36	38	38
Trafalgar House	280	26	32	34	4	10	13
(°298)	300	11	18	23	10	20	22
	330	3	8	12	34	42	42
T.S.B.	90	11	14	15	1	2½	3½
(°99)	100	3½	6	8	4	5½	7½
	110	1	2½	3½	13	13	14
Utd.Biscuits	240	20	24	32	3	7	9
(°254)	260	8	14	20	12	16	18
Ultramar	200	15	26	33	12	20	25
(°203)	220	8	16	23	24	30	38
	240	4	11	15	42	47	50
Woolworth	220	33	42	50	2½	7	9
(°250)	240	15	28	35	8	13	17
	260	7	17	22	18	23	25

Option		Nov	Feb	Apr	Nov	Feb	Apr
Ladbroke	390	55	62	–	3	7	–
(°435)	420	30	40	48	11	17	19
	460	11	21	25	38	40	40

Option		Nov	Feb	May	Nov	Feb	May
Brit Aero	460	33	50	60	17	24	31½
(°478)	500	14	30	39	38	43	55
BAA	245	20	–	–	4	–	–
(°256)	255	13	–	–	8½	–	–
	260	–	18	24	–	15	17
BAT Inds	390	45	57	65	6	10	16
(°429)	420	25	38	45	16	20	28
	460	8	19	25	43	47	50
Brit. Telecom	220	20	24	29	5	8	10
(°230)	240	6	13	17	14	18	21
Cadbury Schweppes	300	40	52	–	4	10	–
(°332)	330	18	33	39	16	20	25
	360	9	18	25	38	38	43
Guinness	300	21	32	37	8	12	16
(°314)	330	5	15	20	24	26	32

Option		CALLS Nov	CALLS Feb	CALLS May	PUTS Nov	PUTS Feb	PUTS May
LASMO	360	42	62	72	11	19	26
(°389)	390	23	45	53	23	33	40
	420	11	28	40	45	52	57
P. & O.	500	33	50	–	10	18	–
(°524)	550	10	25	33	40	43	50
	600	4	13	18	90	90	95
Pilkington	180	23	26	–	3	6	–
(°197)	200	10	15	22	10	15	16
	220	3	7	12	26	28	29
Plessey	140	13	16	21	5	9	11
(°145)	160	4	8	12	18	21	24
	180	1	4	7	37	38	38
Prudential	140	–	21	24	–	4	8
(°155)	150	9	–	–	6	–	–
	160	5	8	10	13	14	15
Racal	260	33	–	–	9	–	–
(°281)	280	20	31	40	15	20	25
	300	10	21	30	27	31	35
R.T.Z.	390	42	57	67	9	16	22
(°413)	420	23	37	50	18	30	37
	460	7	20	30	50	55	62
Vaal Reefs	60	10	13	16	2½	4½	6
(°$66)	70	4	7½	10	6	9	11

Option		Sep	Dec	Mar	Sep	Dec	Mar
Amstrad	200	9	17	25	7	12	15
(°201)	220	2½	10	17	22	24	26
Barclays	360	34	45	–	1½	6	–
(°390)	390	–	–	35	–	–	28
	395	7	22	–	12	20	–
Beecham	460	17	31	44	5	18	22
(°469)	500	2	13	25	33	41	43
BTR	260	11	19	27	5½	9½	12
(°269)	280	1½	9	17	19	21	23
Blue Circle	420	11	28	43	12	20	24
(°426)	460	2	12	23	44	46	48
	500	1	5	11	84	84	84
Dixons	140	12	18	24	2½	6	9
(°149)	160	2	8	14	14	15	17
	180	1	3½	6	33	35	36
Glaxo	950	48	73	105	8	35	45
(°988)	1000	18	47	78	29	60	70
	1050	4	–	–	67	–	–
Hawker Sidd.	460	43	53	65	3	10	14
(°495)	500	11	27	42	15	27	32
	550	1	10	20	57	60	68
Hillsdown	260	7	18	25	7	11	14
(°259)	280	1½	8	15	22	24	24
	300	½	4	8	42	42	42
Hanson	130	11½	15½	17	½	3	4
(°141)	140	3½	8¼	11	2½	6¼	7¾
	160	½	1¾	3¾	20	20½	21½
Lonrho	240	18	28	32	2	6½	12
(°255)	260	5	15½	18	10	16	22
Midland Bk	360	28	40	–	2	7	–
(°385)	390	6	22	28	10	16	25
Sears	120	8½	14½	21	3½	8	11½
(°125)	130	3½	10½	16	8½	13	16½
	140	1½	6	10½	16	20	23
Tesco	140	3	7½	13	7	9	11
(°136)	160	½	1½	4½	25	25	26
Trusthouse Forte	200	28	–	–	1	–	–
(°225)	220	12	22	27	4	9	14
	240	3½	12	17	17	20	25
Thorn EMI	550	60	72	–	1	15	–
(°595)	600	15	35	47	17	27	34
	650	3½	15	23	62	59	65
Unilever	420	36	47	60	1¾	7	10
(°452)	460	6½	21	35	13	22	28
	500	1	8	19	48	49	53
Wellcome	460	27	45	60	4	14	19
(°481)	500	5½	22	39	23	33	37

Option		Sep	Dec	Apr	Sep	Dec	Apr
Boots	200	6	13	20	6	12	14
(°198)	220	1	5	12	23	25	27
	240	½	2	6	43	43	44

Option		Oct	Jan	Mar	Oct	Jan	Mar
British Gas	170	8½	–	–	3¾	–	–
(°173)	180	2¾	8½	10½	9½	11½	13½

Option		Sep	Nov	Jan	Sep	Nov	Jan
RHM	360	12	25	25	15	26	32
(°355)	390	6	14	17	38	40	47
	420	1½	6	10	68	70	70

Option		Nov	Feb	May	Nov	Feb	May
Conv. 9½% 2005	98	1 13/32	2 1/16	–	1 3/32	1 9/16	–
(°98)	100	23/32	1 1/8	–	2 9/32	2 13/32	–
	102	11/32	5/8	–	4 1/16	4 1/16	–
Tr. 12% 1995	106	1 9/32	1 13/32	–	23/32	1 1/16	–
(°107)	108	13/32	5/8	–	2	2 1/16	–
	110	5/32	7/32	–	3 5/8	3 9/16	–

Option		Sep	Oct	Nov	Dec	Sep	Oct	Nov	Dec
FT-SE	1650	86	105	112	125	6	15	23	30
Index	1700	43	63	78	90	14	30	36	47
(°1735)	1750	16	35	48	62	34	52	59	68
	1800	4½	16	28	40	75	85	93	97
	1850	1	7	15	23	126	128	128	135
	1900	½	3	7	12	176	178	178	180
	1950	½	1	3	–	226	228	228	–
	2000	½	½	2	–	276	277	277	–

September 9 Total Contracts 34,177 Calls 22,337 Puts 11,840
FT-SE Index Calls 2268 Puts 2524
°Underlying security price.

Figure 7.2(a) London traded options, closing prices, 9 September 1988. (Source: *Financial Times* 10 September 1988.)

The modern success of the option as a financial instrument arrived with the opening of the Chicago Board Options Exchange (CBOE) in April 1973. The CBOE began with option contracts on only 16 blue chip shares, but within 10 years it and 3 other exchanges offered about 9500 different option contracts on 350 securities (out of a total of about 6,000 US listed stocks). The European Options Exchange (EOE) in Amsterdam offers contracts on 20 listed Dutch companies as well as the EOE index, gold and the US guilder exchange rate (Fig. 7.1). The London Traded Options Market (Fig. 7.2), established in 1978 with options written on 10 shares, now offers over 1,000 contracts on 63 shares, 2 gilts and the FTSE Index (August 1988).

The success of the traded option is due to the existence of a regulated secondary market in which contracts may be bought and sold and positions opened and closed without the need to enter the securities market.

The organization of the London Traded Options Market

The purchaser of an option contract is referred to as the 'buyer' while the originator of the contract is called the 'writer'. This avoids any confusion when the buyer sells the option to another investor as the obligation remains with the writer. The market price of an option contract is called the premium, but the price at which the underlying shares may be bought or sold by the investor is known as the 'exercise' price (and sometimes the 'striking' price). Each option contract will also have an 'expiry' date on which the rights of the investor and obligations of the writer cease. The maximum life of a traded option is 9 months and the expiry dates are arranged in a quarterly cycle so that at any one time there will be contracts on the underlying share with 3 different expiry dates. The first cycle of options have expiry dates in January, April, July, and October, the second in November, February, May and August, and the third, December, March, June and September. In Fig. 7.2 prices are quoted for October, January and April. When the October options expire the clearing house for the market will create a new series of options for July expiry. Traded options usually cease on the third or fourth Wednesday of the month in which they are due to expire. Invariably, this also coincides with the end of the Stock Exchange settlement period. However, unlike the Stock Exchange's organization of transactions in securities, the TOM requires cash settlement of all contracts by 10.00 a.m. the day after the bargain has been struck.

Each option contract consists of the rights to buy or sell 1,000 of the underlying shares. This is the case for every class (the term for all the contracts written on a particular share) of option except those for Vaal Reefs, the two gilts and those on the FTSE Index. With a new series, 3 exercise prices are usually created; one at or near the ruling share price and one each at a level some 10 per cent above/below the middle price. A new series of option contracts (all the contracts for any particular class with the same exercise price) will be introduced when:

1. The share price exceeds the highest exercise price for 4 consecutive days or when the share price rises to a level halfway between the highest current exercise price and the next potential series.
2. The share price falls below the lowest current exercise price for 4 consecutive trading days or halfway between the lowest exercise price and the next potential series.

Hence, looking at the contracts quoted on Hanson shares in Fig. 7.2, we can see that the highest exercise price is 160p and if the price of Hanson shares rose to 161p for 4 consecutive trading days or rose to 170p the clearing house would create a new series of options with exercise prices of 180p.

Even though the London TOM has expanded greatly, the number of different securities on which options are written is still a very small proportion of the total number of securities in existence. The criteria used for the selection of suitable shares are as follows:

1. The security must be listed on the Stock Exchange.
2. The company must have experienced no default within the previous 5 years.

3. The company must have a 'substantial' market capital.
4. The market for the share must be liquid in the sense that there is a constant stream of bargains struck for the securities every day.
5. There must be at least 10,000 different shareholders.

In addition, once a class of options has been created there are restrictions on the writing of the contracts:

1. The number of option contracts cannot exceed 10 per cent of the number of securities in issue.
2. The number of uncovered options written cannot exceed 5 per cent of the shares in issue.
3. Any one investor or writer cannot hold or sell more than 1,000 contracts of any one series of a particular class or 2,000 contracts in all the series of any particular class.

These criteria and restrictions are meant to ensure that the market for the options in any one class cannot be manipulated or controlled by any individual or concert party. In selecting a new class of options the clearing house attempts to ensure that at all times contracts may be exercised without any undue influence on the share market itself. Thus, the situation should not arise in which the writer of an option contract cannot fulfil his obligations by buying securities in the stock market, or that an investor cannot buy shares in order to sell them to the option writer. Hence the clearing house ensures that the underlying securities form a large market capitalization and that there are a large number of shareholders.

The restrictions on trading are designed to limit the potential impact of the options market on the stock market. Therefore, no investor through the exercise of either put or call options can hope to influence the market for the underlying shares.

Lastly, commission is charged on the following reducing scale (Fig. 7.2(b)):

1. 2.5 per cent on the value of option contracts up to £5,000.
2. 1.5 per cent on the value of option contracts between £5,001 and £10,000,

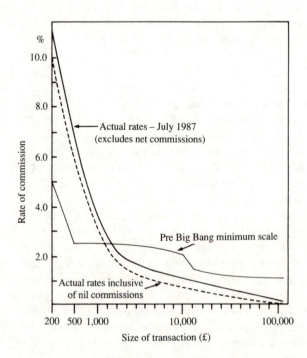

Figure 7.2(b)   Traded options rates of commission. (Source: *Quality of Markets Quarterly*.)

3. 1.0 per cent on the value of option contracts in excess of £10,000. For small bargains there will be a minimum charge which will vary between the different broking firms. In addition to the commission the clearing house also charges £1.50 per contract. If contracts are closed (i.e. sold) by the investor, commission is usually charged at half the rate of that for purchases. It should also be borne in mind that the closing prices quoted by the FT are mid-prices between the bid and offer prices offered by the market-makers.

Motives for buying options

There are 5 broad reasons for buying options:

1. *Equity gearing.*   Traded options allow investors to enjoy (or otherwise) the price movements of the underlying security at a fraction of the cost of buying that security. For example, suppose an investor has correctly anticipated a rise in the price of his or her chosen security. The investor could back his or her judgement by either buying the share itself or if it exists, the option on the share. On 26 September 1985 an investor could have purchased BP shares for 526p (end of trading mid-price) and some 6 weeks later on 11 November sold that same share for 560p. Ignoring transactions costs this represents a profit of 6.5 per cent (which in all probability would have been more than accounted for by brokerage etc.). However, the investor could have purchased call options with an exercise price of 550p and an expiry date in January 1986, for 25p each. On 11 November these could have been sold for 35p each, a profit before transactions cost of 40 per cent. Each contract involving 1,000 rights would have cost £250; if the investor purchased 4 such contracts the total cost would have been £1,000. The commission at 2.5 per cent would have been £25, and a fee of 4 (£1.5) = £6 would have been payable to the clearing house. On the sale of the 4 contracts the investor would have received a revenue of £1,400 less a sales brokerage of £12.50. Therefore, total transactions cost would have been £43.50 and the net profit after costs would have been £366.50.

Over the same period similar and greater profits could have been gained on other securities. For example, Bass shares could have been bought for 567p and sold for 652p, a gross return of 15 per cent (about 7 per cent after costs). On the other hand the December options (exercise price 550p) could have been bought for 42p and sold for 115p, a gross profit of 174 per cent. In addition to the profits made on a rising market the TOM permits investors to try to make profits on a falling market. Again using the same period as the previous two examples, the price of LASMO shares fell from 268p to 240p (due primarily to the falling crude oil price), a fall of 10.4 per cent. However, the investor who had the luck or foresight to predict the fall could have bought November puts with an exercise price of 260p for 10p and sold them for 25p making a gross profit of 150 per cent.

It is worth emphasizing here that because an option has a finite life and expires it can involve the investor in a 100 per cent loss. The above examples have all assumed some prescience on the part of the investor. However, it is very possible that the investor may incorrectly forecast the market as many did in the crash of October 1987.

2. *Limited risk to capital.*   Many options may be purchased at a very small fraction of the cost of the underlying security. If the investor is a purchaser, the risk to capital is therefore limited and known (the case of the writers of options is not so clear cut and will be examined later).

3. *Anticipating cash flows.*   Traded options can be used to secure a predetermined price for a security within a given period in the anticipation of a certain cash inflow. If a specific sum is anticipated in 6 months time, and today's price of the share in which it is intended to invest is considered low or is forecast to rise, then the price may be fixed now by the use of a call option.

On the other hand, if an individual or organization already owns a share on which options may be purchased, and a liability is expected to rise within the near future which can only be met by the sale of the shares, the cash flow from that sale may be secured by the purchase of put options. These two motives may be especially important to the investing institutions such as pension funds and insurance companies which have large inflows and outflows of the capital under their stewardship.

4. *Portfolio insurance.* In the same way that cash flows may be anticipated, the value of the existing portfolio or investment may be secured by buying put options. Favourable movements in share prices may be secured for up to 9 months by buying put options in the relevant securities or by buying put options in the FTSE index. If the portfolio consists of gilts either wholly or in part, options may be purchased in the two gilts on offer: Conv $9\frac{1}{2}\%$ 2005 and Treasury 12% 1995. Thus any adverse price movement in the stock market or the gilts market will be partly or wholly (depending on the degree of insurance purchased) offset by the increase in the value of the put options.

5. *Interest rates.* By enabling the investor to secure the price for future investment at a fraction of the security's price, the TOM allows the investor to invest the majority of his or her capital in the money market in order to take advantage of high interest rates. Existing or anticipated high interest rates may in fact depress share prices and hence call prices thus permitting the investor to buy the option contracts at very favourable prices while at the same time benefitting from the attractive rates on offer in the money markets.

In addition to the above motives we must recognize that the TOM provides a very convenient place for pure speculation. However, before taking any adverse moral position it should be borne in mind that it is only the existence of such risk takers that allow risk-averse (such as those described in motives 4 to 5) investors to effectively sell the risk of their portfolios or investments.

The factors that influence option premiums

Before describing and assessing the binomial and Black and Scholes option pricing models it is appropriate at this point to examine the factors which are expected to influence option premiums and in the next section to have a brief look at the various investment strategies that may be created with options and securities. In Fig. 7.2 the premiums quoted for options on BP shares are as follows:

Ex. P.	Calls			Puts		
	Oct.	Jan.	Apr.	Oct.	Jan.	Apr.
220	20	29	31.5	2	4	7.5
240	7	15	18	8.5	11	17
260	1.5	7	9.5	24	24	31

In Fig. 7.2 the end of trading price of the underlying security, which in this case is 237 p, is to be found in brackets under the name of the share. The TOM has a convenient set of jargon to describe the relationship between the security price and the exercise price. Given that this relationship is the determinant of whether the investor has made a profit or loss (ignoring transactions costs for the moment), it is of primary importance in determining the option premium. The options market has coined three expressions to describe the relationship between the exercise and security prices as follows:

	Calls	Puts
'in-the-money'	$P_s > P_e$	$P_s < P_e$
'at-the-money'	$P_s = P_e$	$P_s = P_e$
'out-of-the-money'	$P_s < P_e$	$P_s > P_e$

where P_s is the security price and P_e is the exercise price.

An in-the-money option allows the investor to exercise immediately and make a gross profit (forgetting premiums, spreads and commissions for the moment). Using the quotation for BP options it can be seen that the 220p calls are in-the-money as the security price is 237p. In the absence of transactions costs and the option premium this series of contracts would permit the investor to buy the shares at 220p from the writer and sell them in the market for 237p thus gaining a gross profit of 17p per share. However, the existence of the option premiums of 20p, 29p and 31.5p for the October, January and April expiry dates eliminates any gross profit. Once the marketmaker's spread and the broker's commission are taken into account the investor will face a sizeable loss if he or she buys and exercises at these prices. However, it remains that in-the-money options are more expensive than at-the-money and out-of-the-money options as the potential for profit is greater.

A convenient way of gauging the extent to which an option is in-the-money is to calculate the 'intrinsic' value. This is simply the security price minus the exercise price for calls (and the exercise price minus the share price for puts). In the case of 220p October BP calls this is $237 - 220 = 17p$. It should be noted that TOM practice does not recognize negative intrinsic values. By definition, all at-the-money and out-of-the-money options have intrinsic values of zero.

The intrinsic value of an option cannot be greater than the premium itself as this situation would provide investors with an instant arbitrage profit. For example, if the price of BP October calls with an exercise price of 220p were only 10p then investors could buy the calls and exercise by buying the shares at 220p making a total purchase price of 230p and selling them back to the market for 237p thus making a profit of 7p per share. In such a situation the demand for the options would rise and, given the restrictions on the creation of option contracts, the price would rise until the profit opportunity disappeared.

However, intrinsic value never accounts for all of the option premiums in the case of in-the-money options and none of the premiums in the cases of at-the-money and out-of-the-money options. The balance is known as 'time' value. This is the price that an investor has to pay for the possibility that the share price may change to make the option in-the-money. For example, taking the October calls and puts we may make the following division between intrinsic and time values:

P_s	P_e	Calls	Intr. value	Time value	Puts	Intr. value	Time value
237	220	20	17	3	2	0	2
237	240	7	0	7	8.5	3	5.5
237	260	1.5	0	1.5	24	23	1

At the time of writing there are 5 weeks before these options are due to expire. Hence, time value is the price paid for the chance that the share price will move sufficiently during the following 5 weeks in order to make the investment profitable. This aspect of option premiums may be seen more clearly if we look at calls and puts with the same exercise price but with different expiry dates. Using the premiums quoted in Fig. 7.1 for BP options with an exercise price of 240p the effect of time can be seen as follows:

Expiry month	Calls	Intr. value	Time value	Puts	Intr. value	Time value
October	7	0	7	$8\frac{1}{2}$	3	5.5
January	15	0	15	11	3	8
April	18	0	18	17	3	14

The time value components of the option premiums quoted get larger as the time to expiry lengthens. However, it should be noted that the relationship between time value and the term to maturity is neither linear nor is it the same for both types of contracts. The difference between the time values for calls and puts may be taken as an indicator of market sentiment about the future progress of the share price. Thus in the above example, investors are willing to pay slightly more in terms of time value for calls than for puts but the difference is so slight that the indicator is in this case quite inconclusive.

The determinants of the time value component are primarily the volatility of the underlying shares and the prevailing and expected interest rates in the money markets.

1. *Interest rates*. One of the motives mentioned was the actual and expected levels of interest rates. As the TOM allows investors to avoid purchasing shares, the higher the actual and expected levels of interest rates the greater the incentive to use options and delay the acquisition of shares in order to benefit from the rates of return prevailing or expected in the money markets. It is also worth noting that as rates rise in the money markets equities by comparison may be seen in a less favourable light, and if this produces a greater level of uncertainty about prices, options combined with the money markets may constitute a refuge for those investors wishing to avoid such doubts.

2. *Volatility*. Despite the influence of interest rates, the movement of the underlying share price is the principal determinant of changes in option premiums. Therefore, the extent to which the share moves in response to stock market, macroeconomic, industrial and company stimuli is very important. Hence, the greater the volatility, the greater the chance, within any given term to expiry, that share price and option premiums will change, thus increasing the probability of a profitable investment. So the greater the volatility of the underlying share, the greater the time value for any given term to maturity is likely to be.

3. *Other influences*: In many cases the absolute size of the price of the underlying share may play a part in determining the option premiums. Hence, shares trading in the region of £10 are likely, *ceteris paribus*, to have larger time values than those trading at £1. Secondly, dividend policy may have an important effect on both the level and degree of volatility of option premiums. It is shown in Chapter 8 that the declaration of dividend payments tends to have a depressive effect on share prices and that the larger the dividend payout relative to the share price the greater the impact on the price. From the foregoing discussion it follows that high dividend payouts are likely to have a larger negative effect than low dividend payouts on option premiums. Lastly, option premiums are likely to be affected by the expectations about the company which issued the underlying shares. Hence, companies which specialize in oil field exploration and development (e.g. LASMO) will be affected by crude oil prices to a greater extent than those companies which, although dependent on oil, have diversified into other areas (e.g. BP and Shell). Another specific influence on both share prices and option premiums is the expectation and likelihood of a contested takeover.

These various factors which influence the value of an option may be summed up in the following functional statement:

$$C_o = f(+S, -EX, +T, +\sigma^2, +rf)$$

This will be developed further in a later section which describes the binomial and Black–Scholes option pricing models.

Investment strategies using options

Having taken a look at the nature of, and influences upon, options, we can now examine the investment strategies which may be created using traded options. If we restrict ourselves to puts and calls on a single security there are 4 simple types of investment strategy to look at:

1. *'Naked' or uncovered positions.* These involve the purchase or sale of a single security or option; i.e. long or short shares, long or written calls and long or written puts.
2. *Hedged positions.* A hedge position is a portfolio consisting of a long or short share and one or more of the available options on that share. The most common type of hedge is the written call combined with an investment in the security itself. Where there are as many options written as there are shares held, the hedge is completely 'covered'. Where the number of shares is exceeded by the number of options written, the position is known as a partially covered hedge. These and the other two hedge positions are described in Fig. 7.3.

Options / Shares	Calls Bought	Calls Written	Puts Bought	Puts Written
Long		Covered call = Written put	Hedged share = Bought call	
Short	Reversed hedge = Bought put			Covered put = Written call

Figure 7.3 Hedge positions.

3. *Spread positions.* These are portfolios consisting of 2 or more options with different expiry and/or exercise dates and rights;
   (a) those with different exercise prices but the same expiry dates are known variously as 'money' or 'vertical' or 'price' spreads;
   (b) those with the same exercise prices but with different expiry dates are known as 'time' or 'horizontal' or 'calendar' spreads;
   (c) lastly there are those portfolios which have all 4 types of option in a single class all with the same expiry date but with 3 different exercise prices, known as 'butterfly' or 'sandwich' spreads.
4. *Combinations.* These are portfolios of written calls and puts or bought calls and puts with the same exercise price and expiry date on the same underlying security. Although there is almost an infinite variety of such combinations only 3 have specific names:
   (a) the 'straddle', consisting of an equal number of puts and calls on the same share, either bought or written;
   (b) the 'strap', made up from bought or written options in a ratio of 2 calls to 1 put;
   (c) the 'strip', composed of written or purchased options in a ratio of 2 puts to 1 call.

The objectives of these various strategies is most clearly illustrated by the use of profit diagrams which show profit or loss at expiry (when all time value disappears) in relation to the price of the underlying share price. There are 6 basic diagrams of unhedged position which, when combined in various ways, give the possible results of the strategies outlined.

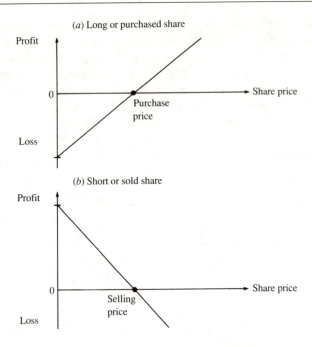

Figure 7.4 Unhedged share profit diagrams.

The two diagrams in Fig. 7.4 are quite straightforward. In the case of a 'long' share (in which the security is purchased and held), each 1p in the share price above the purchase price (S) yields 1p of profit (ignoring transactions costs for the moment). Conversely, each 1p the price drops below the purchase price (S) increases the loss borne by the investor by 1p per share held. The profit diagram of the 'short' share investment reveals the exact opposite relationship between price and profit as the long share investment. An investor selling short is selling shares which he or she does not own. The shares will have been borrowed and sold in the hope and expectation of buying them back at a lower price. For example, an investor might sell for 100p per share one week and if he or she has been proven correct in their expectations may buy the share for say 80p each the following week, thus netting a profit per share of 20p before transactions costs. It is worth noting that although the profit on a long share can be infinitely large, this is not so in the case of a 'short' investment. The lowest price for which shares can be repurchased is zero pence so that an investor can only hope to double his or her investment at the most. However, as there is no limit on the level to which the price of shares may rise, the potential losses are also limitless.

The profit diagrams for options (Figs 7.5 and 7.6) are a little more complex than those for securities as the profit is dependent on more than just the share price at expiry (S). It is also dependent on the exercise price (E) and the option premiums (C for calls and P for puts). The price paid for each option is indicated by the distances OC and OP on the vertical axes for calls and puts respectively. If at expiry the options are out-of-the-money $S < E$ (calls) and $S > E$ (puts) they are worthless and the maximum loss in each case amounts to the option premium itself (C, P). The investments will only be profitable when the following conditions apply:

$$\text{calls, } S > (E + C)$$
$$\text{puts, } S < (E - P)$$

It is worth noting once again that calls have an unlimited profit potential similar to that of the long

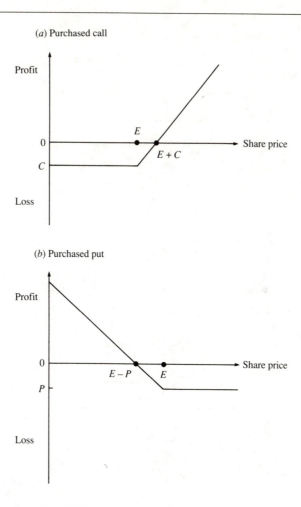

Figure 7.5   Unhedged purchased option profit diagrams.

share while that of the puts is limited to $E - P$; i.e. the maximum is reached when the share price S has reached zero. No more profit may be had as the maximum revenue per option is $E - P - S$ whereas the maximum revenue $(S - E - C)$ for a call is unconstrained. The only limitation on the value of a call option before the expiry date is the price of the underlying security. (Why should anyone pay more for the right to purchase a share than the price of the share itself?)

The profit positions for the writers of options at the point of expiry are the exact opposite of those for the purchasers. The maximum profit in both contracts is the original option premium. The writer of calls faces potentially limitless losses while the writer of puts has a maximum potential loss of $E - P$ (i.e. the price at which the writer has contracted to buy the shares less the option premium).

The simple hedges described in Fig. 7.3 are essentially insurance operations in which profits and losses on each investment tend to offset each other to some extent. For example the covered call is a combination of a written call and a long position in the underlying security. If we assume that exercise price is equal to the purchase price of the shares then diagrams 7.4(a) and 7.6(a) may be combined. If $S > E$ the investor starts to earn profits on the long investment before making losses on the written call. When $S > (E + C)$ the losses incurred on the call are exactly matched by the

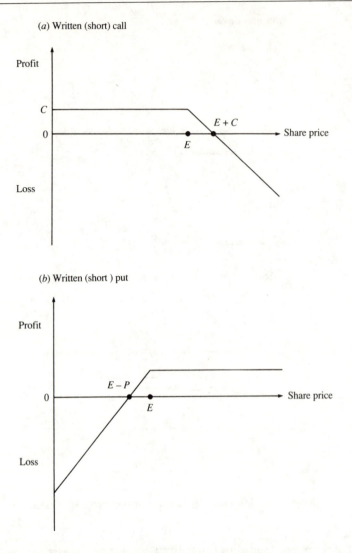

Figure 7.6 Unhedged written option profit diagrams.

profits received from the shares. The net result is a profit equal to the option premium. If $S < E$ the losses incurred on the purchased shares will be offset by the premium received by selling the option. Therefore, losses will only arise when $S < (E - C)$ and will be at a maximum when $S = 0$ and will be equal to $E - C$. The result is shown by the hatched line in Fig. 7.7(a) and is the equivalent of a written put.

Figure 7.7(b) shows the profit position of a 'reverse hedge'. The investor having gone short in a security takes out insurance in the form of a purchased call whose exercise price is equal to the price at which the shares were sold. The cost of the call reduces the profit position when $S < E$ and limits the maximum profit to $E - C$. On the other hand the potential unlimited loss on the short share when $S > E$ is almost exactly offset by the potentially unlimited profit of the purchased call. The net position indicated by the dashed line is the equivalent to that of a purchased put.

There are two remaining hedges which may be constructed using combinations of options and securities. The first is a long share and a purchased put which produces results similar to those of a

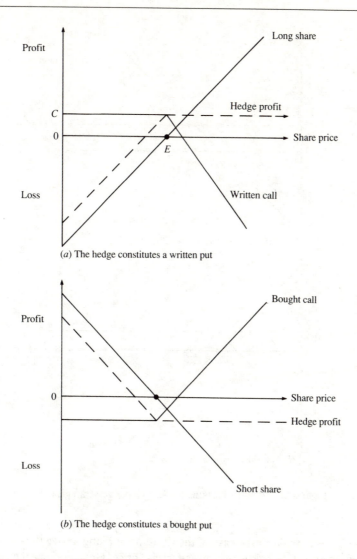

Figure 7.7 Profit diagrams for simple hedge strategies I.

purchased call and the second is a short share with a written put which gives the profit profile of a written call (Fig. 7.8).

Profit diagrams can only be intelligibly drawn for strategies involving investments with the same expiry dates. Therefore, the potential profitability of time spreads cannot be illustrated. However, those for money and butterfly spreads which involve positions with a uniform time of expiry can be drawn. Money spreads are either 'bullish' or 'bearish'. They correspond to the investor's balance of expectations about the movement of the share price during the period up to the expiry date. The bullish spread, as its name suggests, indicates an optimism about the future of the share price whereas the bearish money spread is pessimistic in that the balance of expectations is that the share price is more likely to fall. These spreads consist of written and purchased calls (or puts). The bullish money spread consists of a purchased call with a low exercise price (E_L) and a written call with a high exercise price (E_H). Thus as the share price rises above E_L the purchased call starts to earn profits before the written call makes losses when $S > E_H$. The net result, shown by the dashed

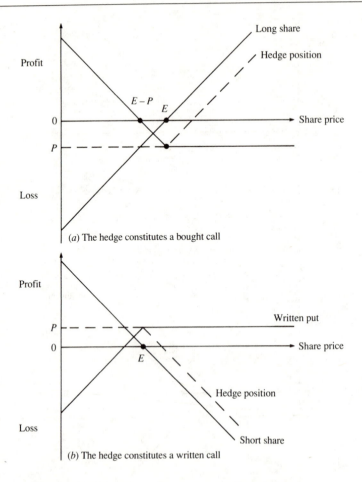

Figure 7.8   Profit diagrams for simple hedge strategies II.

line in Fig. 7.9(a), gives a profit in the case of the share price rising above the lower exercise price and a loss if the share price falls below the lower exercise price. However, in each event the result is strictly constrained.

The bearish money spread (Fig. 7.9(b)) reflects the profit and loss potential of an investor who gives a higher probability to the security price falling than rising but who takes out insurance in case of being wrong. A call is written with a low exercise price (E_L) to make the profit when prices fall as expected. As it has a low exercise price (and is very probably in-the-money) the premium will be high. On the other hand the purchased call with a high exercise price (E_H) which constitutes the investor's insurance policy will have a low exercise price as it is probably out-of-the-money and has no intrinsic value. The resultant profit–loss line shows a maximum profit of $P - C$ and a loss which is determined by the difference between the high and low exercise prices. The written call having the low exercise price starts to make a loss before the purchased call starts to make a profit. As the share price exceeds the high exercise price the profit made on the purchased call exactly offsets any more losses incurred from the written call leaving a constant residual loss.

The rationale for the bearish money spread is easy to see; it limits the potential losses that might be incurred by writing a call. On the other hand the only reason for constructing a bullish money spread is to reduce the premium of a call with a high intrinsic value because of its low exercise price.

(a) Bullish money spread (using calls)

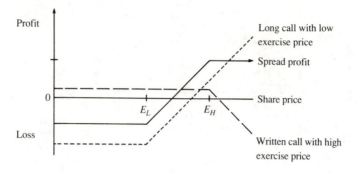

(b) Bearish money spread (using calls)

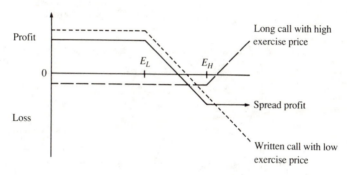

Figure 7.9   Money spreads.

However, bullish and bearish money spreads can be combined to create a potential profit in a situation where the share price is not expected to move and in a situation where the price is expected to move but has equal probabilities of rising and falling. These are known as the butterfly spreads.

The first spread is used where small or no price movements are expected. Three exercise prices are used. The bullish spread has a purchased call on the low exercise price (E_L) and a call written on the middle exercise price (E_M). The bearish spread has a call written on the E_M and a call purchased on the high exercise price (E_H). Hence there are two written calls on E_M and two purchased calls on E_L and E_H. The combined effect is shown in Fig. 7.10(a) where the profit–loss line is shown as an unbroken line.

The butterfly spread can be reversed (Fig. 7.10(b)) to cater for the investor who cannot decide on the balance of his or her expectations. In this situation the investor purchases two calls at E_M and writes two calls, one each at E_H and E_L. The net effect is to produce a loss if the share price does not move beyond the limits set by the high and low exercise prices but a small and limited profit if it does.

Two similar profit–loss lines can be produced with what were earlier called combinations. These are the purchased and written straddles.

Figure 7.11(a) shows the effect of purchasing both a put and a call with the same expiry dates and exercise prices on the same share. The profit–loss line clearly shows that this should be used when

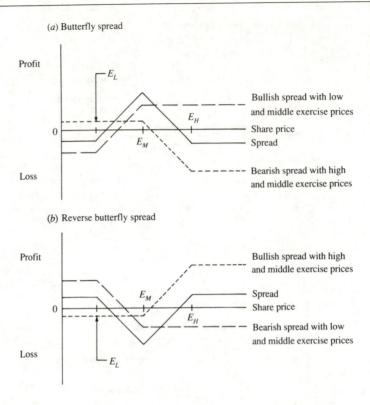

Figure 7.10   Butterfly spreads using calls.

the investor has no clear expectation of the direction of movement of the security's price, only that it will move. The maximum loss $(C + P)$ is incurred if the share price is equal to the exercise price at expiry but profits will be made if it is lower than $E - C - P$ and if it rises above $E + C + P$. This is plainly superior to the reverse butterfly spread illustrated in Fig. 7.10(b) as there are no restrictions upon the potential profit (only in the case of a security price fall where the maximum profit will be $E - P - C$, but which is still superior to the profit made in the same event with the reverse butterfly spread).

The written straddle shown in Fig. 7.11(b) may be used when little or no movement in the underlying security price is expected. Profit is maximized at $C + P$ when $S = E$. However, the investor faces potentially unlimited losses if the share price moves beyond the range of $E + / - (P + C)$. The strategy of the written straddle offers an inferior set of potential returns to the investor compared with the ordinary butterfly spread (Fig. 7.10(a)) as losses can be unlimited.

The binomial valuation model

Having looked at the various strategies for using options it is now time to look at the valuation of options. The above section used the limiting case of value at expiry to illustrate the profit and loss potential of various investment strategies, but given the ability of investors in traded options to sell or exercise before maturity it is essential that there is some way of evaluating options before expiry.

We have already seen that the options market is symmetrical in that only one form of contract is

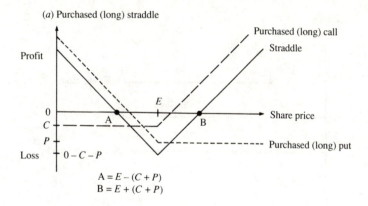

(a) Purchased (long) straddle

$A = E - (C + P)$
$B = E + (C + P)$

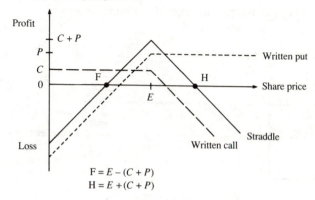

(b) Written (short) straddle

$F = E - (C + P)$
$H = E + (C + P)$

Figure 7.11 Straddles.

needed, either calls or puts. The existence of either permits the creation of the other. However, this ability to mimic financial contracts may be extended to all such using calls, puts, shares and risk-free debentures. At expiry the value of an option may be expressed as follows:

$$C_t = \text{Max}[0, S_t - \text{EX}] \quad \text{or} \quad P_t = \text{Max}[0, \text{EX} - S_t] \tag{7.1}$$

We may define the present value of a pure discount risk-free debenture as follows:

$$B_0 = B_t e^{-(rf)t} \tag{7.2}$$

Riskless and pure discount debentures, shares, calls and puts may now be combined as follows:

$$B = S + P - C \tag{7.3}$$

The right-hand side of the above equation, the combination of a long share and a purchased put, is a manufactured purchased call. This is combined with a written call. The outcome of this combination (shown in Fig. 7.13) is the pay-off on a riskless pure discount debenture.

From the above relationship we can derive the price relationship between calls and puts. For example, suppose the shares of ABC pty are selling for 400p and that options may be purchased and written with an exercise price of 400p. Following Eq. (7.3) we may purchase an equal number of shares and put and write a similar number of calls. Three months after these transactions, suppose the share price will be either 500p or 300p. The pay-offs will be as follows:

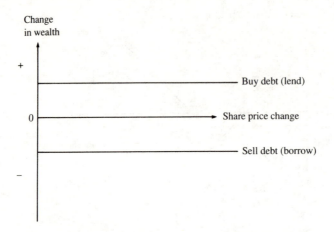

Figure 7.12   The returns and costs of a risk-free debenture.

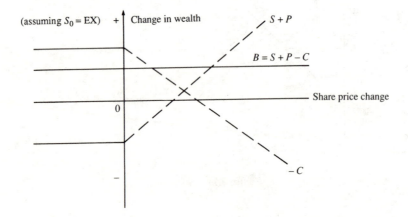

Figure 7.13 $B = S + P - C$.

	$S_t = 500p$	$S_t = 300p$
the long share	500p	300p
put $[(EX - S)]$	0	100p
call $[-(S - EX)]$	−100p	0
pay-off	400p	400p

Regardless of the share price our net wealth will be 400p which according to Eq. (7.3) is equal to the terminal value of a risk-free pure discount debenture. We can now, using the debenture, discount the value of this hedge to the present by using eq. (7.2):

$$B_0 = 400e^{(-0.25)(0.12)} = 400(0.9704) = 388.16$$

Rearranging Eq. (7.3) we have:

$$C_0 - P_0 = S - Be^{(-rf)(t)}$$

$$= 400 - 388.16$$

$$= 11.84 \tag{7.4}$$

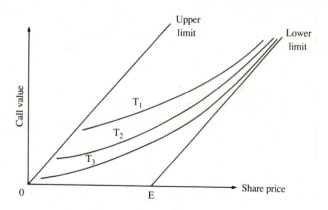

Figure 7.14   The value limits of a purchased call.

The relationship holds that, whatever the price of the call, the price of the put must be 11.84p less. Therefore, if the call was priced at 20p then the put must be priced at 8p (the prices in the traded options market being quoted to the nearest half-penny). Equation (7.4) is known as the put–call parity relationship for European options[2] and in the special case where the share price (S_0) is equal to the exercise price the equation reduces to the following:

$$C_0 - P_0 = S_0(1 - e^{(-rf)(t)}) > 0 \qquad (7.5)$$

In valuing option contracts before maturity, we may intuitively draw the limiting boundaries by observing that a purchased call (Fig. 7.14) never has a negative value so that:

$$C \geqslant 0$$

On the other hand a call cannot exceed the value of the underlying share:

$$C \leqslant S$$

Lastly, the value of the call option cannot be less than the difference between the share price and the exercise price:

$$C \geqslant S - EX$$

We may follow a similar intuitive process for the limits of the value of purchased puts (Fig. 7.15). As in the case of calls, puts can never have a negative value, hence:

$$P \geqslant 0$$

The maximum value of any put is set by its exercise price:

$$P \leqslant EX$$

Lastly, the value cannot be less than the difference between the exercise price and the share price:

$$P \geqslant EX - S$$

Although in chronological terms the Black–Scholes option pricing model came first in 1973, the binomial analyses developed by Cox, Ross and Rubinstein and Rendleman and Bartter provide a conceptually easier introduction to the problem of valuation.[3] The assumptions underlying the binomial approach can be summarized as follows:

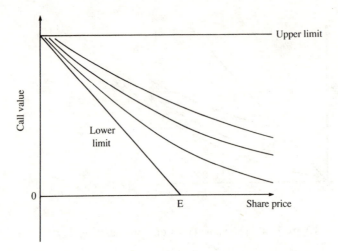

Figure 7.15 The value limits of a purchased put.

1. Perfect capital markets with no taxes or transactions costs.
2. Information is costless and universally available.
3. Short sales permitted;
4. Share prices follow a random walk without any underlying trend.
5. The risk-free rate is constant over the life of the option.
6. No dividends.
7. A one-period time horizon.

Assume that at the end of the investor's time horizon there are two possible end states, the first in which the share price has doubled and the second in which it has halved. Assume also that each of these states has a probability of 0.5. The investor may purchase shares in his chosen company for 200p so that the two states are 400p and 100p—each with an equal probability of occurring (Fig. 7.16). Lastly, assume that the prevailing risk-free rate of return for the duration of the investor's time horizon is 10 per cent. In effect this process describes the existence of two independent multipliers (h, L) which affect the share price. There is no need to specify $L = 1/h$, and as long as $L < 1$, it is quite feasible to permit an infinite upper level for the share price while restricting the lower limit to zero (shares cannot have a negative value as they have limited liability). The only requirement for the upper multiplier is that,

$$h > (1 + rf) \geqslant 1 > L$$

This allows the construction of a riskless hedge in which the pay-offs are the same regardless of the outcome. A portfolio must be constructed by going long in the security and short in the call options so that,

$$hS_0 - mC_h = LS_0 - mC_L$$

where m is the number of calls that must be written to produce a riskless hedge. This equation may be solved for m as follows:

$$m = S_0(h - L)/(C_h - C_L) \tag{7.6}$$

Using the hypothetical data we may calculate a riskless hedge for the investor:

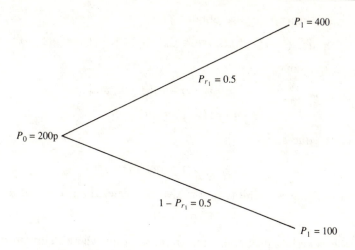

Figure 7.16 A single period binomial stochastic process.

$$S_0 = 200p$$

$$EX = 150p$$

$$h = 2$$

$$L = 0.5$$

$$hS_t = 400p$$

$$LS_t = 100p$$

$C_h = 250p$ (at expiry the value of the option will be $hS_t - EX = 400 - 150 = 250p$)

$C_L = 0p$ (at expiry there is no intrinsic value as $EX > LS_t$)

$$m = S_0(2.0 - 0.5)/(250 - 0) = 300/250 = 1.2$$

Hence, given these probabilities and outcomes the investor may construct a riskless hedge by buying 1 share and writing 1.2 calls. However, as this is a riskless hedge the investor should expect to receive the riskless rate of return. The initial investment is,

$$S_0 - mC$$

so the return should be,

$$(1 + rf)(S_0 - mC)$$

This should be equal to either of the outcomes,

$$LS_0 - mC_L, \quad \text{or} \quad hS_0 - mC_h$$

Therefore, we can write,

$$(1 + rf)(S_0 - mC) = (LS_0 - mC_L) \tag{7.7}$$

Equation (7.7) may be solved to find the value of C, the option at the beginning of the investor's time horizon:

$$C = [S_0(1 + rf - L) + mC_L]/m(1 + rf) \tag{7.8}$$

Substituting for m and rearranging we obtain:

$$C = [C_L(1 + rf - L)/(L - h) + C_h(L - 1 - rf)/(L - h)]/(1 + rf) \qquad (7.9)$$

To simplify Eq. (7.9) assume,

$$p = (1 + rf - h)/(L - h) \text{ and}$$

$$(1 - p) = (L - 1 - rf)/(L - h)$$

Therefore, Eq. (7.9) reduces to,

$$C = [pC_L + (1 - p)C_h]/(1 + rf) \qquad (7.10)$$

p is known as the hedging probability and is always greater than zero and less than 1,

$$0 < p < 1.$$

Hence, p has all the values of a probability and in the situation where all investors are risk averse it can be shown that it is equal to the probability with which we started.

The results of the hypothetical example are as follows:

state 1 payoff, hS_t; $400p - mC_h = 400p - (1.2)250p = 100p$

state 2 payoff, LS_t; $100p - mC_L = 100p - (1.2)0 \quad = 100p$

Using Eq. (7.9),

$$C = [0(1 + 0.1 - 0.5)/(2 - 0.5) + 250(2 - 1 - 0.1)(2 - 0.5)]/(1 + 0.1)$$

$$C = [250(1.1 - 0.5)/(2 - 0.5)]/(1.1)$$

$$C = 90.91p$$

Now we can calculate the initial investment,

$$I = S_0 - mC = 200 - (1.2)90.91 = 90.91p$$

Given that this was a risk-free hedge we can make a check on the process by comparing the outcomes from states 1 or 2 with the result of investing the initial capital at the risk-free rate of return:

$$I_t = I(1 + rf) = 90.91(1.1) = 100p$$

The critical assumption in this model is that the risk-free hedge can earn the risk-free rate of return. Given the price of the underlying security, the risk-free rate of return and the exercise price, the price of the call represents the factor which brings the system into equilibrium. If the risk-free hedge is seen to produce a greater return than the risk-free rate then arbitrage will take place as investors offer to write more calls and so bring down the price of the option. If on the other hand the risk-free hedge's return is inferior to the risk-free rate the supply of investors offering to write calls will contract thus reducing supply and, *ceteris paribus*, reducing the price of the call option. Hence, the price of the option does not depend on the probabilities of the share price rising or falling or by how much it is likely to rise or fall. Even with heterogeneous expectations on the part of investors the process of arbitrage will ensure that they will be in agreement on the price of the option in relation to the parameters S_0, h, L, rf and t even though the average values of h, L and p cannot be observed. For the binomial model to be valid we need only assume that investors prefer more wealth to less wealth (see Chapter 2) so that, given the opportunity, they will engage in arbitrage, and secondly that investors have the ability to construct the risk-free hedge.

The binomial model may be extended by increasing the number of time periods (n) and at the limit where n equals infinity it approaches the deterministic Black and Scholes option pricing model.

The Black and Scholes option pricing model

Black and Scholes[1] make the following assumptions:

1. All markets for securities, options and gilts are frictionless; i.e. no taxes, no transactions costs, no restrictions on short sales, and all securities are infinitely divisible.
2. The risk-free rate of return is constant over the life of the option and is equal to (rf) per unit of time.
3. No dividends (d), $d(S_t, t) = 0$.
4. The standard deviation (σ) of the security's return is constant over the life of the option, $\sigma(S_t, t) = \sigma$ for all t.
5. The distribution of security prices at expiry is log–normal with a mean equal to the risk-free rate and a standard deviation of $\sigma \sqrt{(rf)}$.
6. The prices of securities follow a random walk.

Given the above assumptions Black and Scholes developed a pricing model as follows:

$$C = S_t N(d_1) - (EX)e^{-(rf)t} N(d_2) \tag{7.11}$$

$$d_1 = [\ln(S_t/EX) + (rf + \sigma^2/2)t]/\sigma\sqrt{t} \tag{7.12}$$

$$d_2 = d_1 - \sigma\sqrt{t} \tag{7.13}$$

where t = number of days to expiry/365

σ = standard deviation of the returns of the security

rf = rate of return on 3-month treasury bills

$N(d_1)$ and $N(d_2)$ are cumulative probabilities of a normal distributed variable (z) with a mean of zero and a standard deviation of 1. $N(d_1)$ may be interpreted as the rate of change of the option price divided by the rate of change of the share price. Therefore, we may estimate the share price elasticity of the option by multiplying $N(d_1)$ by the share price divided by the call price:

$$n_c = (dC/dS)/(C/S) = (dC/dS)(S/C) \tag{7.14}$$

This measures the percentage change in the value of the call in response to a given change in the price of the share. It is graphically depicted in Fig. 7.14.

$N(d_2)$ may be interpreted as the probability of the option contract being in-the-money at maturity.

The estimation of call values can now be done using a hand-held calculator. Using the information in Fig. 7.2 for BP and assuming a risk-free rate of interest of 10 per cent we may estimate the call values for an in-the-money option expiring in October with an exercise price of 220p, and an out-of-the-money call with an exercise price of 260p expiring in April:

$EX = 220$p, $S = 237$p, Maturity = October, $t = 42/365 = 0.115$, $rf = 0.118$, $\sigma = 0.27$, $e^{-(rf)t} = 0.9865$

$d_1 = \{\ln(237/220) + [0.118 + (0.27)^2/2](0.115)\}/0.27\sqrt{0.115}$

$\quad = (0.074 + 0.018)/0.092$

$\quad = 1.00$

$$d_2 = 1.00 - 0.092$$

$$= 0.908$$

Using Table A1.2 (page 269) we may convert d_1 and d_2 into cumulative probabilities:

$$N(d_1) = 1 - 0.1587 = 0.8413$$

$$N(d_2) = 1 - 0.1819 = 0.8181$$

(the figure of 0.1819 is arrived at by using the two values in the table that bracket the real value and employing straight-line interpolation). Now the call is estimated using Eq. (7.11):

$$C = 237(0.8413) - 220(0.9865)(0.8181)$$

$$= 199.39 - 177.55 = 21.84$$

rounding to the nearest half-penny, 22p, which is equal to the market value given in Fig. 7.2.

$$EX = 260p, \; S = 237p, \; \text{Maturity} = \text{April}, \; t = 222/365 = 0.608, \; rf = 0.118, \; \sigma = 0.27, \; e^{-(rf)t} = 0.9308$$

$$d_1 = \{\ln(237/260) + [0.118 + (0.27)^2/2](0.608)\}/0.27\sqrt{0.608}$$

$$= -0.093 + 0.094/0.211$$

$$= 0.0047$$
$$d_2 = 0.0047 - 0.211$$
$$= -0.2063$$

therefore,

$$N(d_1) = 1 - 0.4960 = 0.5040$$

$$N(d_2) = 0.4168$$

hence,

$$C = 237(0.504) - 260(0.9308)(0.4168)$$

$$= 119.45 - 100.87 = 18.58$$

rounding to the nearest half-penny, this produces a value of 18.5p. The market value given in Fig. 7.2 is 9.5p. This means that there is a discrepancy of 8p.

Using the put–call parity relationship described in Eq. (7.5) we can now produce estimates for the equivalent puts:

$$P = C + EXe^{(-rt)t} - S \tag{7.15}$$

$$S = 237, \; EX = 220, \; \text{maturity} = \text{October}, \; t = 0.42, \; rf = 0.118$$

$$P = 22 + 220(0.9865) - 237$$

$$= 238.87 - 237 = 1.84$$

rounding to the nearest half-penny, 2p. This is equal to the market value given in Fig. 7.2.

$$S = 237, \; EX = 260, \; \text{maturity} = \text{April}, \; t = 0.608, \; rf = 0.118$$

$$P = 18.51 + 260(0.9308) - 237$$

$$= 260.52 - 237 = 23.52 \; \text{or through rounding, 23.5.}$$

The market value in Fig. 7.2 is 31 and therefore there is a discrepancy between the market and the model of 7.5p.

Empirical evidence

Black and Scholes tested their own model using US data. They noted that the prices indicated by the model differed in various systematic ways from market prices.[4] They came to the following conclusions:

1. The model tends to overestimate the prices of calls on securities that have volatile returns and underestimate the call values of those with non-volatile returns.
2. Options well in-the-money tend to be overpriced and those well out-of-the-money underpriced.
3. Options with lives of less than 90 days tend to be overpriced.

There is, however, little consensus about the direction of these biases. For example, MacBeth and Merville[5] report that the model overprices in-the-money options and underprices out-of-the-money options. On the other hand, Merton[6] has found from practitioners that the model consistently underprices regardless of the option's intrinsic worth. Jarrow and Rudd[7] have advanced two tentative explanations of these apparent discrepancies:

1. The model's performance is better at some times than at others.
2. The model is failing to pick up important determinant characteristics.

In individual cases there may be the possibility of specific characteristics or expectations playing an important role in causing temporary discrepancies between those prices indicated by the model and those set by the market. For example, in the case of BP, LASMO or Shell the expected changes in the price of crude oil can play an important part in determining market prices for options.

Hedging with the Black and Scholes model

In the previous section it was explained that $N(d_1)$ and $N(d_2)$ were cumulative probabilities of a unit normal variable. In addition the section indicated that the intuitive explanation of $N(d_1)$ was that it was equal to the rate of change in the cell price divided by the rate of change in the share price:

$$N(d_1) = dC/dS$$

From our discussion of the binomial model we also know that the value of the hedged portfolio is,

$$V_h = S - mC$$

hence the change in the value of the hedged portfolio per unit of time may be written,

$$\delta V_h/\delta t = \delta S/\delta t - m\delta C/\delta t \qquad (7.16)$$

If we define m as follows:

$$m = \delta S/\delta C = 1/N(d_1) \qquad (7.17)$$

then Eq. (7.16) may be rewritten,

$$\delta V_h/\delta t = \delta S/\delta t - (\delta S/\delta C)(\delta C/\delta t)$$

This reduces to,

$$\delta V_h/\delta t = \delta S/\delta t - \delta S/\delta t = 0$$

Hence, by defining $N(d_1)$ as the reciprocal of the hedge ratio we can ensure that the value of the hedged portfolio does not change during the next time period. Using the estimates for the **BP** options,

$$EX = 220, \ t = \text{October}, \ N(d_1) = 0.8413$$

$$EX = 260, \ t = \text{October}, \ N(d_1) = 0.5187$$

the hedge ratios work out as follows:

$$m = 1/0.8413 = 1.1886$$

$$m = 1/0.5187 = 1.9279$$

therefore, for the options expiring in October we should write 1.1886 option contracts per 1000 shares held and for the options maturing in April we should write 1.9279 contracts per 1000 share held. As fractional contracts cannot be written it is almost inevitable that the hedge will not be perfect. In these two examples, the first would be slightly under-hedged if one contract was written against 1000 shares and in the second case over-hedged as two contracts might be written against each 1000 shares held.

This example illustrates an important consideration which is that not only does the risk of any position increase dramatically with the length of time to maturity but also that the hedge ratio is only valid for very small increments of time. Hence, the use of options to hedge any long position in shares involves a continuous reassessment as time and the share price change.[8]

Evidence on the UK market

Although the TOM was opened in 1978 it was not tested until 1986 when Gemmill and Dickens used the Black and Scholes model to test for mispricing.[9] Gemmill and Dickens argue that such tests examine both the validity of the model and the efficiency of the TOM and that they would have the following implications:
1. If the market was efficient then the model could not produce above normal profits for the user.
2. If the model is an accurate description of the way in which option prices are set and if the market is efficient, then it should produce good predictions of future option prices given the various parameters.
3. On the other hand if the model is good at predicting future option prices and the market *is not* efficient, then the model should produce above normal profits for the user.

Gemmill and Dickens used 5000 observations of option prices for 16 companies which were traded continuously from May 1978 to July 1983. They then analysed over 800 one-month spreads for 62 months and came to the following conclusions:
1. The model successfully identified under- and overpriced options.
2. The model successfully identified trading spreads which earned statistically significant profits above the risk-free rate.
3. Adjusting the model for dividends did not significantly improve its performance.
4. When direct dealing costs, brokerage and VAT were included they tended to help filter out the trades that were only marginally profitable and hence raised the overall profitability.
5. The bid–ask spread was so large that it converted significant profits into significant losses.
6. The market could not be described, as 'potential risk-free profits do not exceed transactions costs'.[10]

Since this study the use of the TOM has increased significantly and, given the growth in options trading, the results may no longer be completely valid.

Notes

1. F. Black and M. Scholes, 'The pricing of options and corporate liabilities', *Journal of Political Economy*, Vol. 81, May 1973.
2. H. Stoll, 'The relationship between put and call option prices', *Journal of Finance*, Vol. 24, December 1969.
3. J. Cox, S. Ross and M. Rubinstein, 'Option pricing: a simplified approach', *Journal of Financial Economics*, Vol. 7, September 1979.
   R. Rendleman and B. Bartter, 'Two stage option pricing', *Journal of Finance*, Vol. 34, 1979.
4. F. Black, 'Fact and fantasy in the use of options', *Financial Analysts' Journal*, Vol. 31, July 1975.
5. J. MacBeth and L. Merville, 'An empirical examination of the Black–Scholes call option pricing model', *Journal of Finance*, Vol. 34, December 1979.
6. R. Merton, 'Option pricing when underlying stock returns are discontinuous', *Journal of Financial Economics*, Vol. 4, January 1976.
7. R. Jarrow and A. Rudd, *Options*, Irwin 1983, Ch 9.
8. This analysis may be extended to calculate both the elasticity and the beta of an option. The elasticity of an option may be defined as,

$$n = (dC_t/dS_t)(S_t/C_t) = N(d_1)(S_t/C_t)$$

The elasticity of the option can be used to calculate the beta of the option,

$$\beta_c = n\beta_m$$

Obviously, like the hedge ratio m, both the elasticity and beta of the option need to be calculated almost on a continuous basis as all three measures are only valid for very small intervals of time. See R. Richardson and R. Singer, 'Instant option betas', *Financial Analysts' Journal*, Vol. 42, September 1986.
9. G. Gemmill and P. Dickens, 'An examination of the efficiency of the London Traded Options Market', *Applied Economics*, Vol. 18, 1986.
10. Ibid. p. 1008.

Questions

1. Explain and discuss the factors which may cause the Black–Scholes model to yield inaccurate results.
2. Using the Black–Scholes model, evaluate the following calls and puts and compare your answers with the market values given below and account for any discrepancies:

	Amstrad	Plessey	FTSE 100
Standard Deviation of Returns	0.53	0.38	0.21
Share Price	149p	253p	2419
Exercise Price	160p	260p	2450
Purchase Date	1/3/89	1/3/89	7/9/89
Expiry Date	21/6/89	21/11/89	21/12/89
Risk Free Rate	12.875%	12.875%	12.875%
Market Value of the Call	13p	27p	50p
Market Value of the Put	19p	24p	70p

3. Why might the use of the 90-day treasury bills be inappropriate for valuing options?
4. Explain and critically discuss the proposition that the Black–Scholes model demonstrates how an option's value is an explicit function of the characteristics of the underlying asset.

5. What criteria must be satisfied before options may be written on a company's shares and explain what these criteria are supposed to achieve?
6. How might the London Traded Options Market be described as being symmetrical?
7. Under what circumstances might a butterfly spread be used?
8. Why would a purchased straddle be preferred to a reverse butterfly?
9. What risks and rewards would an investor incur by writing calls on shares that he or she owns?
10. What sources of inaccuracy would you expect to find when using the Black–Scholes model to estimate the values of traded options?

8. Equities

Introduction

An equity or share is a certificate of ownership and confers on the holder specific rights and privileges which are determined by the Articles of Association (for example the voting rights attached to each class of share), the Memorandum of Association and the Companies Act of 1985 (see Chapter 2). The rights of shareholders may be summarized as follows:

1. Alteration of the 'objects' clause in the Memorandum of Association which determines the business activities of the company.
2. The election and removal of directors and auditors and the definition of their duties and remuneration (if any).
3. The approval or otherwise of the annual accounts and auditors' reports.
4. The authorization of the payment of the dividend (a residual and discretionary income after all the immediate liabilities of the company have been settled).
5. The authorization of an agreed merger.
6. The authorization of any change in share capital—rights issues, placements, scrip issues and repurchases.
7. The right to any residual assets on the liquidation of the company.

In theory, the shareholders have legal control of the company, but in practice this is most often exercised by the directors who between them may have a small minority of the shares with the acquiescence of the institutions which are the major shareholders.

Companies already listed on the Stock Exchange have two basic methods of raising additional equity capital:

1. A rights issue in which the existing shareholders may exercise their pre-emptive rights to subscribe to the new shares in proportion to those already held.
2. A placing in which selected shareholders (usually investing institutions) are invited to buy up to £15 million (this had been limited to £3 million until 1986) of additional equity.

Rights issues have become increasingly unpopular over the last decade or so. They have been criticized for being slow (a minimum of a 3-week offer is involved), cumbersome and expensive. Recent changes in the law and the regulations imposed by the Stock Exchange have allowed companies to ignore pre-emptive rights as long as the permission of the shareholders has been obtained. These changes have been made in response to the development of 'vendor' placings and 'back-door' rights issues during the eighties. A 'vendor placing' is the term given to placings which exceed the customary limit of about 15 per cent of the outstanding value of the company's existing equity. In November 1984 the Dee Corporation raised £180 million in the form of a placing. This was equivalent to some 45 per cent of the value of its existing equity. The new shares were placed with institutions at a discount of 14p to the market price of 174p. The additional capital was used to buy International Stores from BAT. Although there have been some notable examples of this practice (such as Saatchi and Saatchi, and Ward White in 1984) it does not appear to have become commonplace. 1984 was notable for the extension to the rights queue caused by the British Telecom privatization so that the brief emergence of the 'vendor placing' may have been due only to exceptional circumstances.

The practice of 'back-door' rights issues enabled companies to evade the requirements of pre-emptive rights by getting shareholders to agree to a paper issue (an expansion of the authorized capital which, if not being sold to raise additional capital, may be used in a share swap) for the purpose of taking over an investment trust. The trust's assets, which consist of shareholdings in other companies, are then liquidated thus releasing the capital needed by the acquiring corporation.

The new issue market

The new issue market is not a distinct and separate organization within the Stock Exchange, rather it is merely a tag given to the collection of processes by which companies acquire both a listing on the exchange and new equity capital. There are 3 distinct advantages to a company in using equity financing:

1. Ordinary shares do not carry fixed returns to investors and do not have to be redeemed.
2. As equity holders are the residual owners of the company, they constitute a loss-absorbing buffer in the event of liquidation and as such can improve the company's creditworthiness. This is a traditional view of the mix of corporate financing and is discussed at more length later in this chapter when the theories of Miller and Modigliani are discussed.
3. As the market for corporate debentures is rather thin in the UK, equities very often constitute a more liquid market and are thus easier to price and trade. In addition, equities have a greater appeal to many groups of investors as they generally carry a higher expected rate of return.

It is often argued that equities are more marketable as they are a better safeguard against inflation because they will reflect the rise in the nominal value of real assets during an inflationary period. On the other hand there are 3 disadvantages of using equity financing:

1. The issue of equities inevitably results in a spread in ownership initially. However, it also allows the accumulations of holdings and the transfer of ownership and control which may be unacceptable to the owner–managers of small and/or family firms.
2. The issue of equities, although it may improve the creditworthiness of the company, will also reduce the gearing (leverage) in its financing mix and also reduce the tax-shield effect of interest payments due to debt holders, thus lowering the potential rate of return to the owners.
3. Raising equity capital is invariably more expensive than raising debt capital.

There are 5 main methods of making a new issue:

1. *An introduction.* Strictly speaking an introduction to the Stock Exchange merely involves the acquisition of a listing and the permission for the company's existing shares to be traded on the Exchange. Hence, every company applying to the Stock Exchange by whatever process, involves an introduction. The Stock Exchange requires that there be at least 100 shareholders and that 25 per cent of the shares be held by the general public. For a quotation on the USM only 10 per cent of the shares must be in the possession of the general public. The advantages of an introduction for a company are lower costs and the benefit of having the market price of the shares before raising further capital. This second advantage is apparent when one considers the high probability of the underpricing of new assets involved in an offer for sale. This has sometimes been a serious issue of contention during the UK Government's privatization programme of the eighties.

2. *Placings.* The Stock Exchange permits companies to raise up to £15 million in the main market and £5 million in the USM when they come to the market through a placing (companies with existing quotations on the Exchange can also raise £15 million by means of a placing). Although the new capital is selectively marketed by the company through its issuing house (the financial institution, usually a merchant bank, which has been employed to organize the placing) to its clients, the Stock Exchange still requires that 25 per cent of the total shares be with the general public.

3. *An offer for sale.* This involves the disposal of all or part (at least 25 per cent) of the existing

shareholdings to the public and investing institutions through the Exchange. There is no limit on the size of capital that may be raised in an offer for sale by a company coming to the market for the fist time. For example, the British Government raised £3.9 billion before expenses on its sale of British Telecom.[1] This particular issue illustrates the previous point about the probability of mispricing the issue. BT was five-times oversubscribed and the premium on the part-paid issue price at the end of the first day's trading was 43p. It may be argued that this issue was seriously underpriced and that the nation undersold its asset by about £1.3 billion. On the other hand, others have described the issue as a resounding success as all the shares were sold. This sort of difference of opinion resurfaced in October 1987, when the sale of the Government's remaining holding in BP was adjudged a disaster because the issue was greatly undersubscribed leaving a large proportion of the shares with the underwriters who had undertaken to 'insure' the issue.

On average, the underwriters charge a fee equal to 2 per cent of the gross proceeds of the issue and in return guarantee to buy any shares not demanded by the investing public and institutions. Generally, this insurance is organized by a leading merchant bank which will sub-contract a proportion of the insurance to other sub-underwriters for about half of the fee. The remainder is shared between the principal underwriter (about 0.75 per cent) and the broker (0.25 per cent) in the issue. New or secondary issue underwriters have rarely had to take up undersubscribed issues as the timings of such are usually gauged to ensure the full take-up of the shares on offer. The practice of underwriting before the reforms of October 1986 has been described as a method of compensation for the high transactions costs of fixed commissions for large institutional clients. Since the Big Bang the disappearance of fixed commissions has removed the necessity for offering such compensation.[2]

However, the BP secondary issue may also be described as a success for the market as the Government was able to collect the intended capital sum from the underwriters for its divestment. Furthermore, it might be argued that this issue was overpriced and that the nation was able to sell an effectively overpriced collection of assets.

4.   *An offer by subscription (prospectus issue)*. This type of issue involves the issuing company itself offering the shares to the public. The issue may or may not be underwritten and the issuing company may or may not engage the services of a broker for advice and/or to organize the insurance of the issue.

5.   *An offer for sale by tender*. The tender offer involves an offer to the public to bid for the shares but with a minimum subscription price. After the closing date, the organizers will set a 'striking price' which is best for the company.

However, the organizers must ensure as in all other types of issue that the ownership is spread wide enough to create a liquid market. Hence, the tender issue will not necessarily eliminate underpricing although substantially reducing it renders it not too popular with those who like to 'stag' new issues. 'Stagging' is the process by which investors speculate on new issues. New shares are applied for on the expectation that the issue will be underpriced and hence a profit might be made on the difference between the immediate market price and the issue or striking price. For example, the tender issue by the Virgin Group in 1986 resulted in a striking price of 140p (with a minimum price of 100p) and at the end of the first day's trading the market price was still 140p.

On the other hand, the tender offer by Hillsdown Holdings resulted in a stagging profit as the price at the end of the first day of trading was 33p higher than the striking price of 145p (minimum 120p). Some of the early privatization issues such as Britoil and Cable and Wireless were tender issues, but since 1983 this practice has been discontinued.

Table 8.1   New issue methods in the main market. January 1983–March 1986

Amount of new capital	Placings		Offer for sale		Tender		Subscription		Total	
	£ million	(no.)	£ million	(no.)	£ million	(no.)	£ million	(no.)	£ million	(no.)
0m–3m	36.3	(14)	10.2	(4)	5.3	(2)	—		51.8	(20)
3m–5m	3.6	(1)	45.6	(11)	31.5	(8)	5.0	(1)	85.7	(21)
(%) costs[a]	16.5		24.0		16.4		−21.2[b]			
5m–10m	—		170.8	(24)	48.9	(6)	10.0	(1)	229.7	(31)
(%) costs			10.9		17.5		n/a			
10m+	—		5230.1	(25)	815.8	(11)	37.8	(3)	6083.7	(39)
(%) costs			10.0		11.0		−1.4[b]			
Total	39.9	(15)	5456.7	(64)	901.5	(27)	52.8	(5)	6450.9	(111)
(%) costs	16.5		13.6		14.3					

[a] These percentage costs are for new capital issues up to £5 million.
[b] The negative percentage costs for the subscription issues represent a large measure of overpricing which more than compensated for the fees charged by the organizers.
Source: *Bank of England Quarterly*, December 1986, p. 536, Table D.

Raising additional capital and adjusting issued share capital

A company with a listing on the market (either the main or USM market) may return for more equity capital from time to time. Additional capital is raised by either rights issues or placings. Existing shareholders have pre-emptive rights (Companies Act 1980 S17) to buy new shares in proportion to their existing holdings. These rights may be waived by the shareholders at a general meeting so that the new capital may be raised by means of a placing.

Rights issues require a minimum subscription period of 3 weeks to allow existing shareholders the chance to take up their rights. A rights issue not only affects the amount of equity capital at the disposal of the company but also the price of the existing shares. For example, in October 1988 Polly Peck made a rights issue of 1 new share for every 4 held. The market price of the existing shares on the day of the issue was 310p and the subscription price for the new shares was 255p. Suppose an investor held 1,000 shares in Polly Peck. This investment was worth £3,100. The investor has the pre-emptive right to buy 250 of the new shares at 255p each, an additional investment of £637.50.

$$1{,}000 \text{ old shares at 310p each} = £3{,}100.00$$

$$250 \text{ new shares at 255p each} = £\ \ \ 637.50$$

$$\text{Total investment} \qquad = £3{,}737.50$$

The intended ex-rights price may be estimated by dividing the total investment by the total number of shares held:

$$\text{Ex-rights price} = (3100 + 637.50)/(1000 + 250) = 299\text{p}$$

Therefore, if the investor refuses the offer to buy a further 250 shares, the price of his or her existing shares will fall by 11p each.

However, the investor may sell his or her rights to compensate for the fall in the value of the investment, $3{,}100 - (1{,}000)(2.99) = £110$. The value of the right is determined by the difference between the ex-rights price and the subscription price, 299p − 255p = 44p. If all 250 rights are sold then the investor will receive (£0.44) 250 = £110, which compensates for the loss in value of the existing shares.

Rights issues are invariably underwritten in order to ensure that the issuing company receives the additional capital needed. However, it is quite feasible for the issuing company to take the risk that the issue will be undersubscribed, or the company can offer the shares at 'deep discount' to the current market price so that there is little risk that the market price will fall below the subscription price (in which case there would be no incentive for any investor to buy the new shares).

Given the risk associated with the possibility that the market price may fall below the subscription price the timing of a rights issue is extremely important. An example of an unfortunately managed rights issue was that of STC in March 1985. The company's shares had reached a peak in the market in 1984 at over 350p but had fallen quite sharply after this. Companies invariably prefer to time their rights issues to coincide with the annual results and hopefully float the issue on a tide of good news. However, companies are not entirely free to time their issues as the Bank of England imposes a queue when it is concerned that the market may be faced with too many cash calls. The result of this practice by the Bank of England was to force STC to make its rights issue two weeks before the declaration of its 1984 results. In addition, the company didn't have much good news to declare. Profits were static and the market price of its shares was already falling. As a consequence STC explained the issue in terms of the need to maintain research and to cut its level of borrowing. In addition the rewards from this additional investment were not forecast to occur until 1986. The offer was 1 for 5 with a subscription price of 190p (when the market price was 234p). This should have resulted in an ex-rights price of $[(5)(234) + 190]/6 = 227p$ and therefore a value for each right of 227p − 190p = 37p.

However, the market took the news rather badly and cut the price of the existing STC share by 34p on the day of announcement. Three weeks later on 25 March 1985, the price of the old shares was 198p and the rights to buy the new shares were trading at 5p (the apparent shortfall of 3p being caused by the fact that the old shares were due a dividend while the new ones were not). This implied an underlying ex-rights price of 195p after the old shares had gone ex-dividend. Those investors (assume a holding of 1000 shares) who took up their rights would have seen the value of their investment fall from 1000 (2.34) = £2,340 to 1000 (1.98) = £1,980 and would have had to find a further 200 (190) = £380 to invest in the company. Those that refused to take up their rights could have offset their losses by selling their 200 rights at 5p each; i.e. £10. In the months that followed, the news from the company failed to improve and the market price fell below 100p in 1985.

A scrip issue is the alteration of the number of shares in issue. With the shareholders' approval the company converts retained profits into equity by issuing new shares. It is generally thought that highly priced shares are unpopular among investors and that the liquidity of the market for the company's equity can be improved by effectively lowering the price. For example Hanson Plc (formerly Hanson Trust) made two scrip issues during the period 1985–88 when the market price was sustained above 300p.

Thus far we have implicitly valued the right in terms of the new shares. However, it is feasible to value the right in terms of the old shares. As rights are issued in the form of a right for so many old shares held we can calculate the impact of the fractional right on the old share value. In the case of Polly Peck used previously, the company offered 1 right for every 4 old shares held. Put another way, each old share carried with it one-quarter of a right. Therefore taking the data for the day of issue, the market price was 310p and the subscription price was 255p. The value of one complete right was calculated as 44p. Therefore the fractional right attached to each old share is 44p/4 = 11p. A quick formula for the calculation of the value of the fractional right is as follows:

$$v_{r,f} = (P_{o,c} - P_s)/(n + 1)$$

where $v_{r,f}$ = value of the fractional right
$\quad P_{o,c}$ = price of the old share 'cum rights'
$\quad P_s$ = subscription price of the new shares
$\quad n$ = number of old shares needed to acquire 1 right

Hence in the Polly Peck example,

$$V_{r,f} = (310p - 255p)/(4+1) = 11p$$

There is one further way of looking at and estimating the value of a right (both complete and fractional). This is to treat the right as a call option which confers the right to purchase the share at an exercise price equal to the subscription price. We may use the Black and Scholes option pricing model developed in Chapter 7. The following equations need to be estimated:

$$d_1 = [\ln(P/EX) + (rf + \sigma^2/2)t]/\sigma\sqrt{t}$$

$$d_2 = d_1 - \sigma\sqrt{t}$$

$$C = (P)N(d_1) - (EX)N(d_2)(e^{(-rf)t})$$

where P is the market price (310p), EX is the exercise or subscription price (255p), rf is the risk-free rate of interest (0.12 per cent), σ is the standard deviation of the security which in the case of Polly Peck is (0.59), t is the time to expiry as a fraction of a year ($21/365 = 0.058$), C is the estimated value of the call which in this case is the value of a complete right, and e is the natural logarithm base (2.7183). The terms ($N(d_1)$ and $N(d_2)$) are cumulative probabilities of a normally distributed unit variable.

$$d_1 = [\ln(310/255) + (0.12 + 0.59^2/2)(0.058)]/0.59\sqrt{0.058}$$

$$= (0.195 + 0.017)/0.142$$

$$= 0.212/0.142 = 1.492$$

$$d_2 = 1.492 - 0.142 = 1.35$$

$$e^{(-rf)t} = 2.7183^{(-0.12)(0.058)} = 0.9931$$

Using Table A1.2 (Appendix 1) we can find the values of $N(d_1)$ and $N(d_2)$,

$$N(d_1) = 1 - 0.0681 = 0.9319$$

$$N(d_2) = 1 - 0.0885 = 0.9115$$

hence the value of the call is estimated as follows:

$$C = 310(0.9319) - 255(0.9115)(0.9931)$$

$$= 288.89 - 230.83$$

$$= 58.06p$$

Galai and Schneller[3] have shown that the value of the fractional right is obtained by dividing the call value by $(n+1)$. Therefore, the value of the fractional right in this example is 58.06p/$(4+1) = 11.61$. This result is marginally bigger than the previous traditional estimate of 11p. This is basically a reflection of the potential profitable benefit of a call.

In 1979 Marsh[4] published a study which attempted to assess the price effects of rights issues and consequently the semi-strong efficiency of the London Stock Exchange. This consisted of testing the validity of two competing hypotheses. The first, which can conveniently be called the traditional theory, is known as the 'price pressure hypothesis', and holds that rights issues will cause a temporary depression in the price as the issue has increased the supply of shares. The second, which may be thought of as the 'efficient markets' theory, is called the 'substitution hypothesis'. This asserts that the demand for a company's equity may be assumed to be flat (perfectly elastic) for all practical purposes and hence increases in supply will have no discernible effect on the price. Two similar studies for the NYSE produced somewhat contradictory results. The first, by Scholes,[5] found no evidence for the price pressure hypothesis in 696 issues made between 1926 and 1966. The second, by Smith,[6] found a small price fall of 1.4 per cent in the 2 months before the issue which was followed by a compensating rise in the 2 months after the issue. This result has been interpreted as indicating a small degree of price pressure. However, it would be fair to conclude that neither of these studies has shown the NYSE to be less than semi-strong efficient.

Marsh conducted a cross-sectional test on a sample of 997 rights issues that were between 1962 and 1975. In addition, a time series test was carried out on a random sample of 254 of these issues. Marsh found that on average there was a fall of 0.9 per cent for a short period after the shares went ex-rights. On the other hand, he found that the shares more than recovered (1.8 per cent) during the following month. Therefore, as in the Smith study,[6] the results indicated a marginal amount of price pressure which could not be used as a basis for trading on rights issues announcements as the effect would be swamped by transactions costs.

Marsh[4] has also used the Black and Scholes option valuation model to assess the underwriting fees charged in the UK stock market during the period 1962 to 1975. Marsh notes that some 90 per cent of all rights issues during this period were underwritten and that apart from the principal underwriter (usually the organizing merchant bank) there were invariably 100–200 sub-underwriters. During this period there were 671 rights issues known to have been underwritten of which only 35 resulted in a loss for the underwriters. This loss (profit) may be calculated by subtracting the 'loss from taking up unsubscribed shares' from the 'fees paid'. The loss from taking up the unsubscribed shares is calculated as the difference between the market price on the last day of the offer and the subscription price,

$$n(P_{i,m} - P_{i,s})$$

where n is equal to the number of shares taken up by the underwriters, $P_{i,m}$ is the market price on the last day of the offer, $P_{i,s}$ is the subscription price. This will be partially or totally compensated by the underwriting fees F, and the return may be expressed as a percentage of the subscription price as follows,

$$\{[n(P_{i,m} - P_{i,s}) - F]/P_{i,s}\}(100/1)$$

The average loss in the 35 cases was 4.2 per cent. The mean underwriting fee was 1.4 per cent of the issue's nominal value. This means that looking at the process in an ex-post fashion, the underwriters made a return of 1.11 per cent.

However, this says nothing about the under- or overpricing of their insurance services. Marsh argued that the only way in which an objective judgement could be made was to compare actual fees charged with those predicted by an ex-ante model. The one chosen was the option pricing model developed by Black and Scholes. On the assumption that the fees charged for underwriting rights issues were a form of call option premium, Marsh compared the fees with the fractional values predicted by the model. His results indicated that in 88 per cent of the 539 (this represents a subset of the sample of 671 referred to previously, the missing 132 issues arising because the dates of the underwriting contracts could not be firmly established so that they were excluded from the tests) issues studied, the underwriters earned positive excess returns. This conclusion of overpricing was tempered by the observation that the underwriting fee may include payment for services in addition to the traditional insurance component of underwriting.

Before looking at the idea that the overpricing of underwriting contracts as payment for other services it is worth noting that Marsh observed that 'bear' markets tended to lead to marginally higher excess returns to underwriters, while no large or small company effects could be discerned. On the other hand Marsh did find that there was a statistically significant drop in the excess returns after 1968. However, the results did not suggest any paramount reason for this shift.

Marsh observed that companies tend to retain the services of their financial advisers over extended periods and therefore the underwriting is but one of many such financial services. Hence, changing underwriters could mean substantial costs as all the other services might have to be shifted to some new institution. However, given the comparatively low-cost alternative to underwriting—deep discount issues—the insistence of corporate financial officers on using underwriters suggests some traditional but illogical practice which is not going to change overnight.[7]

In the case of rights issues and underwriting there seems to be a perpetual divide between academic analysts and theorists and the practitioners. For example, Newbould argued in 1971:

> Some companies incur unnecessary underwriting costs, presumably because of a lack of appreciation of the mechanics of a rights issue. ... In a rights issue, of course, there is no loss to the company, investors or underwriters, unless the rights price becomes negative (for example, because of a substantial general decline in share prices). Since the issue price can be fixed so that it is virtually impossible for the rights price to become negative, companies which pay underwriting commission on a rights issue are making an expensive *ex gratia* payment.[8]

It is worth remembering that a deeply discounted rights issue is merely one which has had some of the qualities of a scrip issue added to it. The end result will be no different whether the shareholder takes up his or her rights or sells them in the market; the end value of the holding will remain unchanged. Hence, to issue new shares at a substantial discount to the market price and then underwrite it would appear to be a case of double indemnity in which the primary insurer is assured of a very small probability of having to make a compensation payment.

Interpreting published financial data on equities

The return on any form of investment may be defined as follows,

$$r_{i,t+1} = (P_{i,t+1} - P_{i,t} + D_{i,t+1})/P_{i,t}$$

where r is the return on security i in time $t+1$, P is the price of security i in periods t and $t+1$, and D is the income which may accrue to that security during period $t+1$. This definition was first developed and used in Chapter 2 and it can be applied directly without alteration to equities. As in Chapter 2 it is worth stressing that for predictive valuation purposes $P_{i,t+1}$ and $D_{i,t+1}$ are uncertain quantities. However, the principal source of public information are the share quotes published in the press every day and these tend to concentrate on measures other than the holding period return described above. The most informative are those published by the *Financial Times*, (Fig. 8.1).

If we take one of the quotes in Fig. 8.1 as illustrative we may look in more detail at the information which is published:

(1)	(2)	(3)	(4)	(5)	(6)	(7)	(8)	(9)	(10)
£11$\frac{15}{16}$	947	Imp. Chem.	£1	£10$\frac{7}{8}$		41.0	2.4	5.0	9.8

(1) High price 1988; this is the highest level which the share price reached in 1988.

CHEMICALS, PLASTICS

£35$\frac{3}{8}$	£25	Akzo Fl.20............	£35$\frac{1}{4}$	$-\frac{1}{8}$	vQ33%	3.5	5.3	5.4
352	288	Alida Holdings...... γ	340	−2	9.25	2.8	3.6	13.2
144	106	Allied Colloids 10p... β	135	−3	2.3	Φ	2.3	Φ
65	51	✠Amer Plastic Tech $0.001 γ	53	−2	LQ2.5c	Φ	2.9	Φ
506	441	Amersham Intl...... β	455xd	−1	10.0	Φ	2.9	Φ
*42	27	Astra Holdings 5p.. γ	33	......	K0.87	3.2	3.5	13.5
£85$\frac{3}{4}$	£73$\frac{1}{4}$	BASF AG DM50.....	£80$\frac{5}{16}$	$-3\frac{13}{16}$	vQ20%	Φ	3.9	Φ
159	130	BTP 10p............ γ	159	+1	6.2	Φ	5.3	Φ
£93$\frac{3}{4}$	£79$\frac{5}{8}$	Bayer AG DM 50.....	£90$\frac{1}{4}$xd	$-\frac{1}{8}$	vQ20%	2.3	3.5	12.4
183	148	Blagden Inds......... γ	178	+3	7.7	1.6	5.8	(13.1)
158	118	Brent Chems 10p... β	157	......	5.2	1.9	4.4	14.3
70	51	✠Cambridge Isotope 1c.. γ	56	......	LQ0.9c	6.2	1.0	18.2
227	169	Canning (W.)........ β	225	−1	5.3	3.5	3.1	11.1
189	172	Chemoxy Intl. 10p. γ	173	+1	L4.9	2.7	3.8	12.2
347	285	Coalite Group....... β	332xd	+4	9.8	Φ	3.9	Φ
358	296	Coates Bros.......... β	319	......	7.7	3.7	3.2	10.0
27	21	Cory (Horace) 5p.... γ	27	......	0.75	1.2	3.7	29.0
211	173	Croda Int. 10p...... β	206	......	9.0	1.8	5.8	12.4
54	50	✠Delmar Group..... γ	53	......	2.15	2.4	5.4	10.1
118	83	Doeflex 10p......... γ	83	......	3.45	2.6	5.5	9.4
194	147	Ellis & Everard..... β	194	......	†h4.67	2.7	3.2	15.1
£11$\frac{7}{8}$	975	Engelhard U.S.$1.00..	£11$\frac{3}{4}$	......	52c	−	2.4	−
190	150	Evode Group......... β	189	−1	4.44	2.8	3.1	15.4
274	206	Foseco Minsep...... β	260	......	10.6	1.7	5.4	(12.5)
88	70	✠Gaynor Group 10p... γ	83	......	†2.67	2.7	4.3	11.1
85	68	✠Granyte Surface 10p γ	76	−2	3.0	2.4	5.3	10.7
255	226	Halstead (J.) 10p... γ	236	......	†6.5	3.4	3.7	10.6
£28$\frac{7}{8}$	£24$\frac{1}{2}$	Hercules Inc‖..........	£27$\frac{1}{2}$	$+\frac{1}{8}$	Q$1.60	−	0.3	−
249	136	Hickson Intl......... β	240	......	5.63	2.8	3.1	15.4
£89$\frac{1}{2}$	£78$\frac{5}{8}$	Hoechst AG DM50...	£85$\frac{1}{8}$	$-\frac{1}{4}$	Q20%	1.9	3.7	−
£368	£280	Do.Fin.10pcUn.Ln....	£368	......	Q10%	−	2.7	−
£11$\frac{15}{16}$	947	Imp. Chem. £1...... α	£10$\frac{7}{8}$	......	41.0	2.4	5.0	9.8
439	350	Laporte Inds. 50p.. α	436	−2	12.0	2.3	3.7	13.5
*257	157	Leigh Interests 5p.. β	248	−5	5.65	Φ	3.1	Φ
*197	137	Do. 6pc Cv. Red. Prf...	196xr	+11	6%	−	4.1	−
149	118	MTM 5p............. β	143	−2	3.0	3.2	2.8	13.9
697	612	Montedison ADR L1000.	612	......	4%	Φ	0.3	Φ
63	51	Morceau Hldgs.......	63	......	♦1.0	−	2.1	−
£18$\frac{1}{2}$	£11$\frac{3}{4}$	Novo Inds. 'B' Kr. 20..	£18$\frac{1}{2}$	$+\frac{1}{16}$	vQ20%	4.7	1.8	12.0
£21$\frac{7}{8}$	£14$\frac{1}{4}$	Perstorp AB 'B' Sk10..	£21$\frac{1}{2}$	......	Q24%	4.9	1.0	20.0
166	130	Plysu.................. γ	163	......	2.3	Φ	1.9	Φ
96	88	✠Porvair 2p.......... γ	91	......	L2.34	3.8	3.4	(7.4)
74	43	Ransom (Wm.) 10p... γ	57	......	†1.15	2.3	2.7	21.7
207	173	Rentokil 10p........ β	200	−1	3.28	3.4	2.2	16.8
£169	£111	Schering AG DM50..	£162$\frac{3}{4}$	$+\frac{3}{4}$	Q24%	2.7	2.3	15.8
172	121	Sutcliffe Speakman.. γ	139	......	−	−	−	22.4
75	58	Thurgar Bardex 10p.. γ	69	−1	2.25	2.4	4.3	12.6
63	58	✠Transrap Hldgs. 10p γ	61	......	b2.0	2.0	4.4	15.6
123	110	Viking Pack. 10p... γ	115	−1	†3.5	2.0	4.1	16.2
618	500	Wardle Storeys 10p.. β	603	......	†9.0	3.6	2.0	18.7
56	36	✠Wentworth 10p... γ	43	......	1.75	1.7	5.4	14.6
330	270	Wolstenholme Rink.. γ	330	......	10.25	3.1	4.1	10.5
266	213	Yorkshire Chems.... ?	252	+1	7.0	3.2	3.7	10.9
133	106	Yule Catto 10p...... γ	130	......	3.0	2.7	3.1	15 0

Figure 8.1 The *Financial Times* Share Service (25/6/1988).

(2) Low price 1988; this is the lowest price seen during 1988.
(3) Name of the security or stock; this is the name of the issuing company and may indicate whether the security is something other than an equity.
(4) Nominal price of the share; this is the nominal value which is used for accounting purposes in the annual accounts. If this figure doesn't appear, as in the case of Amersham International, the nominal value is always 25p.

The foreign companies traded have the nominal values expressed in the native national currencies; for example, the shares of Dutch chemicals company Akzo have a nominal value of 20 florins. In some cases, as in that of Imperial Chemical Industries, this nominal value is followed by one of three greek letters; α, β, γ. These refer to the level designated by SEAQ. The α shares are invariably the most heavily traded and the γ shares the least traded of the three (those without designations tend to be either the securities of small companies or those of infrequently traded foreign companies such as Hoescht AG).

(5) Market price of the share at the end of the previous day's trading.
(6) Price change on the day.

(7) Dividend net of basic rate personal income tax; the cross in front of the dividend indicates that the interim dividend has 'since been increased or resumed'. At the time of this quote the basic rate of income tax was 25 per cent so that we can calculate the gross dividend payment. The net dividend (ND) of 41p is equal to 0.75 (gross dividend, GD), therefore,

$$GD = ND/0.75 = 41/0.75 = 54.67p$$

(8) Coverage ratio, this is the earnings per share (EPS) divided by the gross dividend,

$$coverage = EPS/GD, \ EPS = GD \ (coverage)$$

therefore we have,

$$EPS = 54.67(2.4) = 131.2p$$

It is worth noting that dividends are paid to shareholders net of basic rate income tax. Therefore, should the shareholder be subject to a higher rate of tax he or she will have to make additional payments to the Inland Revenue.

(9) Gross dividend yield ($GDY\%$); this is the gross dividend expressed as a percentage of the market price (P),

$$GDY\% = (GD/P)100$$

therefore we have,

$$GDY\% = (54.67p/1087.5p) \times 100 = 5.03$$

This result is marginally different from the value given in the quote but may be explained by arithmetic error.

(10) Price/earnings (P/E) ratio; this is based on the latest annual earnings and is calculated by dividing the market share price by the last declared figure for earnings per share. In this case the value is 9.8 and calculated on the previous year's EPS. The EPS calculated above is based on half-year figures as the net dividend figure is only an interim rather than a full annual payment. However, using the P/E ratio we can calculate the previous annual earnings per share as follows:

$$P/E = P/EPS,$$

$$EPS = P/(P/E),$$

therefore we have,

$$EPS = 1087.5/9.8 = 110.97p.$$

However, it should be noted that P/E ratios are calculated on a 'net' distribution basis in which EPS is calculated after taxation and without relief from advanced corporation tax. Hence the figure of 110.97p calculated for the last published results is not strictly comparable with that (131.2p) calculated for the half-yearly figures.

The P/E ratio may be interpreted as the price investors are willing to pay for a unit of earnings. In the example of ICI the ratio was 9.8 and so we may assume that investors were willing to pay 9.8p for 1p of earnings. Looking at Fig. 8.1 we can see a wide range of P/E ratios for the chemicals and plastics firms listed by the *Financial Times*; the highest is 29.0 and the lowest is 5.4. This ratio gives investors a common yardstick to measure the attitude of the market as a whole to all companies regardless of size or industry by reducing the comparison to the simple question 'How much is the market willing to pay for a unit of earnings?'.

There have been several attempts to build predictive models which describe the relationship between share prices and accounting variables, prominent among which has been the price–earnings ratio. One of the more interesting examples of this genre was that published by Whitbeck and Kisor in 1963.[33] They tested a set of assumptions about the attitudes of investors and hence the impact of the P/E ratio. They advanced the proposition that investors prefer high earnings growth rates, low variability of those growth rates, and high dividend payout ratios. There is nothing revolutionary in these assumptions. After all, the first two merely restate the assumptions made earlier in Chapter 2 that investors prefer a higher expected return at the lowest possible risk. However, the third assumption is more contentious. It reflects one side of the debate concerning the importance or otherwise of dividends in the process of the market's valuation of companies, and is discussed in more detail later in this chapter. Whitbeck and Kisor made the observations on 135 shares quoted on the NYSE. They produced a multiple regression equation as follows:

$$P/E = 8.2 + 1.5X_1 + 6.7X_2 - 0.2X_3$$

where X_1 is the forcasted earnings growth rate, X_2 is the dividend payout ratio and X_3 is the standard deviation of the historical earnings growth rate. They tested their model by observing the difference between the theoretical and market values of a firm's P/E ratio and the share price progress in the subsequent three months. They found that where the market value was 85 per cent or less of that predicted by the model, shares outperformed the market. In the opposite case where the market value was greater by 15 per cent or more than the theoretical value of the P/E ratio they found that shares underperformed the market. However, for shares whose market values were in the range 15 per cent either side of the theoretical value, the predictive power of the model was weak.

A British example of this kind of exercise was published by Weaver and Hall in 1967.[34] Their model set out to predict the mean dividend yield. They proposed that it was a function of the mean payout ratio, the predicted short-term earnings and long-term dividend growth rates, the variability of the historical earnings growth rates and the historical earnings growth rate.

Many of the published regression models are quite successful in analysing past data. However, this success does not seem to have been repeated in terms of prediction and their use as bases for mechanical trading rules. One of the major difficulties identified by Whitbeck and Kisor was the need to continually reset the model parameters over time. This requirement alone would preclude most individual investors from using such models. Furthermore, it is logical that models which can yield an investment strategy capable of beating a process of random selection and 'buy-and-hold' would not be published until they ceased to be profitable for their creators.

However, the *P/E* ratio still retains considerable popularity among investors. As suggested above, we can be fairly confident that the basic determinants of the size of the *P/E* ratio are the expected future earnings and their associated risk. Traditionally, a low ratio is interpreted as indicating that investors as a whole expect rather low levels of future earnings or that those earnings are subject to a high level of risk. Conversely, a high *P/E* ratio is presumed to show that the market expects high and/or non-volatile earnings from the company. However, in a semi-strong efficient market as the International Stock Exchange in London we should not expect to find any evidence for *P/E* ratio being a reliable predictor of returns or volatility of returns. It is far safer to regard the *P/E* ratio as an indicator of market sentiment about the future prospects of a company rather than a basis for a systematic forecasting technique of future earnings.

Equity valuation

It is time now to look at the sections of financial theory which are relevant for the valuation of securities. Initially, the techniques will be presented in a world of certainty. When the basic concepts have been established the assumption of certainty will be removed.

Since the privatization of BT in 1984 the problem of company valuation and the pricing of shares has received much informed and uninformed comment. Why did Euro Tunnel price its 'units' (each unit consists of a share and warrant in both Euro Tunnel PLC and Euro Tunnel SA) at 3.50 rather than 2 or 4 or any other price? Why initially did the stock market react favourably to the increased dividend declared by Lloyds Bank after it had made a loss of £224 million in the financial year 1986–87? A daily newspaper (26 February 1988) reported 'Despite the losses Sir Jeremy has sanctioned a 10% increase in the dividend which will be paid from reserves. That more than anything stopped the shares from sliding. However, after an initial 5p rise they still managed to fall a touch below today's opening 270p on further consideration of the results.'[9] 'On further consideration' it can be seen that the fact that the dividend had to be paid out of reserves reduced the amount of assets available to the bank for investment. Hence, not only did this decision reduce the value of the company (i.e. post-dividend compared to pre-dividend), but by reducing the capital the company could invest, it reduced the future earnings that could be expected by the shareholders. Hence, a distribution of dividends from the company's reserves may be more likely to reduce prices than to support them.

In order to try to make sense of the potential multitude of factors that might be considered in valuing shares we need a theoretical framework which, although it may be (and is) criticized, will give the discussion and analysis a starting point. The point of departure is the general valuation model that has been developed out of discounted cash flow (DCF) techniques.

$$P_0 = C/(1+r) + C/(1+r)^2 + C/(1+r)^3 + \ldots + C/(1+r)^n \qquad (8.1)$$

$$= \Sigma C/(1+r)^t \qquad (8.2)$$

where n is the number of periods under consideration (anywhere between 1 and infinity), C is the cash flow, t is an individual observation, and r is the required rate of return for the security under analysis. In Eqs (8.1) and (8.2) two simplifying assumptions have been made. The first is that the required rate of return is constant over the period under consideration. The second is that the cash flow is constant over the whole period and that C represents both dividend payments and capital gains (losses) where necessary. However, these assumptions may be easily dropped although the equation loses a certain amount of neatness,

$$P_0 = C_1/(1+r_1) + C_2/(1+r_1)(1+r_2) + \ldots + C_n/(1+r_1)(1+r_2)\ldots(1+r_n) \qquad (8.3)$$

This basic model postulates that the current price (P_0) is a present value and is determined by the discounted future income that the share earns. As this model stands it is rather cumbersome even with the simplifying assumption of a constant required rate of return. It may be simplified by assuming that the share is held to infinity. Hence the cash flow term must be redefined as dividends only and replaced by D. Equation (8.1) may be written as follows,

$$P_0 = D[/(1+r) + 1/(1+r)^2 + 1/(1+r)^3 + \ldots + 1/(1+r)^n] \qquad (8.4)$$

multiply both sides of the equation by $(1+r)$,

$$P_0(1+r) = D[1 + 1/(1+r) + 1/(1+r)^2 + \ldots + 1/(1+r)^{n-1}] \qquad (8.5)$$

subtract Eq. (8.5) from Eq. (8.4),

$$P_0(1+r-1) = D[1 - 1/(1+r)^n] \qquad (8.6)$$

as n approaches infinity $1/(1+r)^n$ approaches zero and so Eq. (8.6) simplifies to,

$$rP_0 = D \qquad (8.7)$$

rearranging,

$$P_0 = D/r \qquad (8.8)$$

and,

$$r = D/P_0 \qquad (8.9)$$

It is worth noting here that Eq. (8.9) is the reciprocal of the P/E ratio.

However, it is unlikely that dividends will remain static to infinity. One way of removing this restrictive assumption is to assume a constant rate of growth (g) of dividends into the future. Although this replacement assumption seems rather unrealistic, it does approximate what many corporate finance officers would like to achieve. Therefore, Eq. (8.3) will be modified as follows,

$$P_0 = D_0(1+g)/(1+r) + D_0(1+g)^2/(1+r)^2 + D_0(1+g)^3/(1+r)^3 + \ldots + D_0(1+g)^n/(1+r)^n \qquad (8.10)$$

This simplifies to,

$$P_0 = D_0[(1+g)/(1+r) + (1+g)^2/(1+r)^2 + \ldots + (1+g)^n/(1+r)^n] \qquad (8.11)$$

Multiply both sides by $(1+r)/(1+g)$,

$$P_0(1+r)/(1+g) = D_0[1 + (1+g)/(1+r) + \ldots + (1+g)^{n-1}/(1+r)^{n-1}] \qquad (8.12)$$

subtract Eq. (8.12) from Eq. (8.11),

$$P_0\{[(1+r)/(1+g)] - 1\} = D_0\{1 - (1+g)^n/(1+r)^n\} \qquad (8.13)$$

Assuming $r > g$, as n approaches infinity $(1+g)^n/(1+r)^n$ approaches zero,

$$P_0\{[(1+r) - (1+g)]/(1+g)\} = D_0 \qquad (8.14)$$

This simplifies as follows,

$$(1 + r - 1 - g) = D_0(1+g)/P_0 \qquad (8.15)$$

As $D_0(1+g)$ is equal to D_1,

$$r - g = D_1/P_0 \qquad (8.16)$$

and by rearrangement,

$$P_0 = D_1/(r-g) \qquad (8.17)$$

$$r = (D_1/P_0) + g \qquad (8.18)$$

Despite corporate financial officers' best intentions, firms tend to go through various stages of growth. Most recently, we have seen the rapid growth of the electronics companies tend to slow down (Fig. 8.2).

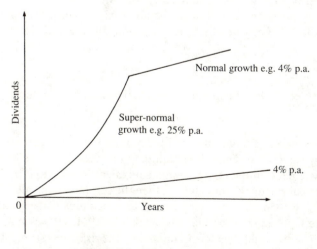

Figure 8.2 Corporate growth rates.

Equation (8.10) or (8.11) may be adjusted to incorporate changing growth rates as follows,

$$P_0 = \Sigma D_0(1+gs)^t/(1+r)^t + D_{n+1}/(r-gn)(1/(1+r)^n \qquad (8.19)$$

The first term on the right-hand side is the sum of the dividend income for n periods which has grown at a compound rate of $(1+gs)$, the 'super-normal' growth rate. The second term on the right-hand side of Eq. (8.19) is the value in period n of the dividend income to infinity which is assumed to grow at the 'normal' rate, $(1+gn)$, discounted back to the present. For example, suppose we have a company from which we expect a dividend growth of 25 per cent for the next 5 years. From then on a 'normal' rate of dividend growth of 5 per cent is expected. If this year's dividend was 10p and the shareholders' required rate of return is 10 per cent, what is the present value of the share?

Present Value of Dividends

$10(1.25)/(1.1)$	$= 11.36\text{p}$
$10(1.25)^2/(1.1)^2$	$= 12.91\text{p}$
$10(1.25)^3/(1.1)^3$	$= 14.67\text{p}$
$10(1.25)^4/(1.1)^4$	$= 16.68\text{p}$
$10(1.25)^5/(1.1)^5$	$= 18.95\text{p}$
Sum	$= 74.58\text{p}$
$[18.95(1.05)/(0.1-0.05)][1/(1.1)^5]$	$= 247.08\text{p}$
Present Value of the Share	$= 321.66\text{p}$

Having outlined the basic techniques for evaluating securities, we may now remove the assumption of certainty. This may be done by two methods. The first is to calculate the risk-adjusted discount rate and apply it to the unadjusted cash flows. In the case of securities we may use the capital asset pricing model developed in Chapter 5,

$$E(r_i) = rf + \beta(E(r_m) - rf) \qquad (8.20)$$

where the expected return on security i, $(E(r_i))$ is determined by multiplying the security's beta coefficient by the market risk premium and adding the result to the risk-free rate of interest. The result may then be used to discount the unadjusted cash flows.

The second method requires the cash flow to be adjusted by 'certainty equivalents' and the results discounted by the risk-free rate of interest. Algebraically we may describe the method as follows,

$$P_0 = \Sigma D_t a_t/(1+rf) \qquad (8.21)$$

where a_t is the certainty equivalent for period t. It may be defined as follows,

$$a_t = (1+rf)/(1+r_i) \qquad (8.22)$$

where rf and r_i are the risk-free rate of return and the required rate of return for the security (for example, determined by Eq. (8.20)). Thus if the required rate of return for a security is 19 per cent and the risk-free rate is 12 per cent then the certainty equivalent is equal to $(1.12/1.19) = 0.9412$. If during the next year the parameters do not change, then the certainty equivalent for year 2 will be equal to $(1.12)^2/(1.19)^2 = 0.8858$. Therefore, if the mean expected dividend in years 1 and 2 are 10p and 12p, then they are equivalent to certain dividends of $(0.9412)10 = 9.412\text{p}$ and $(0.8858)12 = 10.63\text{p}$ respectively. These should then be discounted by the risk-free rate of interest to produce the present values of $9.412\text{p}/(1.12) = 8.4\text{p}$ and $10.63\text{p}/(1.12)^2 = 8.47\text{p}$ respectively.

If we use the risk-adjusted discount rate of return we will obtain the identical results, 10p/1.19=8.4, and 12(1.19)²=8.47.

In practice, the easiest conceptually and to apply, is the risk-adjusted discount rate and consequently may be preferred to the certainty equivalent method with its intermediate stage of producing the equivalent certain cash flow.

The financial mix and the dividend decision

We can now build on the techniques presented in the last section to examine two contentious issues in investment (and corporate) finance. The first concerns the effect of the company's employment of debt on its share price and the second is the relevance of dividend payments.

Capital structure and valuation

What might be called the traditional view of the effect of the capital structure on the price of shares is that there is an optimal debt–equity mix which will maximize the value of the company's securities. This is based on the belief that the cost of equity does not rise sufficiently to offset the use of cheaper forms of financing; i.e. debt. Therefore, the overall cost of capital will fall and the value of the firm will be maximized at some optimum capital structure. This optimum is not 100 per cent debt financing as equity is regarded as a safety cushion which will absorb any losses which might be incurred during the ordinary course of trading and/or liquidation. Hence, the smaller the amount of equity the more likely it is that debt holders may have to bear some part of any losses. However, the traditional view argues that this factor only makes itself felt after a substantial proportion of total financing is in the form of debt. These propositions are depicted graphically in Fig. 8.3.

The traditional view was challenged by Modigliani and Miller in 1958.[10] They argued that the level of gearing used by the firm should not affect the cost of capital or alter the value of the firm as the risk borne by shareholders and debenture holders was dependent on how the firm used the capital not on how the firm raised the capital. In other words, what matters is the way in which funds are invested. Therefore, as the firm takes on more of the cheaper form of financing, debt, the cost of equity should rise so as to offset the advantage and maintain a constant cost of capital

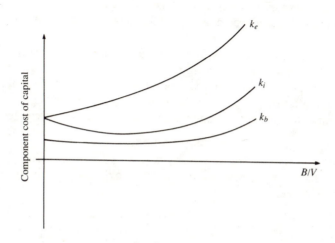

Figure 8.3 The traditional view of the effect of capital structure on the value of the firm.

regardless of the debt–equity ratio. That this should happen is no accident according to Modigliani and Miller. The means by which the cost of equity rises to offset exactly the use of cheaper debt is an arbitrage process and arises out of rational investors taking advantage of profitable opportunities if the market values companies according to factors other than their returns and the riskiness of the returns.

The assumptions on which Modigliani and Miller base their model are very important and hence they must be described before proceeding to a formal development. The assumptions are as follows:

1. Perfect capital markets in which information is costless and available to all investors, no transactions costs, all securities are infinitely divisible, and investors are rational wealth-preferring economic agents.
2. Homogeneous expectations of company earnings and that there is no growth (or otherwise) in those earnings into perpetuity.
3. No corporate taxation. This assumption will be removed at a later stage.
4. Companies are classified by returns, and all companies with an equivalent return have the same business risk.

Our point of departure in tracing the Modigliani and Miller exposition must be the observation that the value of a firm within a given class of business risk is given by the following equation,

$$V = E(Y)/r_i \qquad (8.23)$$

where V is the value of the firm, $E(Y)$ is the expected future income in perpetuity, and r_i is the weighted average cost of capital of the firm which may be defined,

$$r_i = w_e r_e + w_b r_b \qquad (8.24)$$

where r_e and r_b are the costs of equity and debt respectively, and where w_e and w_b are the weight of financing from equity and debt respectively.

Assume an investor is confronted by the choice of investing in one of two companies which are identical in every respect except for the way in which they have been financed. The first company (U) has all equity financing while the second (G) has used some debt in its financial structure.

The potential returns may be described as follows:

1. The investor buys a proportion x of the equity in the geared company G. The investment may be described as xS_g. The return expected from this investment may be written $x(E(Y) - k_b B)$. Where $E(Y)$ is the expected income (defined as earnings before interest and taxes), B is the market value of debt used by the company in its financial structure and k_b is the rate of interest born by that debt.
2. In order to construct an equivalent investment in the ungeared firm, the investor must purchase a proportion x of the outstanding equity and partially finance this with a loan equal to xB of the geared company's debt. The investment may be written as $xS_u - xB$. The return will be equal to $xE(Y) - xk_b B$, as the returns to equity $(xE(Y))$ have to pay for the cost of the loan $(xk_b B)$. By requiring the investor to buy a proportion of debt in the geared company we can write,

$$xS_u - xB = xS_g \qquad (8.25)$$

therefore, if this is true for a proportion, we can show that by dividing both sides of Eq. (8.25) by x, it will be true for the whole,

$$S_u - B = S_g \qquad (8.26)$$

and therefore,

$$V_u = V_g \qquad (8.27)$$

as $S_u = V_u$, and $S_g + B = V_g$.

If these conditions do not hold there will be a diversion in the market valuations of the equity of the two companies and profitable arbitrages would arise. For example, consider the following numerical example:

		ABC Ltd	XYZ Ltd
$E(Y)$	Earnings before interest and tax	40 000	40 000
k_bB	Interest payable on debt		15 000
$E(E)$	Earnings available to equity	40 000	25 000
k_e	Equity required rate of return	0.16	0.14
S	Market value of equity $(E(E)/ke)$	250 000	178 571
k_b	Debt required rate of return		0.10
B	Market value of debt		150 000
V	Value of the firm $(S+B)$	250 000	328 571
k_i	Overall required rate of return	0.16	0.12
B/V			45.65%

Modigliani and Miller argue that this situation cannot persist for long as it offers arbitrage profits to the individual investor. Suppose our investor had purchased 5 per cent of the equity of XYZ Ltd for 8,928.55, his or her expected return would be $(0.14)(8,928.55) = 1,250$. This can be improved upon by selling the shares of XYZ Ltd and borrowing an amount equal to 5 per cent of the market value of XYZ Ltd's debt; i.e. $(0.05)(150,000) = 7,500$. The investor now has a total of $8,928.55 + 7,500 = 16,428.55$ to invest. He or she may now buy 5 per cent of the equity of the ungeared firm, ABC Ltd, for 12,500 and receive an expected return of 2,000 $[(0.05)(40,000)]$. After paying the interest costs (10 per cent of 7,500), the investor is left with a net return of 1,250 which is the same as before. However, with this alternative strategy, the investor can enjoy the income from an extra 3,928.55, which, if invested in ABC Ltd, will generate additional earnings of 628.57. This would constitute an improvement of just over 50 per cent on the original return on the investment in XYZ Ltd.[11]

Given the above potential for arbitrage profits, it was argued that if enough investors acted on this opportunity, the price of ABC Ltd would rise and that of XYZ Ltd would fall in response to the changing pattern of demand.

We can see from these arguments and from Fig. 8.4 that the capital structure theory has distinct implications for the price of equity. Although it is argued that the total value of the firm will remain

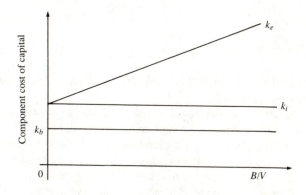

Figure 8.4 The Modigliani and Miller view of the effects of capital structure.

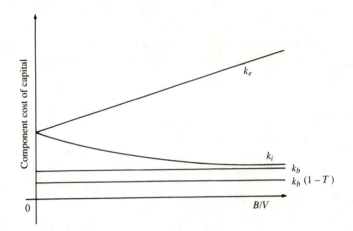

Figure 8.5 Modigliani and Miller with a proportional corporation tax and bankruptcy costs.

constant, it is shown that this will be so because the price of equity will fall so as to offset the impact of using debt. Hence, the implication is that the price of equity will fall in direct proportion to the increase in the use of debt in the financial structure.

However, once taxation and bankruptcy effects are introduced the capital structure will have an effect on the overall value of the firm (Fig. 8.5). In addition, it will have an impact on the price of the firm's equity which is in excess of the contribution of debt to the financial mix. For example, if a proportional corporation tax is introduced the above example may be reworked as follows:

1. The investor buys a proportion x of the equity in the geared company G. The investment may be described as xS_g. The return expected from this investment may be written $x(E(Y)-k_bB)(1-T)$. Where T is the proportional corporate tax rate.

2. As before the equivalent investment in the ungeared firm is given by $xS_u - x(1-T)B$. The return will be equal to,

$$xE(Y)(1-T)-x(1-T)k_bB=x(E(Y)-k_bB)(1-T) \qquad (8.28)$$

The returns from the two investment decisions are equal; hence we may write,

$$xS_g=xS_u-x(1-T)B \qquad (8.29)$$

this reduces to,

$$S_g+B=S_u+TB \qquad (8.30)$$

hence,

$$S_g=S_u+TB-B \qquad (8.31)$$

The effects of the capital mix on share prices and equity required rates of return may be seen from the examples presented in Table 8.2.

It is noticeable that in all 3 cases presented in Table 8.2, the share price declines as the required rate of return increases. This highlights the significance of the debate as far as equity valuation is concerned. It is not a debate about declining share values or rising rates of return but a debate about the rates of decline and increase. If we compare the traditional case with that of Modigliani and Miller with corporate taxes, it is clear that the latter position indicates a linear price decline while that of the traditional view suggests a more progressive decline. However, if bankruptcy considerations are added to the case of Modigliani and Miller with taxes the results will tend to

Table 8.2 The effect of capital structure on share prices

Debt	R_b	$R_b(1-T)$	R_e	R_i	Net inc.	V_e	V_b	V_i	Share prices	(V_b/V_i)
(a) The traditional view and the optimal debt equity mix										
0	0.1	0.06	0.16	0.16	30 000	187 500	0	187 500	1.88	0
50 000	0.1	0.06	0.16	0.14	27 000	168 750	50 000	218 750	1.69	0.23
100 000	0.15	0.09	0.20	0.15	21 000	105 000	100 000	205 000	1.05	0.49
150 000	0.2	0.12	0.30	0.16	12 000	40 000	150 000	190 000	0.4	0.79
(b) Modigliani and Miller without taxes										
0	0.1		0.16	0.16	50 000	312 500	0	312 500	3.13	0
50 000	0.1		0.17	0.16	45 000	262 500	50 000	312 500	2.63	0.16
100 000	0.1		0.19	0.16	40 000	212 500	100 000	312 500	2.13	0.32
150 000	0.1		0.22	0.16	35 000	162 500	150 000	312 500	1.63	0.48
(c) Modigliani and Miller with a proportional corporation tax										
0	0.1	0.06	0.16	0.16	30 000	187 500	0	187 500	1.88	0
50 000	0.1	0.06	0.17	0.14	27 000	157 500	50 000	207 500	1.58	0.24
100 000	0.1	0.06	0.19	0.13	24 000	127 500	100 000	227 500	1.28	0.44
150 000	0.1	0.06	0.22	0.12	21 000	97 500	150 000	247 500	0.98	0.61

Assume 100,000 shares and net operating income of 50,000.

R_b	Cost of debt
$R_b(1-T)$	Cost of debt × (1 – corporation tax)
R_e	Cost of equity
R_i	Weighted average cost of capital
Net inc.	Net income
V_e	Value of equity
V_b	Value of debt
V_i	Value of the whole firm

look like the traditional view once more. It can be argued that the imperfections of the market will become increasingly important after firms have exceeded their 'debt capacity' and lenders of funds no longer perceive the equity financing as an adequate cushion in the event of liquidation. Hence, the costs of debt may rise as this 'bankruptcy consideration' is taken into account.

The empirical investigations of Modigliani and Miller[12] were conducted on examples of oil and electric utility companies. They found that gearing did not significantly increase the overall cost of funds to the firm. However, other studies, for example that by Masulis,[13] have cast doubt on the universality of the results of Modigliani and Miller.

Masulis studied the effect of changes in corporate structure effected by debt–equity swaps and vice versa in which there was little or no net cash inflows or outflows from the firm. Masulis took a sample of 133 US cases of recapitalizations which involved a change in the amount of equity capital of 25 per cent or less (and a corresponding change in the amount of debt). The model and tests gave the following results:

1. Changes in share prices are positively related to changes in gearing.
2. Changes in firm valuation were found to be consistent with the tax-based models of capital structure.

The dividend decision and security valuation

The second major debate in security valuation concerns the significance (if any) of the dividend decision. This second debate was also started in earnest by an article written by Miller and Modigliani which argued that dividends were irrelevant for the purposes of security valuation.[14] They basically posed the question that, if all other financial decisions were held constant, what effect would changing the dividend payout ratio have on the value of the firm's equity? They pointed out that given the firm's investment policy, the dividend decision is really a decision about how to finance the investment policy. It is axiomatic that dividends have to be financed and if funds are used to pay shareholders it may be that alternative sources of capital must be tapped to provide for the investment policy. They attempted to demonstrate that equity value is dependent on the success or failure of the firm's investment policies rather than any deliberate policy concerning dividends.

The first part of this section will present some of the available evidence about the practice of paying dividends while the second part will present a discussion of the debate regarding their relevance in valuation.

Taken together Tables 8.3 and 8.4 indicate some sort of policy for dividend payout ratios on behalf of the commerical companies in the UK. Although Table 8.3 shows considerable increases in the nominal amount of dividends paid these increases are accompanied by a significant decrease in the aggregate payout ratio. This is explained when the nominal amounts paid out are adjusted for inflation, (Table 8.5).

The evidence of Table 8.5 lends itself to a policy of a constant real dividend. However, at company level, other policies are more often mentioned:

1. Constant nominal dividend.
2. Constant payout ratio; i.e. a constant proportion of earnings are paid out to shareholders. However, in practice although earnings vary, it is not always observed that dividends fall as earnings fall.

The evidence[15] suggests that most firms have a 'target payout ratio'. On the other hand they are reluctant to reduce the dividend in response to a fall in distributable earnings. Consequently, the pattern of dividend payouts for firms which follow some target may resemble a ratchet effect which is only broken when the firm's performance is bad for several consecutive periods. In addition, increases are only made when the firm is confident that the new level can be maintained for the foreseeable future.

Table 8.3   UK dividend payout ratios

Year	Profits available (£ million)	Dividends (£ million)	Payout ratio for dividends (%)
1960	3 629	926	26
1961	3 414	1 057	31
1962	3 225	1 063	33
1963	3 917	1 199	31
1964	4 453	1 399	30
1965	4 815	1 586	33
1966	4 426	1 509	34
1967	4 143	1 463	35
1968	4 895	1 434	29
1969	5 434	1 554	29
1970	5 529	1 378	25
1971	6 498	1 530	24
1972	7 948	1 524	19
1973	10 343	1 381	13
1974	10 795	1 246	12
1965	11 083	1 329	12
1976	15 272	1 532	10
1977	19 155	1 749	9
1978	21 752	1 929	9
1979	28 504	3 364	12
1980	24 870	3 260	13
1981	26 036	3 225	12
1982	26 275	3 592	14
1983	33 889	4 446	13
1984	41 562	5 408	13

Source: CSO Economic Trends, 1986, HMSO, Table 173.

Table 8.4   Percentage compound annual growth rates

	1960–64	1965–69	1970–74	1975–79	1980–84
GDP (a)	4.8	6.2	13.5	17.3	14.9
Distributable Profits	4.2	4.1	14.7	21.4	7.8
Dividends (b)	7.7	3.0	3.7	20.9	10.0
RPI	2.6	4.3	9.6	15.5	9.5

(a) At factor prices.
(b) Adjusted for the changes in corporation tax after 1973.
Source: CSO Economic Trends, various years, HMSO Tables A, B, 8, 114, 173.

Table 8.5   Profits and dividends adjusted for inflation[a]

Year	Profits available (£ million)	Dividends (£ million)	Payout Ratio (%)
1960–64	35 330	10 561	30
1965–69	37 605	12 011	32
1970–74	45 972	9 400	20
1975–79	52 257	8 084	15
1980–84	48 385	9 020	19

[a] 1984 = 100.
Source: CSO Economic Trends, 1986, HMSO, Table 173.

After interviewing US corporate managers Lintner was able to describe their behaviour in terms of the following model,

$$D_1 = T(EPS_1)$$
(8.32a)

where D_1 is the dividend paid in period 1, T is the target payout ratio and EPS_1 is the earnings per share in period 1. Changes in the dividend could then be described as,

$$D_1 - D_0 = T(EPS_1) - D_0$$
(8.32b)

However, Lintner found that managers were reluctant to shift the new dividend up to the new target level in one jump, preferring to have something in hand so that dividend growth could be maintained if the subsequent earnings showed no growth. Therefore, the change in the dividend was dependent not solely on the target payout ratio but also on some adjustment factor, a,

$$D_1 - D_0 = a[T(EPS_1) - D_0]$$
(8.32c)

By substituting for the values of D_0 and so on, this model can be generalized as follows,

$$D_t = aT(EPS_t) + aT(1-a)(EPS_{t-1}) + aT(1-a)^2(EPS_{t-2}) + \ldots + aT(1-a)^n(EPS_{t-n})$$
(8.32d)

This implies that dividends are a weighted average of past earnings in which the most recent earnings figures are the most important in determining the level of current dividend.

Fama and Babiak[16] tested this model and found that, on average, firms in the USA have a target ratio of about 0.5 and an adjustment rate of 0.33. They also estimated the probabilities of dividend increases and decreases under certain circumstances (Table 8.6).

Table 8.6   **Distributions of dividend increase/decrease**

Direction of earnings changes			Percentage of firms		
t	$t-1$	$t-2$	$+D$	No change	$-D$
+	+	+	81	8	11
+	+	−	67	15	18
+	−	+	58	17	25
−	+	+	54	15	32
+	−	−	49	18	34
−	+	−	45	19	36
−	−	+	35	17	48
−	−	−	25	25	50

Source: E. Fama and H. Babiak,[16] p. 134.

The foregoing strongly suggests that dividend policy and practice contains important information for the shareholder. However, increases in dividends do not provide completely unambiguous messages to shareholders.

Dividend increases can mean any of the following:

1. Good investment prospects. The management have confidence in future earnings growth and the maintenance of the target payout ratio.
2. Sound financial management which increases the cash payout when the firm has no adequate investment opportunities; this may reflect an expectation of worsening economic performance in the near or distant future.
3. Changes in the management team and consequent changes in investment policy which may or may not have yielded benefits at the time of the dividend increase.

The foregoing has concentrated on increases (decreases) in dividends and makes no comment on the actual payout ratio itself. The important result is that in an uncertain world companies like to maintain a stable payout ratio over the long run. As the actual cash payout varies according to the firm's performance rather than changes in the long run payout ratio, the information content of dividends says nothing about the significance of the size of the payout ratio in the valuation of securities.

Modigliani and Miller begin their discussion of equity valuation by looking at the effect of dividends on the current prices of shares, 'Do companies with generous distribution policies consistently sell at a premium over those with niggardly payouts? Is the reverse ever true? If so, under what conditions? Is there an optimum payout ratio or range of ratios that maximizes the current worth of shares?'[18]

They make the following assumptions:
1. there is perfect knowledge; i.e. certainty;
2. no transactions costs;
3. no taxes;
4. atomistic supply and demand;
5. rational behaviour on the part of investors in which they prefer more wealth to less and are indifferent to whether an increment to their wealth takes the form of an unrealized capital gain or a cash dividend payment.

The model starts with a definition of a simple one-period return:

$$r_t = (p_{t+1} - p_t + d_t)/p_t \tag{8.33}$$

where, p is the price, d is the dividend, r is the rate of return, and t and $t+1$ are time subscripts. This may be rearranged to produce an equation determining price in period t,

$$p_t = [1/(1+r_t)](d_t + p_{t+1}) \tag{8.34}$$

If n is defined as the number of shares in issue in period t and m is the number of any new shares issued in period $t+1$, Eq. (8.34) may be rewritten as follows:

$$V_t = [1/(1+r_t)](D_t + np_{t+1}) \tag{8.35}$$

where $V_t = np_t$ and $D_t = nd_t$. We may define the total value of the firm's equity in period $t+1$ as $p_{t+1}(n+m) = V_{t+1}$. Therefore,

$$V_t = [1/(1+r_t)](D_t + V_{t+1} - mp_{t+1}) \tag{8.36}$$

The need for the firm to issue new shares will be determined by its income, investment plans, and dividend policy:

$$mp_{t+1} = I_t - (Y_t - D_t) \tag{8.37}$$

where I_t is the investment in period t and Y_t is the firm's total net profit in period t. We may now substitute Eq. (8.37) into Eq. (8.36):

$$V_t = [1/(1+r_t)]\{D_t + V_{t+1} - [I_t - (Y_t - D_t)]\} \tag{8.38}$$

Equation (8.38) simplifies as follows:

$$V_t = [1/(1+r_t)](V_{t+1} - I_t + Y_t) \tag{8.39}$$

Hence, dividends have been eliminated from the valuation equation. The present value of the firm is now dependent on the firm's results of its past investment policies (Y_t) and the prospects of its current investment decisions (I_t). We may now generalize this result so that the present value of the firm is independent of any future dividend decisions. For example, using the same logic and assuming a constant required rate of return, V_{t+1} may be defined as follows:

$$V_{t+1} = [1/(1+r_{t+1})](V_{t+2} - I_{t+1} + Y_{t+1}) \tag{8.40}$$

Equation (8.40) may be substituted into Eq. (8.39) for V_{t+1} and after some manipulation we get,

$$V_t = (Y_t - I_t)/(1+r)^t + (Y_{t+1} - I_{t+1})/(1+r)^{t+1} + V_{t+2}/(1+r)^{t+1} \tag{8.41}$$

This may be generalized as follows:

$$V_t = \sum \frac{(Y_t - I_t)}{(1+r)^t} + V_{t+1}/(1+r)^{n+1} \tag{8.42}$$

As n approaches infinity so V_{t+1} will approach zero and will cease to be an important component of the valuation equation. This leaves the current price of the share being equal to the present value of the difference between net income and investment into infinity. Modigliani and Miller conclude that:

> Like many other propositions in economics, the irrelevance of dividend policy, given investment policy, is 'obvious, once you think about it'. It is, after all, merely one more instance of the general principle that there are no 'financial illusions' in a rational and perfect economic environment. Values there are determined solely by 'real' considerations—in this case the earning power of the firm's assets and its investment policy—and not by how the fruits of earning power are 'packaged' for distribution. ... Given a firm's investment policy, the dividend payout policy it chooses will affect neither the current price of its shares nor the total return to its shareholders.[18]

At this point it is necessary that we pay some attention to the phrase 'rational and perfect economic environment'. The first point to make is that dividend policy and share valuation take place under conditions of uncertainty. Not only is the future uncertain, but information about the present is not free and is not available to everyone. Gordon[19] has emphasized these real world imperfections and has argued that dividend policy is important because dividends represent a more certain return than reinvested profits. Hence, a pound paid out is worth more than a pound retained and reinvested. However, this implicitly assumes that the investor may be able to reinvest the dividend for the same return at a lower risk than the firm (or for a higher return for the same risk) which, given the asymmetry of information, cannot be the case unless the firm itself has an inferior investment policy, in which case the investor would be advised to withdraw his or her investment from the firm completely. Therefore, if the firm is efficient with regard to its investment policy, the investor must accept the same level of risk as the firm in order to achieve the same expected return. Under these circumstances the dividend must lose the supposed qualities of uncertainty.

It has been and still is argued by many market practitioners that dividends do have an effect on market prices because of their information content. Share prices do react to company announcements of dividend changes. Earlier in this chapter, a quote from a newspaper[9] was presented which commented on the market's favourable reaction to the announcement from the Chief Executive Officer of Lloyd's Bank that its dividend would be increased by 10 per cent. However, further analysis of the company's results showed that a loss had been made and that the whole dividend (including the increase) was to be paid out of reserves. This caused the price of the shares to fall back. Although this constitutes a piece of anecdotal evidence, it serves to illustrate the point about the value of the information content of dividends.

The example poses the question 'what was more important'? The increase in the dividend and presumably the optimistic implication about the bank's future earning ability or the possibility that past investment policies were proving to be injudicious? In other words did the dividend increase embody different and superior information to that published in the accounts? Investors spend considerable amounts of effort, time and money in their investigations into the firms behind the shares. They analyse managements, investments and future income streams. They make forecasts of the results of the firms' past and present investment activities. Hence, the possibility arises that the information content of the dividend decision may contradict the information presented in other sources.

However, empirical evidence on the information content of dividends is not consistent. Graham and Dodd and others have observed an apparent relationship between dividends and share prices.[20] Cragg and Malkiel provided evidence that professional analysts were no more accurate than naive earnings forecasting methods over 5-year horizons.[21] It has also been argued that the dividend payment represents tangible evidence of management's expectations which should be based on superior knowledge to that of investors. Ross[22] has taken this line of reasoning further by arguing that because managers' remuneration is linked to the value of the firm, they will make decisions which maximize that value. Therefore, dividends should be expected to contain information.

On the other hand, those who support the efficient market theory (EMT) have made substantial cases for the irrelevance of dividends. For example, Richards[23] has used the methods of Cragg and Malkiel to show that over a 1-year time horizon professional analysts perform 'reasonably well'. The implication of this is that dividends do not carry significant new information, merely a confirmation of present conditions which are already known from other sources of information. In addition to these results, much of the work done on the EMT has concerned the existence or otherwise of a financial illusion. Thus, the work of Fama et al on the significance of scrip issues indicated that the issues themselves did not tell the market anything it did not already know from its analysis of the company's performance during the 30 months before the split.[24] Similarly, studies using their methodology of cumulative average residuals have shown that earnings announcements are correctly anticipated.[25]

The use of the capital asset pricing model has had similarly contradictory results. For example Bar-Yosef and Kolodny, and Litzenberger and Ramaswamy have found dividends to be significant while Black and Scholes have found them to be without significance.[26] The inconclusive nature of the empirical tests may suggest something about the validity of the tests themselves rather than the significance or otherwise of dividends. The fact remains that dividends exist and have existed since shares were first sold to the investing public. If dividends are insignificant as Modigliani and Miller have suggested, then this requires that corporate financial officers act irrationally. However, this persistent irrationality is inconsistent given the evidence for the efficiency of stock markets. This paradox has been considered by Dyl and Hoffmeister[27] who used the concept of duration (see Chapter 10) to show that there might be a relationship between dividends and beta. They conclude that firms pay dividends to influence the riskiness of their equity and that the higher the dividend payout ratio, the lower the total and systematic risk of the shares. They also suggest that the possible existence of the relationship might explain the inconsistent results obtained from studies of the effects of dividends using the capital asset pricing model.

Dividends and taxes

When the assumption of no taxes is dropped the relevance of dividends depends on the neutrality of the taxation system.[28] In the situation where the tax system is more favourable to capital gains, then there is an incentive not to pay dividends. In addition, a sharply progressive personal tax system will make dividends a relatively unattractive source of income for the marginal tax payer compared to capital gains which may be taxed at a flat rate. The effect of a progressive personal taxation system may be exacerbated by high levels of price inflation in which the rate of increase in personal allowances lags behind the rate of change in prices and incomes.

These conclusions have been formally demonstrated in articles by Farrar, Selwyn and

Brennan.[29] Brennan adapted the capital asset pricing model to try to gauge the effects of dividends and taxes on the returns to shareholders:

$$E(R_{i,t}) - R_{rf} = a_1 + a_2 + a_3(d_{i,t} - R_{rf})$$ (8.43)

where

$E(R_{i,t})$ = expected before tax return on security i in period t,

R_{rf} = before tax return on the risk-free asset

a_1 = constant

a_2 = coefficient of the security's systematic risk,

a_3 = difference between marginal income tax and capital gains tax

$d_{i,t}$ = dividend yield

If a_3 is found to be both positive and statistically significant then the model suggests that dividends are undesirable and that rational shareholders should prefer to take their returns in the form of capital gains. However, there are problems with Brennan's original model. By using the CAPM the model introduces the problem of unstable betas (see Chapter 6).

Secondly, the principal method of correcting this fault by concentrating on portfolio betas which are more stable, then obscures the effects on market values, risks and returns for individual shares.

However, these defects were largely solved by Litzenberger and Ramaswamy who concluded that risk-adjusted returns are higher for those securities offering higher dividend yields. In other words, the payment of high dividends depresses the security's price which means that investors require a higher income rate of return to induce them to hold those securities paying high dividends.[24] Using a similar methodology, Poterba and Summers found similar results for UK firms.[30]

Dividend clienteles

The clientele effect was first suggested by Modigliani and Miller in their original 1961 article when they pointed out:

> If, for example, the frequency distribution of corporate payout ratios happened to correspond exactly with the distribution of investor preferences for payout ratios, then the existence of these preferences would clearly lead ultimately to a situation whose implications were different, in no respect, from the perfect market case. Each corporation would tend to attract to itself a 'clientele' consisting of those preferring its particular payout ratio, but one clientele would be as good as another in terms of the valuation it would imply for firms.[31]

Elton and Gruber[32] attempted to measure clientele effects by measuring the extent to which share prices fell when they went ex-dividend. In addition they estimated the implied income tax brackets associated with each dividend payout level. Their starting point was to set up a model in which there were no opportunities for arbitrage by specifying an equality between those investors taking their returns solely in terms of capital gains by selling before the share went ex-dividend, and those who sold after the share went ex-dividend and thus collected their return in capital gains and dividends:

$$P_t - T_g(P_t - P_0) = P_t - T_g(P_{t+1} - P_0) + d(1 - T_i)$$ (8.44)

where

$$P_0 = \text{purchase price}$$

$$P_{t+1} = \text{price of the share after it goes ex-dividend}$$

$$T_g = \text{rate of capital gains tax}$$

$$T_i = \text{rate of personal income tax}$$

Equation (8.44) may be rearranged to give,

$$(P_t - P_{t+1})/d = (1 - T_i)/(1 - T_g)$$

In this form the ratio of the share price decline to the size of the dividend may be used to estimate the personal income tax of the investor given a rate of capital gains tax.

Using US data for the period April 1966 to March 1967 (4,148 observations), Elton and Gruber were able to conclude from their findings that the lower the dividend yield the higher the implied personal income tax rate and that there was a clientele effect. This result was also found by Litzenberger and Ramaswamy in their 1982 article.[26]

Notes

1. This may be compared with the third tranche of 1.5 million shares in Nippon Telephone and Telegraph (NTT) sold to the Japanese public and investing institutions for a price of Y1.9 million (£8,600) each in October 1988. This capitalizes NTT on a P/E ratio of 130 and at £138 billion which is roughly equivalent to the total capitalization of the West German stock markets. It is also worth noting in this case that the second tranche of NTT shares was sold in November 1987, just after the crash in world stock markets, at a price of Y2.55 million per share. Since the sale of the second tranche, the price of NTT has never approached Y2.55 million giving the investors (mainly individuals) no chance to sell their holdings. Hence, the third tranche has been sold primarily to the investing institutions as the demand from individuals has dried up.

2. B. Riley, 'The long view: stardom could prove unfortunate', *Financial Times*, 31 October 1987.

3. D. Galai and M. Schneller, 'The pricing of warrants and the value of the firm', *Journal of Finance*, Vol. 33, December 1978.

4. P. Marsh, 'Equity rights issues and the efficiency of the UK stock market', *Journal of Finance*, Vol. 34, September 1979.
   P. Marsh, 'Valuation of underwriting agreements for UK rights issues', *Journal of Finance*, Vol. 35, June 1980.

5. S. Scholes, 'The market for securities: substitution versus the price pressure and the effects of information on share prices', *Journal of Business*, April 1984.

6. C. Smith, 'Alternative methods for raising capital: rights versus underwritten offerings', *Journal of Financial Economics*, Vol. 5, 1977.

7. A sample of this unfinished debate may be seen in the following publications:
   S. M. Keane, 'The significance of the issue price in rights issues', *Journal of Business Finance*, Vol. 4, 1972.
   M. Lee-Jones, 'Underwriting of rights issues: a theoretical justification', *Journal of Business Finance*, Vol. 3, 1971.
   A. J. Merrett, J. Howe and G. D. Newbould, *Equity Issues and the London Capital market*, Longman, 1967.

G. Newbould and E. Wells, 'Underwriting of rights issues—a theoretical justification: a reply', *Journal of Business and Finance*, Vol. 3, 1971.

8. G. Newbould and E. Wells, op. cit. 7, p. 20.

9. The purpose of this quote is to illustrate rather than to criticise any particular newspaper, hence the name of the paper has been withheld. Similar comments can be found in all of the daily papers which have sizeable financial sections.

10. F. Modigliani and M. Miller, 'The cost of capital, corporation finance and the theory of investment', *American Economic Review*, Vol. 48, June 1958.
'The cost of capital, corporation finance and the theory of investment: reply', *American Economic Review*, Vol. 49, June 1959.
'Corporate income taxes and the cost of capital: a correction', *American Economic Review*, Vol. 53, June 1963.

11. Assuming the shares of ABC ltd and its overall value remained unchanged, the equilibrium required rate of return for XYZ ltd may be found by treating its equity as a residual. Hence, the equity of XYZ ltd would be worth £250,000–£150,000 (the market value of XYZ ltd's debt) = £100,000. The rate of return would then be calculated as £25,000/£100,000 = 25 per cent. However, this is unrealistic as the changing distribution of demand and supply would affect the equity prices and values of both firms.

12. F. Modigliani and M. Miller, 'Some estimates of the cost of capital to the electric utility industry: 1954–57', *American Economic Review*, Vol. 56, June 1966.

13. R. Masulis, 'The effects of capital structure change on security prices: a study of exchange offers', *Journal of Financial Economics*, Vol. 8, 1980.

14. M. Miller and F. Modigliani, 'Dividend policy, growth, and the valuation of shares', *Journal of Business*, Vol. 17, October 1961.

15. J. Lintner, 'Distribution of incomes of corporations among dividends, retained earnings and taxes', *American Economic Review*, Vol. 46, May 1956.

16. E. Fama and H. Babiak, 'Dividend policy: an empirical analysis', *Journal of the American Statistical Society*, Vol. 63, December 1968.

17. M. Miller and F. Modigliani, 'Dividend policy, growth, and the valuation of shares', *Journal of Business*, Vol. 17, October 1961. p. 411.

18. Ibid., p. 414.

19. M. Gordon, 'Dividends, earnings and stock prices' *Review of Economics and Statistics*, Vol. 41, May 1959, and 'The savings, investments and valuation of the corporation' *Review of Economics and Statistics*, Vol. 48, 1966.

20. B. Graham and D. Dodd, *Security Analysis: Analysis and Techniques*, 3rd edn, McGraw-Hill, 1951; M. Gordon op. cit. 19; G. Fisher, 'Some factors influencing shares prices', *Economic Journal*, Vol. 71, 1961.

21. J. Cragg and B. Malkiel, 'The consensus and accuracy of some predictions of the growth of corporate earnings', *Journal of Finance*, Vol. 23, March 1968.

22. S. Ross, 'The determination of financial structure: the incentive signalling approach', *Bell Journal of Economics*, Spring 1977.

23. R. Richards, 'Analysts' performance and the accuracy of corporate earnings forecasts', *Journal of Business*, Vol. 32, July 1976.

24. See Chapter 4.

25. For example see R. Ball and P. Brown, 'An empirical evaluation of accounting income numbers', *Journal of Accounting Research*, April 1968; A. Riding, 'The information content of dividends: another test', *Journal of Business Finance and Accounting*, Vol. 11, Summer 1984.

26. S. Bar-Yosef and R. Kolodny, 'Dividend policy and capital market theory', *Review of Economics and Statistics*, 1976; R. Litzenberger and K. Ramaswamy, 'The effect of personal

taxes and dividends on capital asset prices', *Journal of Financial Economics*, Vol. 7, 1979; F. Black and M. Scholes, 'The effects of dividend yields and dividend policy on common stock prices and returns', *Journal of Financial Economics*, Vol. 2, May 1974; R. Litzenberger and K. Ramaswamy, 'The effects of dividends on common stock prices: tax effects or information effects?', *Journal of Finance*, Vol. 37, 1982.

27. J. Dyl and J. Hoffmeister, 'A note on dividend policy and beta', *Journal of Business Finance and Accounting*, Vol. 13, Spring 1986.

28. R. Stapleton, 'Taxes, the cost of capital and the theory of investment', *Economic Journal*, Vol. 82, 1972; R. Stapleton and C. Burke, 'Taxes, the cost of capital and the theory of investment. A generalisation to the imputation system of dividend taxation', *Economic Journal*, Vol. 85, 1975. See also the Government publication 'Reform of Corporation Tax', Cmnd. 4955.

Stapleton has provided a framework within which the effects of taxation and dividends have on the valuation of companies and their securities may be analysed. His original analysis concerned the simple proportional corporate taxation system where dividends were taxed at the investor's marginal tax rates. Stapleton simplifies the analysis by assuming personal income tax rates are the same for all investors (w). In addition, the analysis assumes that capital gains are realized and thus constitute taxable income for investors and are subject to a tax rate (g). The rate of return (r) in a taxless system may be defined as,

$$r = (D_1 + P_1 - P_0 - C_1)/P_0 \qquad (8.45)$$

where D_1 is the total dividend payment in period 1, C_1 is any new capital raised by the company through rights issues in period 1, and P is the market value of the company in periods 0 and 1. If we now introduce a corporation tax (h) and the personal taxes, Eq. (8.45) becomes,

$$r(1-w) = [D_1(1-w) + (1-g)(P_1 - P_0 - C_1)]/P_0 \qquad (8.46)$$

Equation (8.46) may be manipulated to produce an expression for P_0,

$$P_0 = \frac{D_1(1-w)}{[r(1-w)+(1-g)]} + \frac{P_1(1-g)}{[r(1-w)+(1-g)]} - \frac{C_1(1-g)}{[r(1-w)+(1-g)]} \qquad (8.47)$$

Define $(1-w)/(1-g)$ as 'a' which is a personal tax factor which will be less than unity when income tax exceeds capital gains tax and vice versa. When the personal tax factor is applied to the rate of return (r), the result (ar) is the appropriate parameter for discounting dividends and new issues. Equation (8.47) may be simplified further if we make the following definitions:

$$a/(1+ar) = (1-w)/[r(1-w)+(1-g)], \text{ and } 1/(1+ar) = (1-g)/[r(1-w)+(1-g)].$$

The equation may now be reduced to,

$$P_0 = [(aD_1 - C_1)/(1+ar)] + P_1/(1+ar) \qquad (8.48)$$

The valuation of the company in period 1 may be similarly defined,

$$P_1 = [(aD_2 - C_2)/(1+ar)^2] + P_2/(1+ar)^2 \qquad (8.49)$$

Substituting (8.49) into (8.48),

$$P_0 = [(aD_1 - C_1)/(1+ar)] + [(aD_2 - C_2)/(1+ar)^2] + P_2/(1+ar)^2 \qquad (8.50)$$

Successive substitutions for $P_3, P_4, \ldots, P_n$ give,

$$P_0 = [(aD_1 - C_1)/(1+ar)] + [(aD_2 - C_2)/(1+ar)^2] + \ldots + [(aD_n - C_n)/(1+ar)^n] \qquad (8.51)$$

Equation (8.51) defines the value of the firm as a tax adjusted net cash flow in perpetuity to the shareholders. In the special case where the personal income tax rate is equal to the capital gains tax the equation reduces to a simple difference between what is paid to shareholders and what is raised from shareholders. In the case where $w > g$, $a < 1$ and the tax system is biased towards retentions. On the other hand in the case where $w < g$, $a > 1$ and the system favours higher payouts.

If we assume a 100 per cent payout ratio, the dividend payment to shareholders may be defined as,

$$D_t = Y_t + C_t - (1-h)I_t + B_t \tag{8.52}$$

where D_t is the dividend payment in period t, Y_t is the cashflow in period t net of capital expenditure but gross of tax allowable interest, I_t is the interest charge payable in period t, $(1-h)I_t$ is net interest liability, and B_t is the amount of cash raised in new loans raised in period t. The desired relationship between market capitalization (P_0) and cash flows is produced by substituting Eq. (8.52) into (8.51). Generalizing the result for n terms, we have,

$$P_0 = [a\Sigma Y_t/(1+ar)^t] + [a(1-h)\Sigma I_t/(1+ar)^t] + [\Sigma B_t/(1+ar)^t]$$
$$- [(1-a)\Sigma C_t/(1+ar)^t] \tag{8.53}$$

On the other hand, Eq. (8.51) may be transformed by substituting for C_t,

$$C_t = D_t + (1-h)I_t - B_t - Y_t \tag{8.54}$$

and generalizing the result for n terms,

$$P_0 = [\Sigma Y_t/(1+ar)^t] - [(1-a)\Sigma D_t/(1+ar)^t] - [(1-h)\Sigma I_t/(1+ar)^t] \tag{8.55}$$

Stapleton interprets these results as follows:
1. Equation (8.53) implies that an increase in cash flow (Y_t) with unchanged new issues and debt leads to a rise in dividends. This in turn will increase the market value of the firm by 'a' times the present value of the increment to the cash flows.
2. Equation (8.54) implies that if additional cash flows are used to reduce issues of new debt and equities, the value of the firm will increase by the full present value of the incremental cash flows.
3. Given a constant cash flow, increases in dividends which necessitate increases in new equity (leaving new debt constant) will reduce the market value of the firm by $(1-a)$ times the present value of the dividend increase.

Stapleton and Burke modified the above analysis after the 'imputation' system of corporation tax was introduced in the UK in 1973. The objective of the imputation system was to eliminate the discrimination against dividends which was thought to be caused by the old system's double taxation of dividend income—first by the corporation tax paid by the firm and second by the personal income tax paid by the shareholder. Under the imputation system the firm pays corporation tax at a single rate on all profits whether distributed or not. In the case of any profits distributed as dividends, the company is required to make an advance payment of corporation tax to the Inland Revenue at a rate of 25/75 of the dividend paid. The advance payments are then set off against the firm's corporation tax liability. Lastly, the shareholder receives the dividend net of basic rate income tax and gets a tax credit to that effect. However, as dividends are taxed at the individual's marginal rate of tax he or she may still be liable for tax on the dividend income. Stapleton and Burke conclude that as the tax credits given by the imputation system are equal to the standard rate of personal income tax, it is biased towards dividend payouts.

29. D. Farrar and L. Selwyn, 'Taxes, corporate financial policy and return to investors', *National Tax Journal*, December 1967; H. Brennan, 'Taxes, market valuation and corporate financial policy', *National Tax Journal*, December 1970.

30. J. Poterba and L. Summers, 'New evidence that taxes affect the valuation of dividends', *Journal of Finance*, Vol. 39, December 1984.
31. op. cit. 14, p. 431.
32. E. Elton and M. Gruber, 'Marginal stockholder tax rates and the clientele effect', *Review of Economics and Statistics*, Vol. 52, February 1970.
33. V. Whitbeck and M. Kisor, 'A new tool in investment decision making', *Financial Analysts' Journal*, May 1963.
34. D. Weaver and M. Hall, 'The evaluation of ordinary shares using a computer', *Journal of Institute of Actuaries*, Vol. 93, 1967.

Questions

1. Much criticism was voiced when the issuers of the British Steel share issue announced that the advisory price for the issue would be 60p. Despite concern that this price was too low the opening market price for the newly issued shares was only 60.5p. In what circumstances might such a course of events occur? In what ways did the British Steel offer differ from other privatization issues?

2. If a portfolio manager is considering investing in a company for 5 years, how much should he be prepared to pay if he finds out from his broker that the company is expected to perform as follows:

Year	1	2	3	4	5
Earnings ('000's)	40	30	50	40	60
Investment ('000's)	0	5	10	5	0
Debt–equity ratio %	50	50	50	50	50
Payout ratio %	50	67	40	50	40

The price in 5 years time is expected to be 75p, the beta for the company's equity is 1.2 and there are 400,000 shares extant with no expectation of any additional issues over this period. The risk-free rate is currently 10 per cent and the expected market rate of return is 15 per cent and neither is expected to change over the 5-year investment period. What price would the portfolio manager be prepared to pay for these shares given a holding period of 5 years?

3. Critically discuss the proposition that the generally perceived importance of dividend payments constitutes a financial mirage.

4. An efficient market has been described as one in which 'the theories of Miller and Modigliani hold true'. How far does the empirical evidence for the US and UK markets support the efficient market hypothesis?

5. Using your own numerical examples critically discuss the proposition that the market value of a company is not dependent on its level of gearing and that the financing decision is essentially concerned with marketing the company to the investment community rather than a process of maximizing its value.

6. Can Lintner's behavioural model and the findings of Fama and Babiak be reconciled with the dividend irrelevance model of Miller and Modigliani?

7.(a) If investors require an expected return of 8 per cent p.a., what prices would they expect to pay for the following:
   (i) a share which pays an annual dividend of 30p which is expected to remain the same for the foreseeable future.
   (ii) a share which pays an annual dividend of 20p but which is expected to grow by 5% p.a. for the foreseeable future.
   (iii) a share which pays an annual dividend of 10p which is expected to grow by 6% p.a. for the next 10 years and 4% p.a. thereafter.
   (b) If the expected return rises to 15 per cent what would they expect to pay for the above shares?

8. How might market imperfections such as taxes and transactions costs affect a firm's dividend policy and the market value of the firm?

9. How might the Black–Scholes option pricing model be used to value rights issues?

10. Consider the following 3 groups of 3 equities each,

Group I		Group II		Group III	
Share	Price	Share	Price	Share	Price
A	301p	D	251p	G	215p
B	430p	E	303p	H	373p
C	595p	F	370p	I	330p

Group I shares have low systematic risks and are expected to earn a return of 10 per cent. Group II shares have a higher systematic risk and therefore are expected to yield 12 per cent. Lastly, Group III shares have the highest systematic risk and are expected to give a return of 14 per cent.

(a)   If all 9 shares currently pay a dividend of 30p, what are the expected growth rates in each case?

(b)   On the basis of the results obtained in part (a) critically discuss the effects of the rate of dividend growth and systematic risk on equity prices.

9. Government and corporate debt

Introduction

Corporate and government debt ('debentures' and 'gilts') confers no ownership on holders, only a fixed or predictable income and a fixed or predictable redemption value. Holders have no voting rights and cannot make any contribution to the management of the corporation except *in extremis* when they can force liquidation if their contractual income has not been paid. During the eighties the holders of debt from those countries which found it difficult to make interest payments found it impossible to take effective remedial action. This lack of ultimate sanction is the principal difference (apart from degrees of risk) between corporate and government debt.

The vast majority of UK and US government debt is issued with fixed coupons (the actual cash payment made to holders) and redemption values. Consequently, unlike equities, the income stream from debt is usually known. However, the unit price at any time is a function of the prevailing interest rates and the risk associated with the corporation or government which issued the security.

The British Government issues two other types of debt: index-linked gilts and convertibles. Index-linked gilts offer investors coupons and redemption values in real terms. They are linked to the rate of inflation in the retail price index (RPI). Therefore, the apparently low coupons offered, between 2 and 3 per cent, have to be adjusted by the rate of inflation to obtain the nominal coupon and hence the actual amount of cash paid out. For example, if an index-linked gilt offers a 2 per cent coupon, C_r, and the relevant rate of inflation, IR (this is covered in more detail below), is 5.5 per cent then the nominal coupon, C_n, will be:

$$(1 + C_n) = (1 + IR)(1 + C_r)$$

$$= (1 + 0.055)(1 + 0.025) = 1.081,375$$

or 8.1375 per cent; i.e. a payment of 8.1375 per unit held. The redemption value is also linked to the rate of inflation so that, taking the above rate of inflation as being relevant, the original 100 would have been increased to 105.5 (100)(1.055).

The rate of inflation used is the RPI and each index-linked issue has a base level for the calculation of the effects of inflation on coupons and redemption values. This is taken as the RPI value 8 months before issue and each coupon is adjusted on the basis of the inflation which occurred during the half-year which ended 8 months before the coupon is due to be paid. Therefore, the cash amount of the next coupon is always known.

The present structure of the gilts market

The principal objective of the Bank of England in restructuring the gilt-edged market was to minimize the cost of raising debt finance for the Government. To this end the Bank attempted to use the reorganization of the Stock Exchange to introduce further competition into the methods by which government debt was sold.

In 1985 the Bank set about reorganizing the market for government debt. It began by inviting applications for marketmakers in gilts who would undertake to provide continuous two-way prices under any trading conditions. In order to reduce the supervisory role of the Bank itself, it intended to recruit marketmakers solely from those firms and institutions who were already members of the International Stock Exchange (and therefore subject to the regulatory framework of the ISE). The principal qualification, other than membership of the ISE, imposed by the Bank was and is 'capital adequacy'. In its discussion papers the Bank explicitly avoided reference to any minimum capital requirements. Instead the Bank stated its intention to monitor and regulate the ratio of risk exposure to capital. In this way the Bank attempted to avoid the situation of a gilt-edged marketmaker being in financial difficulties because it did not have the capital resources to cover any contingent liabilities incurred during operations in the market.

Before October 1986 the Bank of England approved 29 marketmakers for the gilts market but before the new system came into operation the Bank of America and Union Discount withdrew leaving 27 starters. This has ensured the realization of the Bank's principal objective—that of increased competition and the minimization of the cost of funding the Government's financing requirements. Although the number of marketmakers has not substantially changed in the 3 years since the Big Bang the membership has. The membership has changed as the financially weaker institutions have dropped out (Lloyds Bank, Orion Royal, Hill Samuel, Pru Bache, Citicorp, Morgan Grenfell, Hoare Govett) and new ones have joined (notably the Japanese firms of Nomura and Daiwa). Including the 2 new entrants, there were 22 marketmakers in gilts at the beginning of 1989. There were also 5 (6 were originally appointed but in 1988 a firm called Tullets dropped out) 'inter-dealer brokers'. These are firms which arrange deals between the marketmakers themselves and allow them to unwind positions which they might have otherwise found difficult. They are essential for the maintenance of the market's liquidity.

The Bank also laid down the requirements for its own operations in the market:
1. To receive and accept, at its discretion, bids from marketmakers, both during and outside market hours, for stock.
2 To receive and undertake, at its discretion, proposals to switch stock from marketmakers.
3. To bid for, at its discretion, stock of less than 3 months maturity and index-linked stock offered by marketmakers.
4. To purchase, at its discretion, other stocks offered by marketmakers.

The Bank also intended to continue the tax arrangements available to gilt-edged jobbers under the old system:
1. Marketmakers are able to claim against their tax liabilities the full amount of any trading losses made by buying stock cum dividend and then selling it ex-dividend regardless of the interval between purchase and resale.
2. Marketmakers are able to offset against dividends received any dividends paid by them on stock they have purchased.

In tandem with the structural changes made to the membership of the gilt-edged market the Bank has revamped the payment and transfer systems. The Central Gilts Office (CGO) provided marketmakers with computerized accounts which facilitated the transfer of stock before the change of ownership was recorded at the Bank. It also ensured that payment was assured by the buyer's settlement bank to that of the seller on the same way as the transfer of stock.

Table 9.1 shows the average numbers of transactions per day in the gilts market during 1986.

Table 9.1   Average numbers of transactions per day in 1986

		Jan.–Oct.	Nov.–Dec.
Credits to CGO Accounts		1400	1250
Debits to CGO Accounts		1400	1350
Member to Member movements		1100	2850
	Total	3900	5450

The Bank noted that the increase in the member-to-member movements in November and December 1986 reflected additional transactions being made through the inter-dealer brokers.

Returns on equities and fixed interest stocks

By virtue of having a prior claim on assets and having a fixed and legally enforceable income and redemption, fixed interest debentures are usually assumed to offer less risk to the investor. Hence, given that they are held to bear less risk, we should expect a lower return. Merrett and Sykes[1] produced estimates of equity and fixed interest yields for UK securities between 1919 and 1966 (Table 9.2).

Table 9.2   Annual returns on UK equities and fixed interest investments 1919–66

	Equities (–) return		Fixed interest (–) return	
	Real	Money	Real	Money
1919–39	12.4	10.3	6.5	4.6
1939–49	0.3	5.9	−2.2	3.3
1949–66	7.4	11.2	−4.6	−1.0
1919–66	8.0	9.7	0.6	2.3

Source: A. Merrett and A. Sykes, Tables 2 and 4.

The figures of Table 9.2 may be updated using the work of Ibbotson et al.[2] (Table 9.3).

Table 9.3   Annual US $ adjusted percentage returns 1960–80

	UK		USA		Japan	
	Equities	Debt	Equities	Debt	Equities	Debt
1960	0.13	−0.47	0.83	10.74	38.5	8.37
1961	12.56	4.72	27.52	2.66	−13.03	6.18
1962	4.76	13.19	−9.29	5.94	4.68	−0.02
1963	22.8	5.04	21.04	2.33	8.87	19.24
1964	−5.14	−1.18	16.71	4.15	10.93	8.45
1965	12.66	4.8	15.26	−0.26	21.39	12.24
1966	−2.07	5.27	−8.21	1.09	9.04	8.02
1967	16.57	−11.43	30.45	−4.29	−4.85	6.25
1968	51.34	1.55	14.95	2.21	26.43	7.84
1969	−12.52	1.63	−9.86	−4.63	34.15	6.65
1970	−5.72	8.64	−1.0	14.36	−6.35	7.26
1971	47.99	28.61	18.16	10.52	46.55	21.3
1972	3.93	−12.53	17.71	5.81	126.56	14.24
1973	−23.44	−7.05	−18.68	2.3	−20.13	6.43
1974	−50.33	−2.63	−27.77	0.17	−15.65	−1.35
1975	115.06	9.62	37.49	12.29	19.84	10.35
1976	−12.55	−9.06	26.68	15.58	25.8	14.56
1977	56.49	53.66	−3.03	2.99	15.7	42.7
1978	14.63	6.64	8.53	1.17	53.33	30.26
1979	22.2	16.05	24.18	2.28	−11.69	−17.72
1980	38.8	28.01	33.22	3.05	29.7	22.25

Source: R. Ibbotson, R. Carr and A. Robinson,[2] Tables III and VII, pp. 69 and 74.

Ibotson et al. summarized their results as shown in Table 9.4.

Table 9.4   Summary of equity and fixed interest percentage annual returns 1960–80

Country	Equities Compound	Arith. mean	St. dev.	Fixed interest Compound	Arith. mean	St. dev.
Europe	8.4	9.6	16.2			
France	6.2	8.1	21.4	5.3	6.0	12.3
Germany	8.3	10.1	19.9	10.3	10.6	9.2
Holland	9.3	10.7	17.8	7.6	7.9	8.1
UK	10.0	14.7	16.2	5.9	6.8	14.9
USA	8.7	10.2	17.7	4.2	4.3	5.4
Canada	10.7	12.1	17.5	3.3	3.5	6.3
Japan	15.6	19.0	31.4	10.6	11.2	8.1
World	9.3	10.5	15.8			

Source: R. Ibbotson, R. Carr and A. Robinson,[2] Tables II and VI, pp. 65 and 73.

The evidence presented in Tables 9.3 and 9.4 lends weight to the statement that being less risky we should expect less return from fixed interest investments whichever country is being considered.

Issuing gilt-edged stock

The Bank uses two main methods of issuing gilt-edged stock:

1. *Tender offers*—these may involve either the issue of completely new stocks or substantial tranches of existing stocks. An example of the former (Fig. 9.1) was advertised in the press on 31 May 1988 when 400 million of 2 per cent index-linked stock was offered to the public. All tenders had to be lodged with the Bank by 10.00 a.m. on Thursday 2 June 1988 with a down payment of £40 per £100 nominal bid for.

It is noteworthy that in this case the advertisement makes no reference to a minimum tender offer, the latter being the general policy of the Bank in respect of this class of stock (see Fig. 9.2). All other gilt-edged (conventional fixed coupon stock) tender offers stipulate a minimum price for offers. However, despite the slight difference in the way that the stocks are offered to the public, the method of allocation is the same. A striking price is arrived at which will be in excess of the minimum offer price if the issue is oversubscribed otherwise at the minimum tender price, and the issue is allocated in proportion to the size of the bids regardless of the price bid (except those that underbid the striking price). The only point to note in this system of allocation is that those who bid in excess of the striking price will have priority in allocation where the issue has been oversubscribed.

The Bank customarily announces the issue of new stock on a Friday and dealings usually start in the secondary market on the following Thursday. However, it should be borne in mind that on announcement, a 'grey' market may start in which the issue may be traded before it is issued. This is not uncommon and it has occurred with many of the privatization issues in the equity market. All tender issues are underwritten by the Bank and issues that are undersubscribed are taken up by the Bank and used as 'tap' stock which may be sold into the secondary market at the discretion of the Bank. The Bank's usual policy in this regard is to sell into a rising or stable market.

However, the Bank may buy in a falling market if the market is considered to be erratic and unstable. In this event the Bank only buys stock offered to it by marketmakers at prices slightly below those ruling in the market. Normally this activity is not noticed by the investing public, only by those market professionals intimately concerned with the gilt-edged market. In this activity the

TENDERS MUST BE LODGED AT THE BANK OF ENGLAND, NEW ISSUES (F), NEW CHANGE, LONDON, EC4M 9AA NOT LATER THAN 10.00 A.M ON THURSDAY, 2ND JUNE 1988, OR AT ANY OF THE BRANCHES OR AGENCIES OF THE BANK OF ENGLAND NOT LATER THAN 3.30 P.M. ON WEDNESDAY, 1ST JUNE 1988.

ISSUE BY TENDER OF £400,000,000

2 per cent INDEX-LINKED TREASURY STOCK, 1994

PAYABLE AS FOLLOWS:

Deposit with tender	£40.00 per cent
On Monday, 18th July 1988	Balance of purchase money

INTEREST PAYABLE HALF-YEARLY ON 16TH MAY AND 16TH NOVEMBER

1. The Stock is an investment falling within Part II of the First Schedule to the Trustee Investments Act 1961. Application has been made to the Council of The International Stock Exchange for the Stock to be admitted to the Official List.

2. THE GOVERNOR AND COMPANY OF THE BANK OF ENGLAND are authorised to receive tenders for the above Stock.

3. The principal of and interest on the Stock will be a charge on the National Loans Fund, with recourse to the Consolidated Fund of the United Kingdom.

4. The Stock will be registered at the Bank of England or at the Bank of Ireland, Belfast, and will be transferable, in multiples of one penny, by instrument in writing in accordance with the Stock Transfer Act 1963. Stock registered at the Bank of England held for the account of members of the Central Gilts Office Service will also be transferable, in multiples of one penny, by exempt transfer in accordance with the Stock Transfer Act 1982 and the relevant subordinate legislation. Transfers will be free of stamp duty.

5. The Stock may be held on the National Savings Stock Register.

6. If not previously redeemed under the provisions of paragraph 15, the Stock will be repaid on 16th May 1994. The value of the principal on repayment will be related, subject to the terms of this prospectus, to the movement, during the life of the Stock, of the United Kingdom General Index of Retail Prices maintained by the Department of Employment, or any Index which may replace that Index for the purposes of this prospectus, such movement being indicated by the Index figure issued monthly and subsequently published in the London, Edinburgh and Belfast Gazettes.

7. For the purposes of this prospectus, the Index figure applicable to any month will be the Index figure issued seven months prior to the relevant month and relating to the month before that prior month; "month" means calendar month; and the Index ratio applicable to any month will be equal to the Index figure applicable to that month divided by the Index figure applicable to June 1988.

8. The amount due on repayment, per £100 nominal of Stock, will be £100 multiplied by the Index ratio applicable to the month in which repayment takes place. This amount, expressed in pounds sterling to four places of decimals rounded to the nearest figure below, will be announced by the Bank of England not later than the business day immediately preceding the date of the penultimate interest payment.

9. Interest will be payable half-yearly on 16th May and 16th November. Income tax will be deducted from payments of more than £5 per annum. Interest warrants will be transmitted by post.

10. The first interest payment will be made on 16th November 1988 at the rate of £0.7727 per £100 nominal of Stock.

11. Each subsequent half-yearly interest payment will be at a rate, per £100 nominal of Stock, of £1 multiplied by the Index ratio applicable to the month in which the payment falls due.

12. The rate of interest for each interest payment other than the first, expressed as a percentage in pounds sterling to four places of decimals rounded to the nearest figure below, will be announced by the Bank of England not later than the business day immediately preceding the date of the previous interest payment.

13. If the Index is revised to a new base after the Stock is issued, it will be necessary, for the purposes of the preceding paragraphs, to calculate and use a notional Index figure in substitution for the Index figure applicable to the month in which repayment takes place and/or an interest payment falls due ("the month of payment"). This notional Index figure will be calculated by multiplying the actual Index figure applicable to the month of payment by the Index figure on the old base for the month on which the revised Index is based and dividing the product by the new base figure for the same month. This procedure will be used for each occasion on which a revision is made during the life of the Stock.

14. If the Index is not published for a month for which it is relevant for the purposes of this prospectus, the Bank of England, after appropriate consultation with the relevant Government Department, will publish a substitute Index figure which shall be an estimate of the Index figure which would have been applicable to the month of payment, and such substitute Index figure shall be used for all purposes for which the actual Index figure would have been relevant. The calculation by the Bank of England of the amounts of principal and/or interest payable on the basis of a substitute Index figure shall be conclusive and binding upon all stockholders. No subsequent adjustment to such amounts will be made in the event of subsequent publication of the Index figure which would have been applicable to the month of payment.

15. If any change should be made to the coverage or the basic calculation of the Index which, in the opinion of the Bank of England, constitutes a fundamental change in the Index which would be materially detrimental to the interests of stockholders, Her Majesty's Treasury will publish a notice in the London, Edinburgh and Belfast Gazettes immediately following the announcement by the relevant Government Department of the change, informing stockholders and offering them the right to require Her Majesty's Treasury to redeem their stock. For the purposes of this paragraph, repayment to stockholders who exercise this right will be effected, on a date to be chosen by Her Majesty's Treasury, not later than seven months from the last month of publication of the old Index. The amount of principal due on repayment and of any interest which has accrued will be calculated on the basis of the Index ratio applicable to the month in which repayment takes place. A notice setting out the administrative arrangements will be sent to stockholders at their registered address by the Bank of England at the appropriate time.

16. Tenders must be lodged at the Bank of England, New Issues (F), New Change, London, EC4M 9AA not later than 10.00 A.M. ON THURSDAY, 2ND JUNE 1988, or at any of the Branches or Agencies of the Bank of England not later than 3.30 P.M. ON WEDNESDAY, 1ST JUNE 1988. Each tender must be for one amount and at one price which is a multiple of 5p. Tenders will not be revocable between 10.00 a.m. on Thursday, 2nd June 1988 and 10.00 a.m. on Tuesday, 7th June 1988. TENDERS LODGED WITHOUT A PRICE BEING STATED WILL BE REJECTED. Separate arrangements have been made under which gilt-edged market makers may tender by telephone to the Bank of England not later than 10.00 a.m. on Thursday, 2nd June 1988.

17. A separate cheque representing a deposit at the rate of £40.00 for every £100 of the NOMINAL amount of Stock tendered for must accompany each tender; cheques must be drawn on a bank in, and be payable in, the United Kingdom, the Channel Islands or the Isle of Man.

18. Tenders must be for a minimum of £100 nominal of Stock and for multiples of Stock as follows:—

Amount of Stock tendered for	*Multiple*
£100—£1,000	£100
£1,000—£3,000	£500
£3,000—£10,000	£1,000
£10,000—£50,000	£5,000
£50,000 or greater	£25,000

19. Her Majesty's Treasury reserve the right to reject any tender or part of any tender and may therefore allot to tenderers less than the full amount of the Stock. Tenders will be ranked in descending order of price and allotments will be made to tenderers whose tenders are at or above the lowest price at which Her Majesty's Treasury decide that any tender should be accepted (the allotment price). All allotments will be made at the allotment price: tenders which are accepted and which are made at prices above the allotment price will be allotted in full; tenders made at the allotment price may be allotted in full or in part only. Any balance of Stock not allotted to tenderers will be allotted at the allotment price to the Governor and Company of the Bank of England, Issue Department.

20. Letters of allotment in respect of Stock allotted, being the only form in which the Stock (other than amounts held in the Central Gilts Office Service for the account of members) may be transferred prior to registration, will be despatched by post at the risk of the tenderer, but the despatch of any letter of allotment, and any refund of the balance of the amount paid as deposit, may at the discretion of the Bank of England be withheld until the tenderer's cheque has been paid. In the event of such withholding, the tenderer will be notified by letter by the Bank of England of the acceptance of his tender and of the amount of Stock allocated to him, subject in each case to payment of his cheque, but such notification will confer no right on the tenderer to transfer the Stock so allocated.

21. No allotment will be made for a less amount than £100 Stock. In the event of partial allotment, the balance of the amount paid as deposit will, when refunded, be remitted by cheque despatched by post at the risk of the tenderer; if no allotment is made the amount paid as deposit will be returned likewise. Payment in full may be made at any time after allotment but no discount will be allowed on such payment. Interest may be charged on a day-to-day basis on any overdue amount which may be accepted at a rate equal to the London Inter-Bank Offered Rate for seven day deposits in sterling ("LIBOR") plus 1 per cent per annum. Such rate will be determined by the Bank of England by reference to market quotations, on the due date for the relevant payment, for LIBOR obtained from such source or sources as the Bank of England shall consider appropriate. Default in due payment of any amount in respect of the Stock will render the allotment of such Stock liable to cancellation and any amount previously paid liable to forfeiture.

22. Letters of allotment may be split into denominations of multiples of £100 on written request received by the Bank of England, New Issues, New Change, London, EC4M 9AA on any date not later than 14th July 1988. Such requests must be signed and must be accompanied by the letters of allotment.

23. Members of the Central Gilts Office Service may, subject to the provisions of the agreement governing their membership of that Service, surrender a partly-paid letter of allotment to the Central Gilts Office for cancellation and for the Stock comprised therein to be credited to the member's account. The member who is shown by the accounts of the Central Gilts Office as being entitled to any Stock shall, to the exclusion of all persons previously entitled to such Stock and any person claiming any entitlement thereto, both be treated as entitled to such Stock as if that member were the holder of a letter of allotment and be liable for the payment of any amount due in respect of such Stock. A member will be entitled at any time prior to registration to withdraw, in multiples of £100, Stock credited to the member's account and to obtain a partly-paid letter of allotment comprising such Stock, and such member shall be liable for the payment of all amounts becoming due thereafter in respect of such Stock unless and until that letter of allotment is surrendered to the Central Gilts Office for cancellation as aforesaid.

24. Letters of allotment must be surrendered for registration, accompanied by a completed registration form, when the balance of the purchase money is paid, unless payment in full has been made before the due date, in which case they must be surrendered for registration not later than 18th July 1988; registration of Stock held for the account of members of the Central Gilts Office Service will be effected under separate arrangements.

25. Tender forms and copies of this prospectus may be obtained at the Bank of England, New Issues, New Change, London, EC4M 9AA, or at any of the Branches or Agencies of the Bank of England; at the Bank of Ireland, Moyne Buildings, 1st Floor, 20 Callender Street, Belfast, BT1 5BN; or at any office of The International Stock Exchange in the United Kingdom.

Government statement

Attention is drawn to the statement issued by Her Majesty's Treasury on 29th May 1985 which explained that, in the interest of the orderly conduct of fiscal policy, neither Her Majesty's Government nor the Bank of England or their respective servants or agents undertake to disclose tax changes decided on but not yet announced, even where they may specifically affect the terms on which, or the conditions under which, this Stock is issued or sold by or on behalf of the Government or the Bank; that no responsibility can therefore be accepted for any omission to make such disclosure; and that such omission shall neither render any transaction liable to be set aside nor give rise to any claim for compensation.

BANK OF ENGLAND
LONDON

27th May 1988

THIS FORM MAY BE USED
TENDER FORM

This form must be lodged at the Bank of England, New Issues (F), New Change, London, EC4M 9AA not later than 10.00 A.M. ON THURSDAY, 2ND JUNE 1988, or at any of the Branches or Agencies of the Bank of England not later than 3.30 P.M. ON WEDNESDAY, 1ST JUNE 1988.

ISSUE BY TENDER OF £400,000,000

2 per cent Index-Linked Treasury Stock, 1994

TO THE GOVERNOR AND COMPANY OF THE BANK OF ENGLAND

I/We tender in accordance with the terms of the prospectus dated 27th May 1988 as follows:—

Amount of above-mentioned Stock tendered for, being a minimum of £100 and in a multiple as follows:—

Amount of Stock tendered for	*Multiple*
£100—£1,000	£100
£1,000—£3,000	£500
£3,000—£10,000	£1,000
£10,000—£50,000	£5,000
£50,000 or greater	£25,000

1. NOMINAL AMOUNT OF STOCK

£

Amount of deposit enclosed, being £40.00 for every £100 of the NOMINAL amount of Stock tendered for (shown in Box 1 above):—

2. AMOUNT OF DEPOSIT (*a*)

£

The price tendered per £100 Stock, being a multiple of 5p *(tenders lodged without a price being stated will be rejected):—*

3. TENDER PRICE (*b*)

£ : p

I/We hereby engage to pay the balance of the purchase money when it becomes due on on any allotment that may be made in respect of this tender, as provided by the said prospectus.

I/We request that any letter of allotment in respect of Stock allotted to me/us be sent by post at my/our risk to me/us at the address shown below.

__________ 1988

SIGNATURE ....
of, or on behalf of, tenderer

PLEASE USE BLOCK LETTERS

MR/MRS MISS	FORENAME(S) IN FULL	SURNAME	DT
FULL POSTAL ADDRESS:—			
	POST-TOWN	COUNTY	POSTCODE

a **A separate cheque must accompany each tender. Cheques should be made payable to "Bank of England" and crossed "New Issues". Cheques must be drawn on a bank in, and be payable in, the United Kingdom, the Channel Islands or the Isle of Man.**

b **Each tender must be for one amount and at one price which is a multiple of 5p.**

Figure 9.1 Advertisement for the issue by tender of 2% index-linked stock on 31 May 1988. (Source: Bank of England.)

TENDERS MUST BE LODGED AT THE BANK OF ENGLAND, NEW ISSUES (T), WATLING STREET, LONDON, EC4M 9AA NOT LATER THAN 10.00 A.M. ON WEDNESDAY, 15TH JULY 1987, OR AT ANY OF THE BRANCHES OR AGENCIES OF THE BANK OF ENGLAND NOT LATER THAN 3.30 P.M. ON TUESDAY, 14TH JULY 1987.

ISSUE OF £500,000,000

3 per cent TREASURY STOCK, 1992

FOR TENDER AT A MINIMUM TENDER PRICE OF £85·50 PER CENT

PAYABLE IN FULL WITH TENDER

INTEREST PAYABLE HALF-YEARLY ON 11TH JUNE AND 11TH DECEMBER

This Stock is an investment falling within Part II of the First Schedule to the Trustee Investments Act 1961. Application has been made to the Council of The International Stock Exchange for the Stock to be admitted to the Official List.

1. THE GOVERNOR AND COMPANY OF THE BANK OF ENGLAND are authorised to receive tenders for the above Stock.

2. The principal of and interest on the Stock will be a charge on the National Loans Fund, with recourse to the Consolidated Fund of the United Kingdom.

3. The Stock will be repaid at par on 11th June 1992.

4. The Stock will be registered at the Bank of England or at the Bank of Ireland, Belfast, and will be transferable, in multiples of one penny, by instrument in writing in accordance with the Stock Transfer Act 1963. Stock registered at the Bank of England held for the account of members of the Central Gilts Office Service will also be transferable, in multiples of one penny, by exempt transfer in accordance with the Stock Transfer Act 1982 and the relevant subordinate legislation. Transfers will be free of stamp duty.

5. Interest will be payable half-yearly on 11th June and 11th December. Income tax will be deducted from payments of more than £5 per annum. Interest warrants will be transmitted by post. The first interest payment will be made on 11th December 1987 at the rate of £1.2247 per £100 of the Stock.

6. Tenders must be lodged at the Bank of England, New Issues (T), Watling Street, London, EC4M 9AA not later than 10.00 A.M. ON WEDNESDAY, 15TH JULY 1987, or at any of the Branches or Agencies of the Bank of England not later than 3.30 P.M. ON TUESDAY, 14TH JULY 1987. Tenders will not be revocable between 10.00 a.m. on Wednesday, 15th July 1987 and 10.00 a.m. on Monday, 20th July 1987. Separate arrangements have been made under which gilt-edged market makers may tender by telephone to the Bank of England not later than 10.00 a.m. on Wednesday, 15th July 1987.

7. Each tender must be for one amount and at one price. The minimum price, below which tenders will not be accepted, is £85·50 per cent. Tenders must be made at the minimum price or at higher prices which are multiples of 5p. Tenders lodged without a price being stated will be deemed to have been made at the minimum price.

8. Tenders must be accompanied by payment in full, i.e. the price tendered (minimum of £85·50) for every £100 of the nominal amount of Stock tendered for. A separate cheque must accompany each tender; cheques must be drawn on a bank in, and be payable in, the United Kingdom, the Channel Islands or the Isle of Man.

9. Tenders must be for a minimum of £100 Stock and for multiples of Stock as follows:—

Amount of Stock tendered for	Multiple
£100—£1,000	£100
£1,000—£3,000	£500
£3,000—£10,000	£1,000
£10,000—£50,000	£5,000
£50,000 or greater	£25,000

10. Her Majesty's Treasury reserve the right to reject any tender or part of any tender and may therefore allot to tenderers less than the full amount of the Stock. Tenders will be ranked in descending order of price and allotments will be made to tenderers whose tenders are at or above the lowest price at which Her Majesty's Treasury decide that any tender should be accepted (the allotment price), which will be not less than the minimum price. All allotments will be made at the allotment price: tenders which are accepted and which are made at prices above the allotment price will be allotted in full; tenders made at the allotment price may be allotted in full or in part only. Any balance of Stock not allotted to tenderers will be allotted at the allotment price to the Governor and Company of the Bank of England, Issue Department.

11. Letters of allotment in respect of Stock allotted, being the only form in which the Stock may be transferred prior to registration, will be despatched by post at the risk of the tenderer, but the despatch of any letter of allotment, and the refund of any excess amount paid, may at the discretion of the Bank of England be withheld until the tenderer's cheque has been paid. In the event of such withholding, the tenderer will be notified by letter by the Bank of England of the acceptance of his tender and of the amount of Stock allocated to him, subject in each case to payment of his cheque, but such notification will confer no right on the tenderer to transfer the Stock so allocated.

12. No allotment will be made for a less amount than £100 Stock. In the event of partial allotment, or of tenders at prices above the allotment price, the excess amount paid will, when refunded, be remitted by cheque despatched by post at the risk of the tenderer; if no allotment is made the amount paid with tender will be returned likewise. Non-payment on presentation of a cheque in respect of any Stock allotted will render the allotment of such Stock liable to cancellation. Interest at a rate equal to the London Inter-Bank Offered Rate for seven day deposits in sterling ("LIBOR") plus 1 per cent per annum may, however, be charged on the amount payable in respect of any allotment of Stock for which payment is accepted after the due date. Such rate will be determined by the Bank of England by reference to market quotations, on the due date for such payment, for LIBOR obtained from such source or sources as the Bank of England shall consider appropriate.

13. Letters of allotment may be split into denominations of multiples of £100 on written request received by the Bank of England, New Issues, Watling Street, London, EC4M 9AA on any date not later than 13th August 1987. Such requests must be signed and must be accompanied by the letters of allotment. Letters of allotment, accompanied by a completed registration form, may be lodged for registration forthwith and in any case they must be lodged for registration not later than 17th August 1987.

14. Tender forms and copies of this prospectus may be obtained at the Bank of England, New Issues, Watling Street, London, EC4M 9AA, or at any of the Branches or Agencies of the Bank of England; at the Bank of Ireland, Moyne Buildings, 1st Floor, 20 Callender Street, Belfast, BT1 5BN; or at any office of The International Stock Exchange in the United Kingdom.

Government statement

Attention is drawn to the statement issued by Her Majesty's Treasury on 29th May 1985 which explained that, in the interest of the orderly conduct of fiscal policy, neither Her Majesty's Government nor the Bank of England or their respective servants or agents undertake to disclose tax changes decided on but not yet announced, even where they may specifically affect the terms on which, or the conditions under which, this Stock is issued or sold by or on behalf of the Government or the Bank; that no responsibility can therefore be accepted for any omission to make such disclosure; and that such omission shall neither render any transaction liable to be set aside nor give rise to any claim for compensation.

BANK OF ENGLAND
LONDON

10th July 1987

THIS FORM MAY BE USED

TENDER FORM

This form must be lodged at the Bank of England, New Issues (T), Watling Street, London, EC4M 9AA not later than 10.00 A.M. ON WEDNESDAY, 15TH JULY 1987, or at any of the Branches or Agencies of the Bank of England not later than 3.30 P.M. ON TUESDAY, 14TH JULY 1987.

ISSUE OF £500,000,000

3 per cent Treasury Stock, 1992

FOR TENDER AT A MINIMUM TENDER PRICE OF £85·50 PER CENT

TO THE GOVERNOR AND COMPANY OF THE BANK OF ENGLAND

I/We tender in accordance with the terms of the prospectus dated 10th July 1987 as follows:—

Amount of above-mentioned Stock tendered for, being a minimum of £100 and in a multiple as follows:—

Amount of Stock tendered for	Multiple
£100—£1,000	£100
£1,000—£3,000	£500
£3,000—£10,000	£1,000
£10,000—£50,000	£5,000
£50,000 or greater	£25,000

1. NOMINAL AMOUNT OF STOCK
£

Sum enclosed, being the amount required for payment in full, i.e. the price tendered (minimum of £85·50) for every £100 of the nominal amount of Stock tendered for (shown in Box 1 above):—

2. AMOUNT OF PAYMENT (a)
£

The price tendered per £100 Stock, being a multiple of 5p and not less than the minimum tender price of £85·50:—

3. TENDER PRICE (b)
£   :   p

I/We request that any letter of allotment in respect of Stock allotted to me/us be sent by post at my/our risk to me/us at the address shown below.

_____ July 1987

SIGNATURE...
of, or on behalf of, tenderer

PLEASE USE BLOCK LETTERS   DT

MR/MRS MISS	FORENAME(S) IN FULL	SURNAME
FULL POSTAL ADDRESS:—		
POST-TOWN	COUNTY	POSTCODE

a A separate cheque must accompany each tender. Cheques should be made payable to "Bank of England" and crossed "New Issues". Cheques must be drawn on a bank in, and be payable in, the United Kingdom, the Channel Islands or the Isle of Man.

b The price tendered must be a multiple of 5p and not less than the minimum tender price. If no price is stated, this tender will be deemed to have been made at the minimum tender price. Each tender must be for one amount and at one price.

Figure 9.2 Advertisement for the issue by tender of 3% treasury stock 1992. (Source: Bank of England.)

THIS NOTICE DOES NOT CONSTITUTE AN OFFER FOR SALE AND THE STOCKS LISTED BELOW ARE NOT AVAILABLE FOR PURCHASE DIRECT FROM THE BANK OF ENGLAND. OFFICIAL DEALINGS IN THE STOCKS ON THE INTERNATIONAL STOCK EXCHANGE ARE EXPECTED TO COMMENCE ON MONDAY, 1ST AUGUST 1988.

ISSUES OF GOVERNMENT STOCK

The Bank of England announces that Her Majesty's Treasury has created on 29th July 1988, and has issued to the Bank, additional amounts as indicated of each of the following Stocks:

£100 million   **2 per cent INDEX-LINKED TREASURY STOCK, 2006**
£100 million   **2½ per cent INDEX-LINKED TREASURY STOCK, 2016**

The price paid by the Bank on issue was in each case the middle market price of the relevant Stock at 3.30 p.m. on 29th July 1988 as certified by the Government Broker.

In each case, the amount issued on 29th July 1988 represents a further tranche of the relevant Stock, ranking in all respects *pari passu* with that Stock and subject to the terms and conditions applicable to that Stock, and subject also to the provision contained in the final paragraph of this notice; the current provisions for Capital Gains Tax are described below.

Application has been made to the Council of The International Stock Exchange for each further tranche of stock to be admitted to the Official List.

Copies of the prospectuses for 2 per cent Index-Linked Treasury Stock, 2006 dated 3rd July 1981 (as amended by the supplement to the prospectus dated 9th March 1982) and 2½ per cent Index-Linked Treasury Stock, 2016 dated 14th January 1983 may be obtained at the Bank of England, New Issues, New Change, London, EC4M 9AA. The Stocks are repayable, and interest is payable half-yearly, on the dates shown below (provision is made in the prospectuses for stockholders to be offered the right of early redemption under certain circumstances):

Stock	Redemption date	Interest payment dates
2 per cent Index-Linked Treasury Stock, 2006	19th July 2006	19th January 19th July
2½ per cent Index-Linked Treasury Stock, 2016	26th July 2016	26th January 26th July

Both the principal of and the interest on 2 per cent Index-Linked Treasury Stock, 2006 and 2½ per cent Index-Linked Treasury Stock, 2016 are indexed to the General Index of Retail Prices. The Index figure relevant to any month is that published seven months previously and relating to the month before the month of publication. The Index figure relevant to the month of issue of 2 per cent Index-Linked Treasury Stock, 2006 is that relating to November 1980 (274.1); the equivalent Index figure for 2½ per cent Index-Linked Treasury Stock, 2016 is that relating to May 1982 (322.0). These Index figures will be used for the purposes of calculating payments of principal and interest due in respect of the relevant further tranches of stock: as provided for in the prospectuses, the calculations will take account of the revision of the Index to a new base of January 1987 = 100 (on the old base the Index for January 1987 was 394.5).

The relevant Index figures for the half-yearly interest payments on 2 per cent Index-Linked Treasury Stock, 2006 and 2½ per cent Index-Linked Treasury Stock, 2016 are as follows:

	Relevant Index figure	
Interest payable	Published in	Relating to
January	June of the previous year	May
July	December of the previous year	November

The further tranches of 2 per cent Index-Linked Treasury Stock, 2006 and 2½ per cent Index-Linked Treasury Stock, 2016 will rank for a full six months' interest on the next interest payment date applicable to the relevant stock.

2 per cent Index-Linked Treasury Stock, 2006 and 2½ per cent Index-Linked Treasury Stock, 2016 are specified under paragraph 1 of Schedule 2 to the Capital Gains Tax Act 1979 as gilt-edged securities (under current legislation exempt from tax on capital gains, irrespective of the period for which the Stock is held).

Government statement
Attention is drawn to the statement issued by Her Majesty's Treasury on 29th May 1985 which explained that, in the interest of the orderly conduct of fiscal policy, neither Her Majesty's Government nor the Bank of England or their respective servants or agents undertake to disclose tax changes decided on but not yet announced, even where they may specifically affect the terms on which, or the conditions under which, these further tranches of stock are issued or sold by or on behalf of the Government or the Bank; that no responsibility can therefore be accepted for any omission to make such disclosure; and that such omission shall neither render any transaction liable to be set aside nor give rise to any claim for compensation.

BANK OF ENGLAND
LONDON

29th July 1988

Figure 9.2 (*continued*)   Tranchettes.

Bank is acting in the same way as lead managers in the Euroband markets whose duties include the stabilization of the issue's price.

Recently a very similar operation was undertaken by the Bank in respect of the sale of British Petroleum shares by the Government to the public at large. Because the issue was hugely undersubscribed the Bank effectively underwrote the shares by entering the secondary market at a fixed price of 70p (the partly paid issue price being 120p) for a period of 6 months.

2. *Tranchettes*—These are issues of small blocks of existing stocks which are placed in the Bank's own portfolio of gilts for direct sale into the secondary market (see Fig. 9.2).

In the financial year 1985–86 the gross sale of gilt-edged stock amounted to £11.9 billion of which £6.5 billion was accounted for by funding redemptions and official purchases of stock nearing maturity. Therefore there was a net sale of £5.4 billion of new gilts to the private sector. The remaining government funding requirement was met by sales of national savings certificates to the amount of £2.2 billion.

Table 9.5   Analysis of gilt-edged issues in 1985–86

By type of stock (£billion) *full coupon conventionals*	
up to 5 years	1.1
5–10 years	1.9
10–15 years	0.95
over 15 years	7.25
total	11.2
convertible	0.85
low coupon conventionals	1.45
index linked	0.85
total	14.35
By method of issue (£billion)	
Taps: issued by tender	5.2
Taps: issued to the Bank	3.7
total	8.9
Tranchettes[a]	5.45
total	14.35

[a] 12 packages of small amounts of 35 different gilt-edged stocks.
Source: *Bank of England Quarterly*, December 1986.

The market for corporate stocks in the UK

Since the end of the sixties the use of traditional debenture financing by British corporations has been rather limited (see Tables 9.6(a) and (b)).

The striking aspect of Tables 9.6(a) and (b) is the very low levels of loan capital issued in the UK by British corporations between 1973 and 1980 (inclusive). This is in stark contrast to the fifties and sixties when loan capital formed an important part of corporate financing needs. Conventional corporate finance leads us to believe that debt financing is usually cheaper than equity financing.[2] Yet the seventies saw a very significant decline in long-term debenture financing. We may note from Table 9.6(a) that equity financing never exceeded 34 per cent of the total, indeed the primary sources of finance have been bank advances and 'other' (Euroloans etc.) over the entire period covered by the table.

Table 9.6(a) Corporate debt financing 1963–80

Year	Gross requirement £billion	Listed capital issues in the UK Loan cap. £billion	(%)	Share cap. £billion	(%)	Bank borrowing £billion	(%)	Other £billion	(%)
1963	1.2	0.2	(17)	0.1	(11)	0.5	(46)	0.3	(25)
1964	1.5	0.2	(17)	0.2	(11)	0.8	(51)	0.3	(21)
1965	1.3	0.4	(28)	0.0	(4)	0.5	(39)	0.4	(29)
1966	1.1	0.4	(39)	0.1	(13)	0.2	(17)	0.3	(30)
1967	1.0	0.4	(35)	0.1	(6)	0.3	(33)	0.3	(27)
1968	1.4	0.2	(14)	0.3	(21)	0.6	(42)	0.3	(23)
1969	1.5	0.3	(22)	0.2	(12)	0.7	(44)	0.3	(22)
1970	2.1	0.1	(7)	0.1	(2)	1.1	(53)	0.8	(38)
1971	1.9	0.2	(11)	0.2	(9)	0.7	(39)	0.8	(41)
1972	4.1	0.2	(6)	0.3	(8)	3.0	(74)	0.5	(13)
1973	6.2	—	—	0.1	(2)	4.5	(72)	1.6	(25)
1974	6.3	−0.1	—	0.1	(1)	4.4	(70)	1.9	(30)
1975	2.9	—	(1)	1.0	(34)	0.5	(17)	1.4	(48)
1976	4.4	—	—	0.8	(18)	2.4	(55)	1.2	(27)
1977	4.7	−0.1	—	0.7	(15)	3.0	(63)	1.1	(24)
1978	5.1	−0.1	—	0.8	(16)	2.9	(57)	1.5	(29)
1979	6.2	−0.1	—	1.0	(15)	4.9	(79)	0.5	(8)

Capital issues

Year	Gross requirement £billion		Capital issues	Bank borrowing	Other
1980	6.2		1.3	6.0	0.6
1981	3.4		1.7	3.3	2.9
1982	5.6		0.9	1.8	5.0
1983	−1.4		2.2	2.3	−0.1
1984	4.0		1.7	4.0	3.2
1985	4.0		5.0	6.9	1.5
1986	7.8		7.8	8.6	1.2
1987	22.1		17.7	15.2	1.7

Notes: (a) all percentages calculated on unrounded figures; (b) the equity figures for 1978 and 1979 are inflated by the take up of BL shares (£0.4 and £0.1 billion respectively) by the National Enterprise Board. Source: *Bank of England Quarterly*, March 1981, p. 54, Table 19.3 and various issues.

The variation in the popularity of fixed interest financing between the sixties and the seventies may be explained by changes in the tax environment and the levels of inflation experienced during the 1970s:

1. In 1965 the Government of the day introduced corporation tax which reduced the cost of servicing debt. This measure encouraged the use of securitized debt as a major source of cooporate finance. This stimulus lasted until the Finance Act of 1973 which introduced a major revision of the system of corporation tax. This was and still is called the imputation system which ensures that dividend income is only taxed once (a detailed analysis of the effects of this and the original corporation tax system is presented in Chapter 8).

2. During the sixties the rate of inflation experienced in the UK, although higher than that of most international competitors, never rose above 10 per cent. On the other hand, the seventies began with a doubling of the rate of inflation (from 5.6 per cent in 1969 to 11.6 per cent in 1970). This increased to 22.1 per cent in 1974 and subsequently never fell below 10 per cent in that decade. However, what is more important than the actual levels experienced were the levels of expectations and the perception of stability in macroeconomic management. It is a paradox that in the contemplation of using debenture finance expectations of falling inflation are

Table 9.6(b)   Corporate capital issues 1946–85

UK corporate capital issues 1946–85

	Debt £million	(%)	Preference £million	(%)	Equity £million	(%)	Total £million
1946	20.1	15.7	30.5	23.7	77.8	60.6	128.4
1947	32.3	24.1	40.5	30.3	61.1	45.6	133.8
1948	15.6	11	24.9	17.6	100.8	71.3	141.3
1949	34	29.8	30.3	26.5	50	43.7	114.3
1950	71.5	55.6	10.9	8.5	46.2	35.9	128.6
1951	49.1	37.8	19.7	15.1	61.1	47.1	129.9
1952	36.7	28.6	4.1	3.1	87.8	68.3	128.6
1953	53.1	50.4	7.9	7.5	44.3	42.1	105.4
1954	101	49.9	28.3	14	73	36.1	202.3
1955	65.1	27.2	18.9	7.9	154.9	64.9	238.9
1956	76	33.8	3.1	1.4	145.7	64.8	224.7
1957	183.3	54	1.7	0.5	155.2	45.5	340.2
1958	95.2	50.4	1	0.5	92.6	49.1	188.8
1959	119.5	29.6	10.7	2.6	274	67.8	404.2
1960	121.8	25.5	10.4	2.2	345.5	72.3	477.7
1961	141	25.5	2.8	0.5	408.4	74	552.3
1962	173.8	42.1	5.3	1.3	233.9	56.6	413
1963	271.5	60.3	14.7	3.3	163.9	36.4	450.1
1964	234	56.6	10.7	2.6	168.9	40.8	413.6
1965	454.6	90.3	3.2	0.6	45.5	9	503.4
1966	464.2	74.5	16.4	2.6	142.5	22.3	623.2
1967	343.5	81.5	5.7	1.4	72.6	17.2	421.9
1968	289.6	44.1	3.1	0.5	363.7	55.4	656.4
1969	376.5	65.9	0	0	195	34.1	571.5
1970	284.3	80.4	17.2	4.9	51.9	14.7	353.4
1971	340.4	51.3	12.8	1.9	310.4	46.8	663.6
1972	295.6	30.9	10.9	1.1	649.9	68	956.4
1973	42.9	20.4	14	6.7	153.6	73	210.5
1974	42.8	26.4	0	0	119.3	73.6	162.1
1975	212.8	13.5	44.9	2.8	1 320.7	83.7	1 578.4
1976	92.5	8	44.5	3.8	1 023.9	88.2	1 160.9
1977	93.8	9.9	33.9	3.6	819.6	86.5	947.3
1978	8.8	1.3	41.3	6.2	612.5	92.5	662.5
1979	61.4	6.9	34.6	3.9	789.2	89.2	885.1
1980	217.2	19.6	37.1	3.3	853.6	77.1	1 107.9
1981	440.4	16.5	113.1	4.2	2 110.8	79.2	2 664.3
1982	1 016.1	45.9	32.5	1.5	1 165.4	52.6	2 214
1983	525.5	17.7	80.7	2.7	2 370.1	79.6	2 976.3
1984	1 161.7	36.4	78.4	2.5	1 947.5	61.1	3 187.7
1985	2 594.7	32.4	455.2	5.7	4 962.3	61.9	8 012.1

Source: *Midland Bank Quarterly*, various Spring issues.

detrimental. Put very simply, if debentures are issued at high coupon rates which reflect current rates of inflation, then if the rate of inflation falls the company will be stuck with a high coupon burden at a time when inflation no longer boosts its earnings.

3. From Table 9.6(a) it can be seen that bank financing has always played a major part in financing British industrial and commercial companies. During the seventies this form of finance became comparatively more attractive as it offered variable rates of interest (which are tax deductible) and the short nature of these loans was mitigated by the banks' willingness to roll-over these loans on request. Furthermore, by 1980 one study[1] found that almost 60 per cent of bank

lending to the industrial and commercial sectors constituted 'medium-term finance'. These developments were magnified by the changes to the regulation of banks in 1971 ('Competition and Credit Control'). This gave the banks greater freedom in their lending policies to industrial and commercial companies. Another stimulus was the steady influx of foreign financial institutions into London most of which were willing to lend on competitive terms to industrial and commercial companies.[3] In addition to lengthening the terms of the advances, banks began to be flexible about repayment arrangements and began to offer very attractive leasing schemes with which capital equipment could be acquired.[4]

4. The last, but by no means least important, of the factors inhibiting the use of securitized debt as a source of financing was the existence of foreign exchange controls and the investment premium on overseas investments. Apart from discouraging investment abroad this also effectively reduced companies' access to international capital markets.

The valuation of fixed interest stock

As stated earlier in this chapter, the salient qualities of securitized debt are that they offer a known or predictable stream of income and redemption payments. In the absence of any significant listed corporate bond market in the UK (although this may change in the near future and UK corporate financing may become more heterogeneous and develop a bond market as in the USA), this chapter will confine itself to the valuation of government debt. This restriction reduces the problems of analysis considerably as it may be confidently assumed that there is no uncertainty about the payment of coupons or principal.

The general valuation model

As in all valuation problems in corporate and investment finance the valuation of debt concerns the present value of a stream of income.

$$P_0 = E(c)/(1+r_1) + E(c)/(1+r_1)(1+r_2) + \ldots$$

$$\ldots + [E(c) + E(M)]/(1+r_1)(1+r_2)\ldots(1+r_n) \tag{9.1}$$

where P_0 is the price, or rather the present value, of the income stream offered to the investor; $E(c)$ is the expected coupon payable in each period whether annually, or semi-annually; M is the redemption value payed to the investor when the debenture matures: E is the expected value operator; and $r_1, r_2 \ldots r_n$ are the risk-adjusted discount rates which are expected to apply to the future periods in which the income will be received. Where the discount rates are expected to be identical for all future periods and there is no realistic probability that the borrower will default, as in the case of the UK Government, Eq. (9.1) reduces to:

$$P_0 = c/(1+r) + c/(1+r)^2 + \ldots + (c+M)/(1+r)^n \tag{9.2}$$

or

$$P_0 = \sum_{t=1}^{n-1} [c/(1+r)^t] + (c+M)/(1+r)^n$$

This general valuation model may be used either in the case of the investor holding the debenture/gilt to maturity (i.e. M is the redemption value) or if the investor sells before redemption (i.e. M is the present value of the remaining coupons and the redemption value). For example, assume a 10 per cent 3-year gilt is being considered as an investment. It has 6 semi-annual coupons of £5 each remaining, in addition to the redemption payment of £100.[5] Assuming certainty of payment, the general valuation model may be used to estimate the present value of this investment—in fact the price the investor might be willing to pay. If the ruling rate of interest ('risk-adjusted discount rate') for a default-free 3-year investment is 8 per cent then the gilt would be evaluated as follows:

$$P_0 = 5/(1+0.085/2) + 5/(1+0.085/2)^2 + \ldots + (5+100)/(1+0.085/2)^6$$

$$P_0 = 103.9$$

In the traditional method of quoting gilt-edged prices this would appear as $103\frac{29}{32}$. On the other hand, if the relevant rate of interest was 10.5 per cent then the calculation would be as follows:

$$P_0 = 5/(1+0.105/2) + 5/(1+0.105/2)^2 + \ldots + (5+100)/(1+0.105/2)^6$$

$$P_0 = 98.74 \text{ or } 98\frac{3}{4}$$

If the interest rate is expected to change during the remaining life of the investment this may be accommodated using Eq. (9.1). Assume that the investor expects a falling series of rates; 9 per cent in year 1, 8 per cent in year 2 and 7 per cent in year 3:

$$P_0 = 5/(1+0.09/2) + 5/(1+0.09/2)^2 + 5/(1+0.08/2)^3 + 5/(1+0.08/2)^4$$
$$+ 5/(1+0.07/2)^5 + (5+100)/(1+0.07/2)^6$$

$$P_0 = 107.7$$

This general model may also be used to calculate the 'yield to redemption' (R) or the rate of return offered by the investment if the investor holds the debt to maturity. This value is more familiar to students of corporate finance as the 'internal rate of return'. The process merely involves equating the discounted stream of income from the bond with the purchase price (P_0). By successive iterations Eq. (9.1) may be solved for r rather than P_0. Using the previous example, the semi-annual internal rate of return is 5.7 per cent which gives an annualized yield to maturity of $11.46 ((5.73 \times 2)$ which is the method used in such papers as the *Financial Times*), or 11.79 which equals $[(1.05732)^2 - 1]100$ and which compounds the half-yearly rate and is theoretically correct. If the price quoted on the market was £105 the semi-annual yield to maturity would fall to 4.05 per cent implying an annual rate of 8.1 per cent (or 8.26 per cent compounded semi-annually).

Two general conclusions may be drawn from the relationships between prices, coupons and yields:

1. When yields rise prices fall and vice versa. Although this is not a linear relationship (discussed in the next section), it is a useful rule of thumb to recognize that there is an inverse relationship between interest rates and prices.

2. If the coupon exceeds the yield then the price will 'be at a premium to the face value' and vice versa.

However, the above conclusions must be tempered by the effects of the length of maturity of the debenture or gilt under consideration. For example, regardless of the relationship between the coupon and the yield the price of a gilt which has less than 12 months to run will move towards its face value.

In Table 9.7 there are 3 low coupon gilts all of which are within 3 per cent of their face value. Indeed the Transport 3% having gone ex-dividend is only a few weeks from maturity and hence its price is only 28p below its face value. Taking into account the bid–offer spread of the marketmaker and the brokerage fees (if any) there will be no opportunity to make a return on this investment before it matures (the 'xd' notation signifies that the seller rather than the buyer will receive the last coupon).

In this section all that remains to be examined are two special types of debenture. The first,

Table 9.7   Gilt-edged prices 28 May 1988 'shorts'

1988 High	Low	Name	Price	Yield int.	Maturity
99.72	98.19	Transport 3% 78–88	99.72xd	3.01	6.72
100.75	99.91	Treas 9–% 88	100.63	9.44	7.72
102.69	101.75	Treas 11–% 89	102.28	11.24	8.10
101.19	99.88	Treas 9–% 89 cnv	101.00	9.40	8.24
97.38	95.31	Treas 3% 89	97.22	3.08	5.86
102.31	100.69	Treas 10–% 89	102.00xd	10.29	8.46
103.53	101.81	Exch 10% 89	101.5	9.85	8.59
102.00	100.00	Exch 11% 89	102.88	10.70	8.64
97.56	95.19	Treas 5%	86–89	97.44	7.16
104.47	101.75	Exch 10.25% 89 cnv	102.81	9.96	8.04

Notes:
1. The 'interest yield' (also called the flat or running yield) is calculated by dividing the coupon by the quoted 'clean' price (which takes no account of any accumulated rights to coupons). This is important to institutional investors which need to be able to measure the cash flow from their investments in order to meet their contractual liabilities (pension and annuity payments etc.).
2. Those gilts with two dates in their names afford the Bank of England a range of time within which the stock may be redeemed. This allows the Bank to redeem at a point in time which is most advantageous to itself.
3. Two of the gilts have the notation 'cnv' in their titles. This shows that there are options to convert (usually at predetermined times at the discretion of the Bank) into new or other stocks.

Source: *Financial Times*, 28 May 1988.

'undated', have been issued by the British Government and are called 'consols' (coupons at 2% and 4%), War Loan 3%, Conversion 3%, and Treasury (coupons at 3% and 2%). They are perpetual gilts because there is no commitment to redeem them and the coupon (2–4%) rates are so low that in practice it is hard to envisage the circumstances in which the Government would redeem them. Some of these perpetuals were issued at a time of zero inflation or deflation and their coupon represented a real return. However, they now provide an opportunity for the higher rate tax payer who would take most of his or her return in the form of a capital gain rather than income and hence pay tax at the rate of 30 per cent rather than their marginal rate. This advantage was curtailed in the budget of 1989 when the marginal rate of income tax was also applied to capital gains.

The second type of special debenture to be examined are variously called 'discount' bonds or 'zero' bonds. These are more universally common. Most governments use short-term discount bonds (90-day treasury bills in the UK, and the US). These are sold without coupons on a discounted basis. Rarer are long-term discount bonds. They have not been used by the UK corporate sector and there has only been one offering on the UK market during the eighties which was by a US firm.

The term structure of interest rates

The yields to maturity calculated in the previous section are used to construct 'yield curves' such as those depicted in Fig. 9.3.

It has been suggested that a coupon-bearing debenture is analogous to a portfolio of pure discount bills making payments on a number of future dates.[6] If the secondary market for gilts is efficient it will discount different coupon payments made by different gilts at the same point in time

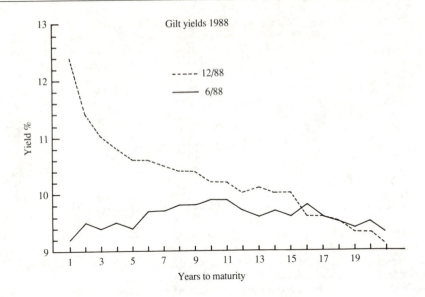

Figure 9.3 Yield curves.

by the same spot interest rate. After all is said and done there is no difference in risk as the debts were issued by the same riskless (for all practical purposes) borrower—the UK Government (or the US Government or the French Government etc). On the other hand a stream of coupons paid by a gilt over a range of different points in time will be discounted by each specific, and usually different, spot rate. Hence, the spot rate may be defined as the price today of money at some point in the future.

The yield to maturity and the yield curve are widely used in all financial bond markets. However, the yield to maturity is not entirely a satisfactory or straightforward measure in the context of the analysis of fixed interest securities. Carleton and Cooper[7] have stated the conceptual dilemma of the yield to maturity very clearly:

> As many people have shown, the concept of yield to maturity, Rn, is an ambiguous concept. For a conventional bond (if not for some hybrid financial contracts or real assets purchases) the expected cash flow pattern implies a unique Rn as a solving—or internal—rate of return. Its economic meaning is moot, however, inasmuch as reinvestment of intermediate cash flows at the solving rate is implied. To borrow a concept from capital budgeting literature, the price of an asset equals its present value only in the sense that its cash flows have been discounted at the market's return requirements. It is true that associated with each bond is a derived Rn, but that does not give us license to say that Rn is a market required rate, exogenous to the individual bond in question.

Even the classical defence of the internal rate of return—that it represents the highest cost of capital that a project can bear rather than a return on investment—seems inappropriate in this case.

The foregoing objections to the yield to maturity may be avoided if the investor arranges for the coupons to be stripped from the debenture or gilt ('stripes'). In this form there is only one payment at the end of the gilt's life and no stream of coupon income to be reinvested at the yield to maturity. Hence, the gilt becomes a zero bond which can be sold at a deep discount to its redemption value and the yield to maturity becomes an accurate and realistic measure of the return on the investment. In this form, the investment is free of the risk of the reinvestment rate for the stream of coupon income falling below the cost of funds.

In fact, the yield to maturity is only one of 3 valuation formulae for gilts:
1. Yield to maturity,

$$P_{0,n}=C/(1+R)+C/(1+R)^2+ \ldots +(C+M)/(1+R)^n$$

where $P_{0,n}$=price in period 0 of an n period gilt

C=cash coupon

M=redemption value

n=number of periods to maturity

R=yield to maturity

2. Spot rates,

$$P_{0,n}=C/(1+r_1)+C/(1+r_2)^2+ \ldots +(C+M)/(1+r_n)^n$$

where r_1 is the spot rate of return for cash flows contracted in period 0 received in period i.
3. Forward rates,

$$P_{0,n}=C/(1+{_0}f_1)+C/(1+{_0}f_1)(1+{_1}f_2)+ \ldots +(C+M)/[(1+{_0}f_1) \ldots (1+{_{n-1}}f_n)]$$

where ${_{t-1}}f_t$ is the forward rate of interest for payments contracted at the beginning of period t and received at the end of period t.

In the broadest meaning, the 'term structure of interest rates' may be defined as the relationship between time and the cost of money. Hence, the term may be used to describe the relationship with time of any of the above types of interest rates. However, given the ambiguity of the yield to maturity, the most economically valid definitions of the term structure involve either spot or forward rates of interest.

There are 3 main theories which purport to explain the term structure of interest rates:
1. The unbiased expectations hypothesis.
2. The liquidity preference hypothesis.
3. The market segmentation hypothesis.
Each of these explanations would appear to focus on part of the whole truth and hence should not be regarded as being in competition with each other. Hence, each makes a contribution to our understanding of the term structure of interest rates or yield curve.

The unbiased expectations hypothesis

This assumes that investors act as though they are risk neutral; i.e. that enough of them are risk neutral to overcome any bias of those who are risk averse. In addition, this hypothesis assumes that the market is perfect in that there are no transactions and information costs. From these premises the unbiased expectations hypothesis holds that expected future interest rates are equal to the forward rates which may be estimated from the observed prices and coupons of existing traded government debt.

The yield to maturity on a gilt, being merely an internal rate of return, gives no indication of expected future annual rates of interest. However, the gilts market, by pricing government debt, implies a 'term structure' of spot and forward interest rates. Given the information about prices, coupons and times to maturity, not only can the redemption yields be calculated but also the forward spot rates. For example, assuming that the coupon is paid once a year (this merely simplifies the numerical exposition without altering the logic of the analysis or the applicability of the conclusions), consider the following information (the first three columns):

Gilt	Coupon	Maturity (years)	Price	Redemption yield	Spot rate	Forward rate
A	10%	1	103.77	6.00%	6.00%	6.00%
B	9.5%	2	104.60	6.96%	7.00%	8.01%
C	11%	3	108.11	7.86%	8.00%	10.03%
D	12%	4	110.75	8.59%	9.00%	12.06%
E	8	5	97.26	8.70%	8.84%	8.20%

Redemption yields (column 4) may be calculated by solving the DCF model for the rate of discount. The redemption, spot and implied forward rates (Fig. 9.4) may be estimated as follows:

1. In year 1 the spot, forward and redemption yields are one and the same. In the case of a one-period investment we may calculate the return as follows:

$$R_1, r_1, {}_0f_1 = (C + M - P_0)/P_0 = (10 + 100 - 103.77)/103.77 = 6.23/103.77 = 6\%$$

2. The yield to maturity may be obtained by solving the following equation:

$$104.6 = 9.5/(1 + R_2) + 109.5/(1 + R_2)^2$$

Therefore the yield to maturity for the 2-year gilt is 6.96%. The spot yield for year 2 may be obtained from the solution of the following equation:

$$104.6 = 9.5/1.06 + 109.5/(1 + r_2)^2, \quad (1 + r_2)^2 = 109.5/95.64 = 1.1449$$

therefore the spot rate for year 2 is = 7%.
The forward rate for year 2 may be estimated from the following:

$$(1 + r_1)(1 + {}_1f_2) = (1 + r_2)^2$$
$$(1 + {}_1f_2) = (1 + r_2)^2/(1 + r_1)$$
$$= (1.07)^2/1.06 = 1.1449/1.06 = 1.08$$

therefore, the implied forward rate for year 2 is 8%.

3. The yield to maturity for the 3-year gilt may be obtained by solving the following:

$$108.11 = 11/(1 + R_3) + 11/(1 + R_3)^2 + 111/(1 + R_3)^3$$

therefore, the redemption yield for a 2-year gilt is = 7.86%.
The spot rate for year 3 may be calculated as follows:

$$r_2, \quad 108.11 = 11/(1.06) + 11/(1.07)^2 + 111/(1 + r_3)^3$$
$$(1 + r_3)^3 = 111/88.12 = 1.26$$
$$\log(1 + r_3) = (\log(1.26))/3$$
$$(1 + r_3) = \text{antilog}(0.0335) = 1.08$$

therefore, the spot rate for year 3 is 8%.
The forward rate for year 3 may be estimated from the following:

$$(1 + r_2)^2(1 + {}_2f_3) = (1 + r_3)^3$$
$$(1 + {}_2f_3) = (1 + r_3)^3/(1 + r_2)^2$$
$$= (1.08)^3/(1.07)^2 = 1.2597/1.1449 = 1.1003$$

therefore, the implied forward rate for year 3 is 10.03%.

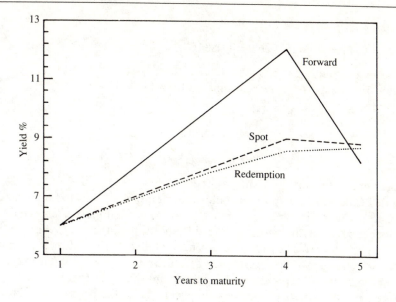

Figure 9.4 Redemption, spot and forward rates.

4. The yield to maturity for the 4-year gilt may be obtained by solving the following:

$$110.75 = 12/(1+R_4) + 12/(1+R_4)^2 + 12/(1+R_4)^3 + 112/(1+R_4)^4$$

therefore, the redemption yield for the 4-year gilt is 8.59%.
   The spot rate for year 4 may be calculated as follows:

$$110.75 = 12/1.06 + 12/(1.07)^2 + 12/(1.08)^3 + 112/(1+r_4)^4$$

$$(1+r_4)^4 = 112/79.42 = 1.4102$$

$$\log(1+r_4) = (\log(1.4102))/4$$

$$(1+r_4) = \text{antilog}(0.0373) = 1.0897$$

therefore, the spot rate for year 4 is 9%.
   The forward rate for year 4 may be estimated from the following:

$$(1+r_3)^3(1+{}_3f_4) = (1-r_4)^4$$

$$(1+{}_3f_4) = (1+r_4)^4/(1+r_3)^3$$

$$= (1.09)4/(1.08)^3 = 1.4116/1.2597 = 1.1206$$

therefore, the implied forward rate for year 4 is 12.06%.
5. The yield to maturity for the 5-year gilt may be obtained by solving the following:

$$97.26 = 8/(1+R_5) + 8/(1+R_5)^2 + 8/(1+R_5)^3 + 8/(1+R_5)^4 + 108/(1+R_5)^5$$

therefore, the redemption yield for the 5-year gilt is 8.84%.
   The spot rate for year 5 may be calculated as follows:

$$97.26 = 8/1.06 + 8/(1.07)^2 + 8/(1.08)^3 + 8/(1.09)^4 + 108/(1+r_5)^5$$

$$(1+r_5)^5 = 108/70.7 = 1.5276$$

$$\log(1+r_5) = (\log(1.5276))/5$$
$$(1+r_5) = \text{antilog}(0.0368) = 1.0884$$

therefore, the spot rate for year 5 is 8.84%.

The forward rate for year 5 may be estimated from the following:

$$(1+r_4)^4(1+{_4}f_5) = (1+r_5)^5$$
$$(1+{_4}f_5) = (1+r_5)^5/(1+r_4)^4$$
$$= (1.0884)^5/(1.09)^4 = 1.5274/1.4116 = 1.082$$

therefore, the implied forward rate for year 5 is 8.2%.

The unbiased expectations hypothesis holds that in a perfect market for money, the forward rates implied from the term structure of spot rates is the best estimate of expected future rates of interest. This does not mean that if the two are different the hypothesis is invalid. Rather, the point is that the forward rates are the best estimate given the available information at the time. Therefore, as the information changes so will the estimates of future rates of interest. Yield curves based on the predictions of the unbiased expectations hypothesis are shown at Fig. 9.5.

The unbiased expectations hypothesis has implications for the behaviour of investors and the shape of the term structure of interest rates:

1. Investors will be indifferent to gilts of different maturities so long as the expected returns are the same regardless of the length of the holding period.
2. Because of the operations of profit maximizing and risk-neutral investors the expected returns will be equal regardless of the term to maturity. Therefore gilts of different maturities are perfect substitutes.
3. The shape of the term structure is determined by the investors' expectations about future short-term interest rates.

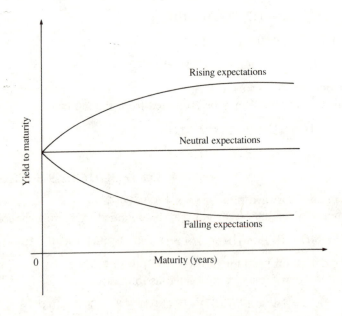

Figure 9.5 Yield curves predicted by the unbiased expectations hypothesis.

The liquidity premium hypothesis

This is based on a major criticism of the unbiased expectations hypothesis; that it is erroneous to assume that investors act as though they are risk neutral. The result is a modified expectations hypothesis which assumes risk aversion rather than neutrality on the part of investors.[8]

In a world of uncertainty and assuming risk-averse investors, this hypothesis holds that unless future spot rates are expected to decline, long-term rates will be greater than short-term rates. This is due to the premiums which must be offered to compensate investors for the increased uncertainty that the longer-term debts entail (see Fig. 9.6). One other factor which seems to play a part in determining the liquidity premiums is the size of the issue itself. Small issues can often be 'illiquid' in the sense that there is no continuous market and hence there is a larger risk to the investor because of greater uncertainty as to the selling price. Thus it may be that this is rewarded by a greater liquidity premium.

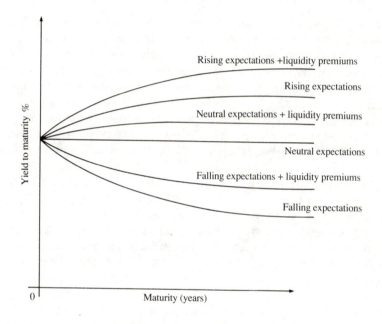

Figure 9.6   Yield curves with liquidity premiums.

This hypothesis not only predicts that lenders will demand a greater premium the longer the term of the loan, but also that borrowers will be willing to pay the premium because the long-term loan will afford them some certainty of interest payments. This hypothesis also implies that debts of different maturities cannot be perfect substitutes and this implication leads to the third hypothesis. One interesting phenomenon in this regard is the limited range within which the yield to maturity of 30-year US Government bonds fluctuates, 8–9.75 per cent. It may be significant that this yield exceeded 9.75 per cent at the time of the October 1987 crash.

The market segmentation hypothesis

If the liquidity premium hypothesis introduced the idea that debts of different maturities are not perfect substitutes, the market segmentation hypothesis takes this one step further by noting that many investors have different but fixed contractural liabilities. Hence, those liabilities will compel the investor to buy debts of specific maturities. Taken to its logical end, this means that each maturity will have its own demand and supply schedules and that the yields across the term structure may not have any systematic relationship with each other.

Evidence

Although investors are segmented by their liabilities to some extent, this does not appear to have any great impact on the shape of the yield curve. However, the existence of liquidity premiums is supported as is the expectations theory. The latter is attested by the existence of downward-sloping yield curves from time to time.

Risk management and debt portfolios

The basic principles of diversification and risk minimization are the same for debt portfolios as for equity portfolios (see Chapters 4 and 5). Investing in debt exposes investors to three types of risk: *Default in respect of coupon or principal* — apart from debt issued by some Third World countries (debt denominated in foreign rather than domestic currencies) the risk of default on government debt is negligible, so it will be ignored for the purposes of this section. On the other hand the risk of default on corporate bonds although generally small is a very real factor in the pricing of debentures. The risk of default is not an absolute event. It ranges from time extensions given by creditors to debtors (in preference to liquidation) to outright liquidation of the assets of the debtor. Time extensions will invariably be preferred to liquidation if liquidation is unlikely to produce much in the way of repayment of capital due.

Default risk constitutes the unsystematic risk of the debenture's total risk. The other types of risk (discussed below) affect all debentures and debt instruments equally and hence constitute systematic risk. Default risk is unsystematic because it is specific to the corporation (or government) itself and relates directly to those variables under management's control.

Default risk is usually assessed by reference to the financial statements of the corporation in question or debenture rating services where available. It is not the function of this volume to explain or describe financial ratio analysis, there are many other corporate finance and managerial accounting texts which cover this topic. The two financial ratios of primary importance to this analysis are the interest coverage ratio and the debt ratio. The first is the ratio of earnings before interest and tax (EBIT) to interest payments, and gauges the ability of the firm to make its contractual payments. It is clear from any study of corporate finance and/or managerial accounting that EBIT is a most volatile result. Hence, healthy ratios which allow for substantial adverse movements in EBIT will reduce the perceived risk of the firm's debentures.

The second ratio, debt-to-equity or debt-to-total assets, measures the proportion of debt used in total financing. Its impact on the pricing and discount rates for equities was discussed in Chapter 8. It is enough to state here that the debt ratio is used in assessing the default risk of corporate debentures. The higher the debt ratio the higher the estimated default risk and vice versa.

Unanticipated changes in interest rates — interest rate risk is the major component of the systematic risk which affects all debentures and government debt. Therefore, it is completely non-specific and beyond the control of the issuers of debt securities. For those issues of debt which bear a fixed coupon, the movement of interest rates after the time of purchase will result in price changes and hence capital gains or losses.

However, although changes in interest rates will affect the prices of all debentures, the impact will not be uniform. It has been shown by Yawitz et al.[9] that price volatility increases at a decreasing rate as the length of time to maturity gets longer (Table 9.8).

Table 9.8   Debenture price variability

Years to maturity	Mean average price change (%)
1	0.242
2	0.447
3	0.605
4	0.743
5	0.857
10	1.158
20	1.519
30	1.681

Source: Yawitz et al.[9]

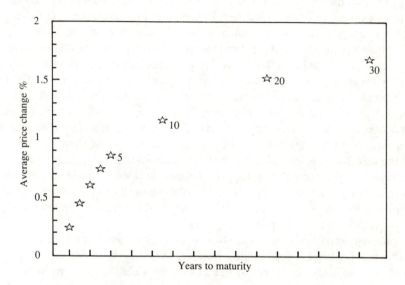

Figure 9.7   Debenture price variability (using the data of Table 9.7).

The curvilinear relationship illustrated in Fig. 9.7 means that even if stock prices are perfectly correlated (the worst case in Markowitz Portfolio analysis—see Chapter 4), a portfolio of gilts of differing maturities will have a lower expected risk than a single gilt whose maturity equals the average maturity of the gilts in the portfolio.

Purchasing power risk(or inflation)—the risk and effect of unanticipated inflation is simple. It will result in a fall in the investor's level of real wealth. Consider a 1-year investment in a gilt which offers a coupon of 8. If the investor anticipates a rate of inflation of 5 per cent then his real wealth at the end of the investment period will be increased by:

$$(1+0.08)/(1+0.05)=1.0286$$

Thus the investor's wealth will be increased by 2.86% if he anticipates inflation correctly. On the other hand, if inflation turns out to be 10%, then the investor's wealth will be reduced by:

$$(1+0.08)/(1+0.1)=0.9818$$

or a reduction of 1.82%.

Given the importance of inflation on the real wealth of investors in gilts or debentures, it is not surprising that long-term interest rates will reflect the market's assessment of future interest rates and its uncertainty about those rates.

Strategies for debenture portfolio management

Given a fixed time horizon for investment in debentures and/or gilts there are four basic types of strategy that an investor can adopt. These may be summarized as follows:

Roll-over—the investor buys a sequence of short maturity gilts until the time horizon is reached. Therefore, if an investor has a time horizon of 5 years he may buy 1-year gilts 5 times in succession. This strategy exposes the investor to interest rate risk as short-term rates may vary more than long-term ones (reinvestment rate risk). However, it does have the advantages of allowing the investor to reassess his strategy in the light of new information, and involves the investor in virtually no price risk in relation to principal. In practice this type of strategy may be employed by institutional investors which have limited time horizons due to important maturing short-term liabilities.

Maturity—the investor purchases either a single gilt with a maturity equal to the required time horizon or a portfolio of gilts whose average maturity is equal to the required time horizon. This strategy exposes the investor to the reinvestment rate risk for coupons received from the original investment (as opposed to the whole investment in the previous strategy). However, the length of the investment will involve the investor in a greater inflation risk than the previous roll-over strategy. If the investor opts for a single gilt of the required maturity, there will be no risk to the nominal repayment of principal. On the other hand, with a portfolio of gilts whose average maturity is equal to the required time horizon, there may be a risk that the level of realization of the longer-maturity gilts will be below the purchase price (of course there is also the 'risk' that the realized principal will exceed the purchase price).

Naive—this strategy involves the purchase of a single gilt or a portfolio of gilts whose maturity or average maturity exceeds the investor's time horizon. Whether the investor opts for a single gilt or a portfolio of gilts the investor is exposed to all of the possible risks; reinvestment rate, inflation, and price risk. The principal advantage of this strategy is that the investor may select high coupon gilts to try to offset the aforesaid disadvantages.

Duration—this strategy uses a different measure, that of 'duration', which is a weighted average of a gilt's remaining life.[10] This option requires the investor to equate the duration of the chosen gilt or portfolio of gilts to his/her preferred time horizon. Duration is calculated as follows:

$$\text{Duration} = D = \frac{\sum_{t=1}^{n} t(C_t)/(1+R)^t + n(C_n+M)/(1+R)^n}{\sum_{t=1}^{n} C_t/(1+R)^t + (C_n+M)/(1+R)^n} \tag{9.3}$$

where t = time subscript

n = number of periods to maturity

C = coupon

M = redemption cash flow

R = yield to maturity (internal rate of return)

Hence, duration is measured in units of time and is a weighted measure of a gilt's remaining life in which each remaining year is weighted by the present value of the coupon paid during that year.

Duration for a gilt with a fixed maturity will decline over time and will always be less than the maturity. In the special case of a perpetual gilt or debenture, duration may be approximated by $(1+R)/R$ and is independent of the coupon.

For example, assume a gilt with a 5-year life paying a coupon of 8 units once a year, with a redemption rate of 8 per cent:

Time	Payment	Present value		Weighted present value	
1	8	$8/(1.08)=$	7.41	$1[8/(1.08)]=$	7.41
2	8	$8/(1.08)^2=$	6.86	$2[8/(1.08)^2]=$	13.72
3	8	$8/(1.08)^3=$	6.35	$3[(8/(1.08)^3]=$	19.05
4	8	$8/(1.08)^4=$	5.88	$4[8/(1.08)^4]=$	23.52
5	108	$108/(1.08)^5=$	73.50	$5[108/(1.08)^5]=$	367.51
		Total $=100$		Total $=431.21$	

Hence the duration of this gilt is equal to $431.21/100=4.31$ years. In this example the redemption yield is the same as the coupon rate and so the gilt must be priced at par. Hence, the denominator must be equal to the par value of the gilt by definition. This is rarely the case but by using the redemption rate to discount the income stream promised by the gilt this presents no problem. For the above gilt paying an annual coupon of 8 with 5 years to run, the durations at various redemption rates are as follows:

Redemption rate (%)	Duration (years)
0	4.43
2	4.4
4	4.37
6	4.34
8	4.31
10	4.28
12	4.25
14	4.22
16	4.19

The table and Fig. 9.8 show duration to be rather insensitive to changes in the redemption rate. It may be observed that the only occasion when duration is equal to maturity is in the case of a zero-coupon debenture whose redemption rate equals its promised rate of return. Therefore, if the gilt in the above example paid no coupon but sold at a price of 68.06, promised a redemption value of 100 in 5 years time (i.e. promising a compound interest on the investment of 8% p.a.), and had a current redemption rate of 8 per cent, its duration would be equal to its maturity; i.e. 5 years.

Figure 9.9 shows the durations for 6 per cent coupon debentures with various times to maturity and yields to maturity. The limit on maturity is independent of the coupon rate and is determined by the yield to maturity as follows:

$$\text{Duration limit}=(1/\text{yield to maturity})+0.5$$

Hence, for a debenture yielding 10 per cent, the duration cannot be greater than 10.5 years.

Duration has also been used to give an indication of the price sensitivity of a debenture or gilt. Hopewell and Kaufman[11] differentiated the price of a debenture with respect to the yield to maturity and developed an expression for the price sensitivity of a debenture:

$$\partial P = -DP(\partial R)/(1+R) \tag{9.4}$$

where, $\partial P =$ change in price

$\partial R =$ change in yield to redemption

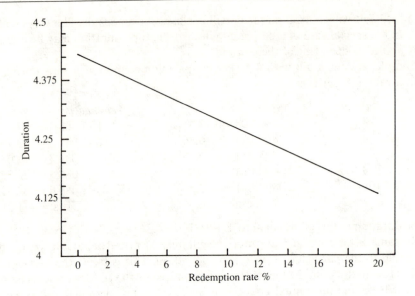

Figure 9.8   Duration and the redemption yield.

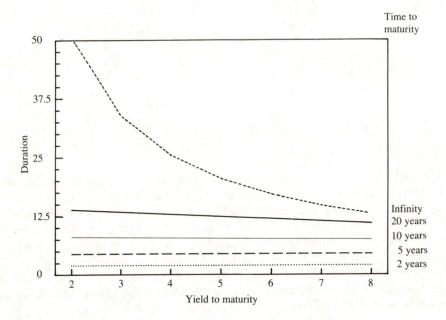

Figure 9.9   Duration and the time to maturity.

Hence, the change in debenture price is a weighted negative function of the change in the yield to maturity where the weight is the duration[10]. This produces a single rule of thumb for debenture pricing; i.e. the longer the duration, the greater the price volatility.

The principal advantage of using an investment policy based on duration is that it is linearly related to gilt or debenture price volatility. Fisher and Weil[12] have shown the duration strategy to be superior to a simple maturity strategy in terms of both achieving promised returns and minimizing the variance of the difference between promised and realized returns (Table 9.9).

Table 9.9 **Standard deviations of the differences between promised and realized returns**

Investment horizon (years)	Rolling over a portfolio of 20-year debentures	Maturity strategy	Duration strategy
5	0.1150	0.0031	0.0026
10	0.1740	0.0170	0.0120
20	0.1820	0.0760	0.0290

Source: L. Fisher and R. Weil,[12] p. 423.

Diversification

So far we have only discussed investments in single fixed interest securities. However, as in equities, there remains the possibility of diversification. It has already been shown that different debentures with different maturities have different volatilities and risks. In domestic terms, diversification may be achieved through the combination of debentures with different maturities. Where the correlations between the price changes of debts with different maturities are less than unity, opportuntities exist for reducing risk by diversification. Given measures of risk, return and covariance portfolios may be constructed by using Markowitz's methodology (see Chapter 4).

Assume that we have the following information about the price variances for the following gilts:

Term to maturity	Variance
2 years	0.25
4 years	0.75
6 years	0.85
10 years	1.25
12 years	1.5

It would be possible to construct portfolios with an average term to maturity of 6 years for example and attempt to improve upon the price risk of an investment in a 6-year debenture. As Yawitz et al.[9] have shown the relationship between maturity and price volatility to be non-linear, even a correlation coefficient of unity will enable us to produce a portfolio which will improve upon the risk of the single debenture.

Portfolio	Respective weights	Correlation coefficient		
		1.00	0.5	0.0
2 and 10 years	0.5 and 0.5	0.65	0.51	0.38
4 and 10 years	0.67 and 0.33	0.9	0.69	0.47
2 and 12 years	0.6 and 0.4	0.62	0.48	0.33
4 and 12 years	0.75 and 0.25	0.91	0.71	0.52

Diversification has a greater potential for risk reduction when it is carried out not only across maturities but with debentures of different default risks.

Thus far we have only considered diversification in a national or domestic setting. However, as with equities, debt portfolios may be constructed internationally in order to achieve greater diversification. Levy and Lerman[13] have shown the benefits of international diversification in debt portfolios to be considerable—US investors being able to double the expected return on a portfolio of US domestic debentures for the same level of risk.

For international diversification to be effective, portfolio managers must look at the covariances and correlations between returns (see Table 9.10).

Table 9.10   International debentures: correlation coefficients of annual US $ adjusted returns 1960–80

Country	Bel.	Den.	Fra.	Ger.	Ita.	Hol.	Spa.	Swe.	Swi.	UK	Jap.	Can.
Denmark	0.54											
France	0.72	0.69										
Germany	0.77	0.22	0.43									
Italy	0.25	0.43	0.53	−0.01								
Holland	0.93	0.45	0.64	0.86	0.36							
Spain	0.31	0.49	0.47	0.04	0.61	0.24						
Sweden	0.63	0.42	0.28	0.34	−0.4	0.63	0.44					
Switzerland	0.9	0.48	0.66	0.85	0.08	0.94	0.17	0.46				
UK	0.09	0.12	0.1	0.12	0.29	0.03	−0.13	−0.24	0.13			
Japan	0.32	0.36	0.28	0.27	0.24	0.25	−0.16	−0.18	0.38	0.5		
Canada	0.16	−0.01	0.01	0.18	−0.22	0.21	−0.1	0.26	0.04	−0.15	−0.17	
USA	0.05	0.22	0.15	0.1	−0.13	0.17	0.07	0.06	0.1	0.08	0.1	0.63

Source: R. Ibbotson, R. Carr and A. Robinson.[2]

Levy and Lerman used the data of Table 9.10 to construct minimum variance portfolios for various levels of return (Table 9.11).

Table 9.11   Efficient bond portfolios from the US investor's perspective

Mean Return (%)	8.00	9.00	10.00	11.00
St. Dev. (%)	4.76	5.72	7.02	9.43
Weights				
Germany	0.2	0.29	0.47	0.34
Spain	0.02	0.02	0.0	0.0
Sweden	0.4	0.4	0.19	0.0
UK	0.01	0.0	0.0	0.0
Japan	0.23	0.29	0.34	0.66
US	0.15	0.01	0.0	0.0
Riskless Rate (%)	1.79	3.81	5.27	8.1
CML slope	1.3	0.9	0.67	0.31

Note: the riskless rate of return is an 'international' average.
Source: H. Levy and Z. Lerman,[13] Table II p. 68.

Levy and Lerman point out that for the period as a whole the risk on a portfolio of US debt was 5.53 per cent which offered an average return of 4.31 per cent while the international portfolio of a similar risk offered 9 per cent.[14] This process was repeated for international equity portfolios. However, it must be emphasized that the period covered in these studies is dominated by the Bretton Woods system of fixed exchange rates and these figures may well be substantially altered in the light of the increased currency volatility of the eighties.

The results for the international equity portfolios were as shown in Tables 9.12 and 9.13.

The results in Tables 9.11 and 9.13 indicated that investors could have secured a high return by gearing an international debenture portfolio which would have a lower risk than an international equity portfolio. Levy and Lerman argue that the dominance of the debenture markets over the equity markets has a function of the predominance of lower and greater numbers of negative

Table 9.12   Equities: correlation coefficients of annual US $ adjusted returns

Country	Bel.	Den.	Fra.	Ger.	Ita.	Hol.	Spa.	Swe.	Swi.	UK	Jap.	Can.
Denmark	0.39											
France	0.56	0.26										
Germany	0.30	0.06	0.27									
Italy	−0.1	0.16	0.4	−0.00								
Holland	0.57	0.34	0.48	0.53	0.03							
Spain	0.21	0.41	0.33	−0.08	0.34	−0.1						
Sweden	0.31	0.28	0.28	0.28	0.13	0.43	0.31					
Switzerland	0.46	0.13	0.44	0.70	0.13	0.66	0.13	0.23				
UK	0.28	0.15	0.43	0.26	0.1	0.67	−0.04	−0.3	0.45			
Japan	0.33	0.83	0.36	0.3	0.31	0.28	0.34	0.34	0.24	0.17		
Canada	0.62	0.34	0.44	−0.04	0.27	0.55	0.26	0.31	0.35	0.36	0.23	
USA	0.39	0.24	0.21	0.21	0.21	0.73	−0.12	0.4	0.45	0.62	0.22	0.71

Source: R. Ibbotson, R. Carr and A. Robinson.[2]

Table 9.13   Efficient equity portfolios from the US investor's perspective

Mean Return (%)	12.00	13.00	14.00	15.50	18.50
St. Dev. (%)	11.87	14.03	15.96	19.32	29.28
Weights					
Belgium	0.10	0.01	0.0	0.0	0.0
Germany	0.22	0.2	0.11	0.0	0.0
Spain	0.17	0.15	0.09	0.0	0.0
Sweden	0.03	0.00	0.0	0.0	0.0
Switzerland	0.0	0.0	0.04	0.11	0.0
UK	0.03	0.07	0.09	0.1	0.12
Japan	0.08	0.2	0.29	0.38	0.88
Canada	0.31	0.38	0.38	0.36	0.0
US	0.06	0.0	0.0	0.0	0.0
Riskless Rate (%)	2.71	4.93	6.48	7.82	12.44
CML slope	0.74	0.57	0.47	0.4	0.21

Source: H. Levy and Z. Lerman,[13] Table III p. 59.

Table 9.14   Debt-equity cross-correlations of annual US $ adjusted returns 1960–80

Debts / Equity	Bel.	Den.	Fra.	Ger.	Ita.	Hol.	Spa.	Swe.	Swi.	UK	Jap.	Can.	USA
Belgium	0.49	0.58	0.57	0.34	0.54	0.41	0.58	0.26	0.34	−0.08	0.19	0.19	0.11
Denmark	−0.09	0.24	0.01	−0.21	0.28	−0.14	0.34	−0.02	−0.11	−0.21	0.17	−0.11	0.14
France	0.25	0.59	0.61	−0.06	0.64	0.15	0.67	0.08	0.2	0.07	0.1	−0.34	−0.07
Germany	0.17	0.15	0.27	0.28	0.2	0.24	0.1	−0.17	0.32	−0.11	0.26	−0.32	−0.12
Italy	−0.34	−0.01	−0.17	−0.53	−0.27	−0.37	0.32	−0.06	−0.33	0.07	0.11	−0.51	−0.24
Holland	−0.05	0.41	0.24	−0.06	0.3	−0.04	0.12	−0.18	−0.00	−0.07	0.14	−0.14	0.09
Spain	−0.17	0.01	−0.1	−0.31	0.44	−0.3	0.53	0.02	−0.36	−0.18	−0.21	−0.26	−0.33
Sweden	0.05	0.39	0.06	−0.18	0.16	−0.01	0.38	0.32	0.00	−0.17	0.01	−0.19	0.02
Switzerland	0.12	0.1	0.3	0.18	0.41	0.17	0.25	−0.17	0.14	0.03	0.12	−0.2	0.08
UK	−0.11	0.43	0.21	−0.16	0.51	−0.19	0.05	−0.39	−0.08	0.52	0.35	−0.18	0.22
Japan	0.09	0.39	0.09	−0.13	0.35	0.00	0.38	0.05	0.06	−0.07	0.41	−0.14	0.16
Canada	−0.13	0.18	0.06	−0.29	0.42	−0.18	0.46	0.07	−0.27	0.03	−0.12	0.17	0.1
USA	−0.24	0.13	−0.07	−0.36	0.25	−0.27	0.07	−0.17	−0.31	0.03	0.11	0.07	0.21

Source: H. Levy and Z. Lerman,[13] Table AIII p. 64.
Calculated from Ibbotson et al.[2]

Table 9.15   Efficient debt and equities portfolios from the US investor's perspective

Mean Return (%)	8.50	10.00	11.50	15.00	18.50
St. Dev. (%)	3.64	4.68	6.38	15.90	29.28
Equities					
Italy	0.04	0.03	0.0	0.0	0.0
Spain	0.11	0.14	0.1	0.0	0.0
UK	0.0	0.0	0.02	0.12	0.12
Japan	0.0	0.0	0.07	0.39	0.88
Canada	0.0	0.0	0.12	0.08	0.0
USA	0.11	0.16	0.05	0.0	0.0
Debt					
Germany	0.33	0.46	0.54	0.41	0.0
Sweden	0.14	0.11	0.0	0.0	0.0
UK	0.02	0.0	0.0	0.0	0.0
Japan	0.07	0.11	0.09	0.0	0.0
Canada	0.07	0.0	0.0	0.0	0.0
SA	0.12	0.0	0.0	0.0	0.0
Riskless Rate	2.12	4.33	7.38	10.53	12.47
CML Slope	1.75	1.21	0.65	0.28	0.21

Source: H. Levy and Z. Lerman,[13] Table IV p. 61.

correlation coefficients in Tables 9.10 and 9.12. They also argue that barriers to international investment might be a cause of these imbalances.[15]

Lastly, using data from the work of Ibbotson et al., Levy and Lerman looked at the risk–return characteristics of portfolios containing a mix of international debt and equity. Their results are shown in Tables 9.14 and 9.15.

Tables 9.14 suggests that there are considerable benefits to be had from international diversification between debts and equities.

It is noteworthy that German debt forms a major part of all the portfolios (Table 9.15) except the last. This reflects the very favourable risk–return characteristics shown in Table 9.4.

Eurobonds

The Eurobond market developed in London (and elsewhere subsequently) in 1963 when Warburgs arranged a $15 million issue for the construction of Italian *autostrade*. (This does not appear to be the first such issue. In 1957 an issue was made for the Belgian oil company Petrofina. However, the Warburg/autostrada issue seems to have been the one to capture the financial imagination.)[16] This market takes advantage of the large sums of currency held outside their countries of origin, a practice begun by the new communist government in China in 1949 which wanted to secure its US dollar earnings from sequestration by placing them on deposit in a Russian-owned bank, the Banque Commerciale pour L'Europe du Nord.[17] At first this sort of deposit was used to make short-term loans but longer-term financing soon emerged.

The Eurobond market constitutes an unregulated source of funding for major corporations and states. Documentation is easier and the bonds are in bearer form which ensures anonymity. Although much of the business is concentrated in London (except the Eurosterling market) the two clearing houses are in Brussels and Luxembourg. Domestic capital markets are affected by national economic and political policies and are restricted to the domestic currency. The Eurobond market allows borrowers to avoid these considerations as they can borrow in any currency (except their own) on the most favourable terms. The lack of formal regulation (although there is informal self-regulation by the participants) allows the market to organize, place or sell the issue and then announce it as a *'fait accompli'* with what has become known as a 'tombstone' advertisement in the financial press. The Bank of England has defined the essential differences between domestically issued debentures and Eurobonds:

	Domestic	Eurobonds
Type	Usually registered	Usually bearer bonds
Security	Often secured	Usually unsecured
Tax	Paid net of UK income tax	Paid gross
Interest	Semi-annual	Annual
Listing	London	London or Luxembourg
Placing	Fixed price on a particular day	Over a period at various prices
Trading	ISE, day after issue	Immediate, OTC by the issuing banks
Issuing Houses	Mainly domestic	Both domestic and overseas.

Source: 'Recent developments in the corporate and bulldog sectors of the sterling bond market', *Bank of England Quarterly*, February 1988, p. 63.

The issues are organized by a merchant bank acting as a 'lead-manager' which is usually assisted by a group of co-managers. The issues are underwritten by a syndicate of financial institutions and sold to the investing institutions and public by a group of selling agents. As this market is international and unregulated it has a rating system which is based on company profit records, company size, and the absence of default. Size is important because it restricts the potential borrowers as small issues tend to lack liquidity (i.e. they are difficult to make markets in and trade)

Table 9.16   Eurobond and foreign bond issues 1981–1984

	1981 $million	(%)	1982 $million	(%)	1983 $million	(%)	1984 $million	(%)
Eurobonds	31 294	100	50 329	100	50 123	100	81 717	100
US $	25 761	82	42 228	84	39 230	78	65 334	80
D-Mark	1 396	5	3 253	7	4 042	8	4 324	5
Sterling	535	2	846	2	2 153	4	3 964	5
ECU	153	—	823	2	2 191	4	2 938	4
Canadian $	688	2	1 200	2	1 067	2	2 147	3
Yen	410	1	598	1	233	—	1 190	1
Other	2 352	8	1 381	3	1 207	2	1 820	2
Foreign	20 514	100	25 199	100	27 050	100	27 800	100
US $	6 856	33	6 025	24	4 735	18	4 294	15
Swiss Fr	8 118	40	11 325	45	13 500	50	13 120	47
Yen	2 723	13	3 317	13	3 851	14	4 872	18
D-Mark	1 196	6	2 109	8	2 618	10	2 419	9
Guilder	439	2	854	3	933	4	860	3
Sterling	911	4	1 129	4	859	3	1 649	6
Other	273	1	440	2	544	2	586	2
Total	51 808		75 528		77 173		109 517	

Note: Care must be taken to distinguish between Eurobonds and foreign bonds. The latter are securitized debts raised in sterling in the London market by non-UK borrowers and are known as bulldogs (the equivalent in the USA are 'yankees' and in Japan, 'samurai'). The former are sterling denominated debts raised outside the UK by borrowers of any nationality.

Source: OECD Financial Statistics Monthly.

so that only those UK companies in the FTSE 100 are able to utilize the Eurobond market. This size criterion also applies to sovereign borrowers. Smaller countries find it hard to raise issues on the market due to fears about liquidity. Some countries have made extensive use of the Eurobond markets. For example, in August 1988 Austria had 12 fixed rate Eurodollar issues outstanding with a nominal value of US $1,567 million with coupons ranging from 7.75 to 14.75 per cent, an Australian Eurodollar issue with a nominal value of A$ 75 million and a coupon of 14.25 per cent, a Canadian Eurodollar issue with a nominal value of C$ 250 million and a coupon of 10 per cent, 2 issues of Euro-ECUs with a nominal value of ECU 225 million and coupons of 7.375 and 10.625 per cent, 6 Euro yen issues with a nominal value of Y180 billion and coupons ranging from 5.25 to 7 per cent, a Euro-sterling issue of £100 million and a coupon of 9 per cent, and lastly 15 Euromark issues with a nominal value of DM 3,375 million and coupons ranging from 5.375 to 9.75 per cent. All of the Austrian issues had AAA ratings from Standard and Poor and Aaa ratings from Moody's.[18]

In addition to the flexibility in terms of regulation and currencies, the Eurobond market has been versatile in the forms that the loans can take. Apart from the original fixed rate issues, the market has now offered floating rate notes (FRNs) which have coupon rates fixed at LIBOR (London InterBank offered rate) plus a small margin since the 1970s. One variant of the FRN is the 'droplock' bond which allows the investor to convert to a fixed coupon whenever the LIBOR rate falls to some predetermined level. The market also offers bonds which have been defined in terms of international units of account such as the ECU or the SDR. Being 'basket currencies' these allow the investor some degree of diversification of exchange risk. Lastly, the market also offers zero bonds in some (mainly US dollars) currencies, which have the attraction of offering the investor a guaranteed yield to maturity. In addition to these types of Eurobond, the market has also produced convertibles (discussed below) and bonds with equity warrants attached.

The above understates the flexibility of this international capital market. It can tailor the loans to suit the wishes of its customers and move with each temporary fashion. For example, during the eighties the market has moved from Eurobonds, to internationally syndicated loans, to 'bought deals' where the lead bank is the only bank, and back to bonds again. In 1986 Euroyen bonds were in high demand, tailored to meet the preferences of the Japanese insurance companies which were important investors. The bonds were adjusted to carry high coupons and were sold at prices some 20 per cent higher than ordinary bonds. This enabled the insurance companies to pay dividends out of current income rather than capital gains thus avoiding capital gains tax.

The existence of this international currency market alongside all of the various national markets has produced the situation where there are two interest rates for every term of loan denominated in every Eurocurrency. This has naturally opened up the possibility of arbitrage between them. In addition it has facilitated financial engineering on an unprecedented scale. For example, suppose a multinational borrower issues a loan in Euromarks at an interest rate of 4.5 per cent. However, the company would prefer to have the capital of the loan denominated in US dollars. It then arranges a swap through an intermediary. The Euromark principal is delivered to a West German bank which guarantees to pay the multinational the Deutschmark-denominated interest rate and raises an equivalent loan in dollars at the LIBOR rate. This dollar-denominated principal is then passed to the multinational which then agrees to meet the interest payments on this dollar loan. The multinational has then effectively borrowed the dollars it wanted at the rate charged to the West German bank which will be lower than that offered if it arranged the dollar loan itself. On the other hand the bank will lend the Deutschmarks domestically at higher rates of interest than it is paying to the multinational. Essentially, the multinational is arbitraging between the Eurobond and the West German interest rates for Deutschmarks. Swaps of this kind (and very much more complex) now account for about 70 per cent of all Eurobond issues.

Convertibles

Convertibles are used to lower the cost of borrowing by adding a desirable characteristic to the loan—that of conversion into equities in some prearranged ratio. Of course UK companies also raise convertible loans in the domestic capital market. These were especially popular during the years of high price inflation during the seventies. The convertibility element allowed investors to participate in any improvement in the equity price and possibly escape the erosion of the real value of the asset through inflation.

The conversion ratio implies a market price for the equity component of the loan which is typically set 20–30 per cent above the market price at the time of issue. For example, the Burton issue had a conversion ratio of 35.7 per 100 (nominal) which implies a price of 280p for the company's equity. In the case of the Burton convertible, the market share price is still below that implied by the conversion ratio and hence none of the loan has been converted as it is not advantageous to do so until the market price exceeds the implied price. The Britannia Arrow issue shows some converson. This is due to the market price rising above the conversion price of 92.59p. The market price of the Britannia Arrow convertible was 119.5, a discount to the conversion value of 5.4 per cent. On the other hand the Racal convertible was priced at 145.5 by the market and thus traded at a premium of 6.2 per cent to the conversion value. (See Table 9.17.)

Table 9.17   Convertible loans raised by UK firms in the domestic capital market

Company	Coupon (%)	Conversion dates	Converwion ratio	Share price	Current conversion value	Amount issued £ million	Amount outstanding £ million
Burton	8.00	1989–2001	35.70	195p	69.2	34.6	34.6
Brit Arrow	9.00	1987–1995	108.00	117p	126.36	30.0	23.0
Racal	7.00	1988–2009	38.5	356p	137.06		

Source: *Stock Exchange Year Book*, 1988–89, share prices 24 February 1989.

The valuation of convertible debt consists of pricing the two separate elements. First there is the straight debt value which is simply the present value of the future income stream discounted by the yield to maturity of an equivalent risk pure-debt issue,

$$B_t = \Sigma C/(1+R)^t + M/(1+R)^n$$

The conversion value of the issue is dependent on the market price of the firm's equity. Brigham[19] has expressed this as follows,

$$K_t = P_0(1+g)^t W$$

where K_t is the conversion value in period t, P_0 is the price of the equity on the data of issue, g is the growth rate of the equity price and W is the conversion ratio.

Skerratt[20] has produced a least squares regression model (using UK data in an attempt to analyse the pricing of convertible loan stock) which is very similar to that developed by Brigham. Skerratt identified 4 variables as being important:
1. The market price of equity.
2. The income differential which Skerratt defined as the excess of the coupon payments over the equity dividends.
3. The period of conversion; the longer this period the greater the opportunity for the conversion price to exceed the value of the issue as a straight coupon-bearing debenture. Expressed in terms

of the option pricing models developed in Chapter 7, this reflects the phenomenon that the longer the exercise period the greater the value of the call element of the convertible issue.

4. The floor variable which is the value of the loan treated as an ordinary debenture without the convertibility characteristic. That this variable was important is not surprising as any device which offers the investor protection against risk would have a market value. Hence, we would expect the floor value to be more valuable to the investor the greater the volatility of the underlying equity's returns.

These 4 factors all had a positive influence on the price. However, Skerratt also found that the length of time before conversion was possible, had a negative effect on the price. Skerratt noted that the state of the market for these convertible loans could play a part in their pricing. He noted that some of the convertibles in his data set had illiquid markets. But he concluded that although this lack of liquidity produced some distortion, it did not alter the underlying relationships.

There are several difficulties in valuing convertible loans which have made it difficult to produce an easily usable theoretical model as in the case of options.

1. There are a number of expiry dates unlike the single date in the case of an option.

2. The act of conversion will affect the dividends paid by the firm to the shareholder. It is for this reason that dividends are often quoted twice; first for the number of shares in issue and secondly on a 'fully diluted basis' which takes into account the potential number of shares that could be in issue if the convertible is completely exercised. However, the act of conversion will have a second effect on the company and its potential to make dividend payments. Conversion into equities will reduce the contractual interest payments and alter the tax shield afforded by the use of debt.

3. Again using the option valuation model as a point of comparison, we know that each option has one exercise price. However, the convertible loan has a number of exercise prices as the market value of the loan will change from date to date.

Conclusions

This chapter has attempted to give an overview of debt financing in the UK markets and has developed some of the more important concepts and models used to analyse debt finance and portfolios of debentures. Although this and the previous two chapters have been concerned with different types of financial investment in isolation, this does not mean that the markets for the different assets and rights are independent of each other. It should be appreciated that for investors it is not merely a question of choosing between different shares or different gilts but also between gilts and equities. Debt and equity markets are inextricably linked and perpetually in competition with each other to attract investment funds. It is clear that the process of internationalization of capital markets is more advanced in the markets for corporate and national debt than in equities. The coexistence of the Eurobond and national debt markets will ensure competition and efficiency because of the arbitrage opportunities that are offered.

However, at the beginning of 1989 the total capitalization of the UK gilts market stood at about £135 billion and for the moment is no longer expanding. Since 1987 the Government's finances have been in surplus and there have been net repayments of government debt. Indeed on Friday, 13 January 1989 the Government held an auction at which it bought back gilts rather than selling them. If this trend continued for very long it would have serious competitive implications for the 22 marketmakers and 5 inter-dealer brokers which currently operate the market. A second development which may be important for the future was the issue of ECU-denominated treasury bills in October 1988. This has implications not just for government financing (lower interest rates) but also for the value of sterling. The continued issue of ECU-denominated treasury bills and gilts depends, in great measure, on the informal membership of the European Monetary System and the Government's success in curbing inflation and reducing, if not eliminating, the UK's foreign trade deficit. But it would be foolish to speculate on the future shape of the gilts market other than to say that the process of change instigated in 1986 and 1987 has not stopped and is unlikely to do so.

Notes

1. A. Merrett and A. Sykes, 'Return on equities and fixed interest securities 1919–66', *District Bank Review*, 1966.
2. R. Ibbotson, R. Carr and A. Robinson, 'International equity and bond returns', *Financial Analysts' Journal*, July–August 1982.
3. In 1957 there were about 100 banks of which the 16 London and Scottish clearing banks accounted for about 86 per cent of the £8 billion banking assets. By 1978 there were 348 banks with assets of £219 billion of which the 9 London and Scottish clearing banks held 23 per cent. See the report of the Wilson Committee on Financial Institutions, Cmnd. 7937, 1980, pp. 66–71 and 393–412.
4. Wilson Committee Report on Financial Institutions, Cmnd. 7937, 1980, Ch. 16.
5. Where the interest rate/discount rate is not expected to change, the stream of coupon income may be treated as an annuity and the redemption payment as a one-off payment to be discounted in the normal way. This considerably reduces the computational effort where there are a large number of coupon payments.
6. S. M. Schaefer, 'The problem with redemption yields', in *Modern Developments in Investment Management*, J. Lorie and R. Brealey (eds), Dryden Press, 1978, pp. 702–710.
7. W. Carleton and I. Cooper, 'Estimation and uses of the term structure of interest rates', *Journal of Finance*, Vol. 31, September 1976, p. 1068.
8. J. Hicks, *Value and Capital*, 2nd edn, Oxford University Press 1946, Ch. XI especially pages 144–7.
9. J. Yawitz, G. Hempel, and W. Marshall, 'Is average maturity a proxy for risk?', *Journal of Portfolio Management*, Spring 1976.
10. This measure was first developed by F. Macauley in *Some Theoretical Problems Suggested by the Movement of Interest Rates, Bond Yields and Stock Prices in the United States Since 1865*, Ayor Co., 1981.
11. M. Hopewell and G. Kaufman, 'Bond price volatility and term to maturity: a generalized respecification', *American Economic Review*, Vol. 63, September 1973.
12. L. Fisher and R. Weil, 'Coping with the risk of interest rate fluctuations: returns to bondholders from naive and optimal strategies', *Journal of Business*, Vol. 27, October 1971.
13. H. Levy and Z. Lerman, 'The benefits of international diversification in bonds', *Financial Analysts' Journal*, Vol. 44, September 1988.
14. Ibid. p. 57.
15. Quite clearly, these results indicate a disequilibrium in the international capital markets. If higher returns with lower risks could have been obtained by gearing debt portfolios than by investing in equities, then this implies a degree of overpricing in the equity markets. Levy and Lerman claim that their coefficients were stable over the 21 periods and hence these disequilibria persisted. This in turn implies legal and tax barriers to the free movement of capital.
16. A. Sampson, *The Money Lenders*, Coronet/Hodder & Stoughton Ltd, 1981, pp. 126–7.

17. Ibid. p. 121.
18. *Weekly Eurobond Guide*, Association of International Bond Dealers, 19 August 1988.
19. E. Brigham, 'An analysis of convertible debentures: theory and some empirical evidence', *Journal of Finance*, Vol. 21, March 1966.
20. L. Skerratt, 'The price determination of convertible loan stock: a UK model', *Journal of Accounting and Finance*, Vol. 1, Autumn 1974.
General References
    Bank of England Quarterlies: June 1985 'The future of the gilt-edged market', pp. 250–255. December 1986 'The future of the gilt-edged market: official operations', pp. 569–574. February 1987 'Gilt-edged settlement: phase 2 of the CGO service', pp. 80–82.
    Report of the Committee to Review the Functioning of Financial Institutions, Cmnd. 7937, 1980.

Questions

1. What advantages are there to using 'duration' as a method of managing a portfolio of debentures?
2. What alternatives are there to using 'duration' as a method of managing a portfolio of debentures and what are the advantages and disadvantages of each?
3. How can index-linked gilt-edged stock over- or undercompensate investors for inflation?
4. Given the following information about prices, coupons and maturities calculate the redemption yields, spot rates and forward rates:

Gilt	Coupon (–)	Price	Maturity (years)
A	14	102.70	1
B	10	100.00	2
C	12.5	107.52	3
D	8.5	97.58	4
E	11	107.79	5

5. What are the implications for the market in UK gilts of the current government budget surpluses?
6. Under what economic and political circumstances could a purely domestic market for corporate debentures be resurrected in the UK?
7. Critically discuss the three main theoretical explanations of the term structure of interest rates.
8. How would you construct the minimum variance portfolio with a maturity of 6 years from the following debentures:

Debenture	Maturity	Standard deviation of returns (–)	Correlation coefficient B	C	D	E
A	2 yrs	5	0.80	0.76	0.72	0.69
B	4 yrs	5.5		0.78	0.74	0.71
C	8 yrs	6.5			0.76	0.72
D	10 yrs	7				0.75
E	12 yrs	8				

Does your minimum variance portfolio improve on an investment in a 6-year debenture which has a standard deviation of 6 per cent?

9. Would your portfolio change if the correlation coefficients for question 8 were changed as follows:

	A	B	C	D	E
A	1	0.95	0.93	0.89	0.87
B		1	0.82	0.78	0.75
C			1	0.80	0.76
D				1	0.78
E					1

10. Why might the portfolios in questions 8 and 9 be improved in terms of both risk and return by diversification into equities and foreign debentures?

10. Mergers, acquisitions and buyouts

Introduction

The eighties have seen the use of mergers and takeovers increase dramatically as a means of corporate growth. Although the actual numbers of such deals has not approached the peaks attained in the sixties, the value of assets involved have nearly reached record levels in real terms. Table 10.1 shows the present boom to be comparable to that of 1967–73 in terms of assets acquired although not in terms of the numbers of acquisitions. This reflects the size of some of the contested takeovers. 1986 was dominated by just 2 acquisitions—Hanson Trust/Imperial Group (£2.564 billion at 1986 prices) and Guinness/Distillers (£2.531 billion at 1986 prices) which between them accounted for about 45 per cent of all assets acquired during the first three quarters of 1986. By comparison, the largest takeovers in the 2 previous peak years, 1968 and 1972, were only worth £1.65 billion (GEC/English Electric) and £1.7 billion (Grand Met/Watney Mann) in 1986 prices.

The study of mergers and acquisitions (hereafter referred to as acquisitions) has usually been included in the sphere of corporate finance. However, acquisitions deserve some consideration in a text concerned with financial investments as they constitute investments which not only affect the wealth of shareholders but, in a more direct market sense, have at least a transient effect on share

Table 10.1(a)   Hanson plc: the Imperial and SCM deals

Imperial	*£ million*
Acquired April 1986	2 500
Disposals	
1986 Anchor Hotels, Imperial Inns, Happy Eater	186
Courage	1 400
Golden Wonder	87
1988 Ross Young	335
Lea and Perrins	199
Others	56
Total disposals	2 264
Net Cost	(236)
Value of remaining business	1 400
SCM	*$ million*
Acquired January 1986	930
Disposals	
1986 SCM Headquarters	36
Pulp and Paper	160
Glidden	580
Durkee Famous Foods	140
1988 Allied Paper	56
Durkee Industrial Foods	185
Others	97
Total disposals	1 255
Net surplus	325

Table 10.1(b)   The composition of Hanson plc March 1989

Britain	Est. trading profit 1989 £ million	Low value £ million	High value £ million
Imperial Tobacco	175	1 085	1 302
British Ever Ready	35	409	569
Allders	34	253	295
London Brick	97	945	1 135
Lindustries	30	298	396
SCM Chemicals	71	554	692
Others	43	466	607
Total	485	4 010	4 996
America			
Smith Corona	38	353	471
Hanson Recreation	23	143	214
USI Lighting	25	201	279
Hanson Building Products	45	363	502
SCM Chemicals	160	1 488	1 984
Office-Group America	21	156	195
Other	78	593	806
Total	390	3 297	4 451
Grand Total	875	7 307	9 447
Cash/Investments		1 750	1 750
Convertibles		1 236	1 236
Total value		10 293	12 433
Stock market valuation			6 950

Assumes £1 = $1.75.
Source: Kitcat and Aitken, *The Economist*, 11–17 March 1989, pp. 84–85.

prices in the market. In addition, they deserve consideration as they constitute a principal method of changing corporate management and investment plans which in turn have a direct bearing on the returns to shareholders.

Although the figures in Table 10.2 do not suggest it, it can be argued that the current wave of merger activity started in 1983 with two pace-setting deals (at least in terms of size). First BTR took over Thomas Tilling for £660 million (at current prices) and a short while later BAT acquired the Eagle Star insurance company for £996 million (at current prices) after a contest with the West German insurance company Allianz which had offered £692 million in October 1983. Thomas Tilling was an industrial conglomerate that included such diverse operations as Heinemann, Cornhill Insurance, Pretty Polly Tights and heavy engineering. It had been put together during the fifties and early sixties but had somewhat lost its ability to generate profits. As a consequence its share price was at a discount to the asset value and BTR was able to dismember the group and sell off the unwanted components at a considerable profit (one part of the group, Cornhill Insurance was sold a few years later for a sum almost equal to half that paid for the whole of Thomas Tilling).

This strategy was repeated later (see Table 10.1(a) and (b)) with considerable success by Hanson Trust when it took over the Imperial Group and SCM in the USA and broke them up by selling the unwanted businesses. Of the Imperial Group, only the original tobacco company remains in the control of Hanson plc.

Table 10.1(b) suggests that the recorded value of mergers in the UK understates the extent of the

Table 10.2 Mergers and acquisitions among industrial and commercial companies

Year	No. of deals	Amount paid (Current prices) (£ million)	FT 500 Ord. Index 1963=100	Constant 1985 m Prices (£ million)
1963	888	352	100	2 429
1964	940	505	134	3 371
1965	1 000	517	146	3 295
1966	807	500	140	3 077
1967	763	822	216	4 928
1968	946	1 946	362	11 145
1969	846	1 069	201	5 794
1970	793	1 122	238	5 730
1971	884	911	164	4 255
1972	1 212	2 532	357	11 023
1973	1 205	1 304	213	5 197
1974	504	508	141	1 749
1975	315	291	64	806
1976	353	427	79	1 064
1977	482	812	117	1 690
1978	567	1 140	146	2 159
1979	534	1 656	187	2 763
1980	469	1 475	155	2 087
1981	452	1 144	107	1 447
1982	463	2 206	178	2 569
1983	447	2 343	150	2 608
1984	568	5 473	294	5 806
1985	474	7 091	309	7 091
1986 (3Q)	443	11 300	400	10 970

Source: J. Scouller, 'The UK merger boom in perspective', *NatWest Bank Review*, 1987, p. 15.

Table 10.3 British investment in the USA 1976–86

Year	Number of investments	Acquisitions	New plant	Plant expansion
1976	36	27	0	0
1977	48	23	4	1
1978	111	47	7	0
1979	141	44	11	7
1980	188	76	23	15
1981	180	70	10	4
1982	182	84	12	1
1983	162	66	13	8
1984	170	76	14	6
1985	176	98	7	6
1986	178	108	5	4
76–86	1 572	719	106	52

Source: US Dept of Commerce, 'Foreign Direct Investment in the United States', various years.

current boom because of the considerable activities of UK companies in the USA and, to a much smaller extent, elsewhere. For example, between 1976 and 1986 just over 300 UK companies acquired 719 US companies (see Table 10.3). Hanson's takeover of SCM has been referred to, but other British firms have been active as well. For example, the Midland Bank acquired the Crocker Bank of California, the Imperial Group took over the Howard Johnson Group (both of these were financial failures as the acquisitions were divested at considerable losses only a few years later). In

1986 Allied Lyons (in an attempt to prevent a repeat of the leveraged bid from Elders IXL in 1985) took over the Canadian drinks group Hiram Walker; the Prudential took over the Jackson National Life Insurance for $608 million and Boots acquired Baxters Travenols Flint Division for $555 million. One of the biggest UK acquirers in the USA is ICI with purchases amounting to some £3 billion (e.g. Stauffer Chemicals and Glidden Paints), yet during the same period (1985–87) the company made no major acquisitions in the UK.

Hamill[1] has suggested that some 60 per cent of all UK direct overseas investment since the late 1970s has been made in the USA.

Although 1572 transactions have been recorded, only 784 have a known monetary value which is $36.7 billion for the period 1976–86. Of the 784 known transactions only 86 (11 per cent) were in excess of $100 million; however, these 86 transactions accounted for over 60 per cent of the total known investment.

The main reasons for this investment in US assets have been as follows:
1. The size and purchasing power of the US market compared with the domestic UK market.
2. The loss of cost advantages of producing outside the USA and exporting to the USA compared with producing within the country itself.
3. The depreciation of the US dollar against sterling (this applies equally to the Japanese yen and the Deutschmark) making the acquisition of assets in the USA cheaper.
4. Concern about possible future protectionist measures.

In the context of British direct investment into the USA it is worth pointing out the obvious; that the two countries share a common language and have similar legal and financial systems.

Practice and regulation for corporate control in the UK market

The main principles of the Code of the City Takeover Panel were outlined in Chapter 1. In this section it remains to discuss some of the practices in the takeover boom of 1985–86 which have given rise to demands for change. At the time of writing (January 1989) the court case on the conduct of the management of Guinness during its acquisition of Distillers is still proceeding. It was this case and others which have led to demands such as,
1. the prohibition of all contested takeover bids;
2. the reference of all bids over a certain size to the Monopolies and Mergers Commission;
3. make it a statutory duty for the beneficial ownership of all nominee accounts to be made public;
4. lower the threshold at which equity stakes have to be declared;
5. make it an offence for pension funds to invest in the shares of their parent companies;
6. make it a statutory requirement that bids have to be made in cash.

Although this list is not comprehensive it covers most of the types of specific demands for reform which have been made during recent years.

The first 2 demands arise out of the increasing value of the assets which are up for sale. It may be observed that the larger the company being bid for the more likely it is that the target will be a household name. This may result in some demand that the bid be referred in the national interest. This tendency may be exacerbated if the potential acquirer is a foreign company. An example of this was the recent contested bid for Rowntree (not particularly large in terms of capitalization, but well known for its brand names) which played the nationalist card without success. It is instructive that Allied Lyons, when the subject of an unwelcome bid in 1985 from Elders IXL, an Australian company, raised the public's (and presumably its own shareholders') awareness of its varied role in the national economy. Thus products which had previously been advertised only under a brand name were henceforth used to advertise the corporation name as well.

Demands 3 and 4 have arisen out of the contests for Guinness and Westland. In both cases, nominee accounts played important roles in the eventual outcomes of each contest. More specifically, in the Guinness case, a nominee account operated by the Henry Ansbacher merchant bank appears to have been instrumental in uncovering the methods used to gain control of Distillers.

The current threshold level for the declaration of beneficial ownership of equity shareholdings is 5 per cent. This particular requirement has long been the subject of demand for adjustment downwards. One of the principal arguments used is that this level is too high and leaves shareholders open to abuse as they are not in full possession of the information that there is an acquisition interest in the company in which they have invested. Hence, they may be persuaded to sell early in the proceedings and be prevented from profiting from the premium which is invariably generated by a bid. What is very clear is that many corporate executives are nervous about this threshold level as it may be used to mask the creation of a shareholding from which a bid for the whole company may be made. This is exacerbated by the interval of 10 days which may elapse between the attainment of the 5 per cent stake and the legal requirement for the beneficial holder to inform the company. During this interval, more shares may be purchased so that by the time the management of the target company is officially informed, the potential acquiror may have built up a stake considerably in excess of 5 per cent. This particular consideration is made more serious by the possibility of concert parties accumulating considerable combined stakes in target companies.

The conduct of company pension schemes has been brought under the spotlight after the revelations of the Guinness bid for Distillers. In this case the Distillers pension fund purchased several million Guinness shares. This along with other purchases may have been instrumental in maintaining a high price for Guinness shares. The importance of this strategy may be seen when it is noted that as an alternative to the cash offer, Guinness management offered Guinness shares to Distillers shareholders in exchange for their shares. Hence, it was to the advantage of the bid that the price of Guinness shares be maintained at as high a level as possible.

The final demand mentioned is intended to avoid the manipulation of the bidder's share price. However, the advent of debt-financed bids (such as that by Elders IXL for Allied Lyons in 1985) has made the all-cash offer somewhat easier to arrange. The alternative of making a rights issue and using the proceeds would tend to warn the potential targets of an impending bid and enable them to marshall their defences in good time. The use of debt may allow the bidder to organize its resources in secrecy which may enable it to surprise the target. In addition it may be that if only cash bids are permitted, manipulation of share prices may still result. Prior to making the bid, sales and short sales of the target's shares may result in a lower market price to the advantages of the bidder.

It is not the function of this section to state what should be the proper regulation of mergers and acquisitions, only to highlight some of the problems. What is indisputable is that whatever system is devised, there will be market practitioners who will try to circumvent it by fair means and foul.

Motives for acquisitions

Acquisition may be divided into 3 broad types:

1. *Vertical*. This type of investment is no longer as common as it once was. It involves a company acquiring control of its suppliers or of those companies to which it sells its products. For example, a motor manufacturer may acquire suppliers of components or retail outlets for new cars. During the fifties a retail seller of cars called the Rootes Group acquired a series of motor manufacturers (the firm was taken over by the American Chrysler Corporation in the sixties).

2. *Horizontal.* This type of acquisition involves expansion in the firm's existing sphere of activity by the purchase of competitors. Thus for example, Saatchi and Saatchi have expanded by buying competitors in the advertising and public relations business.
3. *Conglomerate.* This is diversification as the company expands into various spheres of business activity. An example of this strategy is Hanson plc which has put together a portfolio of assets producing such products and services as building bricks, batteries, office furniture and retailing.

Table 10.4 shows the numbers of these 3 types of acquisition which took place over the period 1954 to 1973.

Table 10.4   Mergers in manufacturing industry

	Utton 1954–65	(%)	Gribbin 1965–73	(%)
Horizontal				
Number	448	69.8	622	78
Value (£ million)	1 549.4	81.1	12 739	71
Vertical				
Number	93	14.3	43	5
Value (£ million)	184.7	9.6	887	5
Diversified				
Number	102	15.9	133	17
Value (£ million)	178.6	9.3	4 212	24

Sources: M. Utton, 'Diversification mergers profit stability', *Business Ratios*, 1969. J. Gribbon, 'The conglomerate merger', *Applied Economics*, 1976.

An alternative three-fold classification of motives is as follows:
1. *Absolute size motives.* These include empire building (often used as an accusation, rarely, if ever, given as a motive), and economies of scale in production, finance, research and marketing.
2. *Relative size motives.* Increases in market penetration and attempts to improve the firm's position compared with that of the competitition.
3. *Financial motives.* Among these are the acquisition of assets at lower prices compared with the cost of creating them from scratch and reduction of the probability of corporate failure through diversification. Within this class we may also include the practice of 'asset stripping' which is a pure profit motive. The acquiring management estimates that it can sell off the constituent parts of the target company for more than it can buy it as a whole. In many cases, the discarded component parts of the target company are used to finance the purchase of the desired division. For example, Hanson plc acquired the Imperial Group in 1985 and sold all of the major divisions except the core business, Imperial Tobacco. By the time such major assets as the Courage Brewery had been sold (to Elders IXL), the desired business had been purchased for a very small net price.

A variant of the themes of profit and growth has been called the 'bootstrap game'. This particular practice, now largely discredited, involved the use of high P/E ratios to simulate corporate growth and give the appearance of growth in earnings per share. For example, suppose there are 3 companies each in a different business but all having an EPS of 50p (see Table 10.5).

The mechanics of the process are quite simple. What is of paramount importance is for the management of company X to maintain a good public relations image so that the market continues to reward the company with a high P/E ratio. In Table 10.5 this has been assumed and whatever acquisitions have been made by Company X, the P/E ratio remains at 20. The transactions and returns are as follows:

Table 10.5 The earnings per share illusion

	Company X1	Company Y	Company X2	Company Z	Company X3
EPS (p)	50	50	60	50	66
P/E ratio	20	10	20	12	20
Share price (p)	1 000	500	1 200	600	1 320
No. of shares (million)	1	1	1.667	1	2.267
Capitalization (£ million)	10	5	20	6	30
Total earnings (£ million)	0.5	0.5	1	0.5	1.5
Offer		2 for 3		3 for 5	
Implied price (p)		667		720	
New shares		666 667		600 000	

1. Company X makes an offer for company Y which due to a lack of public relations or perhaps being in an unfashionable business has a low P/E ratio of only 10. The offer is 2 shares of company X for every 3 of company Y. This values the shares of the target company at 667p (2000p/3 = 667p) and yields a potential profit of 33.4 per cent to the shareholders of company Y. We assume that the offer is accepted. The resulting company, called X2 in Table 10.5, has earnings of £1 million, 1.667 million shares and hence an EPS of 60p (an increase of 20 per cent). Given an unchanged P/E ratio of 20, this gives a market price of 1200p which represents a return of 20 per cent to the existing shareholders of company X.
2. Company X2 makes another bid for another unfashionable company, Z, also with a low P/E ratio. The offer is 3 for 5 implying a price of 720p for the shares of company Z and a profit of 20 per cent for its shareholders should they accept. Assuming they do, the resulting company, X3, has earnings of £1.5 million, 2.267 million shares and an EPS of 66p (an increase of 10 per cent). With a P/E ratio of 20 this gives a price of 1320p and a profit of 10 per cent to the existing shareholders of company X.
3. As a result of these two acquisitions, the shareholders of company X have seen the market capitalization of their company grow by 200 per cent and the price of their shares grow by 32 per cent. However, it will be appreciated that these financial manoeuvrings have resulted in no real changes and unless the management of company X can maintain the growth of EPS, the market will at some point re-evaluate the company and its shares.

The foregoing classifications tend to simplify the motives for acquisition. In addition they tend only to be concerned with the publically announced motives. Newbould's study[2] concludes that acquisition activity can best be explained by a motive to reduce uncertainty. Levinson[3] went further in suggesting that 'between the lines of these rational reasons for acquisitions, often there are two more subtle reasons which are rarely discussed in theses terms: fear and obsolescence.'

Fear stems from the attitude that unless the company grows it will either be taken over or be destroyed by the competition. Hence, acquisition is the solution as it provides speedy corporate growth. Until recent years size was commonly thought to be a deterrent to hostile bids. However, the advent of the leveraged bid has undermined this rationale. Small companies which can obtain the necessary backing have been able to use debt to acquire targets which are much bigger than themselves. Levinson explains obsolescence as a motive stemming from established firms with ageing managements which are perceived as being less able to cope with the changing business environment. Therefore, acquisitions based on this motive are intended to purchase new management rather than the assets they control.

Acquisition as an investment decision

Whatever the stated or unstated motives, an acquisition or merger is an investment decision. It is noticeable from the above discussion of motives that 'maximization of shareholders' wealth' has nowhere been mentioned. Yet this is the prime criteria for investment decisions according to corporate finance textbooks. Newbould's 1970 study of 38 acquiring companies in 1967–68 did not produce one example of a manager citing the 'maximization of shareholders' wealth' as a motive.[4] Yet an acquisition is a financial investment which may use shareholders' funds.

There are 4 main possible methods of acquisition or merger:

1. a purchase of the target company's shares with cash;
2. obtaining the target company's shares with a combination of cash and shares;
3. obtaining the target company's shares with shares only;
4. merging by creating a new company and issuing new shares to the shareholders of the 2 pre-merger companies.

In every case except the first, permission is needed from the shareholders of the acquiring company (or from both companies in the case of an agreed merger) for the issue of new shares which may then be used in the offered exchange for those of the target company.

Whichever method is used the acquisition constitutes an investment which is expected to yield additional income to the acquiring company. However, the new stream of earnings is uncertain and may, if large enough, alter the risk–return characteristics of the acquiring company. For example, the external growth produced by Hanson plc increased the company's market capitalization from £91 million during the first quarter of 1979 to £4,849 million in the last quarter of 1986. From quarter 1 in 1979 to quarter 3 in 1983, the company's systematic risk fell from 1.04 to 0.71 thereafter rising to 0.99 in quarter 4 in 1986. The fall in the total risk of the company's returns has been more consistent, falling from 0.32 to 0.27 between the first quarter of 1979 and the last quarter of 1986.[5]

However, the CAPM yields 2 implications for mergers in a perfect market without transactions costs.[6] In the case of an agreed merger between 2 companies the implications are as follows:

1. Where the companies are efficiently priced by the market so that they lie on the 'securities market line' (SML) and where the earnings stream of the new company is merely the sum of the independent companies' earnings streams, the shares of the new combined company will also lie on the SML. Hence, there can be no benefits from the merger as investors could replicate the situation by creating a portfolio of the shares of the two independent companies.
2. Where the earnings stream of the new company exceeds the sum of the 2 independent companies because of some process of synergy, investors cannot replicate this situation by personal diversification as in the previous case. The potential for synergy may be due to simple rationalization of operations, or greater market power enabling the company to operate on more favourable terms of trade with its suppliers of goods, services or finance.

On the other hand, it must be stressed that the CAPM implies that mergers can only be profitable where there is potential for synergy. However, the essential effect of a contested acquisition is a change of management. With a change in management often comes a change in investment policy which is in addition to any synergistic benefits which may accrue from the transaction. This consideration firmly places the acquisition decision in the realm of overall corporate strategy. Essentially, it is a commitment to external, rather than internal or 'organic', growth. As alternatives the external path to growth is faster but, as we shall see below, it is not necessarily the most profitable. Given that the external growth involves the acquisition, it follows that there should be some form of search and evaluation of target companies.

Newbould's study showed that of the 38 acquiring companies studied, 7 gave as their principal reason for acquisition, the approach by the 'target' company itself.[7] More importantly, Newbould found that the analysis of the targets took less than 4 weeks in 15 of the 38 cases and,

1. DCF techniques were not used;
2. in 8 of the cases asset values were used, and in 4 of these the target's balance sheets were used without adjustment;
3. in 7 cases Newbould found that the acquiring company used the target's market price and were concerned to time the bid to minimize the purchase price;
4. in 5 cases the acquirers compared price–earnings ratios and used a rule that the P/E ratio of the target should not be higher than that of the acquirer so as to avoid any reduction in EPS. Newbould found no common systematic method of target analysis and concluded that decisions were taken quickly without reference to shareholders' welfare.

However, 4 practical difficulties should be borne in mind when analysing acquisition decisions:

1. Target companies rarely if ever constitute a perfect fit for the acquirer. Although it may seem that firms like Hanson and BTR have made an art of dismembering conglomerates, most firms may find no little difficulty in disposing of unwanted assets and employees. Whichever methods are used, the disposals may cause radical changes in the cash flows of the target company.
2. Difficulties for analysts of acquisition decisions may result from the acquirer being motivated by the prospect of using accumulated tax losses to set against its own profits. In the same vein, the existence of an overfunded employee pension scheme may allow the acquirer to declare a contributions holiday, thus boosting the target's cash flow.
3. In many cases the acquisition decision will also involve a financing decision. There aren't many companies which can make such purchases without recourse to issuances of new debt and equity. Either way, the financing decision will alter the financial risk of the company by changing the level of gearing. In addition it may change investor perceptions because of dilution of shareholdings, thus affecting the required return and the market price of the acquirer's shares.
4. Lastly, once the market realizes that there is a target for a bid, the target's share price will tend to rise in anticipation. Rose and Newbould found that in the takeover boom of 1967, the final price could vary by up to twice the pre-bid price with an average premium of 20 per cent in uncontested bids and 55 per cent for contested bids (the overall average being 33 per cent).[8] For example, the price of Distillers shares varied between 289p and 277p during the first 8 months of 1985. By September Argyll had announced its interest in Distillers and on 1 September the price had risen to 360p, an increase of about 30 per cent. The final cash offer made by Guinness was 660p in March 1986, a premium of some 140 per cent over the pre-bid price.

With final acquisition prices being at considerable premiums to the pre-bid prices, the managements of acquiring companies may have to find considerable synergistic benefits and increases in operational efficiency to justify their investments. The existence of these premiums is not confined to the UK market for corporate control. Dodd[9] has estimated that in 60 per cent of the acquisitions carried out in the USA between 1979 and 1982 'the stock market's response to buying companies was significantly negative ... Thus, the skepticism of finance theorists about the size of such premiums is being reinforced by the collective judgement of the market.' This quote leads us to the final section of this chapter which must be a consideration of the evidence for the financial success or failure of acquisitions.

Returns to shareholders: the success or failure of acquisitions as an investment policy

The profitability of acquisitions is a much-debated topic. Despite the wealth of research done on the subject there is no academic consensus on the merits of acquisition-led corporate growth. On the other hand, many corporate managers still seek growth by acquisitions. This section attempts to outline a selection of the work done on mergers and acquisitions and is not comprehensive.

1. *Newbould 1970*: Newbould[10] concluded that 17 of his sample of 38 companies showed no benefits 2 years after the merger and that in the remaining 21 cases, after some initial benefit during the first 2 years, no further benefit was expected within the next 5 years.

2. *Singh 1971*: Singh[11] took a sample of 77 firms which acquired other firms (but excluding those which made further acquisitions within the period studied for profitability) within the same industry over the period 1955–70. Singh concluded that:

   (a) in the year of the acquisition, two-thirds of the acquirors had lower profits than in the years immediately before the investment;

   (b) in the first year after the takeover 56 of the sample had lower profitability than before the investment;

   (c) in the second year after the investment 35 of the firms in the sample experienced lower profitability than before the acquisition.

3. *Utton 1974*: Utton[12] took a sample of 39 firms which pursued a policy of horizontal acquisitions between 1961 and 1965, and then changed their policy and pursued internal or organic growth between 1966 and 1970. This sample was compared with a control group of companies which pursued a consistent policy of organic growth throughout the entire period under consideration. Utton concluded that the control group exhibited a consistently greater profitability than the group which at first pursued external growth.

4. *Kitching 1974*: Kitching[13] interviewed a selection of senior corporate executives of whom 30 per cent were of the opinion that the acquisitions they had been involved with had been failures and a further 17 per cent were disinclined to repeat the policy.

5. *Meeks 1977*: Meeks[14] took a sample of 233 of the larger listed companies which merged once during the period 1964–72. As in the previous 2 studies, pre- and post-merger profitabilities were compared. In his study Meeks took the average profitability over 3 years both before and after the merger. Meeks found that apart from the merger year itself, between half and two-thirds of his sample experienced a decline in profitability during the 7 years after the merger.

The overall impression from the 5 studies is that the odds are better than evens that growth by acquisition will not be as profitable as organic growth. However, it is worth noting that most of these studies have been based on accounting data. This source of data has been criticized as being biased against acquisitions. Appleyard[15] argues that the 'conventional' definition of the accounting rate of return, (net profit before interest and tax/depreciated net assets) cannot capture any benefits to acquisitions as it makes no allowance for sources and costs of finance.

In addition to the charge of bias in the 5 studies Bradley[16] has attempted to show that acquisitions are rational economic decisions in which assets are transferred to more efficient users. Using the cumulative abnormal return (CAR) methodology on US data, Bradley attempted to estimate the risk-adjusted abnormal returns in each of the following cases:

1. successful tender offers;
2. unsuccessful tender offers.

The results of Bradley's findings are shown in Figs 10.1 to 10.4.

It may be seen from the figures that Bradley has distinguished between acquisitions that involved only a single bidder and those in which there were more than one. Figure 10.1 confirms some of the results presented earlier in this chapter. On average, shareholders in the target firm can expect an abnormal return of some 30 per cent. Figure 10.4 shows the opposite and expected results. For the shareholders of the acquiring companies, the CARs were higher when no other bidders were present. However, it is worth noting that Bradley failed to observe any great negative CARs for the shareholders of the acquiring firms.

Bradley also looked at those cases in which the bid was unsuccessful. He notes that other

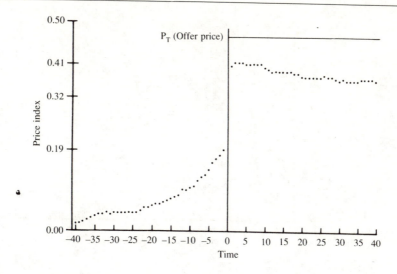

Figure 10.1   CARs to the shares of the targets of successful tender offers. (Source: M. Bradley,[16] p. 375.)

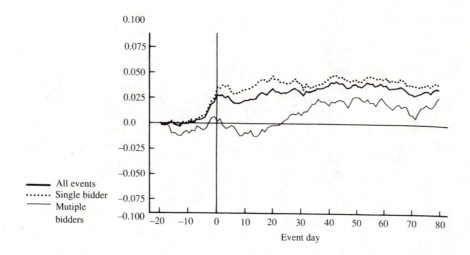

Figure 10.2   CARs to the shares of firms which have made successful tender offers. (Source: M. Bradley,[16] p. 376.)

research has shown that the price increases occasioned by a bid have not been lost after its unsuccessful conclusion, and that this phenomenon has been generally interpreted as evidence that the market had previously undervalued the target implying some inefficiency on the part of the market. However, Bradley puts forward an alternative interpretation of these results, 'Another interpretation of these results is the "kick in the pants" hypothesis. This holds that the target managers were running the firm inefficiently, and the takeover attempt put the fear of God into them. They got their act together and got the revaluation.'[17]

In the case of the shares of the target firms, Bradley concludes that neither of the above hypotheses are supported by the evidence. Figure 10.3 shows that where no subsequent bid is forthcoming, the shares of the target company tend to return to their pre-bid levels. On the other

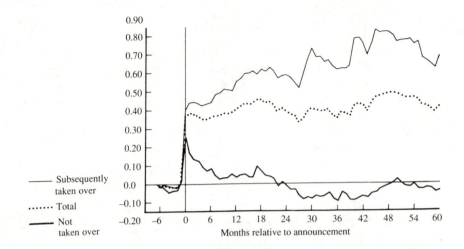

Figure 10.3 CARs to the shares of targets of unsuccessful tender offers. (Source: M. Bradley,[16] p. 377.)

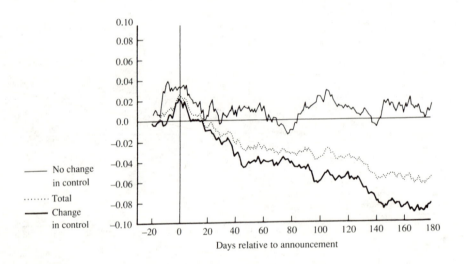

Figure 10.4 CARs to the shares of firms that have made unsuccessful tender offers. (Source: M. Bradley,[16] p. 378.)

hand, the consequences of a failed bid can be deleterious for the shareholders of the unsuccessful bidder. Bradley distinguishes between the cases in which the control of the target is unchanged and those in which it passes to a rival bidder. In this latter case Bradley found large and significant negative CARs. As an interpretation of this phenomenon, Bradley suggests that this reflects the market's assessment that the bidder has lost the potential benefits of synergy and is in an inferior competitive position to the victor of the bid battle.

The first published study of UK acquisition activity using the cumulative average residual methodology was by Firth[18] in 1976. From the data concerning 204 acquisitions during the period 1973–74, Firth found an average abnormal return of 37 per cent to the shareholders of target firms. In a study of 94 takeovers in the brewing industry between 1955 and 1972, Franks, Broyles and

Hecht found that the market anticipated takeover bids by about 3 months and that both groups of shareholders appeared to gain from the acquisition.[19] The authors estimated that the shareholders of the target companies enjoyed abnormal returns averaging about 26 per cent and that the shareholders of the acquiring company experienced small but only temporary positive abnormal returns.

In 1980 Firth[20] published a more wide-ranging study of UK takeover activity between 1969 and 1975. The data consisted of 486 target firms and 563 would-be acquirers. In acquisition terms 355 were successful with the original offer, 79 were successful after a second or counter bid was made and 52 were unsuccessful. Of the 563 would-be acquirers 434 were successful and 129 were not. Using cumulative average residuals methodology, Firth attempted to test two economic and behavioural theories for acquisitions. The first is the neoclassical theory of 'profit maximization' in which acquisitions increase the firm's profitability and hence the shareholders' wealth. The second theory is the 'maximization of managerial utility' which holds that managers seek to achieve a satisfying rather than a maximizing performance. Firth calculated the cumulative average residuals for four groups:

1. acquirers which have made successful bids;
2. acquirers which have made unsuccessful bids;
3. targets which have been the subject of successful bids;
4. targets which have been the subject of unsuccessful bids.

Figures 10.5(a) and 10.5(b) show that Firth found no abnormal returns for bidders in the 12 months before the announcement of the bid. However, during the month of the bid, 80 per cent (successful) and 77 per cent (unsuccessful) of the bidders experienced a statistically significant negative residual. Firth interprets this finding as 'the market regards takeovers as being very expensive for the acquiring firm.'[21] In the case of the successful bidders, their performance after the bid settles down without any significant trend. These results conflict with those of Bradley presented earlier. Whereas in the US successful bidders are found to have positive CARs in the 3 months after the announcement of a bid, those in the UK experience a significant negative residual

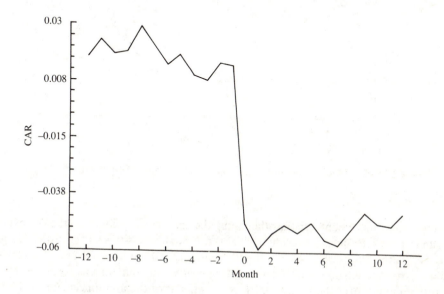

Figure 10.5(a)   CARs for successful acquirers in the UK. (Source: M. Firth,[20] Table 3.)

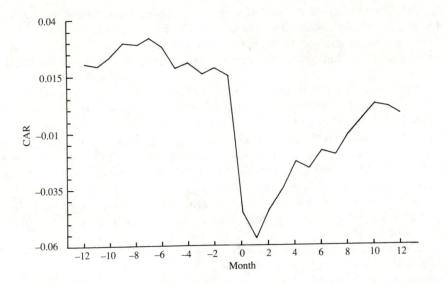

Figure 10.5(b)   CARs for unsuccessful acquirers in the UK. (Source: M. Firth,[20] Table 4.)

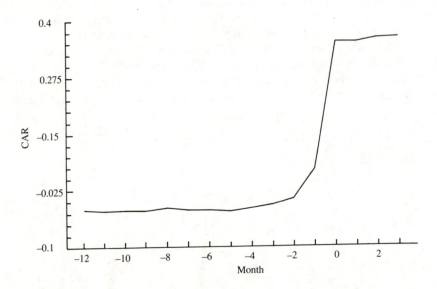

Figure 10.5(c)   CARs for acquired firms in the UK. (Source: M. Firth,[20] Table 1.)

in the month of announcement. On the other hand, the unsuccessful bidders in the UK experience a negative and statistically negative residual which is followed by positive and statistically significant residuals; i.e. beating the market index in the 12 months after the failure of the bid. Bradley's results show that on average unsuccessful bidders suffer negative and statistically negative returns and significantly underperform the market in the 6 months after the announcement of the bid.

Firth extended his analysis of acquisitions by looking at the overall gain or loss in these situations (Table 10.6). This was done by comparing the capitalization of the 2 firms before the

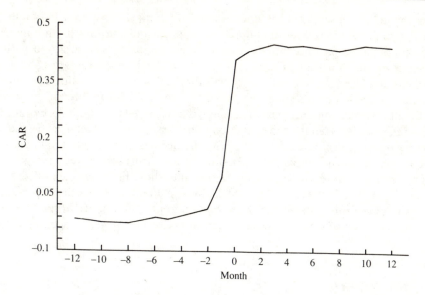

Figure 10.5(d) CARs for target firms which were not acquired in the UK. (Source: M. Firth,[20] Table 2.)

Table 10.6   Firth's overall gain–loss analysis

	Merged firm	Targets	Bidders
Mean Gain or Loss (£ million)	−36.6	1 103.6	−1 140.2
Number of Losses	224	3	350
Number of Acquisitions	434	434	434

Source: M. Firth[20], Table 6, p. 252.

takeover and, in the event of acquisition, comparing the result with the capitalization of the merged firm.

Firth[22] interprets the findings in the following way:

> The table shows that there is virtually a no-gain-loss position attached to takeovers in the United Kingdom in the period 1969–1975. This implies that the stock market is expecting little change in the profitability of firms once they have combined; any possible benefits in the form of synergy or reorganization of the acquired firm are presumably being countered by doubts of whether the offeror has access to management capable of greatly increasing efficiency, and because of the costs in the takeover process.

Firth concluded his study by trying to assess the returns to management from acquisition activity. He pointed out that it has been observed that in both the US and the UK there is a positive correlation between directors' remuneration and the value of assets under their control.[23] Firth regressed the increase in directors' remuneration against the growth of assets in acquiring firms and found a positive and significant relationship. He concluded that although acquisition activity might be expected to lead to a loss of wealth for the shareholders of the bidding firms, it would lead to an increase in welfare for the directors of such companies.

A more recent study by Dodds and Quek[24] concentrated on merger activity in a sample of 70 firms from the industrial sector in the international stock market between 1974 and 1976. The prices of the bidding firms were monitored over a period starting 10 months before the announcement of the merger to 60 months after. CAR methodology was employed, with the major difference of using the Industrial Group Index of the Financial Times Actuaries Share Index (496 shares). Dodds and Quek found positive residuals for the first 25 months after the announcement of the bid, after which they became negative. However, the CARs did not become negative until the 55th month after the bid announcement. The authors interpreted their findings by suggesting that there was a difference between the short- and long-term assessments of mergers. In the short term the market regarded acquisitions as beneficial while in the long term this view was reversed. Dodds and Quek subdivided their sample twice. First into those firms which were 'merger active' and those which weren't. Second, they split their sample into those bidders which offered equity and those which offered cash. In the case of the first distinction, they found that the dispersion of results for the merger-active firms were much higher than that of the non-active firms. They also found that the returns of the firms offering cash tended to underperform those offering equity.

Testing for synergy

Synergy is the reason most frequently cited for acquisitions, yet it is one of the least frequently tested. Much of the US evidence on the profitability of conglomerate mergers has not supported the existence of synergy.[25] One interesting attempt to find evidence for synergy was that by Haugen and Langetieg which observed the performance of an appropriately-weighted portfolio of the 2 firms before the merger and compared the results with the returns from the merged firm after the takeover.[26] The authors defined synergy as being a change in the distribution of returns between the portfolio of the 2 firms before the acquisition and the returns of the merged firm. They argue that there is clearly every reason why this should be so. New management may well be able to change the financial characteristics of the acquired firm. They studied 59 industrial mergers between companies listed on the NYSE between 1951 and 1968. They limited their sample by selecting only those cases in which the transfer of ownership had been effected by a share swap. Each case was matched to 2 other firms which then constituted a control group to eliminate any industry-specific changes which might affect the distribution of returns. The period analysed began 3 years before the merger and ended 3 years after the merger (using monthly data).

As in the other studies Haugen and Langetieg used the market model, but instead of generating CARs they elected to try to detect statistically significant changes in the average returns, standard deviation of returns, and betas. None of the observed changes was significant at the 5 per cent level. However, they added a caveat to their findings:

> It should be remembered, however, that we direct our attention only to changes in the risk attributes of the distribution of stock returns. If the market is efficient, a change in the *profitability* of the assets should be quickly capitalized in the price of the combined company's common stock. A change of this type will go undetected by our analysis.[27]

Conclusions

Mergers and acquisitions have become an important feature of the US and UK stock markets since the fifties. They are generally accepted as a speedier method of obtaining corporate growth than the alternative which is internal or organic investment. However, the motivation or acquisitions in many cases appears to be somewhat confused and confusing, there being unstated motives and fears. In addition, the evidence for the profitability of acquisitions is not conclusive either way. It might be tentatively suggested that the traditional measure of merger profitability using accounting data tends to cast doubts on the policy while the more modern methodology does not.

A new method of changing ownership has emerged during the 1980s. It is the management buyout (MBO) in which the management (part or all of the management and in some cases the workforce as well) of a subsidiary acquires it from the parent company. Two of the most successful have been those of the National Freight Corporation (from the government) and Premier Foods (from Cadbury Schweppes). The latter was effected by a group of management within the division who put up £330,000 and borrowed £96.7 million in 1986 to buy Cadbury's food and beverage division which included such brands as Typhoo Tea, Cadbury's Biscuits, Smash, Marvel, and Hartley's Jam. The management's orginal investment was estimated to be worth about £165 million in March 1989 and the workers who spent £66,000 on shares in the new company had an investment worth about £35 million.

Although, the number of MBOs has varied only in the narrow range 200 to 300 a year between 1982 and 1987, the average size has grown. In the early eighties, many buyouts were only worth £1 million or so, but the last few years have seen MBOs like the £620 million buyout of Reed International's European paper business and the £705 million buyout of the MFI furniture business from the Asda-MFI group. However large these may seem, they are all dwarfed by the leveraged buyout (LBO) of RJR Nabisco for $25 billion organized by the US firm of Kohlberg Kravis Roberts in December 1988. Most MBOs (or management buyins where a non-company management team buys a company or subsidiary, for example the successful bid of £446 million for Harris Queensway by James Gulliver and his consortium in 1988) are financed by debt with very low levels of equity participation. With such a high level of gearing, the management group aim to bring the new company to the Stock Exchange to sell all or part of their stake in order to realize the gains of their investment. Between 1981 and October 1988 there were 125 MBOs floated on the Stock Exchange. These figures may tend to understate the change in the ownership of these assets as some of the new companies are sold without going to the Stock Exchange. For example, in 1989 Premier Brands was considered likely to be auctioned for about £220 million.

Notes

1. J. Hamill, 'British acquisitions in the United States', *NatWest Bank Review*, 1987, p. 2.
2. G. Newbould, *Management and Merger Activity*, Guthshead, 1970.
3. H. Levinson, 'A psychologist diagnoses merger failure', *Harvard Business Review*, 1970, p. 65.
4. op. cit. 2.
5. Given the investment policy of Hanson plc—'Basic Industries'—the reduction in the riskiness of its returns should not be too much of a surprise. Hanson plc now constitutes a portfolio of assets producing goods which may be described as being rather less sensitive to the vagaries of fashion and the business cycle than many others.
6. M. Rubinstein, 'A mean–variance synthesis of corporate finance', *Journal of Finance*, Vol. 28, March 1973.
7. op. cit. 2.
8. H. Rose and G. Newbould, 'The 1967 take-over boom', *Moorgate and Wall Street*, 1967.
9. P. Dodd, 'The market for corporate control: a review of the evidence', in *The Revolution in Corporate Finance*, J. Stern and D. Chew (eds), Blackwell, 1986, p. 356.
10. op. cit. 2.
11. A. Singh, *Takeovers*, Cambridge University Press, 1971.

12. M. Utton, 'On measuring the effects of industrial mergers', *Scottish Journal of Political Economy*, Vol. 21, February 1974.

13. J. Kitching, 'Why acquisitions are abortive', *Management Today*, November 1974.

14. G. Meeks, 'Disappointing marriage: a study of the gains from merger', University of Cambridge, Department of Applied Economics, Occasional Paper 51, 1977.

15. A. Appleyard, 'Takeovers: accounting policy, financial policy and the case against accounting measures of performance', *Journal of Business Finance and Accounting*, Vol. 7, 1980.

16. M. Bradley, 'The Economic consequences of mergers and tender offers', in Stern and Chew, op. cit. 9.

17. Ibid. p. 377.

18. M. Firth, *Share Prices and Mergers*, Saxon House, 1976.

19. J. Franks, J. Broyles and M. Hecht, 'An industry study of the profitability of mergers in the United Kingdom', *Journal of Finance*, December 1977, pp. 1513–1525.

20. M. Firth, 'Takeovers, shareholder returns, and the theory of the firm', *The Quarterly Journal of Economics*, March 1980, pp. 235–260.

21. Ibid. p. 250.

22. Ibid. p. 252.

23. A. Cosh, 'The remuneration of chief executives in the United Kingdom', *Economic Journal*, March 1975.
    G. Meeks and G. Whittington, 'Directors' pay, growth and profitability', *Journal of Industrial Economics*, September 1975.
    D. Roberts, 'A general theory of executive compensation based on statistically tested propositions', *Quarterly Journal of Economics*, May 1956.
    W. Lewellen and G. Maguire, 'A pure financial rationale for the conglomerate merger', *Journal of Finance*, Vol. 26, May 1971.

24. J. Dodds and J. Quek, 'Effect of mergers on the share price movement of the acquiring firms: a UK study', *Journal of Business Finance and Accounting*, Vol. 12, Summer 1985, pp. 285–296.

25. For example, R. Melicher and D. Rush, 'Evidence on the acquisition-related performance of conglomerate firms', *The Journal of Finance*, Vol. 29, March 1974.

26. R. Haugen and T. Langetieg, 'An empirical test for synergism in merger', *Journal of Finance*, Vol. 30, June 1975.

27. Ibid. pp. 1009–1013.

Questions

1. Critically discuss the proposition that 'takeovers and mergers constitute a very costly way of changing managements and investment plans'.

2. What potential benefits can an investor look forward to when the company in which he or she has invested embarks on a policy of diversification by acquisition?

3. Could the investor in question 2 above have obtained the benefits from diversification by acquisition by him- or herself?

4. What is 'junk bond financing'? What implications does it have for the market for corporate control and shareholders and debentureholders of the companies that use it?

5. To what extent is asset stripping a necessary and natural corollary of the creation of conglomerates?

6. Discuss the proposition that firms with low P/E ratios and large and stable cash flows hide value when they diversify into firms with high P/E ratios and erratic cash flows, and that this hidden value only becomes apparent when the conglomerate is taken over and dismembered.

7. Merger and acquisition activity is seen as the result of a free and relatively unencumbered market for corporate control and it is argued that this will produce a more efficient economy. Is this type of argument

compatible with the apparent absence of such a market in the two most successful economies in modern times—Japan and W. Germany?

8. Critically discuss Levinson's idea that the 'fear of being taken over' is the mainspring for many a corporate acquisition.

9. With reference to the takeover battle between Elders IXL and Allied Lyons, what part did advertising 'knocking copy' play in educating shareholders as to the merits or otherwise of the offer?

10. Critically comment on the argument that MBOs are likely to be successful because ownership will improve personal performance. And that just as importantly, the fear of personal bankruptcy due to the inevitably heavy burden of debt will motivate people to do more effective work.

11. Futures and the stock market crashes of 1987

Introduction: speculation and market 'equilibrium'

Speculation may be defined as the purchase or short sale of assets or rights in the expectation of financial gain. It will occur in any market (not just futures markets) in which decisions are taken without the benefit of perfect knowledge. The neo-classical body of microeconomic theory views speculation as one of the primary processes by which equilibrium must be achieved. In this sense, beneficial speculation can take place through arbitrage between different prices for identical assets. In Chapter 1 it was noted that individuals called 'shunters' arbitraged between the various provincial markets and by their efforts price anomalies were removed. In modern financial markets, financial instruments exist to carry this process one step further by allowing speculators to take positions which may exploit the differences between expectations. Futures markets explicitly facilitate this practice by allowing investors to speculate without participating in either production or ownership. It has always been assumed that the successful speculator (if such can be found—that is to say an individual without access to inside information) has superior foresight with which he or she can exploit temporary discrepancies between demand and supply. Therefore, speculators and arbitrageurs (without inside information) are risk takers who are essential for the efficient operation of the market. This was pointed out in Chapter 7 in relation to the traded options markets and this is no less true for futures and forwards markets.

In general, speculators are assumed to buy assets in excess supply and to sell when those assets are in excess demand, thus reducing the variance of price changes. Hence, the speculator's profit is a reward for the assumption of risk. However, it should be appreciated that this type of activity is generally assumed to constitute only a small part of the total transactions activity in the market, if only for the reason that there are not too many individuals who not only have the inclination to take on risk but also have the capital with which to do so.

Therefore, by implication we have established the conditions under which the practice of speculation is a desirable and undesirable occupation. If speculation constitutes more than just a marginal part of the economic activity in a market it will tend to exaggerate, rather than damp down, price swings. In addition, if the majority of speculators' expectations are incorrect their actions will also tend to destabilize the market. However, this may be argued to be a temporary phenomenon at most as those speculators who make incorrect decisions will quickly lose their capital and be eliminated from the market.

There are several prerequisite market characteristics for speculation to occur:
1. the assets must be standardized and homogeneous if possible;
2. the market must be efficient and liquid;
3. the assets must usually be durable or, failing that, have a low storage cost;
4. the assets should usually have a high value in relation to their bulk.

The markets which fulfil these conditions are financial—equities, debentures, options, financial futures—and raw materials—metals (both precious and base), agricultural commodities and oil.

Futures markets

A futures contract is a legally enforceable agreement in which a commitment has been given to buy or sell a specified quantity and quality of assets at a specified price at some specified point in the future. Futures markets standardize the contract in terms of quantity, quality and maturity. Each contract is secured with a down payment, the balance being paid upon delivery. The distinguishing feature of the modern futures market is the clearing house which not only regulates the market but also guarantees each and every contract.

At this juncture it would be useful to outline the differences between futures and forward contracts. These 2 contracts may be distinguished on 4 separate grounds:

1. *The market organization*: futures are traded on an organized exchange where the traders are members of that exchange. Forward markets, such as those for foreign exchange, tend to have no formal market exchange and hence do not have any membership requirements.

2. *The type of contract*: in a futures market contracts are standardized in terms of quantity, quality, and maturity. A forward contract may be an *ad hoc* arrangement specific to a single deal.

3. *The clearing house*: perhaps the most significant part of the modern futures market is the clearing house. Every futures contract has not 2 counterparties, but 3. The third is the clearing house which guarantees every contract. One important exception to this type of organization is the London Metal Exchange (LME) in which there is no clearing house and principals have to guarantee their own contracts.

Figure 11.1 illustrates the essential function of the clearing house. It facilitates the progress of the contract from its inception to its maturity. While it may pass through a large number of owners, the clearing house ensures that the contract does not get mislaid. Thus at each stage and change of ownership, the clearing house acts as both buyer and seller beween the two principals while the obligations remain with the originator and the final owner. Figure 11.1 illustrates a further difference between futures and forward contracts—most futures contracts (98 or 99 per cent) are cancelled before delivery by an equal and opposite trade. In this respect the LME is also somewhat different from the normal futures markets as some 12 to 15 per cent of its contracts are for physical delivery.[1]

4. *The operation of margins and daily settlement rules*: the futures market provides financial safeguards through the mechanism of the clearing house. Not having a clearing house the forward market cannot provide such safeguards. One of the most attractive qualities of a forward or a futures contract is the necessity of only securing the contract with a small deposit, usually known as the margin. For most futures contracts the initial margin is around 5 per cent of the value of the underying asset. However, the clearing house enforces a system of daily cash resettlement in which traders realize the loss they may bear during the day in which it is incurred. For example, suppose a buyer of a futures contract in some physical commodity such as coffee places an initial margin of 5 per cent with his or her broker. If the spot price of coffee falls then the broker will call for an additional margin payment which will be credited to the account of the original seller of the contract. On the other hand, if the spot price of coffee increases then the liability of the originator of the contract increases and the broker can call for a margin payment from the originator and this will be credited to the account of the buyer. If these maintenance margin payments are not met then the broker has the right to close the contract before a loss exceeding the initial margin has been exceeded.

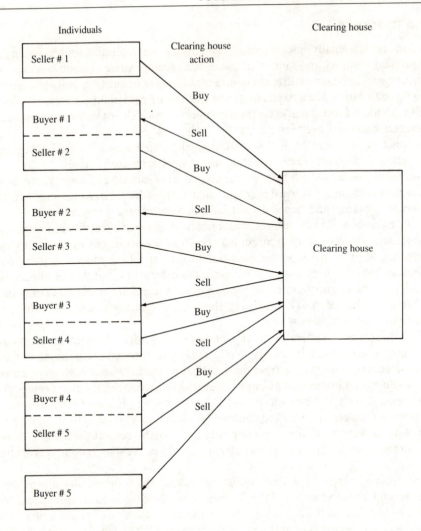

Figure 11.1   Operation of the clearing house.

Spot prices, expected spot prices and future prices

There are two price relationships in futures markets which are of critical importance to the formation of investor expectations and market liquidity. The first of these is called the 'basis' which is the difference between the futures price for the commodity or financial asset and its current cash price (see Table 11.1).

The excess of the futures price over the spot price is known as the 'premium' and in 'normal markets' is just enough to cover the carrying costs such as storage, interest charges, and insurance. Thus in a 'normal market' the basis is positive and is understood to compensate the speculator for the physical costs of speculation rather than to ensure a profit from the movement in prices. In 'normal markets' we may expect to see a progressively higher basis as the time to maturity lengthens and the carrying costs increase. On the other hand the raw and white sugar prices quoted in Table 11.1 show inversion where the futures price is less than the spot price; i.e. the basis is at a

Table 11.1   Basis

(a) Raw Sugar (LCE), spot price $261.8 per ton (London 20/11/1988)

Contract	Price	Basis
March	226	−35.8
May	221	−40.8
August	217	−44.8
October	213.4	−48.4
March	209	−52.8

(b) White Sugar (LCE), spot price $261.5 per ton (London 20/11/1988)

March	266	4.5
May	258	−3.5
August	256	−5.5
October	256.5	−5

(c) Gold (NY), spot price $412 per troy ounce (London 20/11/1988)

October	412.2	0.2
November	413.3	1.3
December	415.4	3.4
February	420.6	8.6
April	425.8	13.8
June	431	19
August	436.5	24.5
October	442.2	30.2
December	447.8	35.8

Source: *Financial Times* 21 November 1988.

discount to the spot price. This is merely a reflection of the expectation of greater supplies of sugar in the future over what is currently available. However, one caveat should be added to this simple relationship. As the producer has taken on the function of carrying the commodity as an inventory for the final user, the basis may be somewhat less than the carrying cost. This difference has been called a 'convenience yield' which has been defined as the 'sum of extra advantages (other than appreciation in the market value) which a manufacturer may derive from carrying stocks above his immediate requirements rather than holding the equivalent value in cash and buying stocks at a later date.[2]

Whereas we can argue that the differences between spot and futures prices are merely the reflection of the expectations of futures demand and supply, the difference between futures and expected spot prices is not so clearly delineated. Hicks and Keynes have argued that futures prices should be slightly less than expected spot prices by an amount equal to a small insurance premium. This condition is called 'normal backwardation' and 'measures the amount which hedgers have to hand over to speculators in order to persuade the speculators to take over the risks of the price fluctuations in question. Ultimately, therefore, it measures the cost of coordination achieved by forward trading; if the cost is very heavy, potential hedgers will prefer not to hedge.'[3] The alternative to this view was formulated by Hardy,[4] in which the futures market is regarded as a casino by speculators who are then prepared to pay an entrance fee for the privilege of taking risks. In this case speculators will bid up futures prices above expected future spot prices.

Normal backwardation has been tested by Telser, Cootner, Dusak, and Chiang.[5] Telser and Cootner attempted to show whether or not futures prices were biased or unbiased estimates of their expected spot prices. However, their results were not conclusive. Even Chiang's more recent study which provides support for normal backwardation does not decisively tip the scales. Dusak used the capital asset pricing model to analyse the systematic risk of futures contracts for wheat, corn and soya beans traded between 1952 and 1967. In each of the contracts, both the systematic risk and the returns were found to be close to zero which does not support the theory of normal backwardation. However, Dusak points out that the institutional conditions in futures markes in the twenties may have been different, which produced conditions of sizeable and positive risks and returns to speculators.

The same methodology was used by Bodie and Rosansky[6] on the data from futures contracts on 23 commodities over the period 1950–76 (see Table 11.2).

Table 11.2   Returns on commodity futures contracts 1950–76

Year	US Equities (%) return	Futures (%) return	Number of commodities	Inflation (%) change
1950	31.71	52.61	—	5.79
1951	24.02	26.71	10	5.87
1952	18.37	−1.22	10	0.88
1953	−0.99	−6.32	10	0.62
1954	52.62	14.88	10	−0.50
1955	31.56	−4.79	13	0.37
1956	6.56	14.75	13	2.86
1957	−10.78	−2.34	13	3.02
1958	43.36	−1.33	13	1.76
1959	11.95	0.54	13	1.50
1960	0.47	−0.09	13	1.48
1961	26.89	1.55	13	0.67
1962	−8.73	0.87	13	1.22
1963	22.80	22.84	13	1.65
1964	16.48	12.13	14	1.19
1965	12.45	10.62	16	1.92
1966	−10.06	14.65	17	3.35
1967	23.98	4.13	19	3.04
1968	11.06	1.24	19	4.72
1969	−8.50	20.84	21	6.11
1970	4.01	11.99	22	5.49
1971	14.31	3.31	23	3.36
1972	18.98	33.71	23	3.41
1973	−14.66	101.54	23	8.80
1974	−26.48	31.96	23	12.20
1975	37.20	−4.01	23	7.01
1976	23.84	12.75	23	4.81
Mean	13.05	13.83		3.43
St Dev	18.95	22.43		2.90

Source: Z. Bodie and V. Rosansky,[6] Tables II, III and IV, p. 29 and p. 31.

Bodie and Rosansky noted the remarkable similarity between the series on risks and returns of equities and futures contracts but also pointed out that they have a negative correlation coefficient of −0.24. They comment that, 'The positive mean excess return on the benchmark commodity futures portfolio seems to lend support to the normal backwardation hypothesis.'[7] Although these results directly contradict those of Dusak, the authors checked the consistency of their data by restricting their sample to wheat, corn and soya bean futures contracts and found that the mean return was close to zero for this subset of their data. Lastly, they used the methodology of the market model to regress the returns of the individual commodity futures returns against the Standard and Poor 500 Index. They found that most of the estimated betas were negative, and were unable to define a securities market line with a positive slope which would have indicated the presence of the normal risk–return relationship.

Figure 11.2 shows another possibility which is known as the 'net hedging hypothesis' which assumes that the balance of expectations and the net position of hedgers and speculators changes over the life of the contract. It suggests that, due to uncertainty at the beginning of the life of the contract, hedgers will be net short while speculators will be net long giving normal backwardation. As the level of uncertainty falls with the nearing maturity of the contract, the hypothesis suggests that the net positions will be reversed. Although unlikely, this change in uncertainty and consequent change in net positions may conceivably occur in agricultural markets. In this situation the farmer hedges and takes a short position while the speculator takes a long position thus producing backwardation which will be reversed as and when the harvest becomes more predictable and the hedgers reverse their initial positions.

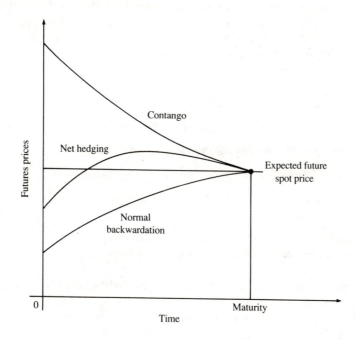

Figure 11.2   Backwardation and contango.

Hedging with commodity futures

Although the concept of a futures contract was introduced with reference to speculators, we have not explicitly considered those for whom the futures markets provide a means of insurance for their economic activities and decisions. Those who use these markets to limit their risk do so by constructing a hedge. Pure insurance against the vagaries of markets is not possible in practice, however, risks may be anticipated and managed by taking positions in assets which will have counterbalancing profits and losses.

Suppose that Agricultural Supplies plc has 300 tons of soya bean meal in storage after the harvest and that it does not want to take the risk of the spot price falling before it sells its produce. It may then enter the figures markets and sell in time t a contract for 300 tons maturing in time $t+1$.

The company has created a hedged position whose expected return may be described as follows,

$$E(r_h) = wE(r_p) + zE(r_f)$$

where, $E(r_h)$ = expected return on the hedged position

    $E(r_p)$ = expected return on the spot position (i.e. the 300 tons of soya bean meal in storage facility)

    $E(r_f)$ = expected return on the commitment to the futures contract

    w = monetary investment to the spot position

    z = monetary commitment to the futures position

If the spot price rises, then the company will make a positive return on the commodity in storage while making a loss on the short position on the futures contract. On the other hand if the spot price falls, the loss on the spot position will be counterbalanced by a positive return on the fugures position. The various hedge positions are shown at Fig. 11.3(a), (b) and (c).

The risk of this hedge may be described as follows,

$$\sigma^2_{(r_h)} = w^2\sigma^2_{(r_p)} + z^2\sigma^2_{(r_f)} + 2wz\rho_{pf}\sigma_{(r_p)}\sigma_{(r_f)}$$

where, $\sigma^2_{(r_h)}$ = variance of the returns on the hedge position

    $\sigma^2_{(r_p)}$ = variance of the returns on the spot investment

    $\sigma^2_{(r_f)}$ = variance of the returns on the futures commitment

    $\sigma_{(r_p)}$ = standard deviation of the returns on the spot investment

    $\sigma_{(r_f)}$ = standard deviation of the returns on the futures commitment

    ρ_{pf} = correlation coefficient between the returns on the spot investment and those on the futures commitment

This equation is merely an application of the formula used by Markowitz (see Chapter 4) to estimate the expected variance of returns on a portfolio of risky assets. This equation may be manipulated to give the minimum-risk hedge by solving for z (see Chapter 4), the amount of the commodity that the firm should sell short in the futures market.

$$z = (-w)[(\rho_{pf})\sigma_{(r_p)}]/\sigma_{(r_f)}$$

where the variances of the returns in the spot and futures markets are equal, $(\rho_{pf})\sigma_{(r_p)}/\sigma_{(r_f)}$ is equal, by definition, to unity and the minimum-risk hedge is obtained by selling short in the futures market an amount equal to that held in storage. In the theoretical situation where the spot and futures markets are perfectly correlated (as implicitly assumed above), it is possible to construct the perfect hedge in which the minimum risk is reduced to zero. In reality this is not so and the above analysis will produce a recommendation to over- or under-hedge by selling short an amount in excess or inferior quantity to the physical commodity held.

The futures market may be used as follows: suppose a cocoa producer anticipates a harvest of 5,000 tons and expects a price of 820 per ton (currency units are unimportant). In order to ensure the anticipated revenue of 4.1 million (5,000)(820), the producer may go to the futures market and sell futures contracts for 5,000 tons at a price of 820 per ton. Suppose the harvest comes in as expected (unlikely) but that the spot price has risen to 850 per ton because of difficulties elsewhere, the farmer will have made a profit of 30 per ton on his physical commodity (in the sense of making

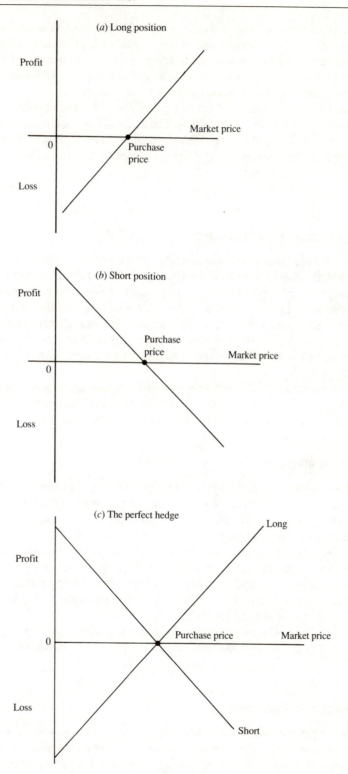

Figure 11.3 Returns on a commodity hedge using futures contracts.

more than expected) but will now make a loss of 30 per ton on the futures contract when he comes to reverse the trade. On the other hand, if the spot price had fallen to 790 per ton due to advantageous harvests elsewhere, the producer will have made a loss of 30 per ton (in the sense that the price was less than expected), but he may make a profit on the futures market when he comes to reverse the trade by buying back the contract at 790 per ton.

The above example constitutes a selling hedge in which the supplier takes out insurance against the vagaries of the market; i.e. price falls. The other side of the coin is the buying hedge in which the end-user of the commodity may seek to secure a future price and insure against price rises. Chocolate manufacturers may stabilize the price of the supplies of their raw materials in the future by buying futures contracts.

Futures market efficiency

Unlike equity markets, futures markets do not exist for the purpose of raising capital. However, like equities markets they do have a pricing function and like traded options markets they provide a means of transferring risk. Hence, it is important that futures markets have some degree of pricing efficiency in order to properly perform their functions. Just as demonstrable pricing inefficiency in equity markets would impair their abilities to raise and allocate new capital, so demonstrable pricing inefficiency in futures markets would impair their abilities to transfer risk. Academic interest in the efficiency of futures markets has concentrated on the terminology and methodology of Fama's work.[8]

The first observation to make about the distributions of returns from futures contracts is that they are leptokurtic—flat tailed with a predominance of observations about the mean.[9] Two types of efficiency have been tested in futures markets—the weak and semi-strong forms.

Weak form efficiency

Taylor has found evidence of 'persistent autocorrelation' in the returns on futures contracts in the London cocoa and coffee markets which suggest trading strategies based on forecasting returns may yield superior returns to a simple buy-and-hold strategy. However, Taylor found no 'persistent autocorrelation' in the returns from the futures contracts in the 3 currencies tested— sterling, Deutschmarks, and Swiss francs.[10] These results confirm those of Stevenson and Bear who found the random walk hypothesis inadequate to explain the distributions of returns for futures contracts in corn and soya beans traded on the Chicago Board of Trade between 1951 and 1967. Their work also showed that trading based on mechanical filter rules could produce superior returns to the buy-and-hold strategy.[11]

Lastly, although other authors have also rejected the random walk hypothesis as a description of commodity futures markets, some have not taken this to mean that futures markets are necessarily inefficient.[12]

Semi-strong form efficiency

There have been 2 principal methods employed to test for semi-strong efficiency in futures markets. The first assumes that all the relevant publicly available information for any particular commodity is in the forecast errors of closely related commodities. Therefore, the current forecast error should be uncorrelated with past errors if the market is semi-strong efficient. This method regresses the current forecast error for a particular commodity contract (i.e. the difference between the current spot price and a lagged futures price for a maturing contract) upon recent forecast errors for identical and similar commodities. However, any rejection of the null hypothesis in this approach does not necessarily mean that the market may be accepted as semi-strong efficient, it may imply that the data and the predictive model have been mis-specified.

The second method involves the construction of an econometric model to predict spot prices of the market under examination. The results are then compared with the futures prices. The implicit assumption in this method is that if the market is semi-strong efficient, the futures prices should perform as well as the econometric model in predicting spot prices—that is to say that above normal returns cannot be gained from the analysis of the current set of publicly available information.

This latter approach was used by Leuthold and Hartmann for the market in hogs in the USA. They constructed an econometric model using the rates of hog slaughter, sow farrowing and income as explanatory variables. Although they found the futures price to be a better predictor than their model for the spot prices of hogs, they rejected the semi-srong hypothesis because they found the series of futures prices to be predictable and capable of being used as the basis for a profitable trading strategy.[13]

The first method was used by Goss to evaluate the semi-strong efficiency of some of the markets (copper, tin, lead and zinc) in the London Metal Exchange.[14] The data used consisted of the futures contract prices for spot and 3-months delivery for all 4 metals between July 1971 and June 1979. Goss estimated the following equation:

$$A_{t+k} - P_{t+k} = a + \Sigma b(A_t^J - P_{t-k}^J) + u_t$$

where, A_t = monthly average spot price in sterling per metric ton

P_t = monthly average futures (3-months) price in sterling per metric ton

t = time in months

$k = 1, 2, 3$, months

$j = 1$ = copper; $= 2$ = tin; $= 3$ = zinc; $= 4$ = lead

The hypothesis tested in each case was that the regression coefficients a and b were not significantly different from zero.[15] Tests on the individual markets supported semi-strong efficiency in the copper, tin and zinc markets,. However, when the exercise was repeated for all 4 metals together, Goss found that the regression coefficients were significantly different from zero, thus rejecting the semi-strong version of market efficiency for the LME. Goss suggested that this inconsistency may be explained by the 'exclusion of some agents from high-price units of information.'[16]

Similar results were found by Bird when he examined the LME for weak form efficiency over the period 1972–82. However, when he divided his data into two subperiods, 1972–75 and 1976–82, he found that the former period only exhibited strong serial tendencies allowing the profitable application of filter strategies.[17]

Although the authors cited so far have tended to argue that the LME is not weak form efficient in the sense that Fama originally defined, this view is not without criticism. For example, Gilbert[18] has argued that Goss's methodology of used monthly averaged data is incorrect and that the weak form efficiency of the LME should rightly be tested with daily data.

Financial futures

So far the discussion in this chapter has been concerned with commodity futures. However, like all other financial markets, the futures markets are in a state of continual evolution. The new products and instruments of the eighties have been financial futures and options on futures. The field of financial futures is expanding rapidly and the markets have shown themselves to be very innovative in creating new tradable instruments. Hence, this section will give a brief overview of the principal contracts before concentrating on the market index futures contracts which may have played such an important part in the stock market events of October 1987.

Basically a financial futures contract is an agreement to buy or sell a set quantity of a financial asset at a pre-set date in the future at a pre-set price. As in commodity futures, the standardization of contracts enables the users and speculators to open and close positions by making opposite and offsetting contracts which obviate the need to take delivery. For example the purchase of a 3-month sterling contract requires the purchaser to take delivery of a deposit of £500,000 in 3 months time. On the other hand, the seller of such a contract will have to make a deposit of £500,000 in 3 months time.

In the UK the major development in the field of financial futures trading was the creation of the London International Financial Futures Exchange (LIFFE) in September 1982. This followed the considerable successes of the US exchanges which had been trading various financial futures since the middle of the 1970s. LIFFE offers the following contracts:

1. Three-month Eurodollar interest rate. The trading unit is US$ 1 million and the contract comprises a 3-month Eurodollar deposit facility arranged by the seller at one of a list of banks designated by the Exchange. The delivery day is the second Wednesday of the delivery month. The quotation is $100.00 minus the annual rate of interest in basis points (1 basis point = 0.01 per cent). The minimum price movement is 1 basis point ($25) and the maximum is 100 basis points ($2,500). The initial margin is $2,000.
2. Three-month sterling interest rate. This is the same as the previous contract except that the unit of trade is $500,000 and the minimum and maximum price movements are 1 (£12.50) and 100 (£1,250) basis points respectively.
3. Twenty-year gilt. This is a notional gilt with a 20-year maturity, a coupon of 9 per cent and a unit value of £50,000. The contract specifies that delivery should be made with any real gilt with 15–25 years to maturity in multiples of £50,000 nominal.
4. 7–10 year notional gilt, £50,000.
5. 6 per cent long-term notional Japanese Government Bond, Y100 million.
6. 8 per cent US Treasury Bonds, $100,000.
7. 6 per cent notional German Government bond, DM250,000.
8. FTSE Index, £25 per index point.
   LIFFE also offers the following options on futures contracts:
1. Long gilt futures options.
2. US Treasury bond options.
3. FTSE Index futures options.
4. £/$ options, 25,000, cents per 1.

Trading is by 'open outcry' and is restricted to the floor of the Exchange and takes place between 8.30 a.m. and 3.15 p.m.

Stock index futures

Stock index futures leapt to prominence in 1988 after the publication of the *Presidential Report on Market Mechanisms* in the wake of the October 1987 stock market crash. Before going on to look at the crash itself and the part played by stock index futures, this section will take a look at this type of contract. There are four such contracts in the USA, one based on the FTSE in the UK and lastly one based on the Japanese stock market, traded both in Tokyo and Chicago. The best known of these is that based on the Standard and Poor 500 Index. This is composed of 40 utility companies, 20 transport firms, 40 financial institutions and 400 industrial firms. The weights are proportional to the firms market capitalization. The index has base value of 10 for the value of the stocks in the index quoted on the NYSE in 1941–43.

The Standard and Poor 500 futures contract is traded on the Chicago Mercantile Exchange (CME). This contract is an obligation to pay cash equal to 500 times the difference between the index value at the end of the contract and the value at which the contract was originally purchased. For example, suppose on the date of purchase the index stood at 300; if on the date of expiry the value has risen to 330 then the seller of the contract will have to pay the purchaser 500(330–300) or $15,000. On the other hand, if the index has fallen to 250 on the day of expiry, the purchaser will have to pay the seller an amount equal to 500(300–250), or $25,000. No physical delivery of shares is made and the market is controlled by the requirement of margin payments which are held by the CME as deposits in good faith. These margins are varied according to the movement of the index and the net positions of each party to the agreement at any point in time. Hence, if the index has risen above the level at which the contract was struck, then the seller is required to increase his margin payment to the controlling clearing house (and vice versa if the index falls below the level at which the contract was agreed).

The futures contract on market indices allows the institutional investor to realize the nominal profit on his or her portfolio when the market rises (assuming the purchase of such contracts) and to insure against nominal losses on the same portfolio when the market falls (assuming the sale of such contracts).

The pricing of index futures contracts is straightforward. The price is equal to 500 times the index level. Thus, if the index was offered at 300, then the price would be equal to (500)(300), or $150,000. The CME requires a margin payment ('deposit in good faith') of $6,000 from speculators (those without a portfolio of shares) and $2,500 from hedgers (those with a portfolio of shares). This means that in the previous example a speculative purchaser could have made a profit of 250 per cent or a loss of 417 per cent. Hence, the attractions for speculation are clear while those wishing to 'insure' their shares can do so at very little cost compared with the cost of the portfolio itself.

However, it is important to note that the previous paragraph stated that the index was 'offered' at 300. This implies that there is a difference between the offer level of the index and that ruling in the stock market. This is known as the 'premium to the index'. A holder of a share portfolio approximating that estimated by the Standard and Poor 500 index will collect dividends and benefit from (or suffer from) market rises (or market falls) in the form of capital gains (or losses). The purchase of a futures contract on the Standard and Poor 500 index will offer the investor the same range of gains and losses.

Index portfolio return = expiry price − purchase price + dividends
$$r_{ip} = P_2 - P_1 + D \tag{11.1}$$

Index futures contract return = expiry price − purchase price + interest
$$r_{fc} = F_2 - F_1 + I \tag{11.2}$$

If the two investments offer the same return, then
$$r_{ip} = r_{fc}, \text{ and } P_2 - P_1 + D = F_2 - F_1 + I \tag{11.3}$$

At expiry the price of the index (P_2) will be equal to the price of the futures contract (F_2). Therefore,

$$F_1 = P_1 + (I - D) \tag{11.4}$$

Hence, the initial price of the futures contract will be the price of the index portfolio (proxied by

$500 times each index point) plus the difference between the risk-free rate of interest and the dividend yield $(I-D)$. These equations merely take into account the concept of opportunity cost for the purchaser of the futures contract. As the capital gain is the same for both investments it concentrates on the income from each alternative. In the case of the investment in the index portfolio of shares the income will be the dividends received. On the other hand, the futures contract only requires a small percentage of the investor's capital, allowing the remaining bulk to be invested in risk-free government debt.

In addition to the opportunity cost, the price of the futures contract on a market index will also reflect the balance of expectations about the future movements of the market and the fact that the transactions cost of purchasing the futures contract is considerably less than buying the index portfolio of shares.

A portfolio insurance could be established by calculating the 'hedge ratio' which shows the number of futures contracts that should be purchased or sold. Assume an investor has an index portfolio worth $800,000 and the Standard and Poor index stands at 300. The price of each contract will be (500)(300), $150,000, and the initial margin required by the CME will be $2,500. The hedge ratio (HR) may be calculated by dividing the value of the index portfolio by the price of the contract as follows:

$$HR = 800{,}000/150{,}000 = 5.33$$

As fractional contracts cannot be purchased the investor may choose to over-insure by buying or selling 6 contracts or to underinsure by buying or selling 5 contracts. If the investor expects a fall in the market in the near future he may sell futures contracts receiving an initial margin income and, if correct, receiving a cash amount to offset the nominal losses made on the portfolio of shares. On the other hand if the investor has got it wrong, the cash payments he is obliged to pay on the futures contracts will be more or less offset by the rise in the value of the share portfolio.

If the investor expects the market to rise in the near future he may purchase futures contracts in order to realize actual cash gains in addition to the nominal profits made on the share portfolio if he has been correct. The caveat in this last strategy is most important. If the investor has got it wrong and the market falls then, as the purchaser of futures contracts and as the holder of a portfolio of shares, he will lose on both counts. The first strategy mentioned will result in a more or less unchanged wealth position regardless of the accuracy of the investor's expectations.

Options on stock index futures

Black[19] has shown that the Black–Scholes option pricing model may be extended to analyse and price options written on futures contracts. The modified equation set is as follows,

$$d_1 = [\ln(F/E) + (\sigma^2 T)/2]/\sigma\sqrt{T}$$
$$d_2 = d_1 - \sigma\sqrt{T}$$
$$C = [FN(d_1) - EN(d_2)]e^{(r-f)T}$$

where F = forward contract price

$\quad$ E = exercise price

$\quad$ T = time to maturity of the option contract

$\quad$ rf = risk-free rate of interest

$\quad$ σ = standard deviation of the price of the futures contract

This is similar to the model presented in Chapter 7. The principal difference is the omission of the risk-free rate of interest in the calculation of d_1. This is due to the fact that the forward contract requires little or no commitment of cash, as in the case of equities, because they are traded on margins and very few are held to maturity. The restriction of this application to forward contracts rather than futures contracts is due to the fact that futures contracts require daily resettlement of margin payments which act in the same way as dividends. In addition, it must be borne in mind that this version of the Black–Scholes formula should strictly be applied only to non-traded options whereas those written on futures contracts are generally tradable and have the facility for early exercise. Thus, estimates made of the options written on futures contracts using this model will be subject to small errors.

The use of options to create hedged positions has already been covered in Chapter 7 and there is no point in repeating them here as the results will be the same. However, the essential difference between the underlying assets must be borne in mind. The exercise of a call option on equities requires the investor to have the cash represented by the exercise price and the number of securities involved. On the other hand, the exercise of a call option on futures contracts does not require the complete amount of cash as futures are traded on margin. This increases the scope for gearing or leverage available to the speculator and the hedger.

The stock market crash of October 1987

As stated earlier the use of stock index futures, and options on those futures, may have played an important part in the events of October 1987. This section seeks to give a short account of those events before going on to examine some of the explanations and analyses that have subsequently emerged.

Between August 1982 and August 1987 the Dow Jones index of the NYSE rose from 777 to 2,722. The 'bull' market in the LSE lasted longer. From a low of 143 in 1975 the FT 30 index rose to 2,400 in 1987. These patterns were repeated with regional and national variations in all of the world's major stock exchanges. This extended capital appreciation was followed in October 1987 by one of the most severe falls in history. Other markets have collapsed by greater extents but in no case has the fall been so widespread or so quick.

The Presidential Report[20] identifies 2 'triggers' during the week before the crash:

1. On 14 October 1987 the US trade deficit was announced at $15.7 billion, some $1.5 billion higher than expected by the world's financial markets. Almost immediately foreign holders of US government debt began selling in anticipation of capital losses caused by a possible devaluation of the US dollar. As debt prices fell the interest rates in the US rose making the already low dividend returns on equities even more unattractive.

2. The announcement on 14 October 1987 that legislation was being proposed to end the tax benefits associated with corporate takeovers in the US. This had the effect of inducing speculators (the 'arbitrageurs') in takeover shares to sell in anticipation of price falls as the targets became less attractive to the corporate predators. As these shares and the people who speculated in them were a major force in pushing the market up to the heights reached in 1987 it can be seen that a major disinvestment by the speculators would have a serious depressing effect on the market.

The net effect of these 2 'triggers' was that the 'Dow' fell by 95 points on 14 October 1987. Not only did the speculators try to withdraw from the market but the portfolio insurers rushed to sell index futures contracts to try to safeguard their share portfolios. Towards the end of the day portfolio managers also entered the market to sell shares. By Monday, 19 October, confidence had completely vanished and the Dow fell by over 500 points. By the end of that week nearly one-third of the capitalization of the NYSE, the ISE and most other exchanges had evaporated.

The first 8 months of 1987 saw the FTSE 100 rise by 46 per cent and the Nikkei-Dow by 42 per cent. The *Bank of England Quarterly* suggests an earlier date for the beginning of the October crash, 6 October.[21] It notes that the NYSE fell by 92 points (3.5 per cent) in response to some tightening of West German monetary policy and 'rumours of discord between the US and German authorities over the Louvre Accord'. The ISE in London reached its lowest point on 9 November when it was 34 per cent below the level on 5 October. Similar declines took place on the continental exchanges, Paris–34 per cent, Frankfurt–40 per cent, and Zurich–38 per cent. The only major market which didn't experience a loss of such magnitude was Tokyo which fell by a 'mere' 15 per cent at its lowest point. All of these figures are in terms of local currencies. However, at the same time as the markets were falling the exchange rates between national currencies were changing as well, making the returns to those with international investments very different (Table 11.3).

Table 11.3   Change in equity indices in different currencies

| | *Percentage changes from 5/10/87 to 31/12/87* | | |
	London	*New York*	*Tokyo*
In sterling	−28.2	−36.5	−13.3
In US dollars	−16.9	−26.6	+0.3
In yen	−31.4	−39.3	−17.1

Source: *Bank of England Quarterly*, February 1988, page 52.

The Bank of England has also attempted to estimate the price volatility of equities quoted on the ISE (Table 11.4). The Bank calculated the standard deviations of price movements on a day-to-day basis. It noted that this measure could be subject to criticism for not taking intra-day movements into account.

Table 11.4   Price volatilities

	FTSE	*Dow-Jones*	*Nikkei-Dow*
5/10/87–12/11/87			
Close-to-close	4.15	5.49	3.88
Open-to-close	2.08	3.66	
Third quarter			
Close-to-close	0.91	0.93	1.10

Note: Standard deviation as a percentage of index daily price movements.
Source: *Bank of England Quarterly*, February 1988, page 53.

The Bank found no conclusive evidence that the most liquid shares were the most volatile. On the contrary, the most liquid shares (alpha stocks) were no more volatile than the others, and in some cases slightly less. This condition appears to have been maintained regardless of events. Neither the 'Big Bang' nor the 'crash' appears to have made any impact on relative share price volatility.

The Presidential Report goes on to argue that these stimuli set off mechanical sales by portfolio managers who had employed computer programs to monitor the market and react to market movements. The Report cites in evidence of this thesis the observation that on 19 October just 3 portfolio management groups using computer-aided techniques sold $2 billion worth of shares on the NYSE and sold futures contracts representing a further \$2.8 billion worth of shares. These figures must be set in context by recalling that the capitalization of the NYSE fell by about \$1,000 billion.

The Report concludes that what had hitherto been regarded as three separate markets: shares, share index futures and options, were in fact a single market. The Report also argues that a major cause of the severity of the October crash was the lack of confidence in the liquidity of the three markets. As a consequence of this, the Report asserts, the three markets separated and went into 'free fall'. The linkages between the markets which had allowed arbitrage operations to take place lapsed and portfolio managers' abilities to insure their portfolios vanished.

The Report's principal conclusions are that, given that there was effectively only one market (shares, share index futures and options), there should be only one regulatory body and only one clearing house system. In addition, the Report recommends that the desirability of trading breaks (based on maximum permissible price changes) should be considered in an attempt to reduce the potential volatility of the market.

Alternative explanations

During the 10 months before the crash in October 1987 the world's major stock markets rose by an average of 40 per cent. Although not an unprecedented rise, this sort of increase is not all that common. Equities listed on the London International Stock Market were offering gross dividend yield of less than 4 per cent. That meant that once basic rate income tax had been paid, the investments were offering a negative real return in terms of dividend income. Hence, investment could only be made on the expectation of capital appreciation. This expectation could have been based on either the expectation of a major improvement of the company behind the shares, or the anticipation of a takeover bid for the company and an associated increase in the share price, or lastly, the shares could have been bought on a pure speculative motive—that the prices would rise in the future merely because they had risen in the past. If the latter motive predominated in the first 10 months of 1987, then the crash in October of that year may be seen as a rather precipitate adjustment of expectations in financial markets and as such was no different from the crashes described earlier in this chapter. If this analysis holds some truth, then it is not so much the crash itself which necessitates investigation, but the essentially irrational boom that preceded the price collapse.

In Chapter 3 the efficient market theories (EMT) were examined. This body of theory and analysis has as an essential assumption that investors are rational. However, even if correct the above analysis does not invalidate this crucial assumption. It merely illustrates the necessity of investor rationality for the efficient pricing of financial assets.

However, this still begs the question of why this speculative boom happened at all and why it happened in 1987. The first of these questions can only be answered by reference to the psychology of crowds and this has not been satisfactorily answered despite the number of historical case studies which could be used for analysis. An explanation of the second question—why 1987—may well have been answered already. Brian Reading[22] writing in *The Sunday Times* argued that the support operations implemented by the governments of the major industrialized countries to prop up the international value of the US dollar served also to provide an inflationary stimulus. For example, the UK, West Germany and Japan accumulated additional reserves of US dollars worth \$65 billion (\$20 billion, \$15 billion and \$30 billion respectively). He argued that, as a consequence of this, these countries lost control of their money supplies. In the UK this additional supply of money was used to purchase existing physical and financial assets. The supply of these assets is relatively inelastic and does not quickly respond to rising demand, hence the increase in prices.[23]

Table 11.5 Equities: annual returns converted into sterling

	(%) p.a.									
	1970	1971	1972	1973	1974	1975	1976	1977	1978	1979
USA	4.2	7.2	29.2	−13.9	−27.3	59.3	46.8	−17.9	0.0	8.5
Japan	−11.1	44.0	146.2	−19.3	−16.6	39.2	49.3	3.2	44.0	−19.3
UK	−3.5	47.1	16.4	−28.6	−51.3	150.8	2.0	48.6	8.4	10.2
West Germany	−22.7	16.5	29.0	−3.5	16.0	51.2	26.6	10.5*	16.3*	−12.3*
Switzerland	−12.7	19.0	39.5	−2.1	−12.8	63.3	31.4	15.3	13.9	2.3
France	−4.3	−5.2	36.0	8.9	−25.8	68.1	−5.2	−6.1	62.2	17.9
Holland	−5.6	−5.1	40.8	−3.6	−16.7	74.8	38.8	3.8	13.0	9.6
Canada	14.9	6.8	44.9	−1.7	−27.7	33.9	30.8	−13.0	13.2	39.1
Australia	−19.3	−7.3	34.2	−13.0	−32.8	72.7	6.7	−0.8	14.7	31.2

	(%) p.a.							Mean
	1981	1982	1983	1984	1985	1986	1987	1978–1987
USA	18.7	43.7	36.5	33.2	5.4	15.5	−16.9	15.4
Japan	35.3	17.2	41.0	46.6	16.3	86.5	14.3	27.1
UK	13.7	29.2	29.1	31.9	20.4	27.3	7.9	21.1
Germany	13.9	33.9	40.0	20.7	92.7	34.4	−39.8	13.8
Switzerland	12.6	22.3	32.8	12.0	66.3	31.4	−28.5	12.5
France	−11.8	16.1	50.6	34.5	48.9	76.8	−31.5	20.7
Netherlands	7.4	38.6	53.6	40.3	29.6	38.3	−14.3	20.6
Italy	12.5	−4.1	15.5	36.9	88.8	105.0	−38.1	26.1
Canada	12.4	21.4	47.1	16.5	−7.0	8.1	−9.4	14.3
Australia	−4.8	−8.2	74.3	9.6	−3.3	40.4	−13.0	15.6
Singapore	48.0	−1.4	46.4	−8.0	−37.7	42.0	−13.0	13.0
Hong Kong	5.1	−34.5	8.5	84.4	21.5	52.4	−24.4	19.2
World	16.1	31.0	35.0	32.5	18.2	43.6	−5.3	20.2
Europe	15.3	29.7	33.9	32.3	49.7	53.8	−13.4	22.1

*Excluding West German Tax Credit.
Source: Phillips and Drew.

Roll has produced an analysis of the events of October 1987 in which he examines the effects of the institutional arrangements of the various markets and the degree of price collapse which they experienced.[24] In effect, Roll tries to assess the efficacy of trading breaks suggested by the Presidential Report, (see Table 11.6).

In order to test the hypothesis that institutional arrangements had an effect on the severity of the fall in market value, Roll converted each of the highlighted institutional arrangements (auction, official specialists, forward trading, automatic quotation systems, computer trading, options and futures, price limits, transactions taxes, margin requirements and off-exchange trading) into dummy variables (one or zero) and tested them in both univariate and multivariate equations. Although the univariate results showed some of the variables to be significant, the multivariate results showed that none of them could be used as reliable explanatory variables for the severity of the fall in share prices.

Roll then used a world stock market index in a market model and tested each of the national markets. The explanatory power of these results (R^2) was found to be 0.245 on average. However, to test lingering suspicions that institutional arrangements may have had an effect on the magnitude of the October falls, Roll conducted another cross-sectional regression with beta being the dependent variable and the dummies for the institutional arrangements being the explanatory variables. Two arrangements showed themselves to be marginally significant, continuous auctions and forwards trading.

Table 11.6 Stock price index percentage changes in major markets (calendar year 1987 and October 1987)[a]

Country	Local currency 1987	October	US dollars 1987	October	Auction	Computer trading	Price limits
Australia[b]	−3.6	−41.8	4.7	−44.9	C	No	No
Austria	−17.6	−11.4	0.7	−5.8	S	No	5%
Belgium	−15.5	−23.2	3.1	−18.9	M	No	10%/No
Canada[a]	4.0	−22.5	10.4	−22.9	C	Yes	No
Denmark	−4.5	−12.5	15.5	−7.3	M	No	No
France	−27.8	−22.9	−13.9	−19.5	M	Yes	No
Germany	−36.8	−22.3	−22.7	−17.1	C	No	No
Hong Kong	−11.3	−45.8	−11.0	−45.8	C	No	No
Ireland	−12.3	−29.1	4.7	−25.4	C	No	No
Italy	−32.4	−16.3	−22.3	−12.9	M	No	10–20%
Japan	8.5	−12.8	41.4	−7.7	C	Yes	−10%
Malaysia	6.9	−39.8	11.7	−39.3	C	No	No
Mexico[bc]	158.9	−35.0	5.5	−37.6	C	No	10%
Holland	−18.9	−23.3	0.3	−18.1	C	No	Variable
New Zealand[b]	−38.7	−29.3	−23.8	−36.0	C	No	No
Norway	−14.0	−30.5	1.7	−28.8	S	No	No
Singapore	−10.6	−42.2	−2.7	−41.6	C	No	0.5%
South Africa[b]	−8.8	−23.9	33.5	−29.0	C	No	No
Spain	8.2	−27.7	32.6	−23.1	M	No	10%
Sweden	−15.1	−21.8	−0.9	−18.6	M	No	No
Switzerland	34.0	−26.1	−16.5	−20.8	M	No	No
UK	4.6	−26.4	32.5	−22.1	C	Yes	No
USA	0.5	−21.6	0.5	−21.6	C	Yes	No

Key: C = continuous; S = single; M = mixed.

[a] Annual average dividend yields are ranged from 2 to 5 per cent except for Japan and Mexico, which have yields less than 1 per cent on average.
[b] Local currency depreciated against the US dollar during October 1987.
[c] Mexico is the only country whose currency did not appreciate against the US dollar during the course of 1987.

Source: R. Roll,[24] Table I, p. 20, Table III, p. 29.

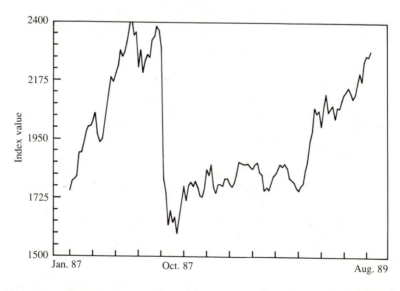

Figure 11.4 The crash of October 1987. (FTSE 100 Jan. 1987–Aug. 1989.)

Portfolio insurance, program trading and the October 1987 crash

Portfolio insurance and program trading have been two of the most publicized financial innovations of the 1980s. Portfolio insurance involves the use of futures contracts and options on those contracts to lock in the value and/or return of a portfolio of equities or debentures. Program trading involves the exploitation of price misalignments between futures and the underlying assets. Both activities rely on real-time computer analysis of prices and computer-directed buy and sell decisions. Both of these techniques have been accused directly and indirectly of causing and/or exacerbating the crash of 1987.

Clarke and Arnott have made an extensive study of the costs and benefits of portfolio insurance.[25] Portfolio insurance is the equivalent of purchasing a put option on a risky asset. However, in practice it is implemented rather differently. Clarke and Arnott describe the process as follows:

> In practice, most insurers use a dynamic hedging approach, changing the effective exposure of the risky assets in the portfolio by using the futures markets. This dynamic strategy is usually designed to approximate the results that would be obtained by purchasing a put option on the portfolio. The strategy, commonly called a synthetic put option, allows one to create insurance with longer time horizons than the maturities of actual put options would allow.[26]

As with all put strategies, the insurance against downside risk is achieved only with the sacrifice of some of the upside potential of the portfolio.

The plots of Fig. 11.5 assume that 100 per cent of the portfolio has been covered by insurance. The results may be modified if only a fraction of the assets are insured. Figures 11.5 and 11.6 illustrate the point that insured portfolios no longer have a distribution of expected returns that remotely resembles a normal distribution.

Bradley and Walsh have applied some of these methods to portfolios of UK equities in a simulation using data from the period January 1978 to December 1981.[27] They found that these strategies cost around 8 per cent of the total portfolio value. Of this 8 per cent, 3 per cent was taken up by transactions costs and the balance was a pure options cost.

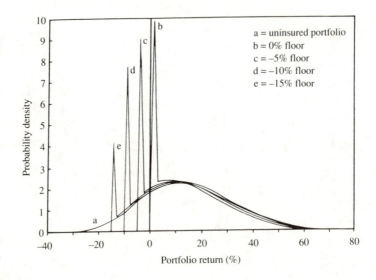

Figure 11.5 Return distributions on uninsured and insured portfolios. (Source: R. Clarke and R. Arnott,[25] p. 40.)

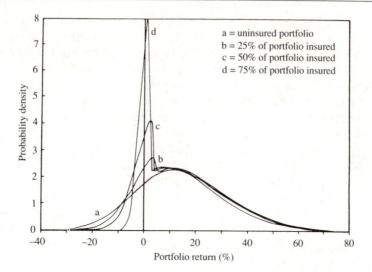

Figure 11.6 Return distributions for various percentages of portfolio insured. (Source: R. Clarke and R. Arnott,[25] p. 41.)

Studies of the effects of portfolio insurance and activity in the futures markets on the US stock market have multiplied since October 1987. The main results of these studies may be summarized as follows:

1. Tosini[28] reported that 16 firms accounted for almost all of the stock index arbitrage and portfolio hedging during October 1987. Furthermore, these activities accounted for 9 per cent and 12/24 per cent respectively, of the activity on the NYSE on 19 October 1987. Tosini also discussed what has become known as the 'cascade' theory. She describes it as follows:

> the scenario is generally expressed as follows: An exogenous shock produces a stock decline; that price decline triggers futures selling by portfolio insurers; such futures selling produces an undervaluing of the futures contract relative to the cash index; stock index arbitrageurs buy the relatively underpriced futures and sell the relatively overpriced stocks; stock prices fall further; declining stock prices induce additional selling by portfolio insurers; and the process begins anew.

Tosini argues that this process may not be an accurate description of market activity as the purchase of futures by the arbitrageurs will tend to have a positive effect on futures prices thus bringing the two markets back towards equilibrium.

2. Rubinstein[29] has argued that the activities of portfolio insurers in the stock market are likely to have had a marginal effect on a situation already created by the twin deficits on the government account and the foreign trade account.

3. Edwards[30] has shown that the evidence available for the period 1972–1986 does not support the hypothesis that futures trading has increased the price volatility of the NYSE.

Conclusions

The pace of development in futures markets is clearly illustrated by the recent developments in the London soft commodity markets. Early in 1987 London's disparate futures markets in soft commodities reacted to the growing competition from American markets by getting together under one roof and introducing options on existing contracts. The new exchange was called FOX—the Futures and Options Exchange. FOX has gone further by cutting the exchange's dealing costs to $1.40 per lot of 50 tons and introducing its automated trading system (ATS) for futures contracts in white sugar which has captured much of the market from competitors in New York and Paris. The ATS system has simplified the process of matching deals to the extent that it only needs on average 500 new contracts a day (instead of the 2,000 or more required by a floor-based trading system) in order to operate a market for a futures contract. In 1989 FOX intends to put its traded options contracts on the ATS trading system as well as new contracts which may be used to arbitrage between raw and white sugar futures.[31]

Changing fashion in response to changing circumstances is just as rapid as technological development and product innovation. In 1987 the Chicago Board of Trade lost almost half of its 1,400 members who left to join the Chicago Mercantile Exchange which had pioneered the development of financial futures. At the CBOT the grain markets were suffering from a succession of surplus agricultural production. However, the market crash of 1987 and the drought of 1988 led to a reversal of the migration as stock index futures became less popular and agricultural contracts offered more scope for speculation.[32]

In the year between the Big Bang and the crash the London stock market experienced a near doubling of equity turnover, £1.1 billion from £0.6 billion, and at 1.8 billion the daily turnover in the gilts market was 50 per cent greater than 12 months before. At the same time the number of contracts in traded options had increased by some 80 per cent to 50,000 a day and transactions in foreign equities were up by 70 per cent to a value of about £500 million a day. On the other hand, average commissions were down to 0.2 per cent for equities and zero for gilts. This compares with the following scales which were in operation just before the introduction of dual capacity:

Equities	*Value of contract (£)*	
	0– 7 000	1.65%
	7 001– 15 000	0.55%
	15 001– 130 000	0.5%
	130 001– 300 000	0.4%
	300 001– 900 000	0.3%
	900 001– 2 000 000	0.2%
	2 000 001 and over	0.125%

Gilts *Value of contract (£)*	*Maturity > 10 years*	*Maturity < 10 years*
0– 2 500	0.8%	0.8%
2 501– 18 000	0.25%	0.125%
18 001– 1 000 000	0.125%	0.0625%
1 000 001– 4 000 000	0.1%	0.05%
4 000 001– 10 000 000	0.05%	0.025%
10 000 001 and over	0.03%	0.015%

For securities having maturities within 5 years, the commission is set at the discretion of agent and principal.

London traded options were charged a fixed rate of £1.50 per contract and an *ad valorem* commission of 2.5 per cent on the first £5,000, 1.5 per cent on the next £5,000 and 1.0 per cent on any excess over £10,000.

The precipitate reduction in commission rates meant that, despite a huge increase in business, income remained more or less the same so that the new marketmaking firms have had to make their profits out of their own dealings in the market. The increase in the market for gilts has been even more intense and marked than in the equities market. At the beginning of the new system 28 firms had applied for and received authorization to make markets in gilts, compared with 40 primary dealers in the US treasury market which is 10 times larger. Before the reorganization of the gilts market there were 3 jobbing firms with 90 per cent of the market. *The Economist* estimated that these 3 firms enjoyed a return of over 50 per cent on a capital investment of about £200 million.[33] At the end of 1987 the surviving 27 marketmakers had made an investment of over 600m and had suffered a return on capital of −8 per cent.

Since the crash in October 1987, turnover in equities has fallen by about 30 per cent (estimates in October 1988 suggest that the fall had increased to 45 per cent) with commission rates still at the low levels established in 1987; thus the financial services industry's high costs remain while its income has fallen. In 1986 members of the Stock Exchange earned £740 million in brokerage income; this jumped to £1.16 billion in 1987 but has fallen back to an estimated £530 million in 1988. The result of these gyrations in commission income is not surprising: it has been estimated that by the middle of 1987 the securities industry in the UK employed about 90,000 people of which 12,000 have since lost their jobs.[34]

Notes

1. G. Gemmill, 'Regulating futures markets: a review in the context of British and American practice', in M. Streit (ed.), *Futures Markets*, Blackwell, 1983, pp. 295–318.
2. G. Blau, 'Some aspects of the theory of futures trading', *Review of Economic Studies, Vol.* 12, 1944–45, pp. 9–14.
3. J. Hicks, *Value and Capital* 2nd edn, Oxford University Press, 1946, pp. 138–9.
4. C. Hardy, *Risk and Risk Bearing*, University of Chicago Press, 1940.
5. L. Telser, 'Future trading and the storage of cotton and wheat', *Journal of Political Economy*, June 1958, pp. 233–255; P. Cootner, 'Returns to speculators: Telser versus Keynes', *Journal of Political Economy*, August 1960; K. Dusak, 'Futures trading and investor returns: an investigation of commodity market risk premiums', *Journal of Political Economy*, December 1973, pp. 1387–1406. E. Chiang, 'Returns to speculators and the theory of normal backwardation', *Journal of Finance*, Vol. 40, March 1985, pp. 193–208.
6. Z. Bodie and V. Rosansky, 'Risk and return in commodity futures', *Financial Analysts' Journal*, Vol. 36, May 1980, pp. 27–39.
7. Ibid., p. 33. Excess return in this context is the difference between the nominal return on the commodity futures portfolio and the returns on the treasury bill rates.
8. E. Fama, 'Efficient capital markets: a review of theory and empirical work', *Journal of Finance*, Vol. 25, March 1970.
9. S. Taylor, 'Trading rules for investors in apparently inefficient futures markets', in M. Streit (ed.), *Futures Markets*, Blackwell, 1983, Table 3, p. 172. Taylor used the data for six markets: cocoa, coffee, sugar, sterling, Deutschmark, Swiss franc. Bodie and Rosansky also suggest from their data that the distributions of returns from futures contracts is positively skewed. Op. cit., p. 30.
10. Taylor, op. cit. 9.
11. R. Stevenson and R. Bear, 'Commodity futures: trends or random walks?', *Journal of Finance*, Vol. 25, 1970, pp. 65–81.

12. T. Cargill and G. Rausser, 'Temporal price behaviour in commodity futures markets', *Journal of Finance*, Vol. 30, September 1975, pp. 1043–1053.

13. R. Leuthold and P. Hartmann, 'A semi-strong form evaluation of the efficiency of the hog futures market', *American Journal of Agricultural Economics*, 1979, pp. 482–489.

14. B. Goss, 'The semi-strong form efficiency of the London Metal Exchange', *Applied Economics*, Vol. 15, 1983, pp. 681–698.

15. Ordinary least squares regression of this equation when it has lagged endogenous explanatory variables and has autocorrelation will produce biased estimators. In order to avoid these problems Goss used the technique developed by D. Hendry in a London School of Economics Mimeograph, 'General Instrumental Variable Estimation of Linear Equations with Endogenous and Lagged Regressors and Autoregressive Errors', 1976.

16. Goss, op. cit. 14, p. 693.

17. P. Bird, 'The weak form efficiency of the London Metal Exchange', *Applied Economics*, Vol. 17, 1985, pp. 571–587.

18. C. Gilbert, 'Testing the efficient markets hypothesis on averaged data', *Applied Economics*, Vol. 18, 1986, pp. 1149–1166. This article produced a fairly lively discussion between Goss and Gilbert over their respective understandings of the operation of the LME and the proper way of testing for weak form efficiency in the LME.

19. F. Black, 'The pricing of commodity contracts', *Journal of Financial Economics*, Vol. 4, September 1976, pp. 167–179.

20. Report of the Presidential Task Force on Market Mechanisms, January 1988.

21. 'The equity market crash', *Bank of England Quarterly*, February 1988, p. 52.

22. Brian Reading, 'The boom that nobody heard', *Sunday Times*, 17 April 1988.

23. For an interesting discussion of stock market panics see E. Renshaw, 'Stock market panics: a test of the efficient market hypothesis', *Financial Analysts' Journal*, Vol. 4, May 1984.

24. R. Roll, 'The international crash of October 1987', *Financial Analysts' Journal*, Vol. 44, September 1988, pp. 19–35.

25. R. Clarke and R. Arnott, 'The cost of portfolio insurance: tradeoffs and choices', *Financial Analysts' Journal*, Vol. 43, November 1987, pp. 35–47.

26. Ibid. p. 36. For a more detailed discussion of portfolio insurance see M. Rubinstein, 'Replacing options with positions in stock and cash', *Financial Analysts' Journal*, Vol. 37, July 1981 and M. Rubinstein, 'Alternative paths to portfolio insurance', *Financial Analysts' Journal*, Vol. 41, July 1985.

27. D. Bradley and M. Walsh, 'Portfolio insurance and the UK stock market', *Journal of Accountancy and Finance*, Vol. 15, Spring 1988, pp. 67–75.

28. P. Tosini, 'Stock index futures and stock market activity in October 1987', *Financial Analysts' Journal*, Vol. 44, January 1988, p. 31.

29. M. Rubinstein, 'Portfolio insurance and the market crash', *Financial Analysts' Journal*, Vol. 44, January 1988, pp. 38–47.

30. F. Edwards, 'Does futures trading increase stock market volatility?', *Financial Analysts' Journal*, Vol. 44, January 1988, pp. 63–69.

31. *The Economist* 3 December 1986, p. 113.

32. *The Economist* 25 February 1989, p. 93.

33. *The Economist* 16 January 1988, p. 7.

34. D. Lomax, 'The Big Bang—18 months after', *NatWest Bank Review*, August 1988.

Questions

1. Comment on and discuss the proposition that with the benefit of hindsight, 'it is obvious that the process of market evolution called the Big Bang in 1986 almost ensured the market crash of October 1987'.
2. What is a clearing house and why is it thought necessary for the proper operation of a futures market?
3. Explain how speculation may be economically beneficial and detrimental under different sets of circumstances.
4. Explain and discuss the difference between backwardation and contango and indicate which is the more likely condition.
5. Were the activities of such institutions as the Tin Council and individuals such as the Hunt brothers consistent with efficiency in futures markets?
6. Explain how index futures may be used to reduce the risk of a portfolio of shares.
7. To what extent did the institutional arrangements exacerbate the volatility of the stock markets in 1987?
8. What evidence is there for the popular belief that portfolio insurance was a major contributor to the severity of the stock market crash in October 1987?
9. Why might investors wish to use the futures market rather than the traded options market to insure their portfolios against the risk of capital loss?
10. What are the implications of the increasing degree of fungibility of futures contracts?

Appendix 1.   Statistical tables

Table A1.1   Standard normal distribution

z	0.00	0.01	0.02	0.03	0.04	0.05	0.06	0.07	0.08	0.09
0.0	0.0000	0.0040	0.0080	0.0120	0.0160	0.0199	0.0239	0.0279	0.0319	0.0359
0.1	0.0398	0.0438	0.0478	0.0517	0.0557	0.0596	0.0636	0.0675	0.0714	0.0753
0.2	0.0793	0.0832	0.0871	0.0910	0.0948	0.0987	0.1026	0.1064	0.1103	0.1141
0.3	0.1179	0.1217	0.1255	0.1293	0.1331	0.1368	0.1406	0.1443	0.1480	0.1517
0.4	0.1554	0.1591	0.1628	0.1664	0.1700	0.1736	0.1772	0.1808	0.1844	0.1879
0.5	0.1915	0.1950	0.1985	0.2019	0.2054	0.2088	0.2123	0.2157	0.2190	0.2224
0.6	0.2257	0.2291	0.2324	0.2357	0.2389	0.2422	0.2454	0.2486	0.2517	0.2549
0.7	0.2580	0.2611	0.2642	0.2673	0.2704	0.2734	0.2764	0.2794	0.2823	0.2852
0.8	0.2881	0.2910	0.2939	0.2967	0.2995	0.3023	0.3051	0.3078	0.3106	0.3133
0.9	0.3159	0.3186	0.3212	0.3238	0.3264	0.3289	0.3315	0.3340	0.3365	0.3389
1.0	0.3413	0.3438	0.3461	0.3485	0.3508	0.3531	0.3554	0.3577	0.3599	0.3621
1.1	0.3643	0.3665	0.3686	0.3708	0.3729	0.3749	0.3770	0.3790	0.3810	0.3830
1.2	0.3849	0.3869	0.3888	0.3907	0.3925	0.3944	0.3962	0.3980	0.3997	0.4015
1.3	0.4032	0.4049	0.4066	0.4082	0.4099	0.4115	0.4131	0.4147	0.4162	0.4177
1.4	0.4192	0.4207	0.4222	0.4236	0.4251	0.4265	0.4279	0.4292	0.4306	0.4319
1.5	0.4332	0.4345	0.4357	0.4370	0.4382	0.4394	0.4406	0.4418	0.4429	0.4441
1.6	0.4452	0.4463	0.4474	0.4484	0.4495	0.4505	0.4515	0.4525	0.4535	0.4545
1.7	0.4554	0.4564	0.4573	0.4582	0.4591	0.4599	0.4608	0.4616	0.4625	0.4633
1.8	0.4641	0.4649	0.4656	0.4664	0.4671	0.4678	0.4686	0.4693	0.4699	0.4706
1.9	0.4713	0.4719	0.4726	0.4732	0.4738	0.4744	0.4750	0.4756	0.4761	0.4767
2.0	0.4772	0.4778	0.4783	0.4788	0.4793	0.4798	0.4803	0.4808	0.4812	0.4817
2.1	0.4821	0.4826	0.4830	0.4834	0.4838	0.4842	0.4846	0.4850	0.4854	0.4857
2.2	0.4861	0.4864	0.4868	0.4871	0.4875	0.4878	0.4881	0.4884	0.4887	0.4890
2.3	0.4893	0.4896	0.4898	0.4901	0.4904	0.4906	0.4909	0.4911	0.4913	0.4916
2.4	0.4918	0.4920	0.4922	0.4925	0.4927	0.4929	0.4931	0.4932	0.4934	0.4936
2.5	0.4938	0.4940	0.4941	0.4943	0.4945	0.4946	0.4948	0.4949	0.4951	0.4952
2.6	0.4953	0.4955	0.4956	0.4957	0.4959	0.4960	0.4961	0.4962	0.4963	0.4964
2.7	0.4965	0.4966	0.4967	0.4968	0.4969	0.4970	0.4971	0.4972	0.4973	0.5974
2.8	0.4974	0.4975	0.4976	0.4977	0.4977	0.4978	0.4979	0.4979	0.4980	0.4981
2.9	0.4981	0.4982	0.4982	0.4983	0.4984	0.4984	0.4985	0.4985	0.4986	0.4986
3.0	0.4987	0.4987	0.4987	0.4988	0.4988	0.4989	0.4989	0.4989	0.4990	0.4990

Table A1.2   Values of the cumulative normal distribution

$-d$	0.00	0.01	0.02	0.03	0.04	0.05	0.06	0.07	0.08	0.09
0.0	0.5000	0.4960	0.4920	0.4880	0.4840	0.4801	0.4761	0.4721	0.4681	0.4641
0.1	0.4602	0.4562	0.4522	0.4483	0.4443	0.4404	0.4364	0.4325	0.4286	0.4246
0.2	0.4207	0.4168	0.4129	0.4090	0.4052	0.4013	0.3974	0.3936	0.3897	0.3859
0.3	0.3821	0.3783	0.3745	0.3707	0.3669	0.3632	0.3594	0.3557	0.3520	0.3483
0.4	0.3446	0.3409	0.3372	0.3336	0.3300	0.3264	0.3228	0.3192	0.3156	0.3121
0.5	0.3085	0.3050	0.3015	0.2981	0.2946	0.2912	0.2877	0.2843	0.2810	0.2776
0.6	0.2742	0.2709	0.2676	0.2644	0.2611	0.2578	0.2546	0.2514	0.2482	0.2451
0.7	0.2420	0.2388	0.2358	0.2327	0.2297	0.2266	0.2236	0.2206	0.2177	0.2148
0.8	0.2119	0.2090	0.2061	0.2033	0.2004	0.1977	0.1949	0.1922	0.1894	0.1867
0.9	0.1841	0.1814	0.1788	0.1762	0.1736	0.1711	0.1685	0.1660	0.1635	0.1611
1.0	0.1587	0.1562	0.1539	0.1515	0.1492	0.1469	0.1446	0.1423	0.1401	0.1379
1.1	0.1357	0.1335	0.1314	0.1292	0.1271	0.1251	0.1230	0.1210	0.1190	0.1170
1.2	0.1151	0.1131	0.1112	0.1094	0.1075	0.1056	0.1038	0.1020	0.1003	0.0985
1.3	0.0968	0.0951	0.0934	0.0918	0.0901	0.0885	0.0869	0.0853	0.0838	0.0823
1.4	0.0808	0.0793	0.0778	0.0764	0.0749	0.0735	0.0721	0.0708	0.0694	0.0681
1.5	0.0668	0.0655	0.0643	0.0630	0.0618	0.0606	0.0594	0.0582	0.0570	0.0559
1.6	0.0548	0.0537	0.0526	0.0516	0.0505	0.0495	0.0485	0.0475	0.0465	0.0455
1.7	0.0446	0.0436	0.0427	0.0418	0.0409	0.0401	0.0392	0.0384	0.0375	0.0367
1.8	0.0359	0.0352	0.0344	0.0336	0.0329	0.0322	0.0314	0.0307	0.0300	0.0294
1.9	0.0287	0.0281	0.0274	0.0268	0.0262	0.0256	0.0250	0.0244	0.0238	0.0233
2.0	0.0228	0.0222	0.0217	0.0212	0.0207	0.0202	0.0197	0.0192	0.0188	0.0183
2.1	0.0179	0.0174	0.0170	0.0166	0.0162	0.0158	0.0154	0.0150	0.0146	0.0143
2.2	0.0139	0.0136	0.0132	0.0129	0.0126	0.0122	0.0119	0.0116	0.0113	0.0110
2.3	0.0107	0.0104	0.0102	0.0099	0.0096	0.0094	0.0091	0.0089	0.0087	0.0084
2.4	0.0082	0.0080	0.0078	0.0076	0.0073	0.0071	0.0070	0.0068	0.0066	0.0064
2.5	0.0062	0.0060	0.0059	0.0057	0.0055	0.0054	0.0052	0.0051	0.0049	0.0048
2.6	0.0047	0.0045	0.0044	0.0043	0.0042	0.0040	0.0039	0.0038	0.0037	0.0036
2.7	0.0035	0.0034	0.0033	0.0032	0.0031	0.0030	0.0029	0.0028	0.0027	0.0026
2.8	0.0026	0.0025	0.0024	0.0023	0.0023	0.0022	0.0021	0.0020	0.0020	0.0019
2.9	0.0019	0.0018	0.0018	0.0017	0.0016	0.0016	0.0015	0.0015	0.0014	0.0014
3.0	0.0014	0.0013	0.0013	0.0012	0.0012	0.0011	0.0011	0.0011	0.0010	0.0010
3.1	0.0010	0.0009	0.0009	0.0009	0.0008	0.0008	0.0008	0.0008	0.0007	0.0007
3.2	0.0007	0.0007	0.0006	0.0006	0.0006	0.0006	0.0006	0.0005	0.0005	0.0005
3.3	0.0005	0.0005	0.0004	0.0004	0.0004	0.0004	0.0004	0.0004	0.0004	0.0004
3.4	0.0003	0.0003	0.0003	0.0003	0.0003	0.0003	0.0003	0.0003	0.0002	0.0002
3.5	0.0002	0.0002	0.0002	0.0002	0.0002	0.0002	0.0002	0.0002	0.0002	0.0002
3.6	0.0002	0.0002	0.0002	0.0001	0.0001	0.0001	0.0001	0.0001	0.0001	0.0001
3.7	0.0001	0.0001	0.0001	0.0001	0.0001	0.0001	0.0001	0.0001	0.0001	0.0001
3.8	0.0001	0.0001	0.0001	0.0001	0.0001	0.0001	0.0001	0.0000	0.0000	0.0000
3.9	0.0000	0.0000	0.0000	0.0000	0.0000	0.0000	0.0000	0.0000	0.0000	0.0000

Appendix 2. Answers to the numerical questions

2.10(a) 75;   (b)   400

4.8   Weight A = 0.38; Weight B = 0.68; Portfolio variance 7.04%; Portfolio return = 4.4%.

4.9   (i)   selling B short, Variance = 15.4%, Return = 9%.
       (ii) selling A short, Variance = 13.2%, Return = 0%.

5.1   Beta = 0.82; Systematic risk = 17.2%; Unsystematic risk = 12.7%; Actual return = 20.5%;
       Expected Return = 17.9%; Abnormal Return = 2.6%; Coefficient of diversification = 0.35.

5.2   Beta = 0.84; Systematic risk = 17.5%; Unsystematic risk = 13.2%; Actual return = 18.5%;
       Expected return = 18.0%; Abnormal return = 0.5%; Coefficient of diversification = 0.36.

6.9(a) Portfolio return = 12.6%; First factor weighting = 0.64; Second factor weighting = 0.72.

8.7(a) (i) 375p;   (ii) 667p;   (iii) 565p
   (b) (i) 200p;   (ii) 200p;   (iii) 540p

8.10(a) A = 0%; B = 3%; C = 5%; D = 0%; E = 2%; F = 4%; G = 0%; H = 3%; I = 5%.

9.4

Year	Redemption yields	Spot rates	Forward rates
1	11.0	11.0	11.0
2	10.0	10.62	10.24
3	9.5	9.25	6.56
4	9.25	9.14	8.83
5	9.0	8.83	7.59

9.8

Portfolio	Variance
A+D	31.1
B+D	31.51
A+E	32.49
B+E	32.73
B+C	32.07
A+C	32.53

9.9

Portfolio	Variance
A+D	34.08
B+D	32.19
A+E	35.94
B+E	33.39
B+C	32.78
A+C	34.99

Bibliography

Abeysekera, S. and A. Mahajan, 'A test of the APT in pricing UK stocks', *Journal of Accounting and Finance* Vol. 17, Autumn 1987.

Alchian, A., 'The meaning of utility measurement', *American Economic Review*, Vol. 43, 1953.

Alexander, G. and J. Francis, *Portfolio Analysis* 3rd edn, Prentice Hall, New York, 1986.

Amsbachtsheer, K., 'Portfolio theory and the security analyst', *Financial Analysts' Journal*, Vol. 28, November 1972.

Amsbachtsheer, K., 'Profit potential in an almost efficient market', *Journal of Portfolio Management*, 1974.

Amsbachtsheer, K. and J. Farrel, 'Can active management add value?', *Financial Analysts' Journal*, Vol. 35, January 1979.

Appleyard, A., 'Takeovers: accounting policy, financial policy and the case against accounting measures of performance', *Journal of Business Finance and Accounting*, Vol. 7, 1980.

Arbel, A. and B. Jaggi, 'Market information assimilation related to extreme daily price jumps, *Financial Analysts Journal*, Vol. 38, November 1982.

Arbel, A. and P. Strebel, 'Pay attention to neglected firms', *Journal of Portfolio Management*, 1983.

Ball, R. and P. Brown, 'An empirical evaluation of accounting income numbers', *Journal of Accounting Research*, April 1968.

Bank of England Quarterly, 'Financing British Industry', September 1980.

Bank of England Quarterly, 'The UK corporate bond market', March 1981.

Bank of England Quarterly, 'The future structure of the gilt-edged market', June 1985.

Bank of England Quarterly, 'The future of the gilt-edged market: official operations', December 1986.

Bank of England Quarterly, 'Gilt-edged settlement: phase 2 of the CGO service', February 1987.

Bank of England Quarterly, 'Recent developments in the swap markets', February 1987.

Bank of England Quarterly, 'Recent developments in the corporate and bulldog sectors of the sterling bond market', February 1988.

Bank of England Quarterly, 'The equity market crash', February 1988.

Banker, 'New York's big bang—10 years after', March 1985.

Banker, 'Games without frontiers?', May 1988.

Bar-Yosef, S. and R. Kolodny, 'Dividend policy and capital market theory', *Review of Economics and Statistics*, 1976.

Berry, M., E. Burmeister and M. McElroy, 'Sorting out risks using known APT factors', *Financial Analysts' Journal*, Vol. 44, March 1988.

Bird, P., 'The weak form efficiency of the London Metal Exchange', *Applied Economics*, Vol. 17, 1985, pp. 571–587.

Black, F., 'Capital market equilibrium with restricted borrowing', *Journal of Business*, Vol. 45, 1972.

Black, F., 'Yes Virginia, there is hope: tests of the value line ranking system', *Financial Analysts' Journal*, Vol. 29, March 1973.

Black, F., 'Fact and fantasy in the use of options', *Financial Analysts' Journal*, Vol. 31, July 1975.

Black, F., 'The pricing of commodity contracts', *Journal of Financial Economics*, Vol. 4, September 1976.

Black, F., M. Jensen and M. Scholes, 'The capital asset pricing model: some empirical tests', in *Studies in the Theory of Capital Markets*, M. Jensen (ed.), Praeger Publishers Inc., New York, 1972.

Black, F. and M. Scholes, 'The valuation of option contracts and a test of market efficiency', *Journal of Finance*, Vol. 27, May 1972.

Black, F. and M. Scholes, 'The pricing of options and corporate liabilities', *Journal of Political Economy*, Vol. 81, May 1973.

Black, F. and M. Scholes, 'The effects of dividend yields and dividend policy on common stock prices and returns', *Journal of Financial Economics*, Vol. 2, May 1974.

Blau, G., 'Some aspects of the theory of futures trading', *Review of Economic Studies*, Vol. 12, 1944–45.

Board, J. and C. Sutcliffe, 'The weekend effect in UK stock market returns', *Discussion Paper in Finance and Accounting*, No. 6, London School of Economics and Reading University, 1987.

Bodie, Z. and V. Rosansky, 'Risk and return in commodity futures', *Financial Analysts' Journal*, Vol. 36, May 1980.

Bradley, D. and Walsh, M., 'Portfolio insurance and the UK stock market', *Journal of Accountancy and Finance*, Vol. 15, 1988.

Bradley, M., 'The economic consequences of mergers and tender offers', in *The Revolution in Corporate Finance*, J. Stern and D. Chew (eds), Blackwell, Oxford, 1986.

Brealey, M., *Security Prices in a Competitive Market*, MIT Press, 1971.

Brennan, M., 'Capital market equilibrium with divergent borrowing and lending rates', *Journal of Financial and Quantitative Analysis*, Vol. 6, 1971.

Brigham, E., 'An analysis of convertible debentures: theory and some empirical evidence', *Journal of Finance*, Vol. 21, March 1966.

Cargill, T. and G. Rausser, 'Temporal price behaviour in commodity futures markets', *Journal of Finance*, Vol. 30, September 1975.

Carleton, W. and I. Cooper, 'Estimation and uses of the term structure of interest rates', *Journal of Finance*, Vol. 31, September 1976.

Chiang, E., 'Returns to speculators and the theory of normal backwardation', *Journal of Finance*, Vol. 40, March 1985, pp. 193–208.

Clarke, R. and R. Arnott, 'The cost of portfolio insurance: tradeoffs and choices', *Financial Analysts' Journal*, Vol. 43, November 1987.

Clayton, G., *British Insurance*, Elek, London, 1971.

Cockerell, H.A. and E. Green, *The British Insurance Business 1547–1970*, Heinemann, London, 1976.

Colker, S., 'An analysis of security recommendations by brokerage houses', *Quarterly Review of Economics*, Vol. 77, 1963.

Cooper, J., 'World stock markets: some random walk tests', *Applied Economics*, Vol. 14, 1982.

Cootner, P., 'Returns to speculators: Telser versus Keynes', *Journal of Political Economy*, Vol. 68, August 1960.

Cowles, A., 'Can stock market forecasters forecast?', *Econometrica*, Vol. 2, 1933.

Cowles, A., 'Stock market forecasting', *Econometrica*, Vol. 13, 1944.

Cox, J., S. Ross and M. Rubinstein, 'Option pricing: a simplified approach', *Journal of Financial Economics*, Vol. 7, September 1979.

Cragg, J. and B. Malkiel, 'The consensus and accuracy of some predictions of the growth of corporate earnings', *Journal of Finance*, Vol. 23, March 1968.

Davies, P. and M. Cannes, 'Stock prices and the publication of second-hand information', *Journal of Business*, Vol. 34, 1978.

Dawson, S., 'The trend toward efficiency for less developed stock exchanges: Hong Kong', *Journal of Business Finance and Accounting*, Vol. 11, 1984.

Dev, S. and M. Webb, 'The accuracy of company profit forecasts', *Journal of Business Finance*, Vol. 3, 1972.

Diacogiannis, G., 'Arbitrage pricing model: a critical examination of its empirical applicability for the London Stock Exchange', *Journal of Business Finance and Accounting*, Vol. 13, Winter 1986.

Diefenbach, R., 'How good is institutional brokerage research?', *Financial Analysts' Journal*, Vol. 28, May 1972.

Dimson, E. and P. Fraletti, 'Brokers' recommendations: the value of a telephone tip', *Economic Journal*, Vol. 96, 1986.

Dodd, P., 'The market for corporate control: a review of the evidence', in *The Revolution in Corporate Finance*, J. Stern and D. Chew (eds), Blackwell, Oxford, 1986.

Dryden, M., 'A statistical study of UK share prices', *Scottish Journal of Political Economy*, Vol. 17, 1970.

Dusak, K., 'Futures trading and investor returns: an investigation of commodity market risk premiums', *Journal of Political Economy*, Vol. 81, December 1973.

Dybvig, P. H. and S. A. Ross, 'Portfolio efficient sets?', *Econometrica*, Vol. 50, 1982.

Dyl, E. and J. Hoffmeister, 'A note on dividend policy and beta', *Journal of Business Finance and Accounting*, Vol. 13, Spring 1986.

Edwards, F., 'Does futures trading increase stock market volatility?', *Financial Analysts' Journal*, Vol. 44, January 1988.

Edwards, R.D. and J. Magee, *Technical Analysis of Stock Trends*, 4th edn, Magee, Boston, Mass., 1958.

Elton, E. and M. Gruber, 'Marginal stockholder tax rates and the clientele effect', *Review of Economics and Statistics*, Vol. 52, February 1970.

Evans, J. and S. Archer, 'Diversification and the reduction of dispersion: an empirical analysis', *Journal of Finance*, Vol. 23, December 1968.

Fama, E., 'The behaviour of stock market prices', *Journal of Business*, Vol. 21, January 1965.

Fama, E., 'Efficient capital markets: a review of theory and empirical work', *Journal of Finance*, Vol. 25, March 1970.

Fama, E., *Foundations of Finance*, Blackwell, Oxford, 1977.

Fama, E. and H. Babiak, 'Dividend policy: an empirical analysis', *Journal of the American Statistical Society*, Vol. 63, December 1968.

Fama, E. and M. Blume, 'Filter rules and stock market trading', *Journal of Business*, Vol. 22, 1966.

Fama, E., L. Fisher, M. Jensen and R. Roll, 'The adjustment of stock prices to new information', *International Economic Review*, Vol. 10, February 1969.

Fama, E. and J. MacBeth, 'Risk, return, and equilibrium: empirical tests', *Journal of Political Economy*, Vol. 81, May 1973.

Farrar, D. and L. Selwyn, 'Taxes, corporate financial policy and return to investors', *National Tax Journal*, December 1967.

Ferber, F., 'Short run effects of stock market services on stock prices', *Journal of Finance*, Vol. 13, 1958.

Firth, M., 'The performance of share recommendations made by investment analysts and the effects on market efficiency', *Journal of Business and Finance*, Vol. 4, 1972.

Firth, M., 'An empirical investigation of the impact of the announcement of capitalisation issues on share prices', *Journal of Business Finance and Accounting*, Vol. 4, 1977.

Fisher, G., 'Some factors influencing shares prices', *Economic Journal*, Vol. 71, 1961.

Fisher, L. and R. Weil, 'Coping with the risk of interest rate fluctuations: returns to bondholders from naive and optimal strategies', *Journal of Business*, Vol. 27, October 1971.

Fitzgerald, M., 'A proposed characterisation of UK brokerage firms and their effects on market prices and returns', *International Capital Markets*, J. Elton and M. Gruber (eds), North-Holland, Amsterdam, 1975.

Fitzgerald, M., 'Media investment advisory service recommendations and market efficiency', *Saloman Brothers Center for the Study of Financial Institutions Working Paper*, No. 159, New York University, 1978.

French, D., 'Stock returns and the weekend effect', *Journal of Financial Economics*, Vol. 8, 1980.

Friedman, M. and L. Savage, 'The utility analysis of choices involving risk', *Journal of Political Economy*, Vol. 54, 1948.

Friend, I. and M. Blume, 'Measurement of portfolio performance under uncertainty', *American Economic Review*, Vol. 60, September 1970.

Galai, D. and M. Schneller, 'The pricing of warrants and the value of the firm', *Journal of Finance*, Vol. 34, December 1978.

Garcia, C. and F. Gould, 'An empirical study of portfolio insurance', *Financial Analysts' Journal*, Vol. 43, July 1987.

Gemmill, G., 'Financial futures in London: rational market or casino?', *National Westminster Quarterly Review*, 1981.

Gemmill, G., 'Regulating futures markets: a review in the context of British and American practice', in *Futures markets*, M. Streit (ed), Blackwell, Oxford, 1983, pp. 295–318.

Gemmill, G., 'The forecasting performance of stock options on the London Traded Options Market', *Journal of Business Finance and Accounting*, Vol. 13, 1986.

Gemmill, G. and P. Dickens, 'An examination of the efficiency of the London Traded Options Market', *Applied Economics*, Vol. 18, 1986.

Gilbert, C., 'Testing the efficient markets hypothesis on averaged data', *Applied Economics*, Vol. 18, 1986.

Girmes, D. and A. Benjamin, 'Random walk hypothesis for 543 stocks and shares registered on the London Stock Exchange, *Journal of Business Finance and Accounting*, Vol. 1, 1974.

Goldman, B. and H. Sosin, 'Information dissemination, market efficiency and the frequency of transactions', *Journal of Financial Economics*, Vol. 7, 1979.

Gordon, M., 'Dividends, earnings and stock prices', *Review of Economics and Statistics*, Vol. 41, May 1959.

Gordon, M., 'The savings, investments and valuation of the corporation', *Review of Economics and Statistics*, Vol. 48, 1966.

Goss, B., 'The semi-strong form efficiency of the London Metal Exchange', *Applied Economics*, Vol. 15, 1983.

Goss, B. and B. Yamey (eds), *The Economics of Futures Trading*, 2nd edn, Macmillan, London, 1978.

Gould, F., 'Stock index futures: the arbitrage cycle and portfolio insurance', *Financial Analysts' Journal*, Vol. 44, January 1988.

Gower, L.C.B., *The Principles of Modern Company Law*, Stevens, London, 1979.

Graham, B. and D. Dodd, *Security Analysis: Analysis and Techniques*, 3rd edn, McGraw-Hill, New York, 1951.

Granger, C. (ed.), *Trading in Commodities*, 4th edn, Woodhead-Faulkner, London, 1983.

Grossman, S., 'Program trading and market voltility: a report on interday relationships', *Financial Analysts' Journal*, Vol. 44, July 1988.

Groth, J., W. Lewellen, G. Schlarbaum and N. Leas, 'An analysis of brokerage house recommendations', *Financial Analysts' Journal*, Vol. 35, January 1979.

Grubel, H., 'The Peter principle and the efficient market hypothesis', *Financial Analysts' Journal*, Vol. 35, November 1979.

Hamill, J., 'British acquisitions in the United States', *NatWest Bank Review*, 1987.

Hamilton, A., *The Financial Revolution*, Penguin, Harmondsworth, 1986.

Hardy, C., *Risk and Risk Bearing*, University of Chicago Press, Chicago, 1940.

Hempel, G. and W. Marshall, 'Is average maturity a proxy for risk?', *Journal of Portfolio Management*, 1976.

Hendry, D., 'General instrumental variable estimation of linear equations with endogenous and lagged regressors and autoregressive errors', *London School of Economics Mimeo*, 1976.

Hicks, J., *Value and Capital*, Oxford University Press, Oxford, 1939.

Hill, J. and F. Jones, 'Equity trading, program trading, portfolio insurance, computer trading and all that', *Financial Analysts' Journal*, Vol. 44, July 1988.

Hirschleifer, J., 'Efficient allocation of capital in an uncertain world', *American Economic Review*, Vol. 54, 1964.

Hirst, I., 'The case for minimum commissions', *Investment Analyst*, January 1982.

HMSO, 'The Banking Act', 1979.

HMSO, 'Report of the Committee to Review the Functioning of Financial Institutions', (the Wilson Committee Report), Cmnd. 7937, 1980.

HMSO, 'The Gower Report on Investor Protection', Cmnd. 9125, 1984.

HMSO, 'The Companies Act', 1985.

HMSO, 'The Companies (Insider Dealing) Act', 1985.

HMSO, 'The Financial Services Act', 1987.

Hodges, S. and M. Brealey, 'Portfolio selection in a dynamic and uncertain world', *Financial Analysts' Journal*, Vol. 29, April 1973.

Hopewell, M. and G. Kaufman, 'Bond price volatility and term to maturity: a generalized respecification', *American Economic Review*, Vol. 63, September 1973.

Jarrow, R. and A. Rudd, 'A comparison of the APT and the CAPM', *Journal of Banking and Finance*, June 1983.

Jarrow, R. and A. Rudd, *Option Pricing*, Irwin, Homewood, 1983.

Jensen, M., 'Random walks: reality or myth–comment', *Financial Analysts' Journal*, Vol. 23, September 1967.

Jensen, M., 'The performance of mutual funds in the period 1945–1964', *Journal of Finance*, Vol. 23, 1968.

Jensen, M., 'Capital markets: theory and evidence', *Bell Journal of Economics and Management Science*, Autumn 1972.

Jensen, M. and G. Bennington, 'Random walks and technical theories: some additional evidence', *Journal of Finance*, Vol. 25, 1970.

Kaiser, R., 'The Kondratieff cycle', *Financial Analysts' Journal*, Vol. 35, May 1979.

Kamara, A., 'The behaviour of futures prices: a review of theory and evidence', *Financial Analysts' Journal*, Vol. 40, July 1984.

Keane, S., 'The significance of the issue price in rights issues', *Journal of Business Finance*, Vol. 4, 1972.

Kendall, M., 'The analysis of economic time series, part I: prices', *Journal of the Royal Statistical Society*, Vol. 116, 1953.

Kindleberger, C., *A Financial History of Western Europe*, George, Allen & Unwin, London, 1984.

King, B., 'Market and industry factors in stock price behaviour', *Journal of Business*, Vol. 22, 1966.

Kirzner, I., *Competition and Entrepreneurship*, University of Chicago Press, Chicago, 1973.

Kitching, J., 'Why acquisitions are abortive', *Management Today*, November 1974.

Kolb, R., *Understanding Futures Markets*, 2nd edn, Scott, Foreman & Co., Glenview, Ill., 1988.

Lee-Jones, M., 'Underwriting of rights issues: a theoretical justification', *Journal of Business Finance*, Vol. 3, 1971.

Leuthold, R. and P. Hartmann, 'A Semi-strong form evaluation of the efficiency of the hog futures market', *American Journal of Agricultural Economics*, 1979.

Levinson, H., 'A psychologist diagnoses merger failure', *Harvard Business Review*, 1970.

Levy, H. and Z. Lerman, 'The benefits of international diversification in bonds', *Financial Analysts' Journal*, Vol. 44, September 1988.

Levy, H. and M. Sarnat, 'International diversification of investment portfolios', *American Economic Review*, Vol. 60, 1970.

Levy, R., 'Conceptual foundations of technical analysis', *Financial Analysts' Journal*, Vol. 22, May 1966.

Levy, R., 'Random walks: reality or myth', *Financial Analysts' Journal*, Vol. 23, January 1967.

Lintner, J., 'Distribution of incomes of corporations among dividends, retained earnings and taxes', *American Economic Review*, Vol. 46, May 1956.

Lintner, J., 'The valuation of risky assets and the selection of risky investments in stock and capital budgets', *Review of Economics and Statistics*, Vol. 47, 1965.

Litzenberger, R. and K. Ramaswamy, 'The effect of personal taxes and dividends on capital asset prices', *Journal of Financial Economics*, Vol. 7, 1979.

Litzenberger, R. and K. Ramaswamy, 'The effects of dividends on common stock prices: tax effects or information effects?', *Journal of Finance*, Vol. 37, 1982.

Lomax, D., 'The Big Bang—18 months after', *NatWest Bank Review*, August 1988.

London Stock Exchange, 'The choice of a new dealing system', July 1984.

Macauley, F., *Some Theoretical Problems Suggested by the Movement of Interest Rates, Bond Yields and Stock Prices in the United States Since 1856*, Ayer Co., New York, 1981.

MacBeth, J. and L. Merville, 'An empirical examination of the Black–Scholes call option pricing model', *Journal of Finance*, Vol. 34, December 1979.

MacDonald, R. and M. Taylor, 'Rational expectations, risk and efficiency in the London Metal Exchange: an empirical analysis', *Applied Economics*, Vol. 21, 1989.

McDonald, J., 'Objectives and performance of mutual funds', *Journal of Financial and Quantitative Analysis*, Vol. 9, June 1974.

McRae, H. and F. Cairncross, *Capital City*, Methuen, London, 1985.

Malkiel, B. and J. Cragg, 'Expectations and the structure of share prices', *American Economic Review*, Vol. 60, 1970.

Markowitz, H., 'The utility of wealth', *Journal of Political Economy*, Vol. 60, 1952.

Markowitz, H., 'Portfolio selection', *Journal of Finance*, Vol. 7, March 1952.

Markowitz, H., *Portfolio Selection*, Wiley, New York, 1959.

Markowitz, H., 'Markowitz revisited', *Financial Analysts' Journal*, Vol. 32, September 1976.

Marsh, P., 'Equity rights issues and the efficiency of the UK stock market', *Journal of Finance*, Vol. 34, September 1979.

Marsh, P., 'Valuation of underwriting agreements for UK rights issues', *Journal of Finance*, Vol. 35, June 1980.

Marshall, A., *Principles of Economics* 8th edn, Macmillan, London, 1920.

Masulis, R., 'The effects of capital structure change on security prices: a study of exchange offers', *Journal of Financial Economics*, Vol. 8, 1980.

Meade, N., 'The random walk in a thin market', *Journal of Business Finance and Accounting*, Vol. 5, 1978.

Meeks, G., 'Disappointing marriage: a study of the gains from merger', University of Cambridge Department of Applied Economics Occasional Paper 51, 1977.

Merrett, A., Howe and G. Newbould, *Equity Issues and the London Capital Market*, Longman, London, 1967.

Merrett, A. and A. Sykes, 'Return on equities and fixed interest securities 1919–66', *District Bank Review*, 1966.

Merton, R., 'Option pricing when underlying stock returns are discontinuous', *Journal of Financial Economics*, Vol. 4, January 1976.

Miller, M. and F. Modigliani, 'Dividend policy, growth, and the valuation of shares', *Journal of Business*, Vol. 17, October 1961.

Mills, T. and M. Stephenson, 'An empirical analysis of the UK treasury bill market', *Applied Economics*, Vol. 17, 1985.

Modigliani, F. and M. Miller, 'The cost of capital, corporation finance and the theory of investment', *American Economic Review*, Vol. 48, June 1958.

Modigliani, F. and M. Miller, 'The cost of capital, corporation fiance and the theory of investment: reply', *American Economic Review*, Vol. 49, June 1959.

Modigliani, F. and M. Miller, 'Corporate income taxes and the cost of capital: a correction', *American Economic Review*, Vol. 53, June 1963.

Modigliani, F. and M. Miller, 'Some estimates of the cost of capital to the electric utility industry: 1954–57', *American Economic Review*, Vol. 56, June 1966.

Moles, P., 'Components of unit trust performance 1966–1975', *Investment Analyst*, Vol. 37, March 1981.

Morgan, E.V. and W. Thomas, *The Stock Exchange*, Elek, London, 1962.

Newbould, G., *Management and Merger Activity*, Guthshead, Liverpool, 1971.

Newbould, G. and E. Wells, 'Underwriting of rights issues—a theoretical justification: a reply', *Journal of Business Finance*, Vol. 3, 1971.

Osbourne, F., 'Periodic structure in the Brownian motion of stock prices', *Operations Research*, 1959.

Osbourne, F. and V. Niederhoffer, 'Market making and reversal on the Stock Exchange', *Journal of the American Statistical Association*, 1966.

Peasnell, K. V. and C. W. R. Ward, *British Financial Markets and Institutions*, Prentice Hall, London, 1980.

Pettit, R. and R. Singer, 'Instant option betas', *Financial Analysts' Journal*, Vol. 42, September 1986.

Poterba, J. and L. Summers, 'New evidence that taxes affect the valuation of dividends', *Journal of Finance*, Vol. 39, 1984.

Radcliffe, R. and M. Gillespie, 'The price impact of reverse splits', *Financial Analysts' Journal*, Vol. 35, January 1979.

Reading, B., 'The boom that nobody heard', *The Sunday Times*, 17 April 1988.

Redhead, K., 'Hedging with financial futures', *National Westminster Quarterly Review*, February 1985.

Rendleman, R. and B. Bartter, 'Two-stage option pricing', *Journal of Finance*, Vol. 34, December 1979.

Renshaw, E., 'Stock market panics: a test of the efficient market hypothesis', *Financial Analysts' Journal*, Vol. 40, May 1984.

'Report of the Presidential Task Force on Market Mechanisms', January 1988.

Richards, R., 'Analysts' performance and the accuracy of corporate earnings forecasts', *Journal of Business*, Vol. 32, July 1976.

Riding, A., 'The information content of dividends: another test', *Journal of Business Finance and Accounting*, Vol. 11, Summer 1984.

Roberts, H., 'Stock market patterns and financial analysis: methodological suggestions', *Journal of Finance*, Vol. 15, 1959.

Robinson, J., 'Merits of the jobbing system', *Investment Analyst*, July 1983.

Roll, R., 'A critique of the asset pricing theory's tests; part I. On past and potential testability of the theory', *Journal of Financial Economics*, Vol. 5, March 1977.

Roll, R., 'The international crash of October 1987', *Financial Analysts' Journal*, Vol. 44, September 1988.

Roll, R. and S. Ross, 'An empirical investigation of the arbitrage pricing theory', *Journal of Finance*, Vol. 35, December 1980.

Roll, R. and S. Ross, 'The arbitrage pricing theory approach to strategic portfolio planning', *Financial Analysts' Journal*, Vol. 40, March 1984.

Rose, H. and G. Newbould, 'The 1967 take-over boom', *Moorgate and Wall Street*, 1967.

Ross, S., 'The arbitrage theory of capital asset pricing', *Journal of Economic Theory*, Vol. 13, December 1976.

Ross, S., 'The determination of financial structure: the incentive signalling approach', *Bell Journal of Economics*, Spring 1977.

Roux, F. and B. Gilbertson, 'The behaviour of share prices on Johannesburg Stock Exchange', *Journal of Business Finance and Accounting*, Vol. 5, 1978.

Rubinstein, M., 'A mean–variance synthesis of corporate finance', *Journal of Finance*, Vol. 28, March 1973.

Rubinstein, M., 'Replacing options with positions in stock and cash, *Financial Analysts' Journal*, Vol. 37, July 1981.

Rubinstein, M., 'Alternative paths to portfolio insurance', *Financial Analysts' Journal*, Vol. 41, July 1985.

Rubinstein, M., 'Portfolio insurance and the market crash', *Financial Analysts' Journal*, Vol. 44, January 1988.

Ruff, R., 'Effect of a selection and recommendation of a "stock of the month"', *Financial Analysts' Journal*, Vol. 19, May 1963.

Rutterford, J., 'Index-linked gilts', *National Westminster Quarterly Review*, 1983.

Rutterford, J., 'The UK corporate bond market: prospects for a revival', *National Westminster Quarterly Review*, May 1984.

Sampson, A., *The Money Lenders*, Coronet/Hodder & Stoughton Ltd, London, 1981.

Santesmases, M., 'An investigation of the Spanish market seasonalities', *Journal of Business Finance and Accounting*, Vol. 13, 1986.

Schaefer, S., 'The problem with redemption yields', in *Modern Developments in Investment Management*, J. Lorie and R. Brealey (eds), Dryden Press, 1978.

Shanken, J., 'The arbitrage pricing theory: is it testable?', *Journal of Finance*, Vol. 37, 1982.

Sharpe, W. F., 'A simplified model for portfolio analysis', *Management Science*, Vol. 9, 1963.

Sharpe, W. F., 'Capital asset prices: a theory of market equilibrium under conditions of risk', *Journal of Finance*, Vol. 19, September 1964.

Sharpe, W., 'Mutual fund performance', *Journal of Business*, Vol. 22, January 1966.

Sharpe, W., *Portfolio Theory and Capital Markets*, McGraw-Hill, London 1970.

Singh, A., *Takeovers*, Cambridge University Press, 1971.

Skerratt, L., 'The price determination of convertible loan stock: a UK model', *Journal of Accounting and Finance*, Vol. 1, Autumn 1974.

Solnik, B., 'Note on the validity of the random walk for European stock prices', *Journal of Finance*, Vol. 28, 1973.

Solnik, B., 'An equilibrium model of the international capital market', *Journal of Economic Theory*, Vol. 8, August 1974.

Solnik, B., 'Why not diversify internationally rather than domestically?', *Financial Analysts' Journal*, Vol. 30, July 1974.

Solnik, B., 'Testing international asset pricing model: some pessimistic views', *Journal of Finance*, Vol. 32, May 1977.

Stapleton, R., 'Taxes, the cost of capital and the theory of investment', *Economic Journal*, Vol. 82, 1972.

Stapleton, R. and C. Burke, 'Taxes, the cost of capital and the theory of investment. A generalisation to the imputation system of dividend taxation', *Economic Journal*, Vol. 85, 1975.

Stevenson, R. and R. Bear, 'Commodity futures: trends or random walks?', *Journal of Finance*, Vol. 25, 1970.

Stock Exchange Report, 'A choice of a new dealing system for equities', July 1984.

Stock Exchange Report, 'The choice of a new dealing system for gilt-edged securities', August 1984.

Stoffels, J., 'Stock recommendations by investment advisory services: immediate effects on market pricing', *Financial Analysts' Journal*, Vol. 22, May 1966.

Stoll, H., 'The relationship between put and call option prices', *Journal of Finance*, Vol. 24, December 1969.

Stoll, H. and E. Whaley, 'Program trading and expiration-day effects', *Journal of Finance*, Vol. 42, 1987.

Streit, M. (ed.), *Futures Markets*, Blackwell, Oxford, 1983.

Taylor, S., 'Trading rules for investors in apparently inefficient futures markets', in *Futures Markets*, M. Streit (ed.), Blackwell, Oxford, 1983.

Telser, L., 'Future trading and the storage of cotton and wheat', *Journal of Political Economy*, Vol. 66, June 1958.

Theobald, M. and V. Price, 'Seasonality estimation in thin markets', *Journal of Finance*, Vol. 39, 1984.

Thomas, W. A., *The Provincial Stock Exchanges*, Frank Cass, London, 1973.

Tobin, J., 'Liquidity preference as behaviour toward risk', *Review of Economic Studies*, Vol. 25, February 1958.

Tobin, J., 'The theory of portfolio selection', in *The Theory of Interest Rates*, F. H. Hahn and F. Brechling (eds), Macmillan, London 1965.

Tosini, P., 'Stock index futures and stock market activity in October 1987', *Financial Analysts' Journal*, Vol. 44, January 1988.

Treynor, J., 'How to rate management of investment funds', *Harvard Business Review*, January 1965.

Upson, R., P. Jessup and K. Matsumoto, 'Portfolio diversification strategies', *Financial Analysts' Journal*, Vol. 31, May 1975.

Utton, M., 'On measuring the effects of industrial mergers', *Scottish Journal of Political Economy*, Vol. 21, February 1974.

Van den Bergh, W. and R. Wessels, 'Stock market seasonality and taxes: an examination of the tax loss selling hypothesis', *Journal of Business Finance and Accounting*, Vol. 12, 1985.

Verrecchia, R., 'On the theory of market information efficiency', *Journal of Accounting and Economics*, 1979.

Ward, C. and A. Saunders, 'Unit trust performance 1964–74', *Journal of Business Finance and Accounting*, Vol. 3, 1976.

Ward, C. and A. Saunders, 'Some disturbing developments in the UK stock market', *Investment Analyst*, 1977.

'Weekly Eurobond Guide', *Association of International Bond Dealers*, 19 August 1988.

Wilson, K., *British Financial Institutions*, Pitman, London, 1980.

Wilson Committee Report on Financial Institutions, Cmnd. 7937, 1980.

Yawitz, J., G. Hempel, and W. Marshall, 'Is average maturity a proxy for risk?', *Journal of Portfolio Management*, Spring 1976.

Zeckhauser, R. and V. Niederhoffer, 'The performance of index futures contracts', *Financial Analysts' Journal*, Vol. 39, January 1983.

Name index

Subject index